PLAYS FOR TWO

ALSO EDITED BY

Eric Lane and Nina Shengold

PLAYS FOR TWO

Edited by *Eric Lane*
and *Nina Shengold*

VINTAGE BOOKS
A DIVISION OF RANDOM HOUSE LLC
NEW YORK

A VINTAGE ORIGINAL, FEBRUARY 2014

Copyright © 2014 by Eric Lane and Nina Shengold

All rights reserved. Published in the United States by
Vintage Books, a division of Random House LLC, New York,
and in Canada by Random House of Canada Limited, Toronto,
Penguin Random House Companies.

Vintage and colophon are registered
trademarks of Random House LLC.

Permissions can be found at the end of the book.

The Library of Congress Cataloging-in-Publication Data
has been applied for.

Vintage Trade Paperback ISBN: 978-0-345-80454-9
eBook ISBN: 978-0-345-80455-6

www.vintagebooks.com

Printed in the United States of America
10 9 8 7 6 5 4 3

CONTENTS

INTRODUCTION

It takes two to tango. Or to perform a duet, fight a duel, or play Ping-Pong. The theatrical version of these close encounters is the two-character play.

Two-handers are a staple of every acting class, providing strong, challenging roles for actors working closely with a partner. Actors love the moment-by-moment scene work these stunning plays offer. Playwrights and audiences enjoy the constantly shifting give-and-take dynamics of two keenly matched characters. And as the economic realities of staging live theater become more and more demanding, plays with smaller casts have become increasingly popular with savvy producers.

We've edited more than a dozen contemporary play anthologies, but this is the first one comprised entirely of plays for two actors. In all our collections, first and foremost, we seek out new plays that excite us; they create vivid worlds and tell compelling stories. The plays are easy to produce, with a wide variety of terrific roles to perform.

While assembling this current collection, we read more than four hundred two-character plays. Ultimately, we chose four outstanding full-length plays and twenty-four shorts. You'll find couples of every sort, swooning or sparring, meeting cute or parting ways. You'll also discover perfect and imperfect strangers, competitors, parents and children, siblings, coworkers, and friends: the whole range of human pairings. In the case of Billy Aronson's hilarious *Negotiation*, even that "human" may be up for grabs.

The full-length selections include David Ives's Broadway hit *Venus in Fur*, a mysterious, funny, erotic battle of the sexes as an aspiring actress pulls out all the stops in her audition for the role of a lifetime. In Steven Dietz's bittersweet *Shooting Star*, former lovers meet by chance in a snowbound airport, revealing two lifetimes' worth of missed connections. Frank Higgins's riveting *Black Pearl Sings!* brings together an African-American convict with a spectacular voice and a folk-song collector who may be her liberator, her exploiter, or something more complex. Anthony Clarvoe's *The Art of Sacrifice* examines the costs of competition as a driven father and his chess-prodigy son play out a high-stakes game of emotional chess.

Many of the collection's short plays seem to be ripped straight from the headlines. Kitt Lavoie's timely *Bank & Trust* puts a human face on recession economics, placing friends and neighbors on opposite sides of a loan default. Neil LaBute's grief-soaked *Strange Fruit* and Paul Rudnick's outrageously funny *My Husband* were both part of an evening called "Standing on Ceremony: the Gay Marriage Plays." Ean Miles Kessler's *Funny Valentine* and Jacob Juntunen's *Saddam's Lions* explore the human fallout of two different wars as a shell-shocked American soldier struggles to connect with a Korean bar girl, and a female Iraq War veteran chafes at her homecoming party.

We also included a wide variety of comedies. Of the many "two people meet in a restaurant" plays that we read, the one that surprised us most and made us laugh loudest was Michael Mitnick's *Hail Caesar!* Actors looking for a romantic comedy are encouraged to pick a scene partner they like a whole lot for Mark Harvey Levine's *The Kiss*, in which two friends explore the mechanics of a great smooch. Doug Wright's black-comedic *Wildwood Park* brings together a high-strung real estate agent, a menacing client, and a mansion property with a very dark past. A feisty senior couple misunderstand their way through an escalating fight in Pete Barry's hilarious *Hearing Aid*.

A couple's strained phone call in Elizabeth Meriwether's *90 Days* is an object lesson in subtext and the frequent disconnect between what we say and what we mean. And in Naveen Bahar Choudhury's *Skin*, an idiosyncratic Bengali hip-hopper and a prickly poet make an unexpected connection in a campus health clinic while awaiting tough news.

For teenage actors, Simon Fill's poignant *The Gift*, Eric

Lane's wry comedy *Lady Liberty and the Donut Girl*, Daria Polatin's subtly etched *That First Fall*, and Kelly Rhodes's cleverly theatrical *Heads and Tails* all provide juicy roles.

José Rivera's *Lessons for an Unaccustomed Bride* brings together a Puerto Rican witch and a religious bride-to-be, each with unexpected strengths and sorrows. Actresses will also find great roles in Edwin Sánchez's pre-wedding drama *Bea and May*, Nina Shengold's anti-nostalgic *Deep Jersey*, and Cori Thomas's moving and poetic *Waking Up*—three plays in which women come face-to-face with mortality and the passage of time.

Actors looking for a good emotional workout can go mano a mano with Marco Ramirez's incandescent, adrenaline-pumping *3:59am: a drag race for two actors* or with David Auburn's *An Upset*, which charts the interpersonal and career arcs of a quick-tempered tennis champion and an up-and-coming contender. Jacqueline E. Lawton's comedic *Finals, Touchdowns, and Barrel Kicks* pairs an athlete and a tutor with an unexpected twist, while Halley Feiffer's brilliantly deadpan *Frank Amends* takes the father-and-son reunion to a whole new level.

At the back of this book, you'll find contact information for the writer, agent, or publisher who represents performance rights for each play. If you wish to perform one of these plays outside the classroom, or to film or record it in any form, you must get permission first. In the Internet age, producing a play without permission is bound to catch up with you: please pay the royalties that the playwrights fully deserve.

Although we've listed the plays by casting needs (m/f, 2 f, 2 m), we recommend that readers browse freely across gender lines. Also, many of the plays in this anthology specify or invite casting of minority actors, and we encourage nontraditional casting wherever possible.

Whether you're looking for a supreme acting challenge; a wonderful play to read, direct, or produce; or inspiration for your own writing, here are twenty-eight stellar scripts that attest to the power of two. Enjoy!

—ERIC LANE AND NINA SHENGOLD

ACKNOWLEDGMENTS

Many people contributed greatly to the creation of this anthology. We'd like to thank the many theaters, literary managers, agents, publishers, playwrights, and friends who led us to these wonderful plays and helped us secure the rights.

In particular, we'd like to thank Sarah Bernstein at Playscripts, Inc.; Craig Pospisil at Dramatists Play Service; Broadway Play Publishing; John McCormack at All Seasons Theatre Group; and our terrific agent at Gersh, Susan Cohen.

Deep gratitude to Actors & Writers, the Drama Book Shop, the Corporation of Yaddo, and the hardworking band at the Stone Ridge post office. As always, we thank our superb editor at Vintage, Diana Secker Tesdell. Red roses to Bob Barnett and Maya Shengold, who bring joy to our lives on a daily basis.

Above all, thanks to the playwrights for sharing your work with us.

FULL-LENGTH PLAYS

VENUS IN FUR

David Ives

Venus in Fur had its world premiere at Classic Stage Company in New York City (Brian Kulick, artistic director; Jessica R. Jenen, executive director; Jeff Griffin, general manager) on January 26, 2010. The production was directed by Walter Bobbie, with set design by John Lee Beatty, costume design by Anita Yavich, lighting design by Peter Kaczorowski, and sound design by Acme Sound Partners. The production manager was La Vie Productions. The production stage manager was Christina Lowe.

THOMAS   Wes Bentley
VANDA   Nina Arianda

Venus in Fur was subsequently produced on Broadway by the Manhattan Theatre Club (Lynne Meadow, artistic director; Barry Grove, executive producer; Florie Seery, general manager) at the Samuel J. Friedman Theatre. The production was directed by Walter Bobbie, with set design by John Lee Beatty, costume design by Anita Yavich, lighting design by Peter Kaczorowski, and sound design by Acme Sound Partners. The production manager was Joshua Helman. The production stage manager was Winnie Lok.

THOMAS   Hugh Dancy
VANDA   Nina Arianda

CHARACTERS
THOMAS
VANDA

For Walter Bobbie

A clash of thunder and a burst of lightning reveal THOMAS *in a bare rented studio. End of an afternoon. A few old metal chairs. A table with a clip-on lamp and a stack of headshots. A ratty prop divan covered with a throw. A metal stand with a coffeemaker and some paper cups. In the middle of the room, an iron pipe disappears into the ceiling. A fuse box hangs on a wall.*

THOMAS: (*Pacing, into his cell phone.*) No. No. Nothing. Nobody. It's maddening, it's a plot. There *are* no women like this. No young women, or young-*ish* women. No beautiful-slash-sexy women. No sexy-slash-articulate young women with some classical training and a particle of brain in their skulls. Is that so much to ask? An actress who can actually pronounce the word "degradation" without a tutor?

(*A roll of thunder.*)

In the book Vanda is twenty-four, for God's sake. Back in those days a woman of twenty-four would've been married. She'd have five kids and tuberculosis. She'd be a *woman*. Most women who are twenty-four these days sound like six-year-olds on helium. *"And I was all like whatever and he was all like, y'know, and I go like whatever and he's like all, y'know?"* Honey—honey—I saw thirty-five actresses today. Even the ones pushing retirement didn't have the stuff. Anybody who does is either shooting a series or she isn't gonna do this for a nickel a week. And the *stupidity*. They bring along props, whole sacks full of costumes. And whatever happened to femininity? Bring along some of *that*, please. Young women can't even *play* feminine these days. Half are dressed like hookers, half like dykes. *I'd* be a better Vanda than most of these girls, all I'd have to do is put on a dress and a pair of nylons. Well, our Vanda's got to be out there somewhere. But at this point . . .

(*Thunder and lightning. The lights in the room flicker.*)

Hello? Hello? Honey? Honey, are you there?

VANDA: (*Offstage.*) Knock knock knock!

(VANDA *enters, in steep high heels, wearing a soaked coat. She carries an enormous bag, a purse, and a battered black umbrella.*)

Am I too late? I'm too late, right? Fuck. *Fuck!*

THOMAS: If you're here for *Venus in Fur*, everybody went home half an hour ago.

VANDA: God, I'm sorry, I'm so, so sorry, I got caught like way uptown and my cell went out. Then my fucking heel gets stuck in one of those sewer-cover-thing-whatevers. Then there's this guy on the train, I don't even want to tell you about him, rubbing up against my ass the whole trip. Then it starts to pour. I get soaked through to the fucking skin. Fuck! Fuck!

(*She throws herself into a chair.*)

God. Just my luck. Fuck . . . *FUCK!*

THOMAS: Are you all right?

VANDA: Yeah, I'm okay. Just my usual luck is all. Thank you, God, once again! Hi. I'm sorry. Vanda Jordan.

THOMAS: Vanda . . . ?

VANDA: See what I mean? I've even got her name! How many
         girls in this town are named *Vanda*? Actually I'm Wanda but
         my parents called me *Vanda*. Anyway, I'm like perfect for
         the part and the fucking train gets stuck in a tunnel while
         this guy's trying to penetrate me. Talk about, like, fate. And
         you are?

THOMAS: Thomas Novachek.

VANDA: Hi. Hey, wait a minute. Thomas Novachek?

THOMAS: Thomas Novachek.

VANDA: You wrote this!

THOMAS: Yes, I did. Well, I adapted it.

VANDA: And you're directing it, too, right?

THOMAS: Within an inch of its life.

VANDA: God, I love your plays! I mean, the ones I know. *Anat-
         omy of Shadows*? Like, *wow. Anatomy of Shadows* was *amazing*!
         I saw it twice!

THOMAS: I didn't write *Anatomy of Shadows*.

VANDA: Right, right. I mean, you know, the other one. God, this
         is embarrassing. Well, *this* play is sure amazing. I mean, the
         parts of it I read. Pretty wild stuff.

(*She takes off the coat, revealing a studded patent leather top, a short
black leather skirt, and a silver-studded dog collar.*)

   Really sexy, huh. Or like, erotic, if you're into humiliation.
   Oh, by the way, I don't usually walk around in leather lin-
   gerie and a dog collar. Usually I'm really demure and shit.

Just thought I'd kinda get into the part. I mean it's basically S&M, right? The play?

THOMAS: Not exactly. And it does take place in 1870.

VANDA: Mm. I guess this isn't too 1870, huh.

THOMAS: No.

VANDA: Who knows, maybe S&M-ers dressed just like this back then.

(*She digs a battered, crushed photo out of her purse.*)

Anyway, here's my headshot. I know the résumé's kinda skimpy. But I'm good. I'm like made for this part, I swear to God. I was amazing as Hedda Gabler.

THOMAS: (*Looking over her résumé.*) I somehow missed the season at the Urinal Theatre. You had an appointment?

VANDA: Yeah, two-fifteen. It's like hours ago, right? Well, better late than whatever.

THOMAS: (*Checks the day's appointment sheets.*) Vanda . . . ?

VANDA: . . . Jordan. People always say is that *real*? "Vanda Jordan"?

THOMAS: I don't see your name.

VANDA: Really? My agent said they set it up and everything. I'm not down there? Two-fifteen. Shit. Thank you, God, once again! Anyway . . .

(*She strips off her top, revealing an amazing bra.*)

Geronimo.

THOMAS: Wait wait wait. What are you doing?

VANDA: (*Stripping off her leather skirt, revealing black panties and garters.*) I brought some costume stuff.

THOMAS: No—Vanda . . .

VANDA: It'll just take me a sec, I swear. I found this great dress. Real period shit.

THOMAS: No. Really. Don't bother . . .

VANDA: What. You mean—like—don't read?

THOMAS: I mean don't read.

VANDA: Yeah, but. Long as I'm here, I might as well like give it a go, right?

THOMAS: There's nobody to give it a go with. The reader's gone home.

VANDA: I'll read with you. It's always an honor to read with the actual author.

THOMAS: Adapter.

VANDA: Getting the play straight from the horse's mouth is always so cool. Come on, what've you got to lose? I'm already—

THOMAS: Stop. *Stop.* To tell you the truth, Miss, um . . .

VANDA: Vanda.

THOMAS: We're looking for somebody a little different.

VANDA: Yeah? What are you looking for?

THOMAS: Well, somebody with a little more, how should I put this . . .

VANDA: Somebody who's not *me*. I'm too young. I'm too old. I'm too big, I'm too small. My résumé's not long enough. Okay.

(*She bows her head and starts to cry.*)

Okay. God, I'm sorry. I'm sorry. It's been like really stressful today. Anyway, how do *you* know who I am or what I can do? Fuck . . . Fuck . . . !

THOMAS: We're going to be scheduling more auditions sometime soon . . .

VANDA: Yeah, but I'm here. Right? Couldn't you try me out, save yourself the time tomorrow or whatever? And save me the time getting here from the middle of nowhere?

THOMAS: Look, Vanda, it's been a very long day. I'm exhausted. I'm kind of frazzled myself, to tell you the truth.

VANDA: (*Putting on her skirt again.*) Okay. Yeah. Okay.

THOMAS: I have someone waiting for me for dinner.

VANDA: Sure.

THOMAS: It's not really optimal conditions for me. This time of day. This kind of day. Late afternoon I always get tired, I unravel a little . . .

VANDA: (*Putting on her raincoat.*) No. Sure. I understand.

THOMAS: Anyway, I think this would be better when I'm fresh. Thank you very much anyway for coming in. And we'll see you again.

(VANDA *heads for the door with her stuff but stops short.*)

VANDA: Yeah, I don't think so. Thank you for saying so, though.
    You seem like a really nice person. It's just—the business,
    you know? The goddamn fucking *business.* Plus I had to put
    out ten bucks at Screaming Mimi's on the fucking dress.

(*Takes a long white fancy dress out of her big bag.*)

    I mean, isn't that real 18-whatever?

THOMAS: It is very 1870-whatever.

VANDA: Isn't that *her*? Like, total Vanda? I figured she'd wear
    one of those long-ass dresses because everybody hated their
    body back then.

THOMAS: Actually, that's a common misconception about the
    nineteenth century.

VANDA: Well, can't I just show it to you, how I look? Please,
    God, please, pretty please?

(THOMAS*'s cell phone rings.*)

THOMAS: Excuse me.

VANDA: Great!

(*She quickly strips down again, to get into the dress.*)

THOMAS: No—wait—Vanda—

(*Into phone.*)

    Hi, honey. Yeah, I lost you, must be the storm.

(*To* VANDA, *waving to her to stop.*)

No! *No!*

(VANDA *keeps on dressing. Into cell phone.*)

No, somebody just walked in. Mm-hm. No, I doubt it. Listen, I'll be heading out in a couple of minutes. I'll pick something up on the way. No, I got the book. I love you, too. Ciao.

(*By now,* VANDA *has gotten into the dress.*)

VANDA: Could you do me up back there?

(THOMAS *does her dress up.*)

Oh, wow. Reading with *Thomas Novachek* . . .

THOMAS: I'm not an actor, so you're not doing yourself any favors. This part needs a real actor.

VANDA: Come on. You're perfect. You *are* Kowalski.

THOMAS: Kushemski.

VANDA: Kushemski. You're *him.*

THOMAS: Not quite.

VANDA: (*As* THOMAS *finishes.*) Thank you, kind sir. So where do we start? I'm up for it, whatever.

THOMAS: Why don't we try the first scene. You have the sides?

VANDA: (*Digging in the big bag and taking out a ragged script.*) Yeah. It got kinda destroyed on the way.

THOMAS: That's the whole script. How did you get that?

VANDA: I dunno. It's what my agent sent me.

THOMAS: How did your agent get it?

VANDA: Wasn't I supposed to get this? What, is it like top secret or something?

THOMAS: Doesn't matter. Have you read it?

VANDA: I kinda flipped through it quick on the train. So what can you tell me? This is like based on something, right? Besides the Lou Reed song? "Venus in Furs"?

THOMAS: This is based on an old German novel called *Venus in Fur*—singular—by Leopold von Sacher-Masoch.

VANDA: I bet you read German. I bet you read it in German.

THOMAS: I did, actually. Anyway, the book was a huge scandal in 1870.

VANDA: Well, sure. Basically it's S&M porn.

THOMAS: It's not S&M porn.

VANDA: You don't think it's porn? Or porn-*ish* . . . ? For medieval times, 18-whatever, I mean?

THOMAS: *Venus in Fur* is a great love story. It's a serious novel. It's a central text of world literature.

VANDA: Oh. I thought from the play it had to be porn. Anyway, you don't have to tell *me* about sadomasochism. I'm in the theater.

THOMAS: The word "masochism" comes from Leopold von Sacher-Masoch, because of this book.

VANDA: "Masochism," "Masoch," I shoulda seen that. Wow. So S&M is like *named* after the guy! Cool!

THOMAS: I'm not sure that's what Sacher-Masoch had in mind.

VANDA: Sure. He thought he wrote a serious novel, everybody else thought it was porn. So like where like are we, like?

THOMAS: We are "like" at a remote inn somewhere in Carpathia, on the eastern edge of the Austro-Hungarian Empire.

VANDA: The Austro-Hungarian Empire . . . Remind me?

THOMAS: Well, it's complicated.

VANDA: But the place is beautiful, right?

THOMAS: It's a health spa for the rich. It's fantastic. At lights-up Kushemski is reading in his room while having his morning coffee. And knock-knock-knock Vanda enters.

VANDA: And that's symbolic, right. For his character? I mean, he's reading?

THOMAS: You know, some people do read, even today. Some-times pages made of actual paper.

VANDA: Ouch. You got me. Oh—is it "*Sev*erin" or "Se*ver*in"?

THOMAS: Se*ver*in.

VANDA: Se*ver*in. And this Kushemski is what. Throw me some, like, adjectives.

THOMAS: He's one of the shiftless rich of his day. Well-traveled. Cultivated. Literate. Intelligent.

VANDA: All in his head.

THOMAS: If you will.

VANDA: "If you will." I love it! I mean when's the last time I heard that? So he's *deestangay.* Kinda like you.

THOMAS: Don't you want to know about her?

VANDA: Oh, I think I know about her. But sure, if you want.

THOMAS: I'd say Vanda is a typical young woman of her time, in spite of her professed principles.

VANDA: In spite of . . . ?

THOMAS: Her professed principles. She's outwardly fairly proper. Probably quite poised. Also cultivated.

VANDA: Well, all that's pretty clear from the pages. What else? Got any like insights about her? Anything I don't know? Never mind, I'll work on it. So I guess this is the so-called divan.

(*The iron pipe:*)

And what's this? A maypole? Phallic symbol?

THOMAS: The remains of a heating system from when this building was a sweatshop.

VANDA: Oh, wait a minute. Wait a minute.

THOMAS: What.

VANDA: (*Digging in her big bag.*) My fur. She's wearing a fur stole when she comes in, isn't she?

THOMAS: She is.

VANDA: (*Takes out a thrift-shop shawl and puts it on.*) There. Okay. Fur. Soft fur. Soft fur . . . So where am I, where do you want me?

THOMAS: Whatever's comfortable.

VANDA: No, tell me.

THOMAS: Why don't you stand there.

(*She does.*)

Further left. No! Further *left.*

VANDA: Oh, *stage* left.

THOMAS: Is there any other kind?

VANDA: Sorry.

THOMAS: Do you want to read the scene over?

VANDA: Nah, let's wing it. How far should we go?

THOMAS: Just to the bottom of page three.

VANDA: That's all? Then you'll kick me out, right?

THOMAS: Let's find our way through this first.

VANDA: In other words, yes. Oh, hey, last thing. These words on page like zero, here? This quotation?

THOMAS: The epigraph.

VANDA: Yeah. *"And the Lord hath smitten him and delivered him into a woman's hands."* What is that?

THOMAS: It's quoted a couple of times in the novel. It's from the Book of Judith.

VANDA: Is that the Bible?

THOMAS: Yes, the Book of Judith is from the Apocrypha of the Bible.

VANDA: Sorry. Not my area. Anyway, it's pretty sexist, isn't it? *"The Lord hath smitten him and delivered him into a woman's hands"*—?

THOMAS: I'm only quoting Sacher-Masoch's book.

VANDA: Yeah, but you included it here on page zero like it's the whole point. Never mind, never mind. None of my business. I'm just an *actrice*. Kinda bright in here. You mind if I change the lights? I hate fluorescents.

(A roll of thunder.)

THOMAS: No. Please. Make yourself at home . . .

(VANDA turns off the fluorescents, goes to the fuse box, and adjusts the lights.)

I didn't realize there was a whole system up there.

VANDA: There. More dramatic. Oh, hey, last thing. It's 18-whatever, do you think Vanda has one of those phony transatlantic accents? Never mind. I'll just try something.

(She shakes herself out for a second, doing vocal exercises.)

KAAA! KA-KA! KA-KA! INK. SPOT. INK! SPOT!— Okay. I'm ready. Turn around. Go on, turn around. You're reading and having your coffee, you don't see me.

(THOMAS *turns his back to her.*)

Okay. Morning in Transylvania. Morning in Transylvania.

THOMAS: Whenever you're ready.

VANDA: Knock knock knock.

THOMAS (*as* KUSHEMSKI): *Come in.*

VANDA (*as* DUNAYEV, *in a perfect, polished accent*): *Herr Doktor Severin von Kushemski—*

(THOMAS *turns around and "sees her."*)

I am Vanda von Dunayev. I'm staying in the room above yours. I'm sorry to disturb you. I found this book in the birch grove last night.

(*Holds out her script.*)

A copy of Faust, *with your bookplate inside. It was sitting at the fountain by that statue of Venus.*

THOMAS (*as* KUSHEMSKI): *Thank you, I was just asking the maid about that.*

VANDA (*as* DUNAYEV): *I would have sent it by maid, but I also found this rather provocative bookmark inside . . .*

(*Takes a "card" from the "book."*)

Is it a Raphael?

THOMAS (*as* KUSHEMSKI): *It's a Titian.* Venus with Mirror. *A favorite painting of mine.*

VANDA (*as* DUNAYEV): *Yes, your* Venus *is as well-thumbed as your* Faust. *Is she faithful?*

THOMAS (*as* KUSHEMSKI): *I'm sorry?*

VANDA (*as* DUNAYEV): *To the original.*

THOMAS (*as* KUSHEMSKI): *To my mind, that woman is Venus. It's a faithful copy of the painting, if that's what you mean.*

VANDA (*as* DUNAYEV): *I can certainly understand your fascination. The plush red velvet. The dark fur outlining her naked body. The bracelets cuffing her wrists. The opulent hair. Her golden breasts. The pretty little Cupid holding the mirror. The picture's ravishing. But is Venus covering herself with the fur—or is she opening the fur to reveal her glories?*

THOMAS (*as* KUSHEMSKI): *We'll never know. Both, I suppose. Well, thank you for returning it.*

VANDA (*as* DUNAYEV): *I also couldn't help noticing this intriguing poem scrawled on the back. "To Venus in Fur." Did you write this poem?*

THOMAS (*as* KUSHEMSKI): *It's just a bit of doggerel . . .*

VANDA (*as* DUNAYEV): *Doggerel. Hardly . . .*

> *"To love and be loved—ah, what bliss!*
> *And yet there glows a greater joy:*
> *The torment of that woman's kiss*
> *Who makes us her slave, her footstool, her toy . . ."*

THOMAS (*as* KUSHEMSKI): *You see? It doesn't even scan properly.*

VANDA (*as* DUNAYEV): *Strong feelings will throw off the strictest meter.*

> *"To her alone prostrate I fall,*
> *That lady cruel who makes men crawl,*
> *Who renders me a cringing cur,*
> *My goddess, my dictator, Venus in fur . . ."*

Interesting sentiments. I'd guard this bookmark well, if I were you.

THOMAS (*as* KUSHEMSKI): *I appreciate your discretion.*

VANDA (*as* DUNAYEV): *Here's your* Faust *with your* Venus, *all safe and sound. And behold. You're complete again.*

(*A pause.*)

Well . . .

THOMAS (*as* KUSHEMSKI): *Would you like to sit down, Frau Dunayev?*

VANDA (*as* DUNAYEV): *Thank you.*

THOMAS (*as* KUSHEMSKI): *May I take your fur?*

VANDA (*as* DUNAYEV): *That's very kind.*

(*He takes the shawl off her.*)

THOMAS (*as* KUSHEMSKI): *It's Tartar, isn't it? Caucasian sable. Probably from Kazakhstan.*

VANDA (*as* DUNAYEV): *Caucasian sable from Kazakhstan. Precisely.—* Kushemski stands there staring at the fur in his hands.

(*She waits for him to stare at the shawl.*)

You're trembling, Herr Kushemski!

THOMAS (*as* KUSHEMSKI): *I'm sorry.*

VANDA (*as* DUNAYEV): *Is everything quite all right?*

THOMAS (*as* KUSHEMSKI): *Yes, fine. May I ring for something?*

VANDA (*as* DUNAYEV): *Some coffee would be lovely.*

THOMAS (*as* KUSHEMSKI): *You can have mine.*

VANDA (*as* DUNAYEV, *mimes taking off gloves*): *How nice. Two sugars, thank you.*

THOMAS: (*Miming it, as he reads the stage direction.*) He pours her coffee.

VANDA (*as* DUNAYEV): *I hope I haven't disturbed you, trodding across your ceiling with my heels.*

THOMAS (*as* KUSHEMSKI): *Not at all. Trod with your heels as hard as you like.*

VANDA (*as* DUNAYEV): *So you're a poet, Herr Kushemski. A dreamer.*

THOMAS (*as* KUSHEMSKI): *A dilettante, if anything. In my life I've stretched a score of canvases but painted nothing. I've written the first chapter of a dozen novels, but never seem to finish. You might say I live the way I paint and write poetry. As an amateur.*

VANDA (*as* DUNAYEV): *Your knowledge of fur seems more than amateur. You knew my stole intimately and you two had only just met.*

THOMAS (*as* KUSHEMSKI): *The love of fur is innate.*—I'll skip all this.

VANDA: No, read it, read it.

THOMAS (*as* KUSHEMSKI, *mechanically speeding through*): *The love of fur is innate. It's a passion given by Nature to us all.*

VANDA: Come on, get into it.

THOMAS (*as* KUSHEMSKI): *The love of fur is innate. It's a passion given by Nature to us all. Who doesn't know the addictiveness of stroking a thick, soft fur? That peculiar tingle. That electricity. What is a cat but a walking galvanic battery with claws? How did the great painters depict power but by trimming their most illustrious subjects with fur? Did Raphael or Titian find a better frame for their mistresses than a mink?*

VANDA (*as* DUNAYEV): *Well said. Yet somehow I suspect that there's more to this love of fur than Renaissance aesthetics. Perhaps your mother swaddled you in sable as a baby. I'm sorry. I'm prying.*

THOMAS (*as* KUSHEMSKI): *Actually, I had an aunt who was very fond of fur . . .*

VANDA (*as* DUNAYEV): *Well, there. That explains everything.*

THOMAS (*as* KUSHEMSKI): *We're all easily explicable. What we're not is . . . easily extricable.*

VANDA (*as* DUNAYEV): *Extricable from . . . ?*

(*A pause.*)

That's the bottom of page three.

(*A roll of thunder.*)

THOMAS: Right. Right. That was good, Vanda.

VANDA: I was just stumbling around, trying to get into it.

THOMAS: You didn't seem to be stumbling.

VANDA: (*Southern drawl.*) Well, that's good actin' for ya! I tell you, I'm a pro.

THOMAS: It was *very* good.

VANDA: Aw, shucks. Now I'm all embarrassed.

THOMAS: I'm not saying it was *perfect* . . .

VANDA: No. Sure.

THOMAS: Let's read on a little. There's his big speech. And we skip to . . .

VANDA: No, read it. Do you mind? It'll rev me up. You're a good actor, Thomas.

THOMAS: I'm just faking it.

VANDA: No, you're really good. Do you have a guy to play Kushemski?

THOMAS: Not yet. We have a few possibilities.

VANDA: You should play him.

THOMAS: Right.

VANDA: No, I mean it. You'd be terrific.

THOMAS: This is hard. I can't believe I put actors through this.

VANDA: You're a playwright. You're a director. It's your job to torture actors.

THOMAS: First-time director.

VANDA: You'd never know it.

THOMAS: I'm only doing this because no director ever seems to get things exactly *right*. Having lived through one misguided production after another . . .

VANDA: That's why you're so perfect. You can *make* it right. You can guide it.

THOMAS: I've got it all plotted out, too. I'm going to use Alban Berg's *Lyric Suite* for transition music.

VANDA: Yeah! Great!

THOMAS: Do you know the *Lyric Suite*?

VANDA: No! But you see? You understand this stuff from the inside, and these people.

THOMAS: I hope I do. Sometimes today I felt as if I didn't know the first thing about them—or this play. There's that moment when the actor turns to you and says, "What should I do, who am I right here?" and you have no idea. You can't remember who *you* are, much less what *they're* supposed to be.

VANDA: Just *play* a director. "Sweetheart, I want this part moving and tragic and blah blah—but funny. And while you're crossing down, could you look out both sides of your head at the same time?"

THOMAS: Play a director. I'll try that.

VANDA: But maybe for Kushemski you should try a little, I don't know, an accent or something . . .

THOMAS: Be more Continental.

VANDA: Be more Continental. Exactly.

THOMAS: (*"Continental."*) Something Continental. Is this Continental, or is it idiotic?

VANDA: That's it! It's a little idiotic, but it's great.

THOMAS: You didn't bring a frock coat along, did you?

VANDA: I did! You want to try it on?

THOMAS: I was only kidding.

VANDA: No, come on, try it on. It'll help you.

(*Digs a black frock coat out of her bag.*)

Here, see if it fits.

THOMAS: It's beautiful. Is it real?

VANDA: They said it's vintage.

THOMAS: (*Checks the label.*) "*Siegfried Mueller, Vienna, 1869*"—?

VANDA: I didn't even notice that. Three bucks. Not bad, huh?

(*She holds it open for him, and he slips the coat on.*)

Whoo! Looks like it was made for you, too. How's it feel?

THOMAS: It feels good. Perfect fit.

VANDA: Sure looks good on you. *Hello, gorgeous!*

THOMAS: How much did the dog collar cost you?

VANDA: This? This is . . . left over from when I was a prostitute.

(*Pause.*)

I'm just kidding! Just kidding! Anyway, let me give you a run-up.—*Somehow I suspect that there's more to this love of fur than Renaissance aesthetics. Perhaps your mother swaddled you in sable as a baby. I'm sorry. I'm prying.*

THOMAS (*as* KUSHEMSKI): *Actually . . .*

VANDA: And this is hard for him, right?

THOMAS: It should be.

VANDA: So give it a shot.—*I'm sorry. I'm prying.*

THOMAS (*as* KUSHEMSKI): *Actually . . . I had an aunt who was very fond of fur . . .*

VANDA (*as* DUNAYEV): *Well, there. That explains everything.*

THOMAS (*as* KUSHEMSKI): *We're all easily explicable. What we're not is . . . easily extricable.*

VANDA (*as* DUNAYEV): *Extricable from . . . ?*

THOMAS (*as* KUSHEMSKI): *What we are. What the world has made us. And the thing that fixes us only takes an instant. "The overturning of a dragonfly's wing," to quote one of the Greeks. One innocent instant and you are different, forever . . . How's the coffee?*

VANDA (*as* DUNAYEV): *I've hardly tasted it, but it's excellent so far.*— And that's symbolic, right? I mean, he's the coffee. She's only had a sip, but he's got her like all intrigued.

THOMAS: Aw, shucks. You saw right through me.

VANDA (*as* DUNAYEV): *Did you have an "innocent instant," Herr Kushemski?*

THOMAS (*as* KUSHEMSKI): *I did, actually, very early on. But this is of no interest to you—*

VANDA (*as* DUNAYEV): *No, I'm enthralled. It's like one of those English mystery stories. I await the mysterious aunt who was fond of fur.*

THOMAS: I really can skip this next speech.

VANDA: No, read it, I want to hear.—*I await the mysterious aunt who was fond of fur.*

THOMAS (*as* KUSHEMSKI*): I was an impossible child. Sickly as an infant and spoiled by my parents. I spent my childhood reading in the library and tormenting the servants—and our cat. Then when I was twelve, an aunt of mine came for a visit. The Countess was a regal woman. Voluptuous, imperious, and terrifying. She refused . . . in a . . .*

(*He breaks off. A pause.*)

VANDA: What.

THOMAS: Nothing. It's just—it feels different, actually saying the words. Out loud. It's not like tapping the words onto a screen at two-oh-two A.M.

VANDA: No, you're doing fine, you're doing good. Your aunt's come for a visit. And she is what . . . ?

THOMAS (*as* KUSHEMSKI*): A regal woman. Voluptuous, imperious, and terrifying. She refused in a thousand ways to indulge my moods, and I took against her for her majestic disdain. I needled her rudely, I insulted her, I called her Messalina. Well, she took her revenge. My parents went off one day and my aunt comes striding into the library. She's wearing an enormous Russian cape of black fox fur. On her head, a diamond tiara. And in her hand, a length of fresh green birch. The cook and the scullery maid follow close behind. My aunt throws off her fur and rolls up her sleeves, revealing sleekly muscled arms. I try to escape, but the other two women grab me, overwhelm me, they fling me down onto the fur and pull down my pants. I try to be heroic, but those two hold me hand and foot while my aunt lays into me with the cane. The birch whistles in the air again and again as the blows descend. The backs of my legs and my naked backside are on fire, the lashes are like acid eating into a copper etching plate, each stroke laid on by a true artist. Meanwhile the servant women urge her on and mock me. They call me a little girl and laugh at my tears. I struggle, but it's no use. My aunt keeps whipping until I'm weeping outright, sobbing and begging her for mercy. When she's done, she forces me to kneel and thank her for punishing me. Makes*

*me kiss the very rod with which she chastised me. Then, threatening
to return for more, she takes her leave. All of this witnessed by the
two laughing servants—and our cat. From that hour forward, a fur
could never be just a fur, nor a length of birch an innocent switch.
You see, in that moment, in that room, by that woman I was made.*

VANDA (*as* DUNAYEV): *And did she return?*

THOMAS (*as* KUSHEMSKI): *You might say she did. For every night
thereafter my Countess-Aunt visited me in my dreams, wearing a
black fox fur and carrying a birch cane to continue her punishment.
Each night she visits me still. An exquisite despot.*

VANDA (*as* DUNAYEV): *You poor, poor man.*

THOMAS (*as* KUSHEMSKI): *Am I? In a way, I couldn't be richer, knowing all I know, having been taught at her feet.*

VANDA (*as* DUNAYEV): *What have you learned?*

THOMAS (*as* KUSHEMSKI): *That there can be nothing more sensuous
than pain or more pleasurable than degradation. The Countess had
become my ideal, you see. Ideal woman, ideal mate. An avatar of
the goddess of love herself. I've been on the hunt for her double ever
since—and for a woman of her delicious cruelty. And on the day I
meet that woman, I shall marry her.*

VANDA: Thomas, that speech, it's brilliant.

THOMAS: Thank you. I spent enough time on it.

VANDA: So, actually, this play's, like, all about child abuse.

THOMAS: No, this play is *not* about *child abuse.* Jesus Christ! This
idiotic urge these days to make everything about some trivial social issue!

VANDA: Child abuse isn't exactly trivial—

THOMAS: No, it's not trivial, but you are being *trite*. Let's not be *trite,* all right? This is not anthropology, or sociology. This is a play.

VANDA: Yeah, but—

THOMAS: Don't generalize. There's a lot more going on here than "corporal punishment issues."

VANDA: Okay. Sorry.

THOMAS: This stupid, impoverished world we live in! Why are we so eager to diminish ourselves? Why do we want to reduce ourselves to *examples* of something? As if we were nothing but proof of Freud, or proof of whatever dime-store psychology is in *People* magazine this week. What are you going to throw at me next, *"race, class, and gender"*?

VANDA: You oughta write all that up and send it to the *Times.*

THOMAS: I did. They didn't print it. Anyway . . .

VANDA (*as* DUNAYEV): *Well, you are certainly unique, Herr Severin von Kushemski. But I'd be careful if I were you. When you obtain your ideal she may be crueler than you care for.*

THOMAS (*as* KUSHEMSKI): *I'm willing to take the risk. In any case, there you have me. Whatever that makes me.*

VANDA (*as* DUNAYEV): *I know what you are. You're a supersensualist. An ascetic voluptuary.*

THOMAS (*as* KUSHEMSKI): *And you, Frau Vanda von Dunayev, who or what are you?*

VANDA (*as* DUNAYEV): *I'm a pagan. I'm a Greek. I love the ancients not for their pediments or their poetry, but because in their world Venus could love Paris one day and Anchises the next. Because they're not the moderns, who live in their mind, and because they're the opposite of the Christians, who live on a cross. I don't live in my mind, or on a cross. I live on this divan. In this dress. In these stockings and these shoes. I want to live the way Helen and Aspasia lived, not the twisted women of today, who are never happy and never give happiness. Who won't admit that they want love without limit. Why should I forgo any possible pleasure, abstain from any sensual experience? I'm young, I'm rich, and I'm beautiful, and I shall make the most of that. I shall deny myself nothing.*

THOMAS (*as* KUSHEMSKI): *I certainly respect your devotion to principle.*

VANDA (*as* DUNAYEV): *I don't need your respect, excuse me. I'll take happiness. My happiness, not society's happiness. I will love a man who pleases me, and please a man who makes me happy—but only as long as he makes me happy, not a moment longer.*

THOMAS (*as* KUSHEMSKI): *To a man, there's nothing crueler than a woman's infidelity.*

VANDA (*as* DUNAYEV): *To a woman, there is: the enforced fidelity of men.*—Can I move around?

THOMAS: Yes, move.

VANDA (*as* DUNAYEV): *A man always wants a woman who's sensual, but not one who's sensual with any other man. You want us to provide pleasure. How can we without honing the necessary skills?*

THOMAS (*as* KUSHEMSKI): *A fine argument for promiscuity.*

VANDA (*as* DUNAYEV): *A fine argument for integrity. In our society, a woman's only power is through men. Her character is her lack of character. She's a blank, to be filled in by creatures who at heart despise her. I want to see what Woman will be when she ceases to be man's slave. When she has the same rights as he, when she's his equal in education and his partner in work. When she becomes herself. An individual.*—God, old Vanda's seriously ahead of her time, isn't she.

THOMAS: Leopold von Sacher-Masoch was. Vanda, how did you learn all those lines?

VANDA: I dunno. I'm a pretty quick study.

THOMAS: A quick study, flipping through it on the train? You know it by heart!

VANDA: But hey, you said Vanda's proper in spite of her, what was it, professed something.

THOMAS: Her professed principles.

VANDA: Yeah. So you don't think she believes all this?

THOMAS: She says she does. Women's rights, yadda yadda.

VANDA: But you think she's only putting on a show or something? Like she's lying? I was just wondering why you said "professed principles" and not just, y'know, principles.

THOMAS: It must have been all those beautiful *p*'s.

VANDA: Sold your soul for a mess of *p*'s, huh.

THOMAS: Guilty.

VANDA: Secretly, Thomas? You are *evil*.

THOMAS: Guilty.

VANDA (*as* DUNAYEV): *In our society, a woman's only power is through men* yadda yadda. *I want to see what Woman will be when she's man's equal in education and his partner in work. When she becomes herself. An individual.*

THOMAS (*as* KUSHEMSKI): *You only say that because you yourself are so individual.*

VANDA (*as* DUNAYEV): *A man usually says that to a woman whose individuality he is about to undermine.*

THOMAS (*as* KUSHEMSKI): *If you don't mind my saying so, you are not only a Greek and a pagan—and an individual. You seem to me to be a goddess.*

VANDA (*as* DUNAYEV): *Really? Which one?*

THOMAS (*as* KUSHEMSKI): *Venus.*

VANDA: And Vanda really *is* Venus, right? Am I crazy? She's like Venus in disguise or something, come down to get him. To, like, torture him.

THOMAS: Well . . . Not really . . . Or not exactly . . .

VANDA: Okay, I won't ask. You probably wanted it to be, like, ambivalent.

THOMAS: Ambiguous.

VANDA: Right, right.

THOMAS: Actually, it's the same story as *The Bacchae*, isn't it?

VANDA: Yeah! What's *The Bacchae*? Just kidding. It's an old play, right?

THOMAS: It's an old play.

VANDA: "Citizens of Corinth!" One of those plays? "Behold this mortal man, Testiculus, cursed for his offenses to the gods and totally fucked for all eternity!"

THOMAS: Yes, it's one of those plays. The god Dionysus comes down and reduces Pentheus the king of Thebes to a mass of quivering feminine jelly in a dress.

VANDA: Sounds hot.

THOMAS: The crazed women of Thebes—the Bacchae—tear Pentheus to pieces and Dionysus leaves triumphant.

VANDA: Oh, yeah, yeah, I think I saw that.

THOMAS: Except here it's not Dionysus, it's Aphrodite.

VANDA: Right! Remind me ... ?

THOMAS: Aphrodite is the Greek version of Venus.

VANDA: The same person.

THOMAS: Same goddess.

VANDA: Hail, Aphrodite!

THOMAS: Hail, Aphrodite! Am I insufferably pedantic?

VANDA: Uh-huh. But it's kinda cute. What are we doing?

THOMAS (*as* KUSHEMSKI): *You seem to me to be a goddess.*

VANDA (*as* DUNAYEV): *Really? Which one?*

THOMAS (*as* KUSHEMSKI): *Venus. But could Venus's pagan principles work in our more civil century? And without slaves? The Greeks only lived as freely as they did because they had slaves.*

VANDA (*as* DUNAYEV): *Then I seem to be in need of one. Would you be my slave, Herr Doktor Kushemski?*

THOMAS (*as* KUSHEMSKI): *Happily. Give me a woman honest enough to say, "I am Pompadour, I am Borgia, I am the master to whom you are bound"—and I'll kneel to her.*

VANDA (*as* DUNAYEV): *But where would Aphrodite find her master today?*

THOMAS (*as* KUSHEMSKI): *No man is worthy of dominating a goddess. He's only worthy of being subjugated by her.*

(*He kneels.*)

Subjugate me.

(*A moment. She laughs.*)

VANDA (*as* DUNAYEV): *What, in love with me already?*

THOMAS (*as* KUSHEMSKI): *Profoundly. And suffering as if I'd known you all my life.*

VANDA (*as* DUNAYEV): *Stand up. Stand away from me.*

(*He moves away and stands.*)

I must say you do intrigue me. I like your earnestness and your clarity of thought. Your great knowledge, your depth of feeling. Physically you are not unattractive. But when a man submits to me, I see a trick.

THOMAS (*as* KUSHEMSKI): *This is no trick. Only love me.*

VANDA (*as* DUNAYEV): *You see? Orders already.*

THOMAS (*as* KUSHEMSKI): *Marry me.*

VANDA (*as* DUNAYEV): *I'm a frivolous woman, Herr Kushemski. You'd have to be very brave to love me. I've told you my principles and how I live.*

THOMAS (*as* KUSHEMSKI): *I only know that I want you to be my wife.*

VANDA (*as* DUNAYEV): *You don't really know a thing about me.*

THOMAS (*as* KUSHEMSKI): *Dominate me.*

VANDA (*as* DUNAYEV): *It's absurd.*

THOMAS (*as* KUSHEMSKI): *In time you'd only try to wrest power from me, as every lover does. Why waste time in the struggle? I hand all power over to you in advance, now and forever. Unconditionally. Dominate me. Do with me what you will. Beat me if you like.*

VANDA (*as* DUNAYEV): *Well, this is certainly novel.*

THOMAS: Stand over there.

VANDA: What?

THOMAS: Stand next to the divan.

VANDA: It feels better from here.

THOMAS: Well, I think you should be over there. You're taking power. Take a power position.

VANDA: (*Stands next to the divan.*) *This is certainly novel.*—No, it feels all wrong.

THOMAS: Stay there and try it.—*I hand all power over to you in advance, now and forever. Unconditionally. Dominate me. Do with me what you will. Beat me if you like.*

VANDA (*as* DUNAYEV, *flatly*): *Well, this is certainly novel.*

THOMAS: You're not trying.

VANDA: You wanted me here, you got me here, I'm saying the line. And hey. It's an audition.

THOMAS: It's also an audition to see if you can take direction. Now *stand there.*

(*She does.*)

> *I hand all power over to you in advance, now and forever. Unconditionally. Dominate me. Do with me what you will. Beat me if you like.*

VANDA: *Well, this is certainly novel.*—God, you're so right. This does feel better.

THOMAS (*as* KUSHEMSKI): *This is the future of men and women. Let the one who would kneel, kneel. Let the one who would submit anyway, submit now.*

VANDA (*as* DUNAYEV): *What do you want, in your heart of heart of hearts?*

THOMAS (*as* KUSHEMSKI): *To be less than nothing. To have no will of my own. To be your property and vanish in your sublime essence. To dress and undress you, to hand you your stockings and put the shoes on your feet.*

VANDA (*as* DUNAYEV): *You call that love?*

THOMAS (*as* KUSHEMSKI): *Of the highest sort. The kind that most people reserve for their god. In love as in politics, one partner must rule. One of them must be the hammer, the other the anvil. I willingly accept being the anvil.*—Should I stop?

VANDA: No, I love it. I love it. God, the insight. Especially about women. Thomas, you really understand women.

THOMAS: Years of study. Where was I?

VANDA: Being the anvil.

THOMAS (*as* KUSHEMSKI): *Great love is born of opposites, not equals. You and I are those opposites, Vanda. I seek pain and you pleasure. And you who seek pleasure must never defer to anyone's feelings. You must enjoy without pity, indulge yourself ruthlessly. You must use a lover as he would use you. You must rule him, you must wring him dry.*

VANDA (*as* DUNAYEV): *You're fantastic.*

THOMAS (*as* KUSHEMSKI): *If you won't take me as your husband then take me as your slave. Treat me with divine cruelty. Punish me— simply for being what I am—and because as a goddess you have the right to.*

VANDA (*as* DUNAYEV): *Why would I ever mistreat a man who loves me?*

THOMAS (*as* KUSHEMSKI): *Because it will make me worship you even more.*

VANDA (*as* DUNAYEV): *I don't want to be worshipped.*

THOMAS (*as* KUSHEMSKI): *That's the first lie that's passed your lips. Every woman wants to be worshipped, just as our Creator does. So create me. Ruin me. Annihilate me.*

(*Cell phone rings.*)

Excuse me.

(*Into phone.*)

Hi. No, I'm still here. No, everything's good, everything's good. I don't know, maybe in a few minutes. I'll call you when I'm leaving. Great. Ciao, doll.

(*He hangs up.*)

So—

VANDA: Excuse me.

(*Has taken a cell phone from her purse. Into phone.*)

Hi. No, everything's cool. The audition went okay. We'll see. Anyway, I'm at the temp agency, they think they might have something for me. Yeah, Dictaphone typing. A night job, typing till morning. Some legal agency, they gotta get the contract in before morning, blah blah blah. I dunno. Well, that's too bad, isn't it. I said *too bad.* 'Bye.

(*Hangs up.*)

Jesus . . .

THOMAS: Your significant other?

VANDA: Does anybody still say that?

THOMAS: Sorry. What's English for "significant other" these days?

VANDA: "Asshole."

THOMAS: Doesn't matter.

VANDA: You're wondering how come I lied, right?

THOMAS: It's none of my business.

VANDA: What does Vanda say? "Why should I deny myself anything?" I got other fish to fuck. To coin a phrase.

THOMAS: So you're the hammer and he's the anvil.

VANDA: What am I supposed to do, say, Yeah, okay, honey, anything you say? Get led around by the nose? This ain't about love. It's about getting a piece of me. You want the piece, you gotta put up with the rest of me. Isn't that what this play's all about?

THOMAS: Is it?

VANDA: Are you kidding?

THOMAS: I don't know. Am I?

VANDA: Come on. Kushemski loves it, getting led around.

THOMAS: Does he really?

VANDA: Will you *stop* it? You're so goddamn *coy*. It's like being on a fucking dance floor with you.

THOMAS: Do you want some coffee? There's still some made, though it's probably tar by now. I can pour you some. Do you want some? What.

VANDA: You're not coming on to me, are you, Tom?

THOMAS: No—I just wanted to know if you wanted some coffee.

VANDA: Is it "symbolic coffee"?

THOMAS: No, it's real coffee. It's live coffee.

VANDA: You think your wife would approve of you offering me some real, live coffee?

THOMAS: (*Pouring two cups of coffee.*) I'm not married.

VANDA: I thought from the phone . . .

THOMAS: That's my fiancée.

VANDA: Same difference. What would *Fiancée* think? Aren't you the guy who once said in some interview, "Working in the theater is the world's greatest way to get laid"?

THOMAS: I was a kid. It was my first interview.

VANDA: You never been married?

THOMAS: Nope.

VANDA: Living with Mom all these years?

THOMAS: No, there've been plenty of women along the way. Nobody ever worked out, somehow. Till now. You see, I have this very old-fashioned kink.

VANDA: Fox furs?

THOMAS: No. I have to fall in love.

VANDA: That's a pretty serious kink.

THOMAS: The thing is, when I do fall . . .

VANDA: You go the whole nine yards, huh.

THOMAS: Bells and whistles. Spots in front of my eyes. Chaos. Thunderbolts . . .

(*Holds out a cup of coffee for her.*)

So—coffee, or no coffee?

VANDA (*as* DUNAYEV, *taking the cup*): *I could imagine giving myself to one man for life, if he commanded my respect. If he overpowered me with his strength. Overwhelmed me with the force of his being. If he enslaved me. I'm going to tell you a secret, Severin. I would submit to a man like that—and I would be faithful, too. I'd kneel to him and bend my neck to him and be his slave . . . So it seems we're not a very good match, are we? We cancel each other out.*

THOMAS (*as* KUSHEMSKI): *And I say we're created for each other. Don't you feel that, Vanda? Don't you feel it, too?*

VANDA (*as* DUNAYEV): *Let me propose a trial. A business deal, if you will. I'll give you one year to prove that you're the man for me.*

THOMAS (*as* KUSHEMSKI): *A year is a long time.*

VANDA (*as* DUNAYEV): *Ah. So you're dictating the terms now?*

THOMAS (*as* KUSHEMSKI): *I beg your pardon.*

VANDA (*as* DUNAYEV): *Within that year, since you so rashly give me the choice of husband or slave, you will be my slave. Men being what men are, I'll draw up a contract defining the terms.*—So, wow, she's like *ready*, huh. I guess she was always ready, before she even got there.

THOMAS: Was she?

VANDA: Will you *stop* that? You wrote it, you tell me.

THOMAS: I don't know if she was "ready," as you say. And I'm not being coy.

VANDA: I guess you wanted it ambivalent.

THOMAS: Ambiguous.

VANDA: Ambiguous. Or is she just so horny she doesn't care how she gets off?

THOMAS: I hadn't thought of it that way. "Horny."

VANDA: Or, is she cutting him a tougher deal—be my slavey for a year and *then* you get to fuck me? You were trying to be ambivalent.

THOMAS: Ambiguous.

VANDA: Ambiguous.

THOMAS: From his perspective, Vanda may be his last chance. Maybe his only chance.

VANDA: She is? At what?

THOMAS: A normal life. That feels normal to *him*.

VANDA: Yeah. Basically, he's got this beat-me-whip-me kink and he wants to see if she's up for it. He's auditioning her.

THOMAS: She's auditioning him, too.

VANDA: He's an oddity. She's a commodity. Like all women in 1870-whatever. What.

THOMAS: Who *are* you, Frau Vanda Jordan?

VANDA: I'm a pagan. I'm a Greek.

THOMAS: No, really.

VANDA: You're coming on to me again.

THOMAS: Where in the world did you come from? What's your program bio?

VANDA: I'm an army brat. I'm from nowhere.

THOMAS: Where, what city, what state?

VANDA (*as* DUNAYEV): *Since you so rashly give me the choice of husband or slave, you will be my slave. Men being what men are, I'll draw up a contract defining the terms. Do you consent?*

THOMAS (*as* KUSHEMSKI): *To anything you demand.*

VANDA (*as* DUNAYEV): *Here's my hand on it.*—They shake hands.

(*They mime shaking hands from a distance.*)

There's a Greek who's come to town.

THOMAS (*as* KUSHEMSKI): *A Greek . . . ?*

VANDA (*as* DUNAYEV): *A real Greek. He rides a snow-white stallion and wears high black leather boots and has a line of medals across his chest. A strapping fellow, usually with a pair of Negro servants in tow. I want you to find out his name and address, where he comes from, his history, everything about him. I'm going to let this handsome animal pay court to me.*

THOMAS (*as* KUSHEMSKI): *But Vanda—*

VANDA (*as* DUNAYEV): *What's this? Insurrection already?*

THOMAS (*as* KUSHEMSKI): *Forgive me.*

VANDA (*as* DUNAYEV): *Wait for me tomorrow in the birch grove, by the statue of Aphrodite.*

THOMAS (*as* KUSHEMSKI): *At what time?*

VANDA (*as* DUNAYEV): *You can wait for me until I decide to arrive. And don't come unless you've found out about this Greek. Kiss my foot.*

THOMAS: (*Without doing so, just inclining his head.*) He kneels and kisses her foot.

VANDA: I love this moment. Just, bang, "Kiss my foot."—*Now you may put my fur on me.*

(*He wraps the shawl around her but lingers, gripping her shoulders from behind.*)

   Severin, where will all this end?

THOMAS (*as* KUSHEMSKI): *That is in your power, Frau Vanda von Dunayev, not mine. When next I see you, will you . . . ?*

VANDA (*as* DUNAYEV, *pulling away from him*): *Will I what?*

THOMAS (*as* KUSHEMSKI): *Will you wear this? Will you wear fur?*

(*A roll of thunder.*)

VANDA (*as* DUNAYEV): *Thank you for the coffee. Slave.*

(*A pause.*)

   Now I really do need some. Coffee, I mean.

(*She turns the fluorescents back on and pours herself coffee at the stand.*)

   Wow. Old Leo was pretty intense. All they have to do is shake hands and it's like *steamy.*

THOMAS: The joys of a more repressed age. When conversation itself was erotic.

VANDA: When conversation was all they *got.* But this isn't how it happens in the book. I mean . . .

THOMAS: So you know the book. You've read *Venus in Fur?*

VANDA: Okay, so I found a copy and I kinda glanced at it.

THOMAS: You've done your homework. I approve. And you were lying before. "So this play is like based on something or something?"

VANDA: Okay, so I wanted some brownie points. And you say it's not S&M, lemme show you my copy.

(*Digs a book out of her big bag.*)

High-heeled patent-leather boots and a riding crop and a babe's bare ass. That ain't exactly Titian. It's S&M, babe. It's porn. Put that on the poster, you'll sell out.

THOMAS: (*Looking at the book.*) Your *Venus* is as well-thumbed as your script. You didn't just happen to find this and read it, did you. That was a lie, too.

VANDA: Okay, so I kinda knew the book. How come you didn't put in that scene with Venus? When she appears to him at the beginning? Naked under a fur, in front of a fireplace?

THOMAS: I didn't know how to fit it in.

VANDA: Just stick it in at the top—so to speak—before he meets Vanda. You can't do this story without Venus. You could even have the same actress play 'em both. I'll do it. Naked onstage? Fuck. I'll take a freebie.

THOMAS: I'll think about it.

VANDA: Why? We can improv it. Maybe you'll get some ideas. Okay, I'm Venus now.

(*She undoes her dress and steps out of it so that she is again in bra and panties.*)

Imagine me totally naked.

THOMAS: You're not coming on to me now, are you, Vanda?

VANDA: Come on, you're a big boy. Just think of me as *Fiancée*, and improvise.

(*She repositions the divan and strips the throw from it, tossing that on the floor.*)

THOMAS: I've never done this before.

VANDA: That's what all the girls say.

(*A roll of thunder.*)

Just bullshit, in character. Okay, set the scene, where are we. Top of the play.

THOMAS: Well. Kushemski's room. The middle of the night . . .

VANDA: Okay. Middle of the night. Two-oh-two A.M. . . .

(*She turns the fluorescents back off, goes to the fuse box, and adjusts the lights to nighttime.*)

Maybe there's just one candle burning.

(*Lights the clip-on lamp on the table.*)

And the fireplace going, stage right.

THOMAS: Stage left.

VANDA: Stage left. Good. And Kushemski is, what.

THOMAS: I don't know. Reading.

VANDA: *Of course.*

THOMAS: Too trite?

VANDA: If he's gonna be reading when he meets Vanda, he
can't be reading here. Just hand out library cards, why
don'tcha.

THOMAS: He's writing in his diary.

VANDA: I like it. He's sitting at the desk with his back turned.
Maybe the fireplace flickers up and we see Venus in the raw
curled up like a cat, draped revealingly in a fur.

(*She lies back on the divan.*)

So drape me. You're the director.

(*He comes over and drapes the "fur" over her, then starts away.*)

Revealingly.

(*He comes back and re-drapes her, more slowly, lingering a moment.*)

Now go to your desk. Go on. *In character.*

(THOMAS *"assumes character" and goes to the table.*)

Write in your diary. Write something.

THOMAS: I am.

VANDA: *Out loud.* This is *theater.* How else we gonna know what
you are? It's the top of the show, the lights are just coming
up. All we hear is the sound of an old clock. Tick. Tick.
Tick. Tick . . .

THOMAS (*as* KUSHEMSKI): *"October twenty-second, 1870. Two-oh-two A.M. I am staying at a springs surrounded by woods and wilderness. There's no moon tonight, nothing but darkness and silence . . ."*

(VANDA *does a bird whistle.*)

"No, wait. I hear . . ."

(*She whistles again.*)

". . . a sparrow."

VANDA: A nightingale.

THOMAS (*as* KUSHEMSKI): *"A nightingale."*

(VANDA *screeches.*)

". . . and the howl of a lovesick cat. I don't know why I feel so terribly alone, and lonely. Am I going to be this all my life? So sick at heart, so unfulfilled? Will no one draw me out of this abyss that bears my name? Severin von Kushemski."

VANDA (*as* VENUS): *Guten Abend, mein Herr.*

THOMAS (*as* KUSHEMSKI): *Well, well. Have the Germans invaded again?*

VANDA (*as* VENUS): *I hope I do not disturb . . .*

THOMAS (*as* KUSHEMSKI): *Not at all. Hail, Aphrodite!*

VANDA (*as* VENUS): *Zo, you haff not forgotten me?*

THOMAS (*as* KUSHEMSKI): *Forget you? My oldest and dearest enemy?*

VANDA (*as* VENUS): *You are zo sweet. You don't vant to kiss my hand?*

(*He does so.*)

> Nice. *Ja, but Thomas . . . —Did I say Thomas? Whoops!—Ja, but Severin. It's so cold in here. Every time I visit you I am catching cold.*

(*Sneezes.*)

> *You see? Already I have pleggum in ze tubes.*

THOMAS (*as* KUSHEMSKI): *Maybe if you didn't fly around naked all the time.*

VANDA (*as* VENUS): *Ja, but I am Venus. I must be all ze time naked, or who knows me? You don't want to take those off those scratchy clothes and come cuddle? There's room here—under my mink.*

THOMAS (*as* KUSHEMSKI): *No, thank you.*

VANDA (*as* VENUS): *But I brought this mink especially for you, from Olympus. It's heavenly. You see ze label? "Made in Heaven."*

THOMAS (*as* KUSHEMSKI): *Why would I be so interested in your mink?*

VANDA (*as* VENUS): *Oh, Severin, I know your little hobby. Your predilection for fine pelts. It's disgusting. You don't want a woman, you want her coat. You ought to marry a raccoon.*

THOMAS (*as* KUSHEMSKI): *Better a raccoon than any woman I've ever met.*

VANDA (*as* VENUS): *Ja, but ziss mink und me, ve make you ze perfect wife.*

THOMAS (*as* KUSHEMSKI): *Yes. And then you and your mink leave me, to cuddle with some other man. Like any mortal woman would.*

VANDA (*as* VENUS): *Ja, but if—under my mink—I open my thighs . . . you would not have me?*

THOMAS (*as* KUSHEMSKI): *This isn't Pompeii, you know. This is civilization.*

VANDA (*as* VENUS): *And what is that, syphilization?*

THOMAS (*as* KUSHEMSKI): *Civilization means that we don't spread our thighs to just anyone. We have principles.*

VANDA (*as* VENUS): *Ja, ja, you modern men, you crave your principles but also a little paganism on ze side. You want to think by day, but by night you want to dance naked around a fire. Und me, you turn into a demon, you are so afraid of love.*

THOMAS (*as* KUSHEMSKI): *Love. Is that what you're offering?*

VANDA (*as* VENUS): *Eh-heh.*

THOMAS (*as* KUSHEMSKI): *A battle's more like it. The same battle that was on in Pompeii. Joining two people together then setting them at each other's throats. Power, that's what you want. You want to have me, and then put your foot on my neck like every petty tyrant who's ever lived. Well, I have a civilized duty to resist you!*

VANDA (*as* VENUS): *And you still think you can? You think you will not bend to me?*

THOMAS (*as* KUSHEMSKI): *Never.*

VANDA (*as* VENUS): *You dare to resist me?*

THOMAS (*as* KUSHEMSKI): *Yes, I dare.*

VANDA (*as* VENUS): *You little piece of nothing! You dust! You dare to resist a goddess?*

THOMAS (*as* KUSHEMSKI): *The same way I've resisted you for years. Ever since one of your sex first taught me the cruelty of women.*

VANDA (*as* VENUS): *Severin, I will have you crawling to me on your knees. I will have you begging.*

THOMAS (*as* KUSHEMSKI): *Never.*

VANDA (*as* VENUS): *You are mine already, and you will be mine for all time to come.*

THOMAS (*as* KUSHEMSKI): *Never!*

VANDA (*as* VENUS): *Ze proof, as they say, is in ze pudding. Auf Wiedersehen, mein Freund. I'll be back.*—And then, poof, she vanishes!

THOMAS: Wow.

VANDA: Not bad, huh.

(VANDA *changes the lights back.*)

THOMAS: Wow.

VANDA: You could write that up and stick it in just like it is.

THOMAS: So to speak.

VANDA: I thought I'd add a little Marlene Dietrich . . .

THOMAS: No, it was great. It was brilliant. This is a totally different side of Kushemski.

VANDA: Yeah, here he is with Venus in the middle of the night and he's all, *No, no, you bitch.* Next morning with Vanda, he's like, *Take me, pleeeeeze.*

THOMAS: You could bring the lights down on that, lights back up to morning, knock knock knock, and there's Vanda. Like Venus in disguise.

VANDA: Taking her revenge.

THOMAS: It's great.

VANDA: So is it you?

THOMAS: What . . .

VANDA: This. Is it you? Kushemski-Novachek, Novachek-Kushemski.

THOMAS: No, this isn't me.

VANDA: Or maybe you're Vanda.

THOMAS: This play doesn't have anything to do with me.

VANDA: Uh-huh. You're just peeping over the fence. You're just the writer. Sorry. Adapter.

THOMAS: Why do people always think a playwright has to be the people he writes about?

VANDA: Because playwrights do that shit *all the time.* You put me in a play, I'll fuckin' kill you.

THOMAS: Can't I just write characters?

VANDA: Sure. And you just *happened* to find these characters in this ancient German S&M novel, Herr Doktor Novachek.

THOMAS: It's a famous book.

VANDA: So you didn't have an "innocent instant" when you were twelve, in the library?

THOMAS: No.

VANDA: With the cat?

THOMAS: No.

VANDA: Maybe you're still waiting for your big moment.

THOMAS: Look. I thought this relationship was fascinating. Very rich, very complex.

VANDA: Okay.

THOMAS: I thought the story was dramatic. Naturally theatrical.

VANDA: Methinks the lady doth protest too much. No, okay, go on.

THOMAS: Mostly, I loved the size of these people's emotions. Nobody has emotions this size anymore. Outsized emotions. Operatic emotions. Kushemski and Vanda are like Tristan and Isolde. Nobody's in total thrall like this anymore. Nobody's overcome by passion like this, or goes through this kind of rage.

VANDA: Meet some of *my* friends.

THOMAS: All right, fine. Maybe it's me. But there are others who don't know people with emotions like these. Don't we go to plays for passions we don't get in life?

VANDA: I thought we're supposed to go to *life* for passions we're not getting in life.

THOMAS: All right. Fine. I don't know anything.

(*Throws himself on the divan.*)

VANDA: So when you go home, *Fiancée* doesn't tie you to the
   bed and take out a whip?

THOMAS: No.

VANDA: You should ask her, see if *Fiancée* is up for it.

THOMAS: Could you stop calling her *Fiancée*?

VANDA: Sorry. How does your Significant Other feel about this
   play?

THOMAS: She's not crazy about it.

VANDA: She's probably worried you've got this whole kinky side
   and she doesn't want you to put this play on because people
   will think this might be you. Or her.

THOMAS: It isn't. Her *or* me.

(VANDA *pulls her chair over to the head of the divan, like a psychoanalyst.*)

VANDA: But let me guess about . . .

THOMAS: Stacy.

VANDA: Stacy. She's a little younger than you. Good family.
   Grew up in one of those nice old stone houses. Maybe
   Connecticut.

THOMAS: Massachusetts, actually.

VANDA: Southwestern Massachusetts, near the Connecticut border. Twenty minutes from Litchfield. Am I close?

THOMAS: I have to admit.

VANDA: She's tall. Maybe a little bossy, in a nice way. Lots of hair, long legs, big brain. Probably went to Stanford. Am I close?

THOMAS: UCLA.

VANDA: Maybe even a PhD. Well?

THOMAS: She's finishing her doctorate.

VANDA: She's got a dog. Let's see. Maybe a Weimaraner. That you like okay but could secretly do without, named something like . . . something traditional, something Old Testament and manly. Like . . . Seth. Ezra.

THOMAS: Noah. I thought you didn't know anything about the Bible.

VANDA: I bet she's the breadwinner, too. I mean, a room with a pipe in the middle of it? Not exactly the big bucks on Broadway. She probably came with money, but while she finishes up her thesis she's working some nice investment job. Or day-trading and making a fortune. Am I right? I'm right. But hey, you're an artist. She loves that about you. And she just knows you're going to be a great big success someday. Plus she appreciates you for your sensitivity. Maybe you're the first guy she met who's got any. She reads a lot. Same books you do. Likes the opera and the ballet and shit. Like you. At night you talk about what's going on in French philosophy and what's new in *The New York Review of Books*, then you have some nice quiet sex. And nice quiet sex is fine. Though there's this rumbling at the back of your head. This voice that wants something else. I don't know what that is, but . . . *Rumble, rumble, rumble.* Anyway, hey, you're happy. You *like* her. You really, really like her and you two are going to have a nice life talking about French philosophy and what's in *The New York Review of Books* and maybe have a couple of kids who can do that when they grow up. And then you'll die.

THOMAS: Are we that transparent? I don't mean Stacy and me.

VANDA: What does the play say? "We're all explicable. What we're not is extricable." Or didn't you believe that when you wrote it? That line's not in the book. I checked. And you're not Kushemski.

THOMAS: No.

VANDA: Should we read on?

THOMAS: Yes, let's read.

VANDA: When they meet the next day? The birch grove?

THOMAS: Sure.

(*A rumble of thunder. She gets into her dress while he rearranges chairs.*)

This is the fountain and we'll make the pipe the statue of Venus.

VANDA: Hail, Aphrodite!

THOMAS: Hail, Aphrodite!

(*She turns her back for him to do up her dress. He does so. Pause.*)

Do you want to look the scene over?

VANDA (*as* DUNAYEV): *No, Severin. No. No. No. It's not right. All this talk of subjugation and slavery. You've corrupted me with all your talk.*

THOMAS (*as* KUSHEMSKI): *I believe that in your heart of hearts you would enjoy controlling a man.*

VANDA (*as* DUNAYEV): *No.*

THOMAS (*as* KUSHEMSKI): *You might even enjoy torturing him.*

VANDA (*as* DUNAYEV): *No.*

THOMAS (*as* KUSHEMSKI): *Admit your nature.*

VANDA (*as* DUNAYEV): *It's not my nature.*

THOMAS (*as* KUSHEMSKI): *See what your nature is. Or change your nature.*

VANDA (*as* DUNAYEV): *Can I not make you be reasonable?*

THOMAS (*as* KUSHEMSKI): *It's not reason that I'm after. You said you would forgo no possible experience.*

VANDA (*as* DUNAYEV): *And you would have me eat my words.*

THOMAS (*as* KUSHEMSKI): *I'd have you prove you meant them.*

VANDA (*as* DUNAYEV): *Severin, don't you see? Don't you understand you'll never be safe in the hands of a woman? Of any woman?*— Now this part is so sexist it makes me, like, *scream.*

THOMAS: It's not sexist. What's sexist about it?

VANDA: "You'll never be safe in the hands of a woman"?

THOMAS: That *is* from the book.

VANDA: I don't care what it's from. It's sexist. The whole thing's really kinda trite, when you think about it.

THOMAS: What's trite?

VANDA: He gets spanked one day and bingo, he's into whips and chains?

THOMAS: Apparently that's what happened to Sacher-Masoch.

VANDA: Did it happen to you?

THOMAS: *No.*

VANDA: So how do you know?

THOMAS: To me, this is a play about two people who are joined irreparably. They're handcuffed at the heart.

VANDA: Yeah, joined by his kink.

THOMAS: No. By their passion.

VANDA: *His* passion.

THOMAS: You're denying *her* passion. That's sexist, too. She's as passionate as he is, and this play is about how these two passions collide.

VANDA: What age are you living in? He brings her into this, and *she's* the one who gets to look bad, she's the villain.

THOMAS: There are no villains in this piece. It's a plea for people to understand that. Understand there's something out there more powerful than we are, and it can run us or it can ruin us. This is a chemical reaction. Two people meet and ignite each other. Look. I wrote this. I've been studying this. I should think I know what my own play's about. It's not making some general statement about men *or* women.

VANDA: Sex, class, gender, pal.

THOMAS: It's about a woman who recognizes something in herself—possibly—and about a man who until he meets her is forced to hide his true self away.

VANDA: Yeah. This *prig*.

THOMAS: Why are you putting him down like this?

VANDA: She's this very nice, this *innocent* person who comes
wandering in.

THOMAS: You don't understand, you don't understand.

VANDA: She *says,* "You've corrupted me."

THOMAS: *Is* she innocent? Was this desire for domination always
there, or does he bring it out of her?

VANDA: Maybe she's just a woman. This is like some old Victo-
rian Teutonic tract against *Das Female.* He forces her into a
power play and then he blames *her.*

THOMAS: That's not it at all, that's not what this play is about
at all.

VANDA: And *the play* blames her.

THOMAS: It doesn't blame her.

VANDA: You don't *see* that?

THOMAS: How does it blame her?

VANDA: It's blaming her on every page, in every line! What happens at the end? She humiliates him one last time, she gets
Count what's-his-name to whip him, she leaves Kushemski
there with his dick in his hand—and she gets blamed like it
was all her fault! Like he didn't want it in the first place! Like
he wasn't asking for it! I think old Kushemski's hot for the
Count, that's what I think.

THOMAS: How can you be so stupid? Really? How can you be so good at playing her, and be so fucking stupid about her? And about everything else in this play. You fucking idiot. You fucking idiot *woman*. Yes. Idiot *woman*. Idiot *actress*.

(*Pause.*)

VANDA: I think you owe me an apology, buster.

THOMAS: I'm sorry.

VANDA: Excuse me?

THOMAS: I'm sorry. I got a little carried away.

VANDA: Well. Can't take back what's been said.

(*She takes off the dress and gets into her leather skirt, packing up her things to leave, wearing her leather skirt and bra.*)

THOMAS: You might say this play is about . . . beware of what you wish for.

VANDA: Because she might come walking in the door. Don't fuck with a goddess is what it's about.

THOMAS: If you will. Sorry. What's modern for "if you will"?

VANDA: "Whatever."

THOMAS: Whatever.

VANDA: Good thing there's no such thing as a goddess, or you'd be fucked, boy.

THOMAS: All right. Yes. You're right. I take all your points. Could we read on? Would you mind? Please?

VANDA: *Don't you understand you'll never be safe in the hands of a woman? Of any woman?*

THOMAS (*as* KUSHEMSKI): *You and I are adventurers, Vanda. We're explorers of the spirit. We're expanding the limits of human nature.*

VANDA (*as* DUNAYEV): *Your nature is diseased. It was poisoned by the Countess. Now you're reaping the effects.*

THOMAS (*as* KUSHEMSKI): *You adore the effects, just as I do.*

VANDA (*as* DUNAYEV): *No.*

THOMAS (*as* KUSHEMSKI): *You love having me in your power.*

VANDA (*as* DUNAYEV): *No.*

THOMAS (*as* KUSHEMSKI): *Tell me anything you would have me do, anything in the world, and it's done.*

VANDA (*as* DUNAYEV): *I called you a dreamer, but "dreamer" is too petty. You're a fanatic. You're a mad visionary. You'll go to any lengths to realize your dreams.*

THOMAS (*as* KUSHEMSKI): *You are my dreams.*

VANDA (*as* DUNAYEV): *Break off with me, Severin, before it's too late.*

THOMAS (*as* KUSHEMSKI): *Do you love me?*

VANDA (*as* DUNAYEV): *I don't know.*

THOMAS (*as* KUSHEMSKI): *Find out. Prove that you do.*

VANDA (*as* DUNAYEV): *How?*

THOMAS (*as* KUSHEMSKI): *By doing what all lovers do. Hurt me.*

VANDA (*as* DUNAYEV): *No. I find it repulsive. And I despise playacting. I'm not your Countess-Aunt. I am I.*

THOMAS: Try that line again. Defy him.

VANDA (*as* DUNAYEV): *I'm not your Countess-Aunt. I am I.*

THOMAS: Again. With fire.

VANDA: WHAT DO YOU WANT FROM ME, THOMAS? I AM NOT YOUR FUCKING COUNTESS-AUNT, I AM I. WHAT DO YOU WANT?

THOMAS: I don't know.

VANDA: Because I don't think we're talking about this play anymore.

THOMAS: I just want more, is all.

VANDA: Well, I'm not her. I'm just a stupid bitch who walked in here looking for a job. And *I am not your Countess-Aunt, I am I.* How's that?

THOMAS: It's good. It's very good.

VANDA: Look, I don't think I can do this. I'm sorry. It's too much.

(*She starts to gather up her things to go.*)

THOMAS: Stay, Vanda. Stay. Really.

(*She stops.*)

VANDA: Say "please."

THOMAS: (*Drops to his knees.*) Please.

VANDA: You are evil.

THOMAS (*as* KUSHEMSKI): *Don't you understand? You have me completely in your power.*

VANDA (*as* DUNAYEV): *Liar. You're not in my power, I'm in yours. You say that you're my slave but you're the one who's mastered me. You're more insidious than the greatest temptress who ever lived. It's like some wicked plot.*—It's really true, isn't it.

THOMAS: What . . .

VANDA: He keeps saying she's got all this power over him. But *he's* the one with the power, not her. The more he submits, the more control he's got over her. It's weird.

THOMAS: It's intricate.

VANDA (*as* DUNAYEV): *Here's the contract we spoke about. It says that you will show me slavish submission and will follow all my orders without contradiction. That you renounce your identity completely. That your soul and your honor and your body as well as your mind and feelings and spirit belong to me. That you are in short a chattel in the possession of Vanda von Dunayev—forever. Sign on the bottom. Well?*

THOMAS (*as* KUSHEMSKI): *I thought my service was for a year.*

VANDA (*as* DUNAYEV): *Who is drawing up these terms, you or I?*

THOMAS (*as* KUSHEMSKI): *May I read the contract?*

VANDA (*as* DUNAYEV): *Why? Don't you trust me?*

(*He "signs."*)

Good. You will address me from this moment forward as "Madam" and you'll speak to me only when spoken to. You'll bring me all my meals and wait in the hallway for my orders. In the mornings you'll dress me and at night undress me. You will hand me my stockings and put on my shoes. And from now on I'm going to call you "Thomas."

THOMAS: It's Gregor in the script . . .

VANDA: I've changed it.—*From now on I'm going to call you "Thomas." I want you in my footman's livery, wearing my coat of arms.*

THOMAS (*as* KUSHEMSKI): *As a gentleman—*

VANDA (*as* DUNAYEV): *As a gentleman you're bound to keep your word. Did you not just sign a paper swearing that you're my slave?*

THOMAS (*as* KUSHEMSKI): *Your slave, not your butler.*

VANDA (*as* DUNAYEV): *I fail to see the distinction.*

THOMAS (*as* KUSHEMSKI): *Is this a game?*

VANDA (*as* DUNAYEV): *This is what I am. I'm stubborn and I'm will-ful and I'm greedy, and when I start something I finish it. The more resistance I come up against the more determined I become.*

THOMAS (*as* KUSHEMSKI): *But at heart you're noble by nature—*

VANDA (*as* DUNAYEV): *What do you know about my nature except what you've decided about it?*

THOMAS (*as* KUSHEMSKI): *Forgive me. I am despicable.*

VANDA (*as* DUNAYEV): *Give me your passport and your money. Give them.*

(*He gives her his wallet and she tosses it into her big bag.*)

We leave tomorrow for Florence. I'll travel in first class, you in third, as my footman.

THOMAS (*as* KUSHEMSKI): *Third class . . . ?*

VANDA (*as* DUNAYEV): *When we arrive you'll eat and sleep in the servants' quarters. I believe you're going to need this.*

(*She takes a servant's jacket from her bag and holds it out to him.*)

Well, Thomas? What is it?

THOMAS (*as* KUSHEMSKI, *taking the jacket*): *Where will all this end?*

VANDA (*as* DUNAYEV): *End? It hasn't even started.*

THOMAS (*as* KUSHEMSKI): *But Vanda . . .*

(*She mimes slapping his face.*)

VANDA: She slaps his face.—*Who gave you permission to call me that?*

THOMAS (*as* KUSHEMSKI): *Yes, Madam. Thank you, Madam.*

VANDA: She kisses him.

(*She mimes kissing him, coming close to him but not touching him.*)

She strokes his cheek.

(*She mimes stroking his cheek.*)

Did that hurt very much, darling?

THOMAS (*as* KUSHEMSKI): *Exquisitely.*

VANDA (*as* DUNAYEV): *So. Did you find out about this handsome Greek?*

THOMAS (*as* KUSHEMSKI): *The man's name is Alexis. At Athens, he's a Count.*

VANDA (*as* DUNAYEV): *He's beautiful, isn't he.*

THOMAS (*as* KUSHEMSKI): *He's very attractive.*

VANDA: I told you Kushemski's hot for the Count. He's *down* for the Count.—*Get me a box near his at the concert tonight. I'm going to let Count Alexis meet me. Indeed I'm going to let him do whatever he wants with me. What's the matter? I'm free to do as I like, aren't I? Well, slave?*

THOMAS (*as* KUSHEMSKI): *You electrify me.*

VANDA (*as* DUNAYEV): *Silence, you dog! Fetch me a birch cane.*

THOMAS: He brings her a birch cane and she whisks it in the air.

(*He mimes getting and giving her a "birch cane." She "whisks" it in the air.*)

VANDA (*as* DUNAYEV): *Do you hear that whistle? That sound makes my nerves vibrate like tuning forks. Everything inside me wants to see you writhing under the lash. To hear you beg for mercy. To see a so-called man reduced to womanly tears. My heart is in my throat. The air is red. What have you done to me, slave? Well? What have you done to me?*

(*Mimes "whipping" him.*)

What have you done? What have you done? What have you done? What have you done? Blah, blah, blah, blah . . .

THOMAS: What do you mean, blah-blah-blah.

VANDA: What, suddenly Vanda turns into the Wicked Witch of the West? "My nerves are tuning forks. The air is red." The air is purple, maybe. Look, Tom. I like you. I mean, I really, really like you. But I don't think this is gonna fly.

THOMAS: It has to. This is it. This is *the play*. And nobody's going to make me think otherwise. You don't know what you're talking about. You are not a playwright. You're not going to take this play down whether you're in it or not. So fuck you.

VANDA: Okay. It's your call.

(*Lightning and a rumble of thunder.*)

She takes out a knife and holds it to his throat.

(*She produces a knife out of nowhere and holds it to his throat.*)

VANDA (*as* DUNAYEV): *My God, I despise you.*

THOMAS (*as* KUSHEMSKI): *What is this? Vanda, what are you doing?*

VANDA (*as* DUNAYEV): *Do you think I don't understand your scheme? Do you think you could bring me into your little game and use me? Did you think you could subjugate* me?

THOMAS (*as* KUSHEMSKI): *I swear I never meant that, Vanda. I swear.*

VANDA (*as* DUNAYEV): *If you knew how delicious this is. Not just to have some random man in my control, some fool. But a man who's smitten with me, no less.*

(*Throws the knife aside.*)

Y'know, I oughta talk to Actors' Equity. Because if you don't know by now if I got the part . . .

THOMAS: I'd love to give you the part.

VANDA: That's what you say *now*. Do I get the part? And will you put that in writing?

(*Cell phone rings.*)

THOMAS: Excuse me.

(*Into phone.*)

Hi.

VANDA: Go to hell, Stacy!

THOMAS: (*Turning away so that Stacy can't hear.*) Hi. No, I'm still here. I'm just wrapping some things up.

VANDA: He's fucking me, Stacy! He's got me on the floor and he's fucking me up the ass!

THOMAS: (*Into phone.*) I don't know yet, pretty soon.

VANDA: He's fucking me like a Weimaraner!

THOMAS: (*Into phone.*) Why don't you go ahead and eat. I'll call you. Ciao.

(*Hangs up.*)

VANDA: How dare I, right? Or something like that.

THOMAS: How dare you is about right. What was that all about?

VANDA: Excuse me.

(*Into her cell phone.*)

Hi. Yeah. I don't know yet. I *told* you, I don't know. Well, listen, go fuck yourself, all right? I'll come home when I come home. 'Bye.

(*Hangs up.*)

Sorry about that.

THOMAS: There was nobody on the other end, was there.

VANDA: What?

THOMAS: You were faking that. You weren't talking to anybody.

VANDA: I was talking to my *significant other.*

THOMAS: So who is this guy?

VANDA: Who said it's a guy?

THOMAS: Why did you do that?

VANDA: Why is right.

THOMAS: I guess you didn't like me talking on my phone.

VANDA: So, like, *woman's revenge.* For being ignored.

THOMAS: Something like that.

VANDA: Blame the woman.

THOMAS: I'm not blaming.

VANDA: You know, most playwright-slash-directors woulda had me upended on the floor by now.

THOMAS: I guess I'm not like most playwright-slash-directors.

VANDA: Bullshit. You wouldn't fuck me on the floor if you thought you could get away with it?

THOMAS: No.

VANDA: What if I gave you permission?

THOMAS: How do you know so much about Stacy?

VANDA: We met at the gym. She seemed really nice. Gorgeous, too. Wow. Anyway, we're getting undressed, we get to talking—*girl talk*, in the shower—she said she had this boyfriend, a writer, kinda hard to know. I told her I used to be an actress, now I'm an operative—or trying to be—so she paid me a little to come here and look into you. Find out what you're made of, see if you really love her. Kind of a premarital fact-finding mission. Plus bank accounts, credit, and so on. I'm supposed to meet her at the hotel, do a full report. Beautiful body, by the way. Congratulations.

THOMAS: You are a magnificent creature.

VANDA: A man usually says that to a woman whose magnificence he's about to undermine.

THOMAS: Touché. Stacy doesn't shower at the gym.

VANDA: Doesn't she? She looked pretty wet the last time I saw her.—So let's go to the end. You'll need your footman's uniform.

(*She throws the servant's jacket at him. He puts it on. Then:*)

Thomas! You've kept me waiting.

THOMAS (*as* KUSHEMSKI): *I'm sorry, Madam. I was polishing the silver.*

VANDA (*as* DUNAYEV): *Don't you look dapper in that footman's jacket.*

THOMAS (*as* KUSHEMSKI): *Thank you, Madam.*

VANDA (*as* DUNAYEV): *Turn around. Show me.*

(*He does so.*)

> *Oh, yes. Quite irresistible. You could make me lose all sense of rank. You could make me forget that you're nothing but a lackey. But I think that something's still missing . . .*

THOMAS: Where is that? That's not in the . . .

VANDA: I'm improvising.—*I think that something's still missing, Thomas.*

(*She takes off her dog collar and puts it on him.*)

> *Oh, yes. The pièce de résistance. Very fetching. How does it feel?*

THOMAS (*as* KUSHEMSKI): *It feels good, Madam.*

VANDA (*as* DUNAYEV): *I might just fall in love with you, wearing that. What's the matter, why are you looking at me like that?*

THOMAS (*as* KUSHEMSKI): *Does that mean that you don't love me?*

VANDA (*as* DUNAYEV): *Oh, you bore me. Whimpering all the time. You bore me.*

THOMAS (*as* KUSHEMSKI): *Is it the Count? Are you in love with the Count?*

VANDA (*as* DUNAYEV, *throwing herself on the divan*): *Can I help it that he followed me to Florence?*

THOMAS (*as* KUSHEMSKI, *kneeling by her*): *That man doesn't love you. He wants you the way he's wanted a thousand others.*

VANDA (*as* DUNAYEV): *So what if he doesn't love me. Console yourself with that when I take him into my bed.*

THOMAS (*as* KUSHEMSKI): *Your heart is a vast stone desert.*

VANDA (*as* DUNAYEV, *kicking him away*): *Insolent swine! How dare you speak to me in that tone? Bring me my other shoes!*

THOMAS (*as* KUSHEMSKI, *rising and heading for the table*): *Yes, Madam.*

VANDA (*as* DUNAYEV): *Not over there. In the bag, you idiot.*

THOMAS (*as* KUSHEMSKI): *Yes, Madam.*

(*He gets a pair of thigh-high, steeply heeled patent-leather dominatrix boots from* VANDA*'s bag.*)

VANDA (*as* DUNAYEV): *From now on, Thomas, I want you to call me "Mistress." It's more degrading.*

THOMAS (*as* KUSHEMSKI): *Yes, Mistress.*

VANDA (*as* DUNAYEV): *Would you like to put my shoes on?*

THOMAS (*as* KUSHEMSKI): *Yes, Mistress.*

VANDA (*as* DUNAYEV): *I mean on me.*

THOMAS (*as* KUSHEMSKI): *Yes, Mistress.*

VANDA (*as* DUNAYEV): *You may.*

(*Long silence while he does so. When the boots are on her:*)

> *Maybe tomorrow I'll tie you to that post in the yard and prick you with golden hairpins. Or harness you to the plow and drive you with the whip. Would you like that?*

THOMAS (*as* KUSHEMSKI): *Yes, Mistress.*

VANDA (*as* DUNAYEV): *You're doing very, very well, Thomas. I might take you on as my servant permanently.*

THOMAS (*as* KUSHEMSKI): *Will there be anything else, Mistress?*

VANDA (*as* DUNAYEV): *Yes. One more thing.*—Call Stacy and tell her you won't be coming home tonight.

THOMAS: I can't do that.

VANDA: Oh, no?

(*Pulls hard on the dog collar.*)

You can't?

(*He takes out his phone and starts dialing.*)

And you can't tell her why either. No excuses, lame or otherwise.

THOMAS: (*Into cell phone.*) Stacy, it's me.

VANDA: "I won't be coming home tonight."

THOMAS: (*Into phone.*) I won't be coming home tonight.

VANDA: No excuses.

THOMAS: (*Into phone.*) I can't tell you why.

VANDA: Say good-bye.

THOMAS: (*Into phone.*) Good-bye.

VANDA: Now hang up and turn off your phone.

(*He does so. She throws the phone across the room.*)

Isn't it wonderful.

THOMAS: I'm sorry . . . ?

VANDA (*as* DUNAYEV): *Isn't it wonderful. Here, I mean. It's so much cozier than an hotel. Having this place all to ourselves. So nice and secluded.*

THOMAS (*as* KUSHEMSKI): *I hardly know where I am, quite frankly . . .*

VANDA (*as* DUNAYEV): *Why, you've got a whole new life ahead of you now. We do. Minus all those other people. All that chaos. Here all alone where I can do what I want with you, undisturbed. Just the two of us.*

THOMAS (*as* KUSHEMSKI): *The two of us—and your friend the Count.*

VANDA (*as* DUNAYEV): *I do wish you would stop harping on him. I've been too nice to you, Thomas. That's the problem. I haven't disciplined you sufficiently. And now look what you've said, look what you've done—just when I was about to take you into my bed.*

THOMAS (*as* KUSHEMSKI): *You mean, you would have me . . . ?*

VANDA (*as* DUNAYEV): *Yes, I would have you.*

(*She reclines on the divan.*)

Come. Come here. Place your arms around me.

(*He lies in her arms and does so.*)

You see? For an hour I can let you imagine you're a free man again. That you're my beloved, you simpleton. At some point it will dawn on you that you're nothing. That you are in reality whatever I want you to be. A person. An animal. An object. An empty pistol. A blank to be filled in. A void.

THOMAS (*as* KUSHEMSKI, *pulling away*): *I won't. I won't do it. I won't allow it to happen.*

VANDA (*as* DUNAYEV): *I beg your pardon . . . ?*

THOMAS (*as* KUSHEMSKI): *I've written you a letter.*

VANDA (*as* DUNAYEV): *A letter? Ah, yes, breaking off with me, no doubt. Because suddenly you find the degradation you yourself begged for too much to bear.*—I don't know, I just don't have a handle on this scene.

THOMAS: It seems pretty straightforward to me.

VANDA: HOW should it go? No, really, in your head, how does it go?

THOMAS: What's the cue line? What does he say?

VANDA: "I've written you a letter."

THOMAS (*as* DUNAYEV): *A letter? Ah, yes, breaking off with me, no doubt. Because suddenly you find the degradation you yourself begged for too much to bear. Well, Thomas, I have a contract. You've probably carried this letter around for days, afraid to show it to me. So? Where is it? Show me this masterpiece. I could use some entertainment.*

VANDA: That's good, Tom. That's fantastic. Listen. You do her.

THOMAS: No . . .

VANDA: Yes. You be her. You've got more of a handle on her than I do. You know her from the inside.

THOMAS: I don't know the part . . .

VANDA: Of course you do.

(*Lightning and a rumble of thunder.*)

THOMAS (*as* DUNAYEV): *Take this off of me and bring me my fur.*

(VANDA *takes the jacket off him.*)

Carefully, Thomas.

VANDA (*as* KUSHEMSKI): *I'm doing the best I can, Mistress.*

THOMAS (*as* DUNAYEV): *Well, your best as always is not good enough.*

(VANDA *puts on the footman's jacket and brings him the throw.*)

VANDA (*as* KUSHEMSKI, *ceremoniously wrapping the throw around him, as a fur*): *Your fur, Mistress.*

THOMAS (*as* DUNAYEV): *Prepare a bottle of champagne and two glasses. The Count will be here any moment.*

VANDA (*as* KUSHEMSKI): *But, Mistress . . .*

THOMAS (*as* DUNAYEV): *If you don't like my service, then leave. Get out of my sight! You bore me, do you hear?*

VANDA (*as* KUSHEMSKI): *Will you take the Count for a husband?*

THOMAS (*as* DUNAYEV): *I won't lie to you, Thomas. That man makes me tremble.*

VANDA: Beautiful. Cross down.

THOMAS (*as* DUNAYEV): *I find him in my thoughts and I can't shut him out. He makes me suffer yet I love the suffering.*

VANDA: Stop there and turn.

THOMAS (*as* DUNAYEV): *If he asks me to be his wife, I will accept.*

VANDA: You're gorgeous.

THOMAS (*as* DUNAYEV): *You know he's jealous of you? I've told him everything about us.*

VANDA (*as* KUSHEMSKI): *He probably threatened to kill you.*

THOMAS (*as* DUNAYEV): *He made his feelings perfectly clear.*

VANDA (*as* KUSHEMSKI): *He struck you, Vanda? You let him strike you?*

THOMAS (*as* DUNAYEV): *Yes. And I enjoyed it.*

VANDA: More.

THOMAS (*as* DUNAYEV): *Yes. And I enjoyed it.*

VANDA: More! Give it to him!

THOMAS (*as* DUNAYEV): *Yes! And I enjoyed it!*

VANDA (*as* KUSHEMSKI): *Once you were a goddess. Now you'd settle for this mannequin, this imitation man?*

THOMAS (*as* DUNAYEV): *You have no right to accuse me of anything. You wanted cruelty and I've given it to you. And didn't I warn you time and time again? Did I ever hide how dangerous I am, how insane it was to surrender to me? If I enjoy torturing you, that's your doing. Not mine. I am not this. You made me this. And now you blame it on* me?

VANDA (*as* KUSHEMSKI): *If I can't have you, no other man will have you either.*

THOMAS (*as* DUNAYEV): *What melodrama are you quoting?*

VANDA (*as* KUSHEMSKI): *If you marry him, I'll kill you. I'll kill you both. I'll cut your hearts out and throw them to the dogs.*

(*Produces from nowhere an even more dangerous knife and holds it to* THOMAS's *throat. Lightning and thunder.*)

Goddamn you! Goddamn you!

THOMAS (*as* DUNAYEV): *Kill me, Thomas. Kill me. I love this fire in your eyes. I always knew you had it in you. I always knew you were a man. My God, I adore you. Have you had enough of your ideal now? Have I done well? Is this goddess excused? Are you willing now to take your wife? Your honest, faithful, and submissive wife?*

VANDA (*as* KUSHEMSKI, *tossing the knife aside*): *My wife . . . ? You mean . . . ?*

THOMAS (*as* DUNAYEV): *Would you still have me? I don't know how you could love me, I've been so awful to you.*

VANDA (*as* KUSHEMSKI): *You mean you were never serious? It was all an act?*

THOMAS (*as* DUNAYEV): *My darling little idiot—didn't you realize?*

VANDA: Kneel.

THOMAS (*as* DUNAYEV, *kneeling*): *Didn't you see how hard it's been for me to hurt you? When I would have preferred to take your face between my hands and cover it with kisses? We have had enough of this game, haven't we? I played my part better than you ever expected, didn't I? I did all this to save you. To show you how much I loved you. To cure you.*

(*Goes to her, on his knees.*)

I'm the one who should be subjugated. I'm the one who should be bound and whipped. So order me. Subjugate me.

VANDA: Nice.

THOMAS (*as* DUNAYEV, *embracing her knees*): *Oh, Thomas, Thomas, how I love you. I've loved you and wanted you since the first moment I saw you. I couldn't tell you because—I'm not what I seem. I'm weak. I'm so lost, you see.*

VANDA (*as* KUSHEMSKI): *From now on you're going to call me "Master."*

THOMAS (*as* DUNAYEV): *Yes, Master.*

VANDA (*as* KUSHEMSKI): *I think I'll tie you with a pair of your stockings. You want that, don't you?*

THOMAS (*as* DUNAYEV): *Yes, please, Master.*

VANDA (*as* KUSHEMSKI): *Go fetch them.*

(*Lightning and thunder.* THOMAS *goes to the big bag and takes out a pair of stockings.*)

THOMAS (*as* DUNAYEV): *Now do with me what you will. Only promise you'll never leave me.*

VANDA (*as* KUSHEMSKI): *Stand over there.*

(THOMAS *stands against the pipe.* VANDA *ties the stocking to his collar and wraps it around the pipe, affixing him to it.*)

THOMAS (*as* DUNAYEV): *I told you I wanted someone I could bend my neck to. Now I've found him. In you.*

VANDA: Good. *More.*

THOMAS (*as* DUNAYEV): *I wanted this from the moment I first saw you. Humiliate me. Degrade me.*

VANDA: Yes, good good good. Very good. Fantastic. But you know the problem here, Tommy? Any way you cut it, any way you play this, it's degrading to women. It's an insult. It's pornography.

THOMAS: What are you talking about . . . ?

VANDA: Just look at you. Maiden in distress. A mass of quivering feminine jelly. This helpless cunt submissively offering herself to a man. *Beat me, hurt me, I'm just a woman.*

THOMAS: But Vanda—

(*She slaps him.*)

VANDA: Say "thank you" for that. *Thank you.*

THOMAS: Thank you.

VANDA: (*Another slap.*) *Thank you what?*

THOMAS: Thank you, Mistress.

VANDA: (*Forcing him to his knees.*) *How dare you. How* DARE *you!* You thought you could dupe some poor, willing, idiot actress and bend her to your program, didn't you. Create your own little female Frankenstein monster. You thought that you could use *me* to insult *me*?

(*Lightning and thunder, louder.*)

THOMAS: No, Vanda, I swear . . .

VANDA: *We dance to the glory of the gods!*

We dance to the glory of Dionysus!

Hail, the Bacchae!

Hail, the Bacchae!

Hail, you brave women of Thebes!

(*Lightning and thunder, louder. She goes to the door and locks it, then lowers the lights at the fuse box.*)

THOMAS: Goddamnit ...

VANDA: (*Shining the desk lamp into his face.*) How's your world now? Not quite so diminished now, is it?

THOMAS: Fuck. *FUCK!*

VANDA: Strong emotions. Good. Very operatic.

THOMAS: Why did you come here?

VANDA: Was I ever here?

(*She takes a real fur stole from her big bag and puts it on.*)

THOMAS: Who are you?

VANDA: You know who I am. Now say it. *Say it.*

THOMAS: Hail, Aphrodite ...

VANDA: Louder, please.

THOMAS: *Hail, Aphrodite!*

(*Lightning and thunder, louder. She takes a triumphant stance, facing him down the room with her feet planted, legs spread, hands on her hips.*)

VANDA: *"And the Lord hath smitten him and delivered him into a woman's hands."*

THOMAS: *HAIL, APHRODITE!*

VANDA: Good.

(*Lightning, and a deafening crack of thunder. Blackout.*)

END OF PLAY

SHOOTING STAR

Steven Dietz

Shooting Star received its world premiere at ZACH Theatre (Dave Steakley, producing artistic director; Elisbeth Challener, managing director) in Austin, Texas, on February 14, 2009. The production was directed by Steven Dietz; the set design was by Michael Raiford; the costume design was by Blair Hurry; the lighting design was by Jason Amato; the sound design was by Craig Brock; and the stage manager was Ian Scott. The cast was as follows:

ELENA CARSON	Barbara Chisholm
REED MCALLISTER	Jamie Goodwin

Shooting Star was subsequently produced by Trinity Repertory Company (Curt Columbus, artistic director; Michael Gennaro, executive director) in Providence, Rhode Island, on October 16, 2009. The production was directed by Fred Sullivan Jr.; the set design was by Patrick Lynch; the costume design was by William Lane; the lighting design was by John Ambrosone; the sound design was by Peter Sasha Hurowitz; and the stage manager was Robin Grady. The cast was as follows:

ELENA CARSON	Nance Williamson
REED MCALLISTER	Kurt Rhoads

Shooting Star was originally commissioned and developed by the Denver Center Theatre Company and presented as a reading at the 2008 Colorado New Play Summit. The director was Susan V. Booth; the dramaturg was Liz Engelman; the cast featured Nance Williamson as Elena and Mark Chamberlin as Reed.

CHARACTERS
REED McALLISTER, a man in his late forties
ELENA CARSON, a woman in her late forties

PLACE
The terminal of a large middle-America airport.

TIME
2006.

SETTING
Simple. There are no scene changes. Any and all transitions will be
accomplished with lights and sound only.
     The gate area is established with a few banks of airport chairs and
attached side tables. A trash can.
     Perhaps a digital clock signals the time.
     Perhaps a large window upstage depicts, from time to time, the fall-
ing snowflakes.

Note: "ELENA" is pronounced "eh-LAY-na," and often shortened in
conversation to "LAY-na."

> *for Lori and for Jaime*
> *and for all the nights*
> *we played the songs*
> *that are still*
> *echoing*
> *in my head*

> *Guess it's too late to say the things to you*
> *That you needed to hear me say*
> *Saw a shooting star tonight*
> *Slip away*
>
> —*from "Shooting Star" by Bob Dylan*

AUTHOR'S NOTE
In my youth, people told me their dreams—the great things they
were going to do with their lives. These were people, in some cases,
that I've never seen again. And the thing is: I find that I'm still
holding those people to their dreams—unwilling to let them give
up on what they promised me, despite the multitude of unmet
expectations in my own life.

The singer/songwriter Eliza Gilkyson has a lyric that captures this perfectly: "We're coming upon a time in our lives / When the little dreams live but the big dream dies."

We live in a time of "virtual reunions"—employing technology to "connect" us with the past, our history, our youth. In *Shooting Star* I wanted to write a nonvirtual reunion. The real and messy kind. Where the person is standing right there and you can't leave. And who would that person be? Someone from your past. Someone who has your secret. They have your secret because they once had your heart.

They knew you back in the day. Back when you gave your heart away so readily, so fully and foolishly. And on long, lazy mornings in cold rented rooms—or in the candlelit quiet of long-shuttered cafés—you no doubt told this person just exactly what amazing things you were going to do with your life. You laid out your boldest plans in grandiloquent terms—and why not? You were young and in love and what in the great wide world of your own shining future could possibly stand in your way?

We wed the past to humor with good reason. Oh, how we used to dress!—and, god, our hair!—the music we listened to!—man, what were we thinking?! And with any luck, we can usually bundle up our great regrets in this same nostalgic laughter, and then happily move on.

Until we see that face. That person who has the goods on us: who knows exactly how close or far we came to making our life match our dreams. Reunions of this kind—the actual face-to-face variety—are typically built on laughter, banter, remembrance, and alcohol. The one you'll see tonight is no different.

Thanks for being here.

Oh, and it's snowing.

STEVEN DIETZ
AUSTIN, TX
MARCH 2010

ACT ONE

A light rises on REED.

He is a conservatively dressed businessman in his late forties. His serious black luggage and computer bag are on the ground, near him. He probably has some kind of phone thing in his ear.

He speaks to the audience.

REED: The storm began in Canada. Canada is the home of storms. Hockey. Neil Young. All of these things—with the exception of storms and hockey—have made our world a better place. What began as a "typical winter storm" could very soon, according to forecasters, become The Greatest Blizzard of the Century. Of course, there's still a lot of century left in this century, but even so: This is a "weather event" that may launch the careers of dozens of intrepid TV reporters—if they don't freeze to death. Cities are locked down. Cars are abandoned. Roadways look ready to host the luge. And the airports, well . . . (*Looks around.*) the airports are packed. (*His phone rings.*) Sorry. I've got to take this. (*He answers the call, as a light rises on* ELENA. *She is dressed in what can best be called "funky midlife casual": comfortable, attractive, but with a certain rebel/hippie flair. Her colorful luggage and shoulder bag are on the ground near her. She holds a long, beautifully carved rain stick. She speaks to the audience.*)

ELENA: The thing about Ginny is that she tried to warn me. She had thrown her runes or walked her labyrinth—she has this amazing labyrinth on her property—or maybe she'd just done some really good hash—who knows—but, anyway, she calls three days ago and leaves me a voice mail, which I will now quote to you in its entirety:

"White Blanket. Harsh Vista. The Shivering Impossibility of Transport."

I thought it was a telemarketer from the Beat Poet Foundation.

Ginny's a piece of work—one of my oldest friends—the reason I'm making this trip—but she is not right about a lot of things. She's been wrong about all her relationships and all her careers. Wrong about quadrophonic sound, the harmonic convergence, and the powers of echinacea.

So, of course, I called her back and said: "Don't worry, I'm sure things'll clear up by the day I fly."

Famous last words.

REED: (*Ends his call. Re: phone.*) That was Conrad, my boss. The man who feels I lack the sort of "personal gravitas"—the proper "killer instinct" required to succeed in the world of business. And though this is a pointless trip—we're never going to land this account—Conrad is adamant that I be there to "show the flag"—to "keep us on the radar" and "not hand the playing field over to our rivals." And so here I stand: the flag bearer—my job on the line—trying to catch a connecting flight that will rush me to a place *I don't want or need to be.*

12:36 P.M.

ELENA: The storm continues. Snowflakes the size of doilies. And we are stranded in this strange, carpeted purgatory of planes.

Time does not pass. The minutes don't even move. They just . . . *lie there*, looking up at you, like a drunken Shriner who can't find the parade.

ANNOUNCEMENT: (*Voice-over*) A REMINDER, PASSENGERS, THAT HOMELAND SECURITY HAS ESTABLISHED A THREAT LEVEL OF "ORANGE"—PLEASE RE-PORT ANY UNATTENDED BAGS OR SUSPICIOUS BEHAVIOR IMMEDIATELY.

REED: I wasn't going to be the first to acknowledge it. Her plane would probably leave soon. She hadn't seen me, yet—

ELENA: I saw him right away.

REED: —And if she did, I could always disappear into Starbucks and hide behind some mugs.

ELENA: Reed McAllister . . .

REED: What point would there be in approaching her?

ELENA: . . . What are the chances?

REED: There is nothing more . . . *vacant*—nothing more . . . *emotionally nondescript* than meeting someone you haven't seen in a long time in the anonymous confines of an airport. You end up talking out of a shared desire to be *done talking*.

ELENA: He looked exactly the same. His face. Even the hair. Where were the wrinkles?—Where was the grey? (*Or, in lieu of "grey?": "paunch?"*) It was lovely and shocking and completely unfair: like time had somehow *forgotten* to age *him*.

REED: She had really let herself go. Wait—what I mean—what I *don't* mean is that she was heavy or unkempt or looked bad. I mean, I guess, that she had let herself *keep going*. Elena

Carson appeared to be living like we used to live. *Still.* How could she do that? How could anyone do that?

ELENA: I was not going to approach him. I wanted him to go first. Yes, I know how that sounds and I wish it wasn't true—

REED: What would be wrong?—What is lost, really, if I just *turn and walk the other way?*

ELENA: —But, all I'm saying is he better see me and get the hell over here. (ELENA *begins to brush her hair, do her makeup, etc.*)

REED: There are probably dozens of these chance nonmeetings every year—these "small world" near-encounters that do *not* happen and we *don't know about it.* If we had a grid—if we could watch our comings and goings from above like some suddenly attentive God or compulsive preteen video addict, what would we see? We'd see people, day after day and year after year, *just barely missing each other* . . . and moving on nicely through their day, thank you very much—nothing wagered, nothing lost.

The world is not small. Thank God for that. Do you really want to keep bumping into the people that you are *done with?* No, the world is just big enough to allow an endless and necessary series of *near misses,* and for that we should thank our lucky stars.

ELENA: I wanted to be doing something interesting, something of import, when he first saw me. I didn't want to be just another bored, wrinkled, embittered traveler waiting in line to buy a candy bar and a *Cosmo.* (I'd already done that, they were in my bag.) I wanted to be doing something unique, appealing . . . (*Holds her waist in.*) and possibly *thinning.*

So, I sat on the floor. Took off my shoes. And I began to meditate. In my lotus, near the windows, overlooking the snow-covered planes.

With my closed eye, I envisioned inner light and world peace and aeronautic tranquility.

With my slightly open other eye, I kept a lookout.

Where was he? Did he leave? Did he not see me and leave? Or: Did he *see me* and leave?!

Light, peace and tranquility were put on hold as I de-lotused and sort of *crawled* behind a row of open chairs—to a place where I could spy from.

I peeked my head up and looked.

He was gone.

Okay. Well. *That certainly played out to perfection.* And what a fitting example of my entire adult love life we have right here: I hide from the man I really want to see and then wonder why he wasn't man enough to come talk to me. (*Lights expand as* REED *appears behind her—*)

1:09 P.M.

REED: Elena?

ELENA: (*Turns.*) Yes? (*Sees him. A beat.*) Oh my God.

REED: It's Reed.

ELENA: I remember your name.

REED: Okay, good. (*Beat.*)

ELENA: Did you really think I wouldn't remember your name?

REED: I wasn't sure.

ELENA: You're kidding, right? You used to kid. Are you still—

REED: Am I—?

ELENA: —Are you still a kidder?

REED: Sure. Yes.

ELENA: Good.

REED: Anyway, I thought—

ELENA: Thanks for coming over—

REED: You know, they made that announcement about "suspicious behavior" and I saw you over here crawling around on the floor and I thought to myself: *What in the world is that woman doing?* (*She stares at him.*) I'm kidding.

ANNOUNCEMENT: (*V.O.*) PASSENGERS TRAVELING ON FLIGHT 394 TO BOSTON—DUE TO WEATHER CONDITIONS YOUR ADJUSTED DEPARTURE TIME IS NOW TWO FIFTY-FIVE P.M.—

REED: So . . .

ANNOUNCEMENT: (*V.O.*) —PLEASE REMAIN IN THE GATE AREA FOR FURTHER UPDATES.

ELENA: (*Re: announcement.*) Wonderful.

REED: Really? Good.

ELENA: What?

REED: I was going to ask how you've been—

ELENA: Oh, that's not what—

REED: —But you've been "wonderful."

ELENA: Well, sure—

REED: That's great.

ELENA: —I guess I must have been "wonderful" at least a couple times in the past ten or twenty years.

REED: I think it's more like twenty-five.

ELENA: Impossible.

REED: You look good. The same.

ELENA: Thanks. And thanks. (*An odd pause. Finally* . . .) Think this snow'll ever stop?

REED: (*Re: his BlackBerry or something.*) I've been checking the National Weather Service site—the "real-time" updates—

ELENA: (*Nodding.*) Oh, those are the best kind.

REED: —And there's a chance the full brunt of the storm might miss us—

ELENA: Really?

REED: —Or at least give a *window* in the late afternoon when they could get a runway open—

ELENA: That's great.

REED: —And a couple planes out of here.

ELENA: It's odd.

REED: Hmm?

ELENA: I can hear us making conversation. In all our time together, I don't remember us ever having to do that. Do you?

(*Another odd pause.*)

REED: (*Making conversation.*) So . . . where you headed?

ELENA: (*Wry.*) You mean . . . cosmically?—on my life's journey?

REED: Where's your *plane* headed?

ELENA: Boston. My friend Ginny is going through a . . . *thing* . . . with her husband . . . and her wife. It's complicated.

REED: She has a husband and a wife?

ELENA: One's current and one's an ex—but there's some debate about which is which. Lawyers and shrinks and animal rights groups are involved. It's a mess.

REED: (*Re: the rain stick.*) And that . . . what is that again?

ELENA: It's a rain stick. I promised to help Ginny with her "cleansing ceremony." Don't smirk.

REED: I'm not.

ELENA: I know what you think about all that.

REED: No, that's not what I—

ELENA: (*Light.*) It was always just a lot of hogwash to you, and that's okay—I think a lot of it is hogwash, too—but, hey, it makes as much sense to me as Catholicism.

REED: Where in Boston?

ELENA: Oh, I don't know. The old part. Ginny says she has "mature trees."

REED: You've never been?

ELENA: First time. If I ever get there. We may never get anywhere.

REED: I've got to get out.

ELENA: Don't we all.

REED: No, I mean: I *have to get out.* I just had a call—and I know a lot of people here have plans and things, but—really, I just—

ELENA: You've got to get out.

REED: Yes.

ELENA: I understand.

REED: I've got a meeting.

ELENA: How can I compete with that? (*Pointing at other travelers.*) I bet that guy has a meeting, too—

REED: Look, I didn't—

ELENA: —And that bunch of suits and toupees over there, look at 'em: I think those are the Executive Platinum Diamond Elite Preferred guys. They board right before the Nobel laureates. It gives them a little extra time to put their egos in the overhead bin—

REED: Elena, please don't *point at them*—

ELENA: (*Overlapping.*) —And you can bet your life that *they* have a meeting—

REED: —That always bugged me—the way you *point at people in public*—

ELENA: (*Overlapping.*) —And hey, if those meetings don't happen, then things won't get *decided*. And if things don't get decided, well then—*oh, man, I don't even want to go there.* (*Pause.* REED *smiles a bit.*)

REED: This is what I loved about you.

ELENA: No, it's not.

REED: And this is also why we broke up. (*Pause.*)

ELENA: (*True.*) I'd always wondered.

REED: No, you didn't. You knew perfectly well—

ELENA: Listen—

REED: —We talked it all out, in the back booth at Morty's.

ELENA: —I'm just saying—

REED: We were very civilized about it. Our friends were impressed.

ELENA: —When people break up, there is always *the thing they tell each other*—the thing they can agree on—the thing they'll tell their friends.

REED: Right.

ELENA: And then there's the *truth*. That thing they know in their gut. And I don't think people ever tell that to each other. I never told it to you. (*Pause. Tone brightens.*) Where you headed?

REED: Austin.

ELENA: You're not.

REED: Total waste of time, we're never gonna get this account, but my boss wants me to somehow—

ELENA: You ever been to Austin?

REED: No.

ELENA: Bunch of freaks down there. It's Techno-Woodstock, man. Lots of ex-hippies with guitars and iPhones. It's like rooming with Steve Jobs and Stevie Nicks—

REED: Okay . . .

ELENA: —But, hey, I love it. Ten years and counting.

REED: You live in Austin?

ELENA: Be careful down there, Reed: You might get a little Blue on you.

REED: (*Lightly.*) What is that supposed to mean—

ELENA: I'm thinking you probably went a little Red over the years. It happens. People age, have kids, acquire houses and guns—and they start to tilt to the right. (*He is laughing, enjoying this.*) I mean, look at you: You're like "Businessman in a Box." Just add water, stir and serve.

REED: Times change, Elena.

ELENA: "I will never own a navy blue suit. I will never wear a yellow tie with blue dots. I will never carry a black briefcase."

REED: Guilty as charged.

ELENA: "I will never value the health of American capitalism over the fair and humane treatment of its citizens."

REED: God, do you remember everything?

ELENA: Yes. It's *terrible.* I do what I can—drink to excess, smoke a lot of dope—but I still can't forget anything. There was always some latent Red in you—like a stain I could never get out, no matter how much public radio I made you listen to.

REED: You never called me on it.

ELENA: It was my guilty pleasure: bedding a budding Republican . . . *kinky.*

REED: Thanks a lot.

ELENA: And now you live where?—Some bright Red place—

REED: I live—

ELENA: —Like maybe Kansas, Indiana, Arizona—one of those?

REED: —I live in Boston. The old part. You'll like it.

ANNOUNCEMENT: (*V.O.*) ATTENTION, PASSENGERS: THE DEPARTMENT OF HOMELAND SECURITY REMINDS YOU TO NEVER LEAVE YOUR BAGS UNATTENDED. UNATTENDED BAGS MAY BE CONFISCATED BY SECURITY PERSONNEL AND DESTROYED. THANK YOU FOR YOUR COOPERATION.

(REED *has turned his focus to his briefcase, his BlackBerry, etc.*)

ELENA: I need to find a pay phone.

REED: (*With a laugh.*) Perfect.

ELENA: What?

REED: *Of course* you don't have a cell phone.

ELENA: Oh, but I do. I'm very modern, Reed. I got one as a gift—it's somewhere in my apartment—I hear it ring every now and then—but I haven't really been able to find it. How long do those batteries *last,* anyway?

(REED *takes his phone out, sets it between them.*)

REED: Here. Use mine, if you need to.

ELENA: Thanks. (REED *checks his BlackBerry again, looks at his watch, stares out the window . . . all the while his left hand is touching/pulling at his left ear.* ELENA *is aware of this.*) How bad is it? (*Off his look.*) You've got the same "tell" you had in your twenties. When something's wrong—when you're all stressed out—you pull on your left ear, run your fingers behind it. Same old "tell."

REED: (*He has stopped doing what she described.*) That's ridiculous.

ELENA: Didn't you ever wonder why I always knew when something was up?

REED: I just thought you were remarkably intuitive.

ELENA: Sucker. So, what is it?

REED: Nothing. (*Unconsciously, his left hand goes toward his ear again—and he stops himself.*)

ELENA: Reed . . .

REED: It's no big deal. I'm waiting to hear from my daughter. I've left her four messages—but she's not answering her phone—

ELENA: And how—

REED: —She's twelve, really good kid, but we had a—we're going through . . .

ELENA: A *"thing."*

REED: . . . Yes, right, no big deal, but I just need to—

ELENA: Right.

REED: —You know, talk to her.

ELENA: I bet you're a terrific dad. (*Pause. Simply.*) That's what made it hard, you know—way back when. Knowing you'd be such a good dad.

REED: I'm not. Not lately. (*Pause.*) I think about you. Sometimes. When I'm driving. (*And now he takes a book out of his briefcase and prepares to read.* ELENA *is hanging on his words . . . waiting.*)

ELENA: Oh, come on—don't make me drag this out of you!

REED: I'm driving and it's late and I'm scanning for a radio station—and NPR comes on—

ELENA: And you drive off a cliff.

REED: —No, but I change the channel right away—

ELENA: I knew it.

REED: —And then I go home, go online to the NPR site . . . and I make a pledge. I still can't stand those smug voices, those vapid little snippets of music—but hey: Every year I send 'em a little money. And I guess that's because of you. (*He returns to his book. She is staring at him.*) What?

ELENA: *THAT'S what you remember about me?*

REED: Not just that—there's other things—

ELENA: Our apartment—the cats—the old Toyota—our road trip to New Orleans—Sunday breakfast at Morty's—

REED: (*Underlapping from "road."*) —Yes—right—of course—all those things—

ELENA: —And now you're telling me it's all gone, or lost, or put under the heading of "that NPR girl I knew when I was in Madison"? That is so *disappointing.*

REED: Listen—

ELENA: I mean—good for you, Reed—I'm glad you still have a conscience, or a guilty heart or whatever it is that makes you *pay* for something that you don't *use* or *enjoy*—

REED: It's no big deal. Can we just—

ELENA: (*Overlapping.*) —No, really, I applaud you. I listen to that stuff every day—and I've *never pledged a dime.* They're gonna track me down and kill me, I'm sure—

REED: *You've never pledged?*

ELENA: Why would anyone do that?! You can listen for *FREE* and *THEY DON'T KNOW WHO YOU ARE!* Why would you *PAY* for that?—

REED: (*Laughing.*) Oh, this is good . . .

ELENA: (*Overlapping.*) —But the point is: As your ex—as one of your exes—as your former—whatever—lover, girlfriend, partner, soul mate of twenty-two months—I would just like to think you'd remember something *a little more* . . .

REED: What?

ELENA: . . . *wonderful.* Something with some *ache* in it. (*Silence.*)

REED: (*Friendly.*) It's good to see you, Elena. I need to return a few emails—get something to eat—

ELENA: Right, okay—

REED: —But I hope things go well with your friend in Boston and—I don't know—I just—(*Stops.*) I wish we had more time to talk. (*Pause. She stares at him.*) I mean: There isn't—

ELENA: No, of course not.

REED: —I wish there was time to get into all of this again. But there's not.

ANNOUNCEMENT: (*V.O.*) ATTENTION IN THE GATE AREA—PASSENGERS HOLDING TICKETS ON FLIGHT 73 TO AUSTIN—DUE TO WEATHER CONDITIONS THAT FLIGHT IS NOW SCHEDULED TO DEPART AT FOUR THIRTY-FIVE P.M.—PLEASE CHECK THE AIRPORT MONITORS FOR ADDITIONAL UPDATES.

ELENA: I guess there's time.

REED: I'm gonna get a paper. (*Music as* REED *goes, leaving his items [including his cell phone] behind.* ELENA *turns to the audience. Music, under.*)

ELENA: I used to dress him up. Just for fun. He always wore these tan corduroy pants—well, they used to be corduroy, by the time I met him they were thin enough to use as a coffee filter, which we actually did once when we were snowed in and couldn't get to the store. Those old tan pants and one of his faded T-shirts that were all thrift store bargains or giveaways from concerts: Laura Nyro. Neil Young. JJ Cale.

Anyway . . . we'd get some cheap red wine in us . . . and sometimes he'd let me dress him up in some of my dad's old clothes—this old box I had in the back of my closet. There was a nice dark suit, a few hand-painted ties, a white shirt that I would clumsily iron. I'd blindfold Reed . . . dress him in those clothes . . . put him in front of the mirror . . . blindfold off . . . and *voilà!*: My Own Private Businessman.

He'd adopt poses of "Executives on TV and in Magazines"—pretend to take an urgent call, close a big sale. We'd laugh till our sides hurt—and after about thirty seconds of this . . . I'd jump him. Throw him on the bed. And, yes, I was—in fact—*stripping my dead father's clothes off my boyfriend and then bedding him with intent*. And, yes, I spent plenty of years and thousands of dollars—making sure that dozens of therapists could afford their Volvos and Birkenstocks—all in an effort to deal with the emotional fallout of this, however real or imagined. But, oh my God . . . Reed McAllister . . . back then . . . in that dark suit . . . man, you would have jumped him, too. (REED's *phone rings.* ELENA *stares at it. Tries to ignore it. She's tempted to answer it. Decides against this. Changes her mind. Decides to answer it. And just as she begins to reach for it— it stops ringing. She returns to her things, begins to settle in, just as* REED's *phone rings, again, and this time,* ELENA *pounces on it. Into phone.*) Reed's phone. (*Beat.*) He's not here. Who's this? (*Beat.*) Beth-Anne? . . . Oh, *nice to meet you* . . . I'm Elena, an old friend . . . from Madison . . . a thousand years ago . . . (*Listens.*) No, we're snowed in—just bumped into each other here. (*Looks outside.*) Yeah. No word on when they'll get us out. Should I have Reed call you at home? (*Pause, listens.*)

Oh, okay . . . does he know that? (*A longer pause, listens.*) Beth-Anne, listen . . . (*Another pause, listens, her voice hardens.*) Sure. I can do that. See you. (ELENA *ends the call. She carefully puts* REED*'s phone back exactly where it was, as—*)

3:27 P.M.

REED *arrives with two coffees and* The Wall Street Journal.

REED: You would not believe the lines. (*Re: the coffee.*) Cream and two sugars, right?

ELENA: (*Impressed.*) Thank you. (*Re: newspaper.*) Did you buy a bird?

REED: What?

ELENA: *The Wall Street Journal?*

REED: Last one they had.

ELENA: Do you have a cage you need to line?

REED: There is some remarkable writing in this paper, Elena. You should read it.

ELENA: Maybe I should. I'm a great lover of fiction. (*He is still holding her coffee.*)

REED: Can we have a truce?

ELENA: What?

REED: All the political stuff—the Red and Blue nonsense—can we agree to put an end to all of that?

ELENA: Absolutely. (*He gives her a coffee. She sips, and then says . . .*) How many times did you vote for Bush?

REED: (*He glares.*) How many times did you vote for Clinton?

ELENA: One more time than I wanted to.

REED: Okay, we're even. (*Settling into a seat.*) So, let's do the big picture—the Roman numerals: What do you do in Austin?

ELENA: Give me your wallet.

REED: What?

ELENA: People's wallets don't lie. Everything you need to know is in there. (*She puts her wallet in front of him.*)

REED: My mother taught me never to touch a woman's purse or her wallet.

ELENA: And your mother was right, but *I am not your mother*—which I think we proved on numerous occasions. (*Re: her coffee.*) Are you sure you put two sugars in here?

REED: No. I put one—

ELENA: You said—

REED: —Because you always said I should stop you if you tried to add the second one.

ELENA: Please don't IMPROVE ME, Reed! You had your chance to do that, and God knows you tried . . . (*He reaches into a pocket and pulls out a second packet of sugar. Hands it to her.*) Thanks. (*She lifts his wallet.*) Okay: Dig in. (*Before opening the wallets, they each take out their reading glasses. A beat—as they register this—they smile a bit—and then dig into each other's wallet.*)

REED: You do this a lot?

ELENA: Really livens up a blind date, lemme tell you. (*Re: his cash.*) You never did carry enough cash. Look at this: twenty-six dollars? You should at least carry your *age* around in cash.

REED: (*Re: her cash.*) You look pretty good for a hundred and forty-three.

ELENA: (*Item.*) And how do you take such good driver's license pictures? I always look like I just went camping.

REED: (*Item.*) Yes, you do.

ELENA: (*Item.*) Sam's Club—nice—very Red of you. Is your NRA card in here, too?

REED: (*Items.*) Costco. Amnesty International. The *ACLU*!

ELENA: I'm gonna burn some flags later—wanna come?

REED: Truce, remember?

ELENA: Can't you at least have a condom or a phone number written in lipstick— (*Stops, item.*) Oh. Nice.

REED: What?

ELENA: (*Holds up card.*) Executive Platinum Diamond Elite Preferred.

REED: Jealous?

ELENA: Terribly.

REED: (*Business card.*) Lone Star Consumer Data. (ELENA *takes the card from him, casual and dismissive*—)

ELENA: Guy on the plane gave me that— (*A photo.*) Is this the wife? The girl who finally nabbed that dreamy Reed McAllister?

REED: That's Beth-Anne, yes.

ELENA: In Venice. The gondola. The whole bit. Nice.

REED: It's Vegas, actually. There's this casino that has a—

ELENA: Still. She's lovely. And thin. Is your daughter in here?

REED: Keep going. (ELENA *finds another photo.*)

ELENA: Oh, look at her. What a beauty.

REED: Great kid. Honor roll . . . gymnastics . . . church choir. (REED *is staring at the photo of his daughter.*)

ELENA: Did you happen to give her a name?

REED: Kirsten.

ELENA: Pretty. (*A beat. Then* REED *turns his attention back to* ELENA*'s wallet—*)

REED: What about you? Is there a—

ELENA: There's no one. No husband hiding in there. Not now. Nor in the past. And truth be told: The future's not lookin' so *husband-y* either. (*Off his look.*) That surprises you?

REED: "I want a man in a flannel shirt and fifteen little babies"—

ELENA: Oh, God.

REED: "—livin' on the farm with all our friends—a big commune in the woods—no telephones, no TVs—home-schoolin' the kids and growin' our own food and takin' in all the strays: dogs, cats, goats, musicians."

ELENA: Don't remind me.

REED: Why not?

ELENA: Reed—

REED: (*With a laugh.*) What's wrong with that?

ELENA: (*With an edge.*) I think you'd know!—I think you of all
people—

REED: Would know what?

ELENA: (*Overlapping.*) —God, I've had this talk with you about a
thousand times over the past twenty years—but all the other
times you were *not present* and *I was alone in my apartment
finishing off a bottle of wine*—

REED: Lena, what are you—

ELENA: (*Overlapping.*) —But God, Reed: *It was such a lie.* Our
youth. The crap we believed. This picture we had of some
kind of life where we lived on love and work and trust and
helping out our friends—it was so *foolish*, completely *naive*—
and you should have known that.

REED: Why me?

ELENA: You were the realist. My tether to the world.

REED: Okay, listen—

ELENA: "Engage, Elena"—I got so sick of hearing that—"Do
not *withdraw* from the world, Elena—*engage!*"

REED: That was—

ELENA: (*Overlapping.*) —And oh, man, were you ever going to
"engage," remember?!—you were gonna be that "social

advocate"—do all that work for the indigenous peoples of
South America—

REED: Yeah, well, that never—

ELENA: —But all I wanted was to go to the woods and have
babies and get high and cook soup for fifty *and God you should
have slapped me!* (*Pause.* ELENA *takes a deep breath.*) They all
slid back, you know. All our friends from those days. A few
of us—Kate, Mitchell, Sydney—we held out into our thirties . . . and then, one by one, even they slid back into the real
world. Jobs and kids and mortgages. The daily grind of it all.

REED: But you held out?

ELENA: (*Simple, a reverie.*) You haven't lived, really *lived*, until
you've picked the food that you've grown by hand . . . put it
in a pot . . . stirred it and watched it cook all day . . . and then
served it to everyone you love that night. Steam rising into
the faces. The spoons against the bowls. (*She finds a final item
in his wallet: a weathered ticket stub.*) Man . . . how many wallets
has this thing been in?

REED: (*Re: ticket stub.*) Remember that? Joni Mitchell at the
Fieldhouse. We sat right up front. I grabbed the set list when
it was over.

ELENA: (*Thoughtfully.*) Joni Mitchell, at the Fieldhouse . . . wow . . .
doesn't ring a bell.

REED: (*Knows she's kidding.*) Stop it—

ELENA: Was I there?

REED: You and your turquoise velvet boots.

ELENA: Which I still have. Somewhere. I think my cell phone's
inside them. (*They begin to put the items back inside the wallets,*

and—REED *discovers a weathered, folded piece of paper in* ELENA's *wallet.*)

REED: Wait—what's this?

ELENA: Birth certificate.

REED: You carry your birth certificate in your—

ELENA: (*Calm.*) Give me that, please.

REED: Okay . . . (REED *hands* ELENA *the birth certificate.*)

ELENA: I need to tell you something . . . (REED *waits.*) . . . your wife called.

REED: (*Beat.*) *Pardon me?*

ELENA: Beth-Anne—while you were gone. She even *sounds* thin.

REED: You answered my phone?

ELENA: Thought it might be your daughter.

REED: What did you say to her?

ELENA: Not nearly as much as I wanted.

REED: There was no message?

ELENA: She said she'd *text you.* Very romantic, I thought. (REED *immediately checks his BlackBerry [or whatever].*) Does she know about me?

REED: (*Re: BlackBerry.*) There's nothing here . . .

ELENA: "The NPR girl from Madison"—does she know who I am?

REED: Sure—why?

ELENA: She could have at least acted a little threatened.

REED: That's not her style.

ELENA: (*Music as* ELENA *starts off, suddenly.*) I'm hungry—you want something?

REED: Uh, no—I'm— (*And she is gone. Calling after her.*) Lena— (REED *watches her go . . . then turns to the audience. Music, under.*) A lot of what I'm about to tell you can be explained if, when I say something ridiculous, you say to yourself: "Remember: it was the seventies." A great decade for the American cinema. And Peter Frampton. But for the rest of us, well . . . let's just say we all very happily threw away those pants.

Elena and I lived together for nearly two years. We were both in school at Madison—me full-time, and Elena on days when she felt like it. We had a great, funky, threadbare apartment where *Court and Spark* never stopped spinning. The Goodwill sofa. The macramé on the walls. The bricks and boards holding our books—my Kerouac and Vonnegut and Tom Wolfe; her Betty Friedan and Rod McKuen and Carlos Castaneda. On our milk-crate coffee table were the obligatory copies of *Rich Man, Poor Man*; *Love Story*; and *Jonathan Livingston Seagull*—which I wish I could say we owned in some kind of *ironic way* . . . but there was no irony here: We had written notes in the margins; sentences were underlined; pages bent in remembrance.

We had all these things in our life . . . and we had—at Elena's request—an "open relationship." The idea—the concept of this open relationship was the need to transcend the accepted bonds of "emotional ownership" and "societal enslavement." In short it meant that either of you could sleep with anyone you wanted as long as you were "honest" about it with each other. Jealousy, of course, was forbidden. Just turn it off like a switch, right? None of us were married yet—that was the ultimate in social conformity—although you were allowed to have "commitment ceremonies" if you felt so inclined or had parents you needed to appease. And because we weren't married, we weren't really "swingers." We were more like "swappers": Take her, man, she's my lady but if she digs you—take her. She's not mine. There is no "mine," man. She belongs to herself and herself alone. Just like your girlfriend or cousin or stepmother belongs to herself, man . . . and if we find each other in a dark room on a beanbag chair with JJ Cale singing "Magnolia" . . . well, then, hey: *It's beautiful.**

5:41 P.M.

ELENA appears, carrying an armful of snack items: nuts, raisins, M&M's, etc.

She begins opening all the snacks—and dumping them into a large, empty bag from McDonald's.

ELENA: I never thanked you for the car.

REED: The what?

ELENA: When you left Madison—

REED: Right . . .

ELENA: —You left me the car.

REED: It was a pile of rust—it was falling apart—

ELENA: Still—

REED: —I can't believe you kept driving that thing!

---

* Note: If a different song is used on page 142, that title and artist should be mentioned here instead.

ELENA: —It ran another five years.

REED: The "Mood Car."

ELENA: Yes! You remember! Who needed "mood rings"—we had the "Mood Car." I try to tell people, you know—but no one believes the story of our Mood Car—

REED: Would *you*?

ELENA: —They don't believe that that old junker would *start right up* on the coldest winter day. But: If you and I'd had a fight, or were trying to go somewhere we didn't really want to go—

REED: Like your sister's house.

ELENA: —Those were the only times that car WOULD NOT START. Crank that baby all you wanted—if there was some kind of ill will in the air, that engine was never gonna turn over.

REED: (*Nods.*) It was weird.

ELENA: I swear that car could read our thoughts. Like some Stephen King story. *Creepy.* (*The McDonald's bag is now full of all the snacks.* ELENA *closes the top and begins to shake the bag vigorously.*)

REED: (*Over the sound of the shaking.*) There's really been no one?

ELENA: *What?*

REED: Sorry—but I just can't believe you never married.

ELENA: I got too interesting. A woman needs to marry before she gets too interesting. (*She gives the bag a final shake and then opens it, offers the contents to* REED—) Trail mix?

REED: No thanks.

ELENA: (*She eats and talks.*) Women should be told. Their friends
should sit them down in their late thirties and say: "Honey,
I love you—but you're getting *pretty damn interesting.* Maybe
tone it down a bit if you're lookin' to find a mate." (*Eating.*)
I meet men nowadays—and we start to talk and it's nice . . .
but at some point they get this look in their eye . . . they get
real quiet, they sit back . . . and they just *watch me like TV.*
(*She throws a peanut or M&M at him, saying . . .*) You *know* you
want some.

REED: (*He stares at her . . . then he digs his hand into the bag, takes a
handful of "trail mix," eats.*) Good stuff.

ELENA: And almost healthy.

REED: They gave you the bag at McDonald's?

ELENA: It came with my Big Mac and fries.

REED: You were a vegetarian.

ELENA: I've evolved. (*They eat the trail mix.*) Did you know I
worked at Spinning World?

REED: The record store?

ELENA: This was right after you left with all your things in our
one good suitcase—

REED: That was my suitcase.

ELENA: We bought it with the money from my dad.

REED: Yes, and we bought it on *my birthday*, so I naturally
assumed—

ELENA: I would gladly have given you my *baggage*, Reed—I just wanted to keep my *luggage*—

REED: Don't take this wrong, Elena—but back then you didn't know anything about music—

ELENA: I still don't.

REED: —You were still listening to *The Best of Bread.*

ELENA: I still am!—but, listen: I knew they'd never hire me unless I walked in there and pretended I was *you.* So, I sat down across from the owner—

REED: Brad.

ELENA: —That's right—with those huge teeth—

REED: "Brad the Impaler"—

ELENA: —Yep, that's him—and I rattled off all the snobby things you always said about Muddy Waters and Miles Davis and all those guys—

REED: You're kidding?

ELENA: —I riffed on the blues being "passed like a smoldering torch" from Robert Johnson to Eric Clapton—

REED: No way.

ELENA: —And I think I even quoted from that guy Bangs—was that his name?—

REED: *You quoted from Lester Bangs?!*—No wonder Brad hired you.

ELENA: I also wore my tight jeans and tube top.

REED: That would work. Was Felicia still there?

ELENA: Oh, she was there. Ms. Lips and Hips. She was every-where, and with *everyone.*

REED: Wonder what ever happened to her?

ELENA: I'm guessing the Reagan years. I bet a decade like the eighties pretty much did her in.

REED: And where were you then?

ELENA: You mean, emotionally?—Spiritually?—

REED: I mean—

ELENA: —Where did my *soul reside* in those years?

REED: —I mean *on a MAP.* I mean *where were you physically located on planet Earth?*

ELENA: I was traveling—bartending—dating musicians—

REED: You know better than that.

ELENA: Hey, those guys were perfect for me. All those guitar players with long fingers and short memories. I was on this kick. I didn't want to be the center of some guy's universe—

REED: Yes, I remember.

ELENA: (*Overlapping.*) —And the one sure way to do that is to date a musician.

(REED's *phone rings. He quickly checks the caller ID. Frustrated [not the call he wants], he drops the phone back onto the bench, or slams it back into his pocket. The "tell" with his ear starts up again.* ELENA *watches; changes the subject.*)

Can I see your paper? A little Red will go good with my outfit. (*He hands her* The Wall Street Journal. *Offering.*) I've got a *Cosmo* in my bag.

REED: That's okay.

ELENA: You can learn how to get a man by plucking your eyebrows in a "soulful, yet nonthreatening" way.

REED: I'll pass. (ELENA *starts to read.* REED *paces, looks at his watch— and his "tell" continues, bigger than ever.*)

ELENA: God, Reed—do you want to *talk about it*?

REED: (*Looks away.*) There's nothing to—

ELENA: I will never understand this. Here are all these strangers thrown together with time to kill: *They could say anything to each other, get the craziest things off their chest* to some person who they're never going to see again—but they don't do it!

REED: And *you do?*—You chat up strangers, tell them your secrets—

ELENA: All the time!—In fact, I'll tell you something right now—you want to know where I work? (*Lifts the business card.*) I work for Lone Star Consumer Data. I work in a beige cubicle the size of a coffin. And you know what I do there? I do "product polling." With my little headset fastened to my ear, I cold-call people, and I ask them about the shows they watch, the cereal they eat, what kind of toothpaste or deodorant or hemorrhoid creme they use. That's me, baby: *I'm the phone call nobody wants.* (*She hands him the card, as if to say: "There. Your turn." He stares at her. Then:*)

REED: You know, Elena . . .

ELENA: Yes?

REED: . . . polling the consumer is *crucial* to the marketing of any new—

ELENA: Oh, please don't give my job "the benefit of the doubt"!—Like you gave my mom and my brother and our landlord in Madison—

REED: Mr. Fenton was a very—

ELENA: (*Overlapping.*) —Like you gave Disney and Kissinger and Bachman-Turner Overdrive. I don't need you to rationalize it for me, okay?—Because I am a Woman of a Certain Age and a Woman of a Certain Age *can explain away ANY-THING. Especially to herself.* (*She moves to her seat. Sharp.*) So: You want to suffer in silence—you want to *rub your darn ear OFF*—go ahead, it's fine with me. (*She opens the paper, but* REED *suddenly says—*)

REED: When Kirsten was little, just a toddler . . . we'd sometimes have what she called a "bad-bye." A bad-bye was when you dropped her off at day care and she didn't want to stay. She'd cling to your pants with her fists—and if you tried to say good-bye, she'd say, "No—it's not, Daddy—it's not *good*—it's a *bad-bye.*"

ELENA: Smart girl.

REED: Yes . . .

ELENA: I know just how she feels.

REED: . . . And so last night we were at home—I knew she'd still be asleep when I left this morning—and so I was saying good-bye to her last night. I hadn't packed—was feeling rushed—I was scouring the house for those *little plastic bottles*—to put things in for the flight—

ELENA: Yes, that's fun, isn't it?

REED: (*Overlapping.*) —All those regulations—and Kirsten was following me around—and Beth-Anne was—well, we had just not had an easy night.

So, I was throwing clothes—and all the plastic bottles I could find—throwing them in my bag and trying to get my boss on the phone—and Kirsten wouldn't let me be— she kept talking about some new dance class she wants to take—some "Afro-Cuban Hip-Hop" thing—I don't really know exactly *what that is* or what that kind of dancing *looks like*, but I know it's a long drive from our house, at a bad time of day, we'll hit traffic coming and going—and she could hear me hedging on it, getting ready to say no to her—but she keeps pushing me on this—I've now *filled* my bag with little plastic bottles—and all I want is to change the subject *and have a pleasant good-bye.* And she says: "How can you keep me from doing this? If I'm going to be a professional dancer, I have to be able to—" and I interrupt her, and say:

"Kirsten—you're not going to be a professional dancer. So, don't worry about it—because it doesn't matter. You're going to have a *great life*—but there are some things that won't happen. I never became a songwriter; your mother never became an architect; and you're more than likely not going to dance for a living. It's a *dream.* It's a nice dream—but it's not going to happen. So don't worry about it." (*Pause.*)

ELENA: The realist.

REED: Yes.

ELENA: What did she do?

REED: She turned, walked away. I went into her room this morning, five A.M. She was fast asleep. Her hair had fallen across
her face. And her dance clothes, her dance shoes, her dance
bag . . . they were all in the trash. (*Pause.*)

ELENA: Give her time. When girls hate their fathers—it's tem-
porary; it passes. When they hate their mothers, it sticks. (*A
good long silence.*)

REED: God, look at that snow.

ELENA: (*As casually as possible.*) Do you think about us? The decision we made. (*Pause.*)

REED: We were kids, Elena. (ELENA *nods.*) There was—there is
no way we could have—

ELENA: Mm-hmm—

REED: —I mean—we both knew that—we both agreed to
that—

ELENA: Yes—

REED: —We were broke and in school—we were in no position
to be parents—

ELENA: —Right. You're right.

REED: —To raise a child. I mean—you know that, right?—*You
do know that? (Pause.*)

ELENA: It took a long time that morning.

REED: Yes. I'm sorry.

ELENA: No, not the—not the procedure. That was surpris-
ingly . . . efficient. But before that . . . I was in the room,

sitting on the white paper, on the table . . . and you were out in the waiting area—

REED: You had asked me to—

ELENA: —Yes, I know, you offered to come back there with me—God love you—but I didn't need that—just know-ing you were out there was so good, Reed—I was so grateful for that . . . and they explained everything to me. Asked me if I needed a little time alone . . . before they started. And I said . . . yes. Just a few minutes. And they left.

And it was quiet. And the door to my room was slightly ajar. And I heard someone come in through the back door of the building and walk down the hall. A bit of conversation. Then it was quiet again.

I hadn't known there was a back door. I listened . . . so quiet . . . no one in the hall. And I stood up . . . left my room . . . and no one saw me . . . and I saw that door . . . it opened into an alley . . . and from there I could see our car. Our rusty old Toyota.

And I had my purse with me . . . I don't know why . . . and I don't know . . . the next thing . . . I was just . . . I was just walking to our car.

REED: (*Quiet.*) You never told me this . . .

ELENA: I was ready to go home. With that baby—with that child inside of me. I was ready. (*Pause.*) And so I got in the car. And turned the key. (*Pause.*) Our "Mood Car" . . . there's no explaining it.

I pumped the gas, turned the key again and again, pounding on the dashboard, swearing at that goddamn car . . . but . . . no. The answer was no.

And when it was over . . . we walked out together . . . you opened my door and I sat in the car. And you got behind the wheel. Turned the key once. And we were off.

ANNOUNCEMENT: (*V.O.*) ATTENTION IN THE GATE AREA—BOSTON PASSENGERS HENLEY, ZANDER, TRUJILLO, CARSON, AND DAVIS—PLEASE SEE THE AGENT AT GATE B-17.

REED: Carson? I think they said—

ANNOUNCEMENT: (*V.O.*) HENLEY, ZANDER, TRUJILLO, CARSON, AND DAVIS—GATE B-17. (ELENA *has not moved.*)

REED: Elena, that's you—

ELENA: Okay.

REED: —They want you at the gate—

ANNOUNCEMENT: BOSTON PASSENGER CARSON—FIRST INITIAL "E"—PLEASE REPORT IMMEDIATELY TO GATE B-17.

ELENA: (*Simply.*) Watch my things? (*Music, as* ELENA *goes.* REED *talks to the audience.*)

REED: You should know that I wasn't very good at our "open relationship." I probably should have taken advantage of this period of supposedly guilt-free cohabitation. But I didn't. I just wanted to be with Lena.

So, I watched her leave parties with other guys—she'd throw me a glance that said, "Remember our pact—no ownership—no jealousy" . . . and then I wouldn't see her till the next afternoon, taking a nap in our bed, maybe wearing some other guy's sweater. I'd watch her sleep . . . and I'd . . .

seethe. I'd look up at the poster on our wall, which said: "If you love something, set it free. If it comes back to you—*after sleeping with half the men in Wisconsin*—it's yours. If it doesn't, it never was." She'd ask me if I wanted to talk about it—ask me if things were okay, if I was feeling jealous—which of course was a trick question. If I said "No," I was lying. If I said "Yes," I just knew she'd say—

ELENA: I'm getting out. (ELENA *reappears. She is holding a newly printed boarding pass.*) My flight. They think there's a window—just like you said—before the last runway closes. They asked if I was traveling alone, said they needed my seat for some family on standby, and would I be willing to—

REED: You gave up your seat?

ELENA: —Would I mind sitting with the "EP-DEPS"—and I said, "With the who?"—and she said the Executive Platinum Diamond Elite Preferred—and I said: Okay. First class. Cool.

ANNOUNCEMENT: (*V.O.*) PASSENGERS FLYING TO BOSTON ON FLIGHT 394—WE WILL BEGIN BOARDING THAT FLIGHT IN A FEW MINUTES—A REMINDER THAT THIS IS A VERY FULL FLIGHT AND THAT CARRY-ON BAGS MUST BE KEPT TO A MINIMUM.

(*She holds out the boarding pass to* REED. *Offering it.*)

ELENA: Here. Go home.

REED: Lena—?

ELENA: First initial only—they won't know the gender—

ANNOUNCEMENT: (*V.O.*) OUR EXECUTIVE PLATINUM DIAMOND ELITE PREFERRED PASSENGERS ARE

NOW WELCOME TO BOARD FLIGHT 394 TO BOSTON.

ELENA: —And they just switched agents at the gate—the new person won't know—

REED: I can't do that—

ELENA: —And you won't have to show your ID—

REED: —For God's sake, Elena—

ELENA: (*Stronger.*) *Go home, Reed.* You're not gonna make that meeting. You're never gonna land that account. You're the realist, remember?—So *get real.*

REED: *Why are you doing this?*

ELENA: Get out of here and go home while you can. Make it right with your daughter. (*Again, she holds out the boarding pass.*)

REED: I can't.

ELENA: Of course you can—

REED: No—

ELENA: *Why?*

REED: —She may not be there. (*Beat.*) She and her mom. They might be at a friend of Beth-Anne's—outside Boston— couple hours' drive.

ELENA: His name is Richard—right? This friend of Beth-Anne's. This boyfriend.

REED: She told you that? (*Pause, the anger showing.*) I asked her *not to do this*—I don't want Kirsten to go to his house—she'll miss a couple days of school for no good reason—so hopefully Beth-Anne did not—

ELENA: They went. They left this morning. (*Beat. He stares at her.*) You weren't going to tell me? (*He moves away.*)

REED: What can I say? She's tired of me.

ELENA: She *said that*?

REED: I don't blame her. I'm tired of me, too.

ANNOUNCEMENT: (*V.O.*) OUR FIRST-CLASS PASSENGERS ARE WELCOME TO BOARD AT THIS TIME.

ELENA: So you're just *letting it happen—letting her go*?

REED: It's not that simple—

ELENA: Okay, then tell me—

REED: —I mean: What am I supposed to do?

ELENA: Throw something!—Fight for her—give her an ultimatum—

REED: I've tried that.

ELENA: (*Overlapping.*) —Let her know that she's making a huge mistake—

REED: That's SO easy for—

ELENA: (*Overlapping.*) —I mean: Say something, *do something*— don't just be *gutless* about it!—

ANNOUNCEMENT: (*V.O.*) WE'RE READY NOW TO BEGIN GENERAL BOARDING OF FLIGHT 394 TO BOSTON.

ELENA: (*Overlapping.*) —This is not ME, Reed—This is not me you're walking away from—this is your daughter, this is your family—

REED: And what would you know about that?! I mean: Do you hear yourself?! Do you have any idea what a *fraud* you are?!—

ELENA: You have no right to— (*He is gathering up his luggage, etc., ready to get away from her*—)

REED: (*Overlapping.*) —And, God, it's so predictable—you think you're so *original?*—You think you're so *offbeat and weird and unique?!*—Well, sorry to say, *but you're NOT.* Everyone knows someone like you, Elena! That person with All the Advice and All the Answers to Everyone Else's Problems—but whose OWN LIFE is a *total fucking mess.* (*He starts offstage*—)

ELENA: (*Sharp.*) *I didn't do better.* (*He stops. She stares at him, hard.*) Is that what you want to hear? I told you I'd do better—I swore to you that when you left Madison I would do *way better than you.* Find someone who was *so much more . . .* (*Looks for the word, gives up; more quietly:*) *. . . dammit . . . I tried.*

ANNOUNCEMENT: (*V.O.*) PASSENGERS IN ZONES ONE AND TWO ARE WELCOME TO BOARD AT THIS TIME—PLEASE HAVE YOUR BOARDING PASS OUT AND READY FOR THE AGENT.

ELENA: (*She takes out her boarding pass. She walks to a nearby trash can.*) And you're right: I can't make this trip. They don't need me out there—someone with all the answers—even though in Ginny's case *I really do have a very good idea of what she should be doing with her life*—but, hey, as you said: Who needs it? Who needs anything from me? And since you don't want to go see your daughter . . . (*She tosses her boarding pass in the trash.*)

ANNOUNCEMENT: (*V.O.*) ZONE THREE. FLIGHT 394 TO BOSTON. WELCOME ABOARD.

(REED *is staring at her.*)

ELENA: You were going to storm off. I wish you'd do that. There's a really good cry that I'm looking forward to having as soon as you're gone.

REED: How will you get home?

ELENA: I'll just close my eyes. Austin's a state of mind, man.

(REED *looks at her . . . then he goes to the trash can, reaches in, retrieves the boarding pass. He turns to face her.*)

REED: Your "spontaneity."

ELENA: Yes?

REED: I never liked it. (REED *puts her boarding pass in his jacket pocket.* REED *sets his boarding pass near* ELENA'*s things.*) You might as well have mine. In case your telepathy fails.

ELENA: Thanks.

ANNOUNCEMENT: (*V.O.*) BOARDING ALL ROWS TO BOS-TON. ALL ROWS AT THIS TIME.

REED: (*He gathers up his things, once again.*) I never even got your number.

ELENA: It's okay.

REED: I'll Google you.

ELENA: How sweet.

(REED *stares, wanting to say more, as—*)

ANNOUNCEMENT: (*V.O.*) FINAL CALL FOR FLIGHT 394.

REED: Lena—

ELENA: I'll see you when I see you. (ELENA *sits down and opens the newspaper once again.*)

ANNOUNCEMENT: (*V.O.*) DOORS ARE CLOSING. ALL PASSENGERS SHOULD NOW BE ON BOARD. (*Music, as lights isolate* REED.)

REED: I boarded. E. Carson. No problem. Took my seat in first class next to a handsome, single, fifty-something guy with a ponytail, who was reading *The Nation*. He'd made his fortune designing solar-powered homes and was headed to Boston for a "primitive drumming" seminar. His name was Nevada Williams—the man who would have met Elena Carson. Another near miss.

Nevada and I had a lot of time to talk as they de-iced the wings . . . and waited for that "window of opportunity" . . . and then came the homilies from the pilot, the creeping delay, sitting on the runway for more than an hour.

Against all federal regulations, I used my cell phone on an active taxiway—and amazingly, the plane didn't flip over or blow up. I called Kirsten again . . . got her voice mail . . . but I left a message, telling her I was on my way home.

And as I'm saying this on the phone—the plane is starting to move, thank God . . . it is gaining speed . . . and soon we are headed . . . back to the gate.

ANNOUNCEMENT: (*V.O.*) ATTENTION, PASSENGERS: THE FOLLOWING FLIGHTS HAVE BEEN CANCELED:

REED: They shut the airport down. No flights were leaving till morning.

ANNOUNCEMENT: (*V.O.*) FLIGHT 255 TO DETROIT—FLIGHT 72 TO DALLAS—FLIGHT 347 TO WASHINGTON/ REAGAN—FLIGHT 54 TO KANSAS CITY—FLIGHT 271 TO ALBANY—FLIGHT 48 TO SALT LAKE CITY—FLIGHT 288 TO HELENA—FLIGHT 183 TO MADISON. IF YOU DID NOT HEAR YOUR FLIGHT CALLED, PLEASE CHECK WITH THE GATE AGENT AT THIS TIME. (*This announcement gradually fades away, as lights now reveal—*)

10:05 P.M.

ELENA *and* REED, *facing each other across the distance.*

ELENA *now wears a long, beautiful robe that might in fact be a kimono. She is barefoot. Her hair is down or loose.*

REED: You changed.

ELENA: Not nearly enough. (*Beat.*) Sorry about the flight.

REED: We tried. (*Pause.*) How was your cry?

ELENA: I've had better. (*Pause.*)

REED: Want to go to the bar?

ELENA: I want to go to sleep. (*She lies down, covers herself with her coat.* REED *removes a piece of paper from his jacket pocket.*)

REED: They gave me a hotel voucher. Pretty nice hotel, too. The shuttle leaves in an hour.

ELENA: (*She sits up; stares at him.*) One voucher.

REED: Yes. Someone should make use of it.

ELENA: And who are you thinking that someone is?

REED: I'm not sure.

ELENA: May I help you decide?

REED: Is that an offer? If I give it to you—which was my original thought . . . where will I stay?

ELENA: (*Beat. She stares at him.*) I want to go to the bar. (*Music,
as* REED *nods and quickly goes, taking his computer bag with
him, and* ELENA *turns to the audience.*) And we did. And we
drank. And we debated how best this voucher should be
used. After a few airport margaritas, it was agreed that
we would both go. That we would use it together. Reed
called the hotel to make sure there were two beds in the
rooms. "Most rooms," they said—"not all"—"no guaran-
tees." And this began the discussion of what we'd do if we
got there and there was only *one* bed . . . and this discussion, of course, led to more drinks . . . and soon the bar was
closing and the last hotel van had already left the airport,
without us.

WEDNESDAY, 1:23 A.M.

REED *appears—jacket off, tie finally loose. Computer bag on his
shoulder.* REED *is tearing the hotel voucher into many pieces. He
tosses it in the direction of the trash can . . . and it falls like
confetti.*

REED: I tried to get him to stay open—that kid at the bar. He
never even gave last call!

ELENA: It's okay.

REED: Says they're about to "power down"—the whole airport—you know … (*Makes some odd "powering down" kind of sound.*)

ELENA: We didn't need another drink.

REED: Speak for yourself. (*And now* REED *removes from his computer bag a dozen or more small plastic "travel" bottles. They are all filled with various liquids. During the following, he lines up a few of them like soldiers and then just lets the rest fall where they may—*)

ELENA: (*Amazed, with a laugh.*) How did you … ?

REED: The kid went in the back room—talking on his cell. He'd already packed up the cups and glasses … but I had my little bottles. See how these federal regulations come in handy? (*Lifts a tiny bottle, indicates others.*) I think the ones shaped like this are tequila. And those are margarita mix. The rest are mainly whiskey … I didn't know if you still drank Maker's … (*She smiles, selects a bottle—toasts him—and drinks. They settle in. They watch the snowflakes fall … and work their way through the tiny plastic bottles of booze.*)

ELENA: Remember the Bing Crosby Christmas specials?—on TV?

REED: Sure.

ELENA: Those are the *exact same snowflakes* that Bing Crosby used to have. (*They watch some more.*)

REED: I met the perfect man for you. On the plane.

ELENA: No kidding.

REED: Smart, funny. Seemed very nice.

ELENA: *They always do.* Especially on final descent—when they know you'll be out of their life in thirty minutes or less.

REED: Now, look, you've got to—

ELENA: I'll give you a hundred dollars to take off that tie. (*He stares at her. Takes it off.*) And the shirt. That's gotta go, too. (*He takes it off. He wears a white T-shirt underneath.*) T-shirt out. (*He untucks his T-shirt.*) And the shoes. (*He takes off his shoes, as* ELENA *opens his suitcase*—)

REED: What are you looking for?

ELENA: (—*and rummages about. She removes a new, unopened packet of shoe insoles, saying*—) Oh, good choice. These insoles did very well when I polled them.

REED: Get out of there!

ELENA: (*And now she removes a simple sweater from his suitcase.*) Even this—even a bland, conservative sweater is an improvement. (*She tosses him the sweater and he puts it on.*) Didn't you pack any jeans?

REED: There's a pair of khakis—under my loafers.

ELENA: *God help me.*

REED: *What are we doing, Lena?*

ELENA: Everyone's cleared out. We're the last two people at the party, Reed. Remember what you always said about the last two people at a party?

REED: They should make out.

ELENA: Exactly. I always thought it was a very sound theory.

REED: No matter who they were—no matter if they knew each other or liked each other or not—

ELENA: —They should just accept that all other options were off the table—that it was now or never, baby—and they should get their lips on each other.

REED: So that's your plan?

ELENA: I don't have a plan. Look at me— (*She stands, perhaps atop the bench or table.*) No, really, the whole package: *Do I truly look like a person with a PLAN?* (*Pause. He smiles. She stares at him.*) One of my therapists, years ago, he told me that if I ever saw you again I should not, under any circumstances, tell you all the things I've been waiting for years to tell you. Instead, according to him, I should let *you ask me* the things you always wanted to ask. The things you always wondered about.

REED: Who was this guy?

ELENA: Dr. Lance. I was dating his brother. His brother was a drummer. Very capable of not worshipping the ground I walked on. (*Beat.*) So . . . one chance only . . . what do you want to know?

REED: (*Pause.* REED *settles in, turns and faces her directly: Ready.*) How many were there? How many guys? (*A long silence. Finally:*) You don't have to. It's okay.

ELENA: You won't like it.

REED: I won't care. It was years ago. (*Pause.*)

ELENA: The first month or so, after we'd moved in . . . there were a few. You want their names?

REED: I know their names.

ELENA: Right. But after that . . . there were none. None at all. (REED's *first reaction is to smile, laugh.*) Really.

REED: Well, okay, thanks, but that's not true! Jesus, Elena—everyone knows that's not true. *I watched it happen—I saw you—*

ELENA: I know what you saw—

REED: —So, come on!—you've got to admit that—at the very least—

ELENA: I admit I made out in a lot of cars, and I had a lot of passionate talks about George McGovern while some guy tried to put his hand up my shirt. But I didn't sleep with them.

REED: You didn't come home.

ELENA: Lot of nights I went to Kate's house, crashed on her couch.

REED: I don't believe you.

ELENA: Yes. I remember that, too.

REED: So it was just a game?—For two years, some big charade?—This "open relationship"—

ELENA: No—the embarrassing thing is I believed it!—I really believed that people could live without jealousy, without ownership—

REED: Then why would you—

ELENA: —And then you slept with Felicia, and I knew it was a lie. (*This lands.*) Who could blame you? Ms. Lips and Hips. She was a knockout. I watched how she came on to you.

And here I was telling you to be "open to it" . . . and you *were* . . . just that *once*, I know . . . and it was okay, it was no big deal . . . and you never told me . . . and I never asked . . . because what would I say? I had made the rules and now I didn't want to play by them—and, oh God, *I was so jealous I couldn't even see straight.* I wanted to own you and what you felt for me and I didn't want to share that with anybody. (*Beat.*) And you know what they call that? Nowadays, they call that *love.* (*Pause.*) I'd like if you said something.

REED: You came home wearing their sweaters. I hated that.

ELENA: That's not what you said.

REED: Yes, I know. (*Pause.*)

ELENA: And if you'd stayed? If we'd stopped all that nonsense and just been together—the two of us. *If we'd had that child.* What then?

REED: I wasn't even sure if it was—

ELENA: It was. (*Pause.*) She'd be twenty-six years old. (*Beat.*) She or he.

REED: Have a better job than both of us, I bet.

ELENA: Be a snob about music.

REED: Know how to make soup. (*Pause.*)

ELENA: Ginny says that kid would have kept us together.

REED: Doesn't work that way. I thought the same about Kirsten. (*Pause. He turns to her, close.*) Your hair was longer before.

ELENA: A lot of me was longer before.

REED: No—last year—it was nearly to your waist. (*Off her look.*) April, maybe? I was changing planes in Dallas. You were coming out of the bathroom.

ELENA: No way—

REED: You looked great.

ELENA: —You saw me and you didn't say anything?

REED: What would I have said?

ELENA: *The same things you said today!*

REED: I couldn't do it. Not then.

ELENA: Today was *different*?

REED: Of course it was.

ELENA: *Why?*

REED: Today you looked lost. (*She stares at him.*) A year ago— the way you walked, held your head up—you didn't look like you needed anything from anyone. Certainly not me. (*Pause.*) The thing is—the thing maybe Beth-Anne didn't get around to telling you—is that she tried to move in with Richard a year ago . . . and *he didn't want her—he wasn't "ready for that."*

ELENA: And you took her back?

REED: Of course I did. And I know how that sounds—

ELENA: Hey, far be it from me to—

REED: —But we are a *family.* (*Re: wallet.*) We are *the people in those pictures,* goddamnit, and I was not going to let that change.

(*Beat.*) And then last week, she told me she'd been seeing him again.

ELENA: And that's it? It's over?

REED: I don't know.

ELENA: How can you not know?

REED: I've been wrong before. I was wrong about you. (*She leans forward . . . and kisses him . . . on the forehead. It is not quite friendship, not quite romance.*)

ELENA: You should look around. Meet someone.

REED: I've tried. Spent the last couple years on the lookout for an "opportunity affair"—I think that's what the magazines call it—something safe and fleeting, in a faraway city. No one finds out and no one gets hurt.

ELENA: (*Wry.*) And how's that going for you?

REED: Opportunities have been scarce. Until today.

ELENA: We don't count.

REED: Why not?

ELENA: Someone would get hurt. (*With little warning, he kisses her—on the lips.*) Reed . . .

REED: Yes?

ELENA: . . . Don't tease me. Don't do this unless you— (*He kisses her again, interrupting. Now, it's real.*) There's a security camera right above us. (*Of his continued kissing.*) *You like that, don't you?*

REED: Why are you still talking? (*The kisses grow more passionate and continue—*REED *unties her robe/kimono—*ELENA *hurriedly clears an area for them to lie down in—and just as she lies back,* REED *suddenly moves to his briefcase, breathlessly saying—*) You want to hear "Magnolia"?—*

ELENA: What?!

REED: —I've got JJ Cale on my computer— (*He is hurriedly opening his computer and plugging in some tiny speakers—*)*

ELENA: "Magnolia"—I loved that song—*

REED: I remember—

ELENA: —Whenever you put that on I knew you were going to take me to bed—

REED: —You want me to put it on now? (—*But* ELENA *pulls him back to her before he can play the song.*)

ELENA: I want you to shut up, Reed— (*She grabs him—they kiss and fall on top of each other. It grows still more heated—*ELENA *pulling off* REED*'s sweater, etc., as—*)

ANNOUNCEMENT: (*V.O.*) ATTENTION, TRAVELERS: DUE TO A SNOW ADVISORY SITUATION, THIS FACIL-ITY WILL NOW POWER DOWN TO ESSENTIAL SERVICES ONLY— (*And now a huge "powering down" sound is heard—and the lights suddenly grow very dim. The only light is that coming through the windows from outside.* REED *and* ELENA *continue to kiss—hungry, in a fever.*) —IN CASE OF EMERGENCY, PLEASE SEE AN AIR-PORT SECURITY OFFICER OR DIAL 911 FROM ANY AVAILABLE PAY PHONE—WE APPRECI-

---

* Note: If a different song is used on page 142, that title and artist should be mentioned here instead.

ATE YOUR COOPERATION—NORMAL OPER-
ATING PROCEDURES WILL BE RESTORED AT
FIVE A.M.—OUTBOUND FLIGHTS WILL RESUME
SHORTLY THEREAFTER PENDING WEATHER
CONDITIONS AND THE AVAILABILITY OF OPEN
RUNWAYS—ONCE AGAIN, THANK YOU FOR
YOUR COOPERATION.

REED: (*Screams at the P.A.*) WOULD YOU PLEASE SHUT
UP?! (ELENA *is laughing.*) GOD—a man finally gets an
OPPORTUNITY and the FAA has to breathe down his
neck! (ELENA *grabs* REED *and they continue from where they left
off—kissing with great passion . . . and this kissing continues until,
at some point . . . mutually . . . they pull away from each other . . .
stare at each other in silence . . . breathing hard . . . engaged, passionate, curious, lost . . . looking for an answer from each other . . .
which never comes. A long silence. Finally . . .*)

ELENA: (*Quietly.*) We stopped.

REED: Mm-hmm. (*Pause.*)

ELENA: Why did we stop?

REED: I don't know. (*Pause.*) Do you? (*She shakes her head no.
Now they hold each other as* REED's *phone rings.* REED *does not
move.*)

ELENA: (*Re: phone.*) Aren't you going to—

REED: No. Ignore it.

ELENA: Reed, what if it's—

REED: Not now. (*Phone keeps ringing.*)

ELENA: Just let me check—

REED: Lena— (ELENA *pulls away and answers the phone . . .*)

ELENA: (*On phone.*) Hello. (*Beat.*) Hi, Kirsten. (*Listens.*) Yes, everything's fine. Your dad is fine. I'm an old friend of his. Elena. Elena Carson? (*Waits.*) That's okay. There's no reason you should have heard of me. I knew your dad a long time ago—back in college—when he was still a Democrat. (*Nods.*) He told you stories? (*Listens, smiles.*) Oh, I can tell you *a lot more of those.* (REED *is reaching/gesturing for the phone.*) I'm gonna hand the phone to your dad—but first I want to tell you something. Just for a second. Would that be okay? (*She listens. She also looks at* REED—*who finally nods "okay."*) People make promises, Kirsten. People say they'll always be there for each other . . . but they can't always *make that happen.* I couldn't. I had a little girl—even your dad doesn't know this—this was long after he left Madison. I had a girl and when she was born I whispered in her ear that I would never leave her . . . but I couldn't make that happen. I did what I thought was best for her. I gave her away. It was the right thing to do . . . but I'll always wish I'd kept my promise. (*A question.*) Well . . . the name on her birth certificate— which I still carry with me, it's in my wallet—on there it just says "Baby Girl Carson." Her name now is Maggie. (*Nods.*) Right. Her parents gave her that name. She just turned eighteen years old. And a few months ago: She called me. Said she wanted to meet me. So I'm going to Boston to see her, if it ever stops snowing. I've never seen her. Never spoken, except that day when she called. But the thing is . . . she gave me another chance. People need that. Your dad might need that one of these days. (*Nods.*) Good. I'll let him know. He's right here. I know he wants to talk to you. (*Listens, nods.*) Nice to meet you, too. (ELENA *hands the phone to* REED. *We hear him say—*)

REED: (*Into phone.*) Hi, honey . . . (—*And then he turns and moves away, offstage, talking to his daughter.* ELENA *is alone. Music, under: the faint strains of a single cello, playing Bach.* ELENA *slowly looks at the now-cluttered area. She perhaps tosses away some of the alcohol, then . . . sees* REED's *sweater on the ground—she lifts it. She slowly, and carefully, folds it. And places it back in his suitcase, just as* REED *enters, finishing his call. His shirt is back on, buttoned, tucked in, etc. Into phone.*) . . . Sleep well . . . love you . . . good night. (*He ends the call. Looks at* ELENA.) So . . . there's no cleansing ceremony?

ELENA: It's for me. The day before I meet Maggie. It was Ginny's idea. Said bring a rain stick and an open mind. (*Beat.*) Can you imagine?: *Me standing across from my teenage daughter.*

REED: You'll be great. (*Music continues.*)

ELENA: Maggie wants some stories about her dad. I don't have many. His name was Toby. He was a bass player with pretty blue eyes. I only knew him for a few months. But back at the house where he lived . . . he had a cello. And we'd sit on the roof. Drink beer. Count the stars. And Toby would make that cello *talk*. Some carved wood, four strings, a bow moving across them . . . God, the sound that something that simple can make. (*Music fades, as a light isolates* REED.)

REED: The night had only a few hours left in it. Elena did some meditation. She tried to get me to join her, said it would help me relax, maybe sleep. I explained that I achieved the same effect by playing Solitaire on my computer. She breathed and stretched and soon she was curled up on a row of chairs, fast asleep.

And nothing moved. Nothing changed . . . except at some point . . . the snow stopped falling.

5:48 A.M.

Sound of "power on"—and the lights are restored to their original level—

ANNOUNCEMENT: (*V.O.*) ATTENTION, PASSENGERS: THIS FACILITY IS NOW FULLY OPERATIONAL—PLEASE

SEE YOUR GATE AGENT FOR SPECIFIC DE-PARTURE TIMES, AS THERE HAVE BEEN NU-MEROUS CHANGES, CANCELLATIONS, AND REBOOKINGS DUE TO THE WEATHER-RELATED DELAYS—AIRPORT MONITORS ARE LOCATED THROUGHOUT THE TERMINAL FOR YOUR CONVENIENCE— (*As* REED *ties his tie, gathers up his items, etc. He has all his things ready to go . . . except for his computer, which remains open, the speakers still plugged in.*) A REMINDER THAT HOMELAND SECURITY HAS ESTABLISHED A THREAT LEVEL OF "ORANGE"—PLEASE REPORT ANY UNATTENDED BAGS OR SUSPICIOUS BEHAVIOR IMMEDIATELY—THANK YOU FOR YOUR COOPERATION. (ELENA *appears. She is dressed in her original traveling clothes. She holds another new boarding pass.*)

ELENA: Morning.

REED: Sleep okay?

ELENA: Very weird dreams. How was Solitaire?

REED: I kicked ass.

ELENA: Did you cheat?

REED: Of course I did.

ANNOUNCEMENT: (*V.O.*) ATTENTION IN THE GATE AREA—WE ARE READY TO BEGIN BOARDING FLIGHT 394 TO BOSTON.

REED: You're getting out?

ELENA: Looks that way.

ANNOUNCEMENT: (*V.O.*) WE WOULD LIKE TO WELCOME OUR EXECUTIVE PLATINUM DIAMOND ELITE PREFERRED MEMBERS TO BOARD AT THIS TIME.

REED: If you see Nevada Williams, say hello.

ELENA: Who's that?

REED: You'll know him when you see him.

ELENA: (*She lifts her bags, ready to go.*) This is where I ask if you have a card.

REED: Yes. (*He gives her his card.*)

ELENA: (*Reads.*) "Assistant Senior Associate." What's that mean?

REED: It means I do what I'm told. (*A warm look for each other; but no hug, no embrace.*)

ANNOUNCEMENT: (*V.O.*) WE ARE READY TO BEGIN GENERAL BOARDING AT THIS TIME—PASSENGERS SEATED IN ZONE ONE MAY NOW BOARD—

REED: See you when I see you.

(ELENA *starts off—*)

ANNOUNCEMENT: (*V.O.*)—ZONE ONE ONLY, PLEASE— FLIGHT 394 TO BOSTON.

(—*but then turns back, holds out the rain stick.*)

ELENA: This is for you. Show it to Kirsten. Little something from Austin.

REED: You don't need it?

ELENA: I'd rather make you explain it to the guys in first class. (*He smiles. It seems he has more to say, but before he can*—) Bye, Reed. (—ELENA *goes.* REED *stares at the rain stick in his hand. Speaks to the audience.*)

REED: I didn't get out for another three hours. Turned out it was the *third* greatest blizzard of the century—but, hey, there's always next year.

And, truth be told, I hadn't cheated at Solitaire. I hadn't even played Solitaire. I had played this. (REED *pushes a key on his computer and it plays music: a song like JJ Cale singing "Magnolia."*)

When I finally got to Austin, someone else had landed the account, of course. I called Conrad. He said: "You've got to start pulling your weight, Reed. Just so we're clear on that." I said nothing and flew home. Kirsten and I went for pizza. (*Music [instrumental] continues, under, as a light rises on* ELENA, *opposite.*)

ELENA: Maggie and I took a long walk on Ginny's property. Lots of mature trees. And, of course, the labyrinth. Maggie had never seen one. We stood together, at the start of the path—and then we started walking, in opposite directions—walking away from each other in this maze, these strange passageways . . .

REED: Beth-Anne is not coming home.

ELENA: . . . Until it seemed impossible that there would ever be an end.

REED: This is good.

ELENA: But there was an end.

REED: This is for the best.

ELENA: And we were standing together.

REED: Elena called me. After she got back from Boston. For a week, we called—back and forth—had some really good talks.

ELENA: And then we made plans to meet. He was going to be in Houston for some meetings.

REED: She made plans to drive down from Austin. She picked a restaurant.

ELENA: He made the reservation.

REED: We both called each other the day before—just to *confirm it.*

ELENA: Just to *be sure.*

REED: I got dressed at the hotel. Reached for the door. But, I couldn't do it. At the last minute ... I bailed. Didn't even call. I imagined her sitting there, alone. At our table. Wondered how long she sat there and waited. What terrible things she must have told the waiter about me.

ELENA: I sat and wondered what he would have worn. His suit and tie, probably. Maybe some cologne. I'll never know ... because I stayed home. Never went. I wonder how long he waited for me.

REED: We never spoke after that.

ELENA: He knew me young, and I'm glad he did.

REED: I don't expect we will.

ELENA: He knew my dreams—the plans I'd made for my life ...

REED: But, it's okay.

ELENA: . . . And I can't be reminded of that.

REED: I sat on my bed, in that hotel room in Houston. Stared out the window. Then, I took off my jacket and tie. Ordered room service. And called Kirsten.

ELENA: I talk to Maggie nearly every day now.

REED: (REED *lifts the rain stick . . .*) She was telling me about her new dance class.

ELENA: Says she'd like to come see me in Austin, someday. Wants to learn how to make soup.

(*. . . and then he turns the rain stick over and listens to the sound as the music fades, and the lights go to black.*)

END OF PLAY

BLACK PEARL SINGS!

A PLAY WITH MUSIC IN TWO ACTS

Frank Higgins

After a reading at Rockhurst University and a mini-production at the Barter Theatre (Richard Rose, producing artistic director), Abingdon, Virginia, *Black Pearl Sings!* premiered at Stages Repertory Theatre (Kenn McLaughlin, artistic director) in Houston, Texas, on October 19, 2007. It was directed by Brad Dalton; music direction and sound design was by Chris Bakos; scenic, costume, and proper-ties design by Jodi Bobrovsky; lighting design by David Gipson; and the production stage manager was Elisabeth Bancroft Wessel Meindl. The cast was as follows:

PEARL JOHNSON	Alice Gatling
SUSANNAH MULLALLY	Susan Koozin

CHARACTERS
ALBERTA "PEARL" JOHNSON, African-American. About forty.
SUSANNAH MULLALLY, white. About forty.

SETTING
Act 1: A warden's cheap ground-floor office at a women's prison farm in rural southeast Texas, summer of 1933.

Act 2: A Greenwich Village apartment rented by a patron of the arts, January 1934.

SONGS IN THE PLAY: All of the songs are in the public domain. The well-known songs are sung in original folk versions not widely known.

"Down on Me"
"When I Was Single"
"Little Sally Walker"
"Troubles So Hard"
"This Little Light of Mine"
"Curtains of Night"
"Reap What You Sow"
"Do Lord, Remember Me"
"Skin and Bone"
"Hard Times in Old Virginia"
"Blackberries" (a fruit vendor's call)
"No More Auction Block for Me"
"Kum ba Yah"
"Raggedy"
"Don't You Feel My Leg"
"Pay Me My Money Down"
"Keys to the Kingdom"
"Six Feet of Earth"
African song

ACT ONE

SCENE ONE

In the dark, PEARL *begins to sing offstage. Lights up on a warden's office at a prison farm during a fierce Texas summer day in 1933.* SUSANNAH *packs up her autoharp and prepares to leave, but then grows interested in the singing.*

PEARL: *(Offstage.) DOWN ON ME, LORD, DOWN ON ME.*
    SEEMS LIKE EVERYBODY IN THIS WHOLE WIDE
       WORLD IS DOWN ON ME.
    DOWN ON ME, DEAR LORD, DOWN ON ME.

SUSANNAH: Hey! I want whoever that is singing brought in here.

PEARL: *(Offstage.) SEEMS LIKE EVERYBODY IN THIS WHOLE*
    WIDE WORLD IS—

(The singer cuts off. SUSANNAH *pats her neck with a kerchief.* PEARL *enters in black-and-white prison stripes. Her ankles are shackled together and she carries a ball and chain.)*

SUSANNAH: Well. None of the other women . . . wore jewelry. Sit here.

PEARL: I can stand.

SUSANNAH: The warden won't know. I told him stay out. Have the other women told you who I am?

PEARL: No ma'am, but if you be on the parole board? Don't let this thing fool you; I be a good person.

SUSANNAH: No, I don't give paroles.—It's okay to look me in the eye. What's your name?

PEARL: Alberta Johnson. Friends call me Pearl.

SUSANNAH: Well, Pearl—can I call you Pearl?

PEARL: You just did.

SUSANNAH: Why you're in prison is none of my business. But you sing better than the other women. People with good voices usually know a lot of songs.

PEARL: Ma'am, if you can't give me a parole, what *can* you give? I don't need another white woman in a girdle to tell me 'bout God.

SUSANNAH: That's not who I am, although in a way I do save souls—

PEARL: Can you save my daughter? She be in Houston. That be where I was tryin' to git. Maybe you could go save her?

SUSANNAH: No. My name is Susannah Mullally; I work for the Library of Congress. I go around the country to find songs from the *people*. I've found that prisons are a good place to look for old songs. If I find a song we don't already have, I use a machine to record the person.

PEARL: Where be this machine?

SUSANNAH: Car.

PEARL: You drives a car? You the first woman I ever knowed drive her own car. Why you do all this?

SUSANNAH: When a person dies, a library is lost. History isn't just made by kings and presidents. People who pick cotton or cook meals got a lot to do with it too. And there are things they believe in so much they sing them.

PEARL: Like what?

SUSANNAH: I found a song once from an old Shaker woman on her deathbed. *'TIS A GIFT TO BE SIMPLE, 'TIS A GIFT TO BE FREE.* We're lucky I found that song. Shakers don't believe in having sex. Know what that makes Shakers? Scarce. I am trying to keep the songs of your people from dying out like the Shakers. My biggest dream is to find a song that goes back *before* slavery time; that came here from Africa.

PEARL: You a white woman. And this be your dream?

SUSANNAH: If I can find a song that came here on the slave ships, you know what that would do? We can prove to the world that a song can be stronger than even slavery chains.

PEARL: Has you ever been in chains?

SUSANNAH: Pearl, can I be blunt?

PEARL: Blunt saves time.

SUSANNAH: Your warden recommended several women to me, but not you. Until I know someone's got something I can use, I can't waste time lugging in the machine. None of the others had a song I hadn't already heard. You'll have to show me something more than they did. You're old enough, were either of your parents slaves?

PEARL: Yessum.

SUSANNAH: So if they taught you a song from their childhood, that's a song from slavery time. What's the oldest song you know, Pearl Johnson?

PEARL: What you get out of it?

SUSANNAH: I just told you—

PEARL: —You get the joy of savin' our songs. But you can't eat joy. What you get out of it?

SUSANNAH: If I'm lucky, I get my grant renewed. That means I don't have to work as a clerk, or get married.

PEARL: So if I gives you somethin' I got, you get money, but I don't?

SUSANNAH: I'll give you a cigarette for a song.

PEARL: You don't get my soul for a cigarette. If I had money, I could give it to somebody to look for my daughter.

SUSANNAH: I'm not paying till you prove you are special enough to record. And you haven't proved to me you know anything yet.

PEARL: Same for you, ma'am.

SUSANNAH: I'm not an expert on your people yet. But I want to be.

PEARL: Can I be blunt, ma'am?

SUSANNAH: Blunt saves time.

PEARL: You ain't no young woman. By now you oughtta be an expert on *somethin'*. How come you not?

SUSANNAH: We're wasting time, Pearl.

PEARL: I don't wanna sing to no private. I wanna sing to a general who can do somethin' *for* me. And since you want somethin' I got, the least you can do is call me *Miz Johnson*.

(PEARL *starts to leave.*)

SUSANNAH: Wait. Wait! . . . What is it you want to know, Miss Johnson? Ask whatever you want.

PEARL: This job. They pays you money to listen to people sing. Must be a lotta folks wantin' that job. But you got it. So how come you not an expert?

SUSANNAH: I *am* an expert. On songs from the Southern Mountains.

PEARL: Prove to me you be an expert.

SUSANNAH: You may know the melody. People in America put new words to it so it goes like this: *OH DON'T YOU REMEMBER SWEET BETSY FROM PIKE.*

PEARL: That song sung by peckerwoods.

SUSANNAH: Yes. But I have to call them "rural nontraditionally educated Caucasians." Back in the Blue Ridge Mountains of Virginia, I found an old woman; she learned the song with different words with the original tune when she was six. See if you can guess where she learned these words.

(*She sings "When I Was Single / Still I Love Him." She starts with the autoharp, then switches to a capella.*)

> *WHEN I WAS SINGLE I HAD A PLAID SHAWL.*
> *ALL OF THE GIRLS WERE JEALOUS AND ALL.*

AH, BUT STILL I LOVE HIM, I'LL FORGIVE HIM.
I'LL GO WITH HIM WHEREVER HE GOES.

HE COME UP TO OUR FARMHOUSE AND HE
  WHISTLED ME OUT.
THE TAIL OF HIS SHIRT FROM HIS TROUSERS HUNG
  OUT.
AH, BUT STILL I LOVE HIM, I'LL FORGIVE HIM.
I'LL GO WITH HIM WHEREVER HE GOES.

HE GAVE ME A HANDKERCHIEF RED, WHITE, AND
  BLUE
AND SAID I AM LEAVING WHY DON'T YOU COME
  TOO?
BUT STILL I LOVE HIM, I'LL FORGIVE HIM.
I'LL GO WITH HIM WHEREVER HE GOES.

WHEN I WAS SINGLE I HAD A PLAID SHAWL.
NOW THAT I'M MARRIED I'VE NOTHING AT ALL.
BUT STILL I LOVE HIM, I'LL FORGIVE HIM.
I'LL GO WITH HIM WHEREVER HE GOES.

PEARL: Why you excited 'bout that song?

SUSANNAH: The old woman learned it as a child . . . on the
  boat coming *from* Ireland. That's about the time of the Irish
  potato famine. The man gives the woman a handkerchief
  red, white, and blue. He's going to America. Then at the
  end the woman is in America. But she's had to sell or barter
  her plaid shawl for food. The song is a warning that times
  will still be hard in America, and that people have to stick
  together.

PEARL: You get all that from the song?

SUSANNAH: It's the biggest discovery I've ever made. You can
  turn that song into a college teaching job at an Ivy League
  school.

PEARL: Then why you didn't?

SUSANNAH: Do you know any old songs or not?

PEARL: I know some play songs I learnt when I was a chil'. My mama learnt 'em when she was a girl too.

SUSANNAH: That gets us back to slavery time.

PEARL: So how 'bout some money?

SUSANNAH: Song first.

PEARL: We call this "Little Sally Walker."

SUSANNAH: Got it.

PEARL: There's diff'rent Sally Walkers. How's yours go?

SUSANNAH: (*Singing a stiff whitebread version.*) *LITTLE SALLY WALKER SITTIN' IN A SAUCER. RIDE, SALLY, RIDE.*

PEARL: Bad. You got to let your body flow.

SUSANNAH: So let me see you flow.

PEARL: Hard to flow with a ball and chain.

SUSANNAH: Try.

PEARL: First thing, that song is diff'rent for how old you is. The way you sing be fine, if you be five years old. But when you gittin' sweet on a boy, your body talks.

LITTLE SALLY WALKER SITTIN' ON A SAUCER.
RISE SALLY RISE, WIPE YOUR WEEPIN' EYES.

(PEARL *moves her body suggestively.*)

*PUT YOUR HANDS ON YOUR HIPS AND LET YOUR
      BACKBONE SLIP.
NOW SHAKE IT TO THE EAST.
NOW SHAKE IT TO THE WEST.
SHAKE IT TO THE ONE THAT YOU LUH-HUV THE
      BEST.*

SUSANNAH: That shaking is nice. Can I see that all again?

PEARL: Can I see fifty cents?

(SUSANNAH *gives her fifty cents.*)

PEARL: Dance with me. Now let loose your hips. *PUT YOUR
HANDS ON YOUR HIPS AND LET YOUR BACKBONE
SLIP.*

Looser. *NOW SHAKE IT TO THE EAST.
NOW SHAKE IT TO THE WEST.*

Let it flow. *SHAKE IT TO THE ONE THAT YOU LOVE
THE BEST.*

SUSANNAH: I think I've got it.

PEARL: No ma'am. I can tell you ain't never danced nasty.

SUSANNAH: (*The big challenge.*) Sing it again.

(SUSANNAH *dances better than before.*)

PEARL: *LITTLE SALLY WALKER SITTIN' ON A SAUCER.
RISE SALLY RISE, WIPE YOUR WEEPIN' EYES.
PUT YOUR HANDS ON YOUR HIPS AND LET YOUR
      BACKBONE SLIP.
NOW SHAKE IT TO THE EAST.
NOW SHAKE IT TO THE WEST.
SHAKE IT TO THE ONE THAT YOU LOVE THE BEST.—*
      Again.

(*They go right into repeating the verse, and this time* PEARL *shows some new moves, which* SUSANNAH *then mirrors well.*)

PEARL AND SUSANNAH: *LITTLE SALLY WALKER SITTIN' ON
A SAUCER.
RISE SALLY RISE, WIPE YOUR WEEPIN' EYES.
PUT YOUR HANDS ON YOUR HIPS AND LET YOUR
BACKBONE SLIP.
NOW SHAKE IT TO THE EAST.
NOW SHAKE IT TO THE WEST.
SHAKE IT TO THE ONE THAT YOU LOVE THE BEST.*

PEARL: Faster.

(*On the "Rise Sally rise" and "Wipe your weepin' eyes" lines* PEARL *sings and freestyles "Riiiiise, Little Sally" while* SUSANNAH *sings the regular lines.*)

PEARL AND SUSANNAH: *LITTLE SALLY WALKER SITTIN' ON
A SAUCER.
RISE SALLY RISE, WIPE YOUR WEEPIN' EYES.
PUT YOUR HANDS ON YOUR HIPS AND LET YOUR
BACKBONE SLIP.
NOW SHAKE IT TO THE EAST.
NOW SHAKE IT TO THE WEST.
SHAKE IT TO THE ONE THAT YOU LOVE THE BEST.*

PEARL: Better. You dance like that now in public, they gonna throw you in prison.

SUSANNAH: That was okay. What else you know?

PEARL: We ready to make a recordin' yet?

SUSANNAH: Not yet. Sing me the oldest song you know.

PEARL: How I know how old a song is?

SUSANNAH: If your grandmother said she learned a song from *her* grandmother. And maybe her grandmother before that.

PEARL: I wouldn't know 'bout that.

SUSANNAH: I think you do. I think you knew who I was before you came in here. I think you sang that song "Down on Me" knowing I'd hear it, knowing I'd like it, knowing I'd invite you in here. And you've been sizing me up since you came in. I think you're trying to decide how to play me.

PEARL: Well then you think wrong. Ma'am.

SUSANNAH: . . . Then at least give me a song with more meat on it.

PEARL: Meat?

SUSANNAH: Pain. You must know something about pain?

PEARL: Yessum. I must.

(PEARL *sings "Troubles So Hard."*)

> *OH LAWDY NOW, TROUBLES SO HARD*
> *OH LAWDY, TROUBLES SO HARD*
> *DON'T NOBODY KNOW MY TROUBLES BUT GOD*
> *DON'T NOBODY KNOW MY TROUBLES BUT GOD.*
>
> *WENT IN THE ROOM, DIDN'T STAY LONG*
> *LOOKED ON THE BED AND MOTHER WAS*
>   *DEAD.*
>
> *OH LAWDY NOW, TROUBLES SO HARD*
> *OH LAWDY, TROUBLES SO HARD*
> *DON'T NOBODY KNOW MY TROUBLES BUT GOD*
> *DON'T NOBODY KNOW MY TROUBLES BUT GOD.*

WENT IN THE ROOM, DIDN'T STAY LONG
LOOKED ON THE BED MY CHILD WAS DEAD.

OH LAWDY NOW, TROUBLES SO HARD
OH LAWDY, TROUBLES SO HARD.

SUSANNAH: Well. I guess I better get some men to lug in that recording machine.

PEARL: Not yet. Only way I make a recordin' for you is if you check an *ad*-dress for me in Houston.

SUSANNAH: Drive all the way to Houston? And ask questions of people who don't want to talk to me?

PEARL: If you want songs.

SUSANNAH: Don't be silly. Here's a dollar to record that song.

PEARL: Keep it.

SUSANNAH: Three dollars.

PEARL: You can offer me thirty pieces of silver and I'll say no. Now do you want songs, or not?

SUSANNAH: . . . Okay. I'll do it, Miss Johnson.

PEARL: Call me Pearl.

SCENE TWO

A month or so later. A large recording machine sits on a table. SUSANNAH *unpacks a picnic basket while singing and working on her hip-shaking. She dances and shakes well.*

SUSANNAH: *LITTLE SALLY WALKER SITTIN' ON A SAUCER.*
RISE, SALLY, RISE, WIPE YOUR WEEPIN' EYES.
PUT YOUR HANDS ON YOUR HIPS AND LET YOUR
    BACKBONE SLIP.
NOW SHAKE IT TO THE EAST.
NOW SHAKE TO THE WEST.

(PEARL *enters in prison stripes and carrying the ball and chain.*)

SUSANNAH: (*Continues.*) *SHAKE IT TO THE ONE THAT YOU*
LUH-HUV THE BEST.

PEARL: You soundin' happy. You find my daughter?

SUSANNAH: Not yet. But I do have a surprise that might help.

PEARL: What the minister say?

SUSANNAH: Not much. The last time he talked to her she told
him she had money trouble.

PEARL: Girl with no money. This be bad.

SUSANNAH: We don't know that yet.

PEARL: First time you gone to Houston the boardin' house
woman tell you my daughter move. Now the minister say
he don't know where to? No money and she not goin' to
church.

SUSANNAH: Calm down. Maybe she's going to church in a different neighborhood.

PEARL: No. We could move to the moon we come back to the
same church.

SUSANNAH: She's okay; we'll find her. Let's take your mind off it.
Here's a plate and spoon.

PEARL: Did the minister say if she was with a man?

SUSANNAH: No.

PEARL: When somethin' go wrong for a woman, there's a man behind it.

SUSANNAH: Let's eat and I'll tell you my plan that can help us find her. I assume it's been a while since you had . . . blackberry cobbler.

(SUSANNAH *presents it.* PEARL *is overcome.*)

PEARL: Blackberries be my favorite. But I can't eat now.

SUSANNAH: Tell me another place to look and I'll go back to Houston *tonight*. But only if you eat.

PEARL: You make this for me yourself?

SUSANNAH: Let's keep that quiet, okay? Where I come from if a woman can cook they don't let her do anything *but* cook.— I've got a plan to find your daughter through a song; it started with this telegram.

(SUSANNAH *takes out her keys while searching her bag for the telegram.* PEARL *reacts to the keys.* SUSANNAH *pulls out the telegram.*)

The people at the Library of Congress listened to the recordings we made. "Oh Susannah, all of us here thrilled!"— exclamation point—"Pearl *is* a pearl. Authentic doorway to the past. Kudos on your discovery. Make more recordings ASAP." How does it feel to be an authentic doorway?

PEARL: I'd rather find my daughter.

SUSANNAH: This will help. When we make our next batch of recordings—

PEARL: I ain't makin' no more recordin's for you.

SUSANNAH: What?

PEARL: I just a business proposition to you.

SUSANNAH: No, we're friends.

PEARL: We be friend-*ly*. But I be dependin' on you. If you sneeze, to me it's a hurricane. What if I run outta songs you like? You gonna drop me?

SUSANNAH: I'd never do that. You know me by now.

PEARL: All I know 'bout you is you be an expert on cracker music. But you not in the South no more. Somebody take you away? What if somebody take you away now? How I find my daughter then?

SUSANNAH: I will never let anybody take me away from you. And I will never stop searching for your daughter. I promise.

PEARL: You promise. All the stars in the sky at night? Those stand for all the broken promises white people make to colored people.

SUSANNAH: Don't you judge me by the color of my skin. I'm not like everybody else.

PEARL: Prove it.

(SUSANNAH *puts down a glass of water in front of* PEARL.)

SUSANNAH: Drink.

PEARL: The warden don't let nobody colored drink from his glasses.

SUSANNAH: So we'll drink from the same glass.

PEARL: I never seen that happen.

SUSANNAH: Drink.

(PEARL *drinks.* SUSANNAH *then drinks from the same spot on the cup.*)

Satisfied?

PEARL: No. You tell me how you come to be here. Or you get nothin' more from me.

SUSANNAH: . . . I haul that machine up into the Southern mountains on a mule, alone. The other song collectors are too afraid they'll get shot. When I find that song from Ireland, I'm in Heaven. The world is going to learn something. But I'm happy for me, too.

PEARL: You got money for that?

SUSANNAH: I got a job in the Ivy League, I *thought*.

PEARL: Why you didn't?

SUSANNAH: I turn in the recording to the man in charge. He sends it to D.C. But he takes credit for it.

PEARL: Why you didn't tell folks the way it was?

SUSANNAH: I did. But he was older. He was well known. He was a *man*. I thought I'd be the first woman to get a job at Harvard. With Harvard behind me, I'd be able to send out a hundred collectors to save songs. Instead, he gets the Ivy League job, and he does nothing with it. I get offered ten dollars a month more, if I'll be quiet.

PEARL: But you can't be quiet.

SUSANNAH: So I get sent to Siberia. Which in D.C. means Texas.

PEARL: You mean you an outcast? How this be anything but bad news for me?

SUSANNAH: It's not bad news. If I'd gone straight from hillbillies to Harvard, it might never have occurred to me to look for songs in prisons.

PEARL: But you an outcast!

SUSANNAH: We don't meet if I'm not. But, Pearl, I have big plans for you. My father, with all his money, can't do for you what a song can do.

PEARL: You talkin' crazy. How a song find my daughter?

SUSANNAH: I want us to make a special recording today. One that we send to somebody I know.

PEARL: You an outcast who done gone outta her mind.

SUSANNAH: At least I have a plan. Do you have one? Now do you want to work together as a team, or not?

PEARL: . . . Okay.

SUSANNAH: Then eat. I'll get the disks from the car.

(SUSANNAH *puts the keys in her bag and then leaves the bag.*)

We'll find your daughter.

(SUSANNAH *exits.*

PEARL *gets the keys but they won't work in the shackles. She takes a letter opener, picks the lock, and frees herself.* SUSANNAH *enters with the disks to find* PEARL *with the letter opener.*)

SUSANNAH: This is going to be so good—

PEARL: Come away from the door.

SUSANNAH: You put that back on right now.

PEARL: Hush. Which one of these keys makes your car go?

SUSANNAH: You think you can escape?

PEARL: The warden's office be the closest thing to the road. This be my best chance. Which key is it?

SUSANNAH: It doesn't matter. You've never driven a car.

PEARL: I'll figure it out.

SUSANNAH: Really? Because it took me a week to learn the clutch. Before you can back up, the guard will put bullets in your brain.

PEARL: . . . Then you drive.

SUSANNAH: And the guard will just let us walk out?

PEARL: We tell him he better.

SUSANNAH: Don't do this. It ruins my plan to help you.

PEARL: Get movin'.

SUSANNAH: No.

PEARL: Miss Susannah, I got a father in Hell, a mother in Heaven, and a daughter in Houston. And I'm gonna see *one* of 'em tonight.

SUSANNAH: Your daughter doesn't need you dead. My plan gets you out of here *legally*.

PEARL: . . . What plan?

SUSANNAH: Put your leg iron on first.

PEARL: You tell me what is it you think you can do.

SUSANNAH: Get you a parole.

PEARL: I never got a parole before and I been here ten year.

SUSANNAH: The Library of Congress was not in love with you before. But now you can set the world on its ears. So put that back on.

PEARL: No. First you tell me how you get me a parole.

SUSANNAH: We write up a convincing case to the governor on *Library of Congress letterhead*. We point out that you are a *model prisoner*, and that you are a doorway to our past.

PEARL: It can't be that simple.

SUSANNAH: Look at the numbers on that blackboard. As the Depression gets worse the number of prisoners here goes up. The governor would be *happy* to have one less mouth to feed.

PEARL: . . . So whatta we say in this letter?

SUSANNAH: Let me write down the facts about you. You're a woman who wants to find her daughter. The governor is more inclined to parole a woman who has *gentle* qualities. What are you in for?

PEARL: I took a knife and killed a man.

SUSANNAH: Ah.

PEARL: But I wouldn't kill no man 'less he needed it.

SUSANNAH: Well, we'll . . . try to make that a positive.

GUARD'S VOICE: You all right in there?

SUSANNAH: We're fine.

GUARD'S VOICE: I don't hear no singin'.

PEARL: *DIS LITTLE LIGHT OF MINE*
AH'M GONNA LET IT SHINE.

SUSANNAH: Let's start at the beginning. So you were born on an island off South Carolina.

PEARL: *DIS LITTLE LIGHT OF MINE*
AH'M GONNA LET IT SHINE.

SUSANNAH: How did you get all the way here?

PEARL: Coz of the son of a neighborwoman. He left the island when he was a boy.

DIS LITTLE LIGHT OF MINE
AH'M GONNA LET IT SHINE.

He come back for his mother's funeral. He say it's no life, livin' on the island. He say he know coz he work for the railroad and he travel lots of places. So I leave home with him. *LET IT SHINE, LET IT SHINE, LET IT SHINE . . .*

SUSANNAH: You left just like that?

PEARL: He was a convincin' man. He could talk a Baptist into burnin' a Bible. *ALL IN MY CELL AH'M GONNA LET IT SHINE.*

SUSANNAH: So you came to Texas because you thought life was better here?

PEARL: That's right.

SUSANNAH: Good. Texans like to hear that.

PEARL: *ALL IN MY CELL AH'M GONNA LET IT SHINE.*

SUSANNAH: How long have you been here in prison?

PEARL: Ten year. *ALL IN MY CELL AH'M GONNA LET IT SHINE.*

SUSANNAH: And how old's your daughter?

PEARL: Twenny-two. *LET IT SHINE, LET IT SHINE, LET IT SHINE . . .*

SUSANNAH: Uh, Pearl, this man you—who was killed—

PEARL: He not my husband. My husband die of the cancer. The man I kilt was later.

WHEN AH'M IS FREE
AH'M GONNA LET IT SHINE.

SUSANNAH: We have to say something more about this.

PEARL: I couldn't make enough workin' maid and scrubbin' floors. So we moved in wid him. He support us. Till he took to drinkin' more.

WHEN AH'M IS FREE
AH'M GONNA LET IT SHINE.

SUSANNAH: So if you've been here ten years, this man you—who was killed, this happened when your daughter was . . . twelve?

PEARL: *WHEN AH'M IS FREE*
AH'M GONNA LET IT SHINE.

SUSANNAH: Is there anything we can say that can help you with this?

PEARL: He needed killin'.

SUSANNAH: It would help if you could say more.

PEARL: Well I'm not.

SUSANNAH: It's called "extenuating circumstances."

PEARL: Not another word. *LET IT SHINE, LET IT SHINE, LET IT SHINE . . .*

SUSANNAH: The governor's Baptist like you are. Can we at least say why you're Baptist?

PEARL: Coz I heard the other churches sing.

SUSANNAH: Is there anything we can say about . . . repentance?

PEARL: No.

SUSANNAH: We have to end with something positive. Something to personalize you.

PEARL: How 'bout why my mother call me Pearl?

SUSANNAH: Personal anecdotes are good.

PEARL: She tell me, "You irritatin'. A pearl start off as a speck of sand irritatin' the oyster. Most of 'em git throwed away. But I want you to last. A pearl is a speck of sand that stuck with it."

SUSANNAH: That's good. I'll write this up. And then we'll put it together with the recording.

PEARL: Which?

SUSANNAH: We record a song just for the governor. Maybe something his ancestors sang.

PEARL: The slave owners?

SUSANNAH: Did your grandmother teach you any song that the masters sang?

PEARL: I only 'member pieces. Somethin' like "the curtains of night." Somethin' with curtains.

SUSANNAH: I know this song. *WHEN THE CURTAINS OF NIGHT ARE PINNED BACK BY THE STARS.* Is that it? Southern women during the war sang this about their men. See if you can get the melody.

(SUSANNAH *gets her autoharp.*)

There's a second verse about fortune. Fortune is good for us. *I KNOW NOT IF FORTUNE BE FICKLE OR FAIR.* Get the tune. *OR IF TIME ON YOUR MEMORY WEARS.* You are singing for your freedom; now, c'mon.

PEARL: So white women sang that for the rebel soldiers?

SUSANNAH: Yes.

I KNOW THAT I LOVE YOU, WHEREVER YOU
ROAM
AND WILL REMEMBER YOU LOVE IN MY
PRAYERS.

Do you want to be free or not?

PEARL: I ain't singin' that song.

SUSANNAH: But Pearl—

PEARL: If singin' that song's what it take to get a parole, I don't want no parole.

SUSANNAH: Then what do you think you should sing?

PEARL: I think I can make it to your car . . . How sincere a man be this gov'ner?

SUSANNAH: Hard to say. He's a politician.

PEARL: If he be religious, we should try for the better angels of his nature.

SUSANNAH: Make it a good choice: we'll only get one chance.

PEARL: . . . There be a old song we sung in the cotton fields when I was a young'un. The old folks workin' 'longside me sang this. So this be what the slaves be singin' together in the field. Maybe in the fields owned by the ancestors of this gov'ner.

(PEARL *sings "Reap What You Sow."*)

> *YOU GONNA REAP WHAT YOU SOW*
> *YOU GONNA REAP WHAT YOU SOW*
> *SOWIN' ON THE MOUNTAIN, SOWIN' IN THE*
> *VALLEY*
> *YOU WILL REAP JUST WHAT YOU SOW.*

(*She taps the letter opener against the keys to keep time.*)

> *I'M TELLIN' YOU, BROTHER, TO KEEP ON FIGHTIN'*
> *TELLIN' YOU, BROTHER, KEEP RIGHT ON FIGHTIN'*

FIGHTIN' ON THE MOUNTAIN, FIGHT HARDER IN
   THE VALLEY
YOU WILL REAP JUST WHAT YOU SOW.

I'M TELLIN' YOU, SISTER, TO KEEP ON FIGHTIN'
TELLIN' YOU, SISTER, KEEP RIGHT ON FIGHTIN'
FIGHTIN' ON THE MOUNTAIN, FIGHT HARDER IN
   THE VALLEY
YOU WILL REAP JUST WHAT YOU SOW.

SUSANNAH: Perfect.

(PEARL *looks at the keys in one hand and the letter opener in the other as she considers which way to go. She decides.*)

PEARL: Then get the machine ready.

SUSANNAH: Okay.

(PEARL *picks up the ball and chain and places the cuff back around her ankle.*)

PEARL: If you think it's a good idea? Tell the gov'ner the man I cut? I wasn't bein' no threat to society. I cut off his private part . . . I made the world a better place.

SCENE THREE

A month later. Lights up on SUSANNAH *on the telephone.*

SUSANNAH: No, she's not back from the fields yet. But we'll be waiting for your call.—No, I'm not with the warden. He's having lunch at a cathouse.—No, I did not drive him to that.—Tom, I want to make sure you mentioned to the governor—Yes, still got the same eyes. If you could make the point to him—Yes, same dimples. In fact, I've got all the same body parts; they're just not all in the same place. Now as to what the governor will be interested in, if you could just add—Yes, lunch would be nice. Tell your wife to join us; I'd like to meet her.—Europe? Well if she can't make it, we'll, we'll try to make do. Pearl just came in; gotta go.

(SUSANNAH *hangs up. She takes out her anger on something in the office.*

PEARL *enters in muddy prison stripes but no shackles and no ball and chain. She is exhausted and she limps.*)

SUSANNAH: You're hurt.

PEARL: I'm okay.

SUSANNAH: Sit.—Where have you been?

PEARL: Workin' in a swamp.

SUSANNAH: A swamp? Get these off.

PEARL: No.

SUSANNAH: If your feet stay wet you can get trench foot.

PEARL: If the warden see me barefoot on his floor, he tell the gov'ner don't give her no parole.

SUSANNAH: The warden has his hands full. Give me your shoes.

PEARL: You find out anything more in Houston?

SUSANNAH: What's that on your foot?

PEARL: Did you find her?

SUSANNAH: No.—It's moving. You've got a leech on your foot.

PEARL: I'm lucky it's just my foot.

(SUSANNAH *gets a napkin.*)

There's a way to do this so the teeth don't stick in.

SUSANNAH: I know how to remove a leech.

(SUSANNAH *works on the leech.*)

PEARL: Most white women be scarified by a leech. Why you not?

SUSANNAH: The Southern mountains. If you're not careful, your closest friends will be leeches, rattlesnakes, ringworms, and crotch rot.—There.

(*She takes the leech to the door.*)

You put women in a swamp with leeches? Here, guard: lunch!

PEARL: We gotta hope I get that parole. They gonna have the people here clear that whole swamp. Take weeks.

SUSANNAH: If you get a parole, I'll make them let you out today. The governor is looking over your file right now. He'll make his decision within the hour and then Tom will call us.

PEARL: Is it a good sign the gov'ner's assistant let you call him by his first name?

SUSANNAH: Maybe.

PEARL: What is maybe? It be good or not. Which?

SUSANNAH: We knew each other in college.

PEARL: So that be good. So I prob'ly get this parole; I can leave here today and look for my daughter.

SUSANNAH: Whoa.

PEARL: But you know him. You be friends. Somethin's wrong.

SUSANNAH: I don't *know* something's wrong.

PEARL: What you *do* know? Why you iffy?

SUSANNAH: I . . . may have hurt his feelings.

PEARL: You hurt the feelin's of the gov'ner's right-hand man?

SUSANNAH: I'm being criticized by someone who cut off a man's pecker?

PEARL: Why you hurt his feelin's? He do ugly to you?

SUSANNAH: Let's eat. I brought you some hush puppies.

PEARL: My whole life depend on this. Tell me why you hurt his feelin's. And don't hold nothin' back.

SUSANNAH: The women's college and Harvard shared classes. We sat next to each other; he said, "What is it you want? To be equal to a man?" I told him that women who want to be equal to men have no ambition.

PEARL: That's it?

SUSANNAH: And then he sort of called me a name.

PEARL: And?

SUSANNAH: I sort of slapped him, and . . . sort of broke his tooth.

PEARL: We never get that parole.

SUSANNAH: This can still work.

PEARL: She broke his tooth, Lord!

SUSANNAH: Pearl, something I did fifteen years ago will *not* cost you your parole.

PEARL: Then you don't know white men.

SUSANNAH: But I do. If they turn us down, I will drive to that state capitol. I will . . .

PEARL: . . . You'll what?

SUSANNAH: Let's not just sit waiting for the phone to ring. Eat.

PEARL: You'll what?

SUSANNAH: I will do whatever it takes to get you out of here.

PEARL: What's that mean exactly?

SUSANNAH: Nothing.

PEARL: Don't sound like nothin'.

SUSANNAH: Not another word about it, okay? Now eat.

(SUSANNAH *takes hush puppies from her purse.* PEARL *takes them but doesn't eat.*)

PEARL: What about Houston?

SUSANNAH: I found the place she moved to from the boarding-house. But she moved away from there a couple of months ago. Nobody knows where to.

PEARL: You sure they tell you the truth? They mighta not coz you white and they don't want to get her in trouble.

SUSANNAH: Pearl, she hadn't paid her bill. They locked her out of her room.

PEARL: I knew there was trouble. She used to write all the time. When she stop, I knew it meant one thing: a man.

SUSANNAH: We don't know that's why she stopped writing.

PEARL: A man don't like a woman writin' to her mother all the time. There was a man livin' there with her, right?

SUSANNAH: Yes.

PEARL: I knew it. And the minister don't know 'bout this man. That means this man not a man of God. He a con man. And if he can't pay the bill he not even good at that.

SUSANNAH: Pearl, when they locked your daughter out, they took her belongings.

PEARL: They took everything she had?

SUSANNAH: There wasn't much. Just a jewelry box.

PEARL: We gotta git that. No matter what.

SUSANNAH: They wanted a month's back rent for it. But I thought you'd want it.

(SUSANNAH *takes out the box.*)

PEARL: Oh Miss Susannah . . .

(PEARL *takes out an old blue kerchief. The blue is the blue of the Union Army from the Civil War.*)

> This be my grandfather's. It been passed down to my father, and then to me, and then to my daughter.

SUSANNAH: We'll find her. Eat.

PEARL: I can't eat when somebody's decidin' my life.

SUSANNAH: Worrying won't make the phone ring sooner. Dig in.

(SUSANNAH *starts to eat, but* PEARL *takes a moment to pray.*)

PEARL: You don't want to pray with me, Miss Susannah?

SUSANNAH: I don't even know if the *governor* liked listening to me. So God—

PEARL: God not so judgmental as a gov'ner.

SUSANNAH: It's just . . . when I used to pray, the things I prayed for, I never got them.

PEARL: Maybe God did answer your prayers. But his answer was no. . . . I say somethin' wrong?

SUSANNAH: What is it with people who pray all the time? You think God sits around and says, "Ah, Pearl is thanking me for the hush puppies."

PEARL: Yes, I do.

SUSANNAH: God doesn't care about hush puppies.

PEARL: My God cares.

SUSANNAH: As an *adult*, here's what I've learned: if I have to pray, then I haven't done enough preparation. Preparation is my way of praying. If we get the parole, it will be because of my preparation. If I have to pray, then I didn't prepare well enough.

PEARL: You a woman in trouble.

SUSANNAH: I am a woman who gets things done.

PEARL: You a woman who got sent to Siberia.

SUSANNAH: We get along better when we sing.

PEARL: What you pray for before? To be a wife and mother?

SUSANNAH: Why would I want to be married? And end up like my mother?

PEARL: But with no kids, when you die you don't just die. You die out.

SUSANNAH: Not if the songs I've saved live on.

BLACK IS THE COLOR OF MY TRUE LOVE'S HAIR.
HER FACE IS SOMETHING WONDROUS FAIR.

I'm more proud of saving that song than if I'd been the person it was written for.

PEARL: Ah'm gonna sing now.

SUSANNAH: Thank you.

PEARL: Lord, I'm not askin' you this for my soul, but for Miss Susannah.

SUSANNAH: No. I am not a charity case.

PEARL: *DO LORD, DO LORD, LORD, REMEMBER ME.*
DO LORD, DO LORD, LORD, REMEMBER ME.

SUSANNAH: Pearl.

PEARL: *DO LORD, DO LORD, LORD, REMEMBER ME.*
NOW DO, LORD, REMEMBER ME.

SUSANNAH: Don't.

PEARL: *WHEN AH'M SICK AND AH CAN'T GET WELL*
LORD, REMEMBER ME.

SUSANNAH: Pearl.

PEARL: *WHEN AH'M SICK AND AH CAN'T GET WELL*
LORD, REMEMBER ME.

SUSANNAH: Stop.

PEARL: *WHEN AH'M SICK AND AH CAN'T GET WELL*
LORD, REMEMBER ME.
NOW DO, LORD, REMEMBER ME.

SUSANNAH: I want you to stop.

PEARL: *DO LORD, DO LORD, LORD, REMEMBER ME.*
DO LORD, DO LORD, LORD, REMEMBER ME.

SUSANNAH: Stop singing.

PEARL: *DO LORD, DO LORD, LORD, REMEMBER ME.*
NOW DO, LORD, REMEMBER ME.

SUSANNAH: I told you to stop it, didn't I?! It's a beautiful song. We'll record it. You can sing it *for* me then. But don't you dare sing it *about* me.

PEARL: Why you think you don't deserve God's love?

SUSANNAH: Is there significance to that kerchief being blue?

PEARL: Don't you think God knows—

SUSANNAH: Isn't blue a . . . voodoo color?

PEARL: You wanna stay away from voodoo, Miz Susannah. You'll stay healthy.

SUSANNAH: But blue is a big deal, right? Your people think blue keeps evil spirits away?

PEARL: Why you wanna push this?

SUSANNAH: I'm just curious.

PEARL: Why? Does the Liberry of Congress want some voodoo?

SUSANNAH: There *is* another woman collecting voodoo stories.

PEARL: You in competition with her?

SUSANNAH: No, not really.

PEARL: Yes. This be serious. Would it help you if you . . . hear a song about a zombie?

SUSANNAH: There's songs about zombies?

PEARL: Zombies are real. So there's real songs about 'em.

SUSANNAH: You've *got* to let me hear a zombie song.

PEARL: Get in close. We can't let the guard hear it.

(PEARL *sings "Skin and Bone" and draws* SUSANNAH *closer and closer.*)

THERE WAS AN OLD WOMAN ALL SKIN AND BONE,
  OH—OH—OH-OH
SHE LIVED DOWN BY THE OLD CHURCHYARD,
  OH—OH—OH-OH
ONE DAY SHE THOUGHT SHE'D TAKE A WALK,
  OH—OH—OH-OH
SHE WALKED DOWN BY THE OLD GRAVEYARD,
  OH—OH—OH-OH
SHE SAW THE BONES A-LAYING AROUND,
  OH—OH—OH-OH
SHE PICKED ONE UP AND—Huh!!!

(PEARL *scares* SUSANNAH *and laughs.*)

SUSANNAH: That's not funny.

PEARL: I think it *is*.

SUSANNAH: My interest is professional. There has to be some reason you passed that blue kerchief down to your daughter.

PEARL: Why you white people like it so much when somebody colored talks hoodoo?

SUSANNAH: My job is to report.

PEARL: You want my songs and hoodoo both? What else you want? Want me to conjure up a zombie?

SUSANNAH: No.

PEARL: Maybe there's a zombie who sings. The Singin' Zombie. Fact, why don't I conjure me up a whole herd of zombies and break me out of here? Freedom be just a zombie away.

SUSANNAH: You're making me feel foolish.

PEARL: You're makin' my people look foolish.

SUSANNAH: No. That kerchief means something to you. I thought it might.

PEARL: Is that why you paid the back rent? Coz you think it's voodoo?

SUSANNAH: No.

PEARL: Yes. You think this is a magic kerchief.

SUSANNAH: I didn't know what it meant to you. I paid the rent because I thought it was important.

PEARL: You was right. This blue got power. Can't you tell what this blue is?

SUSANNAH: . . . It looks old.

PEARL: In the War That Freed the Slaves, the Union Army, they come to the island right at the start. Drive the Rebels off, free the slaves. Some of the men, they go to fight for the Union. My grandfather be one of 'em. This be the kerchief he wore 'round his neck. This kerchief got the sweat, tears, and blood of my grandfather in it. So yes, this blue kerchief got power. Disappointed to learn the truth?

SUSANNAH: The truth is you believe that things have power. And your daughter doesn't have the power anymore.

PEARL: She got what she need. She got songs.

SUSANNAH: What songs? . . . Pearl, does your daughter have a song you haven't sung for me?

PEARL: You wanna hear what we sing workin' in the swamp this mornin'?

SUSANNAH: Is this the song your daughter has?

PEARL: We sing it when I was a kid on the island poundin' rice.

SUSANNAH: Pearl, what songs does your daughter have?

PEARL: This one. The leader sing a line and everybody answer while they work.

(PEARL *sings "Hard Times in Old Virginia" and claps or stamps her foot on "hard."*)

> *MY OLE MISSUS IS A RICH OL' LADY*
> *(HARD TIMES IN OL' VIRGINIA)*

SUSANNAH: Pearl—

PEARL: *SEVEN SERVANTS AROUND HER TABLE (HARD TIMES IN OL' VIRGINIA)*

SUSANNAH: Have you been holding out on me?

PEARL: *HO! IN OLD VIRGINIA (HARD TIMES IN OL' VIRGINIA)*

SUSANNAH: Is there another song?

PEARL: *HO! IN OLD VIRGINIA*

SUSANNAH: I need to know.

PEARL: *(HARD TIMES IN OL' VIRGINIA)*

(*The telephone rings and startles the women.*)

SUSANNAH: Hello?—Yes. Let me have it—

(SUSANNAH *gives* PEARL *the thumbs-up signal.* PEARL *prays to say thank you.*)

Thank you, and one more thing, Tom. I want the parole to start—I *demand* it start *today*. The women will be working on a chain gang clearing out a *swamp*. I refuse to allow—No—*No*—You're sentencing this great singer to three *days* of *leeches*—I'm sorry.—No, you're right. It's foolish of me to question you. I'm sorry, I'm sorry, yes, we still want the parole. . . . Yes, I owe you.

(SUSANNAH *hangs up.*)

PEARL: Thank *you*, Miz Susannah.

SUSANNAH: Don't thank me yet. It'll take three days for the paperwork to get here from Austin. Until then, you'll have to work.

PEARL: So I'll work. And when I'm out I'll go to Houston. Thank you, Jesus.

SUSANNAH: Pearl, we don't even know if she's in Houston anymore. I wasn't able to find anybody else who knows about her.

PEARL: Maybe they wouldn't talk to you. But they will to me.

SUSANNAH: We can try. We'll have a few days.

PEARL: A few days?

SUSANNAH: We'll need to make our plans to leave. But there should be a few days before that to look again.

PEARL: Leave for where?

SUSANNAH: Pearl, your parole is not unconditional. I made a case to the governor that you are special. So there are things that we're supposed to do during your parole.

PEARL: My parole's not unconditional coz I'm special? Then I don't want to be special.

SUSANNAH: The only reason you *got* the parole is that you're special.

PEARL: So what are the strings?

SUSANNAH: It's important to present you, and your songs, to people who matter.

PEARL: Rich folks. There's rich folks in Houston.

SUSANNAH: But the real power is in New York.

PEARL: But my daughter ain't in New York. Why you not tell me about New York before?

SUSANNAH: I didn't know we were going to get the parole before. One thing at a time.

PEARL: I look for my daughter.

SUSANNAH: We *will*. But do you even have an idea of where to look?

PEARL: Somewhere in Texas.

SUSANNAH: Well, that narrows things.

PEARL: The island. If she's lost everything maybe she try to get home where her people be.

SUSANNAH: I'll call them.

PEARL: They don't got telephones.

SUSANNAH: Then we'll write.

PEARL: Most my people there can't read. If I'm there, I'll find her.

SUSANNAH: We don't know she's there yet.

PEARL: We'll look. We'll find her.

SUSANNAH: We don't have the money to look everywhere. Do you have money? Any at all?

PEARL: No, but you do. I'll pay you back.

SUSANNAH: I have my salary, which isn't much.

PEARL: But your family, they got money.

SUSANNAH: They won't help.

PEARL: But if you tell them what it's for—

SUSANNAH: They won't help. They think of me as dead.

PEARL: They disown you?

SUSANNAH: I disowned them. And the Library will only buy our train tickets to New York.

PEARL: I ain't goin' to New York.

SUSANNAH: The governor *expects* us to go to New York.

PEARL: I be a free woman. I go wherever I want to now and the gov'ner won't know.

SUSANNAH: Not exactly.

PEARL: ... What else you not tellin' me?

SUSANNAH: You have been paroled into my custody. And we need to go to New York.

PEARL: So I be your slave girl now.

SUSANNAH: You are not a slave. And don't you ever say that to me.

PEARL: I have to go where you say? Do what you say? That be a slave.

SUSANNAH: Everything I've done is to help you.

PEARL: And help yourself too.

SUSANNAH: The two can work together.

PEARL: I ain't goin' to no New York. What you gonna do? Put me back in prison?

SUSANNAH: New York means money. Money will help us come back and look for your daughter. Money will support the two of you after we find her. Or do you think you can support her by working in a swamp?

PEARL: ... This morning this white man in a white suit come over to tell me he like my singin'. All the guards be "Yes, sir"-in' him. So you know we was clearin' the swamp for him. I say, "Sir, what you want with this swampland? This be nothin' but gators and skeeters." He say, "This Depression not last forever. This gonna be a golf course." I say, "Sir, this swamp can't be no golf course. And it be too far away from anything." Man say, "You need vision. There only two kinds of people in this world. There's a few people who look to the future, and there's everybody else." So maybe I look to the future too. ... I'll go to New York.

VOICE OFFSTAGE: Pearl! Lunchtime's over! Back in the truck!

SUSANNAH: I'll ask the guard to keep you here.

PEARL: Won't do no good.

(PEARL *starts putting her shoes back on.*)

SUSANNAH: You can't go back. You know what's in that swamp.

PEARL: Yes.

SUSANNAH: I'll get this guard to let you stay; we don't have a recording yet today.—And that song, the call and response, it's very African-influenced.

PEARL: If you say so.

SUSANNAH: Pearl, now that you've got a parole, has that helped jog your memory? About any other old song?

PEARL: No, ma'am.

SUSANNAH: Everybody says I'm a hundred years too late.—I'm going to go turn on the charm. You're done working for the day, so relax.

(SUSANNAH *exits.* PEARL *looks to make sure that* SUSANNAH *is gone, and then softly sings in an African language.*)

PEARL: *AH WAKUH MUH MONUH KAMBAY YAH, LEE LUH, LAY TAMBAY YAH.*

WAKUH MUH MONUH KAMBAYYA, LEE LUH. KAH.

END OF ACT ONE

ACT TWO

SCENE ONE

In the dark, recorded jazz plays to suggest New York. The lights come up on Greenwich Village apartment as SUSANNAH *and* PEARL *enter with their bags.* PEARL, *who has never been so cold, has a scarf around her head. A large carved African head sits somewhere. A bowl of fruit is out on a table with a telegram.*

SUSANNAH: You'll get warm in no time. Bedroom's there with the bathroom off it.

PEARL: (*Looking around.*) Mercy. And you're sure your friend don't mind me bein' here?

SUSANNAH: She insisted. And we won't be overcrowded; she'll stay with another friend.

PEARL: No, that ain't right.

SUSANNAH: Nonsense. She's a *do-gooder.* Rule one: when do-gooders want to do you a favor, let 'em.

PEARL: This do-gooder got a African head?

SUSANNAH: She got that in the Congo. Like it?

PEARL: It not real, right?

SUSANNAH: It's art, not a trophy.

PEARL: Do Africans got white people's heads in their house?

SUSANNAH: I wouldn't know.

PEARL: I need a nap.

(PEARL *assumes the couch will be her bed.*)

SUSANNAH: No, I'll sleep on the couch. You take the bedroom.

PEARL: Your friend don't mind somebody colored sleepin' in her bed?

SUSANNAH: This is Greenwich Village. She's a bohemian.

PEARL: We don't got that word in Texas.

SUSANNAH: Bohemians? They want to be artistic but don't have talent. You sleeping in her bed makes the bed more special to her.

PEARL: Noo.

SUSANNAH: We're in the artistic part of town. Right across the street is a famous house.

PEARL: That thing?

SUSANNAH: The poet Edna St. Vincent Millay lives there. It's the narrowest house in New York.

PEARL: How you know all these things?

SUSANNAH: I lived here; this was my apartment.

PEARL: You and your parents lived here?

SUSANNAH: No, they still live by the big park; I moved here after college.

PEARL: Your parents gonna come to our show?

SUSANNAH: No.

PEARL: Why not?

SUSANNAH: That house? You can stand in the center and reach your arms out and almost touch the side walls.

PEARL: On the island we got cabins only that wide. They get mistook by outsiders for a big outhouse.

SUSANNAH: That's good. Mention that tonight. In fact, you should say more about the island than about Texas. All your oldest songs come from there. And the island's got this exotic name nobody's ever heard before: Hilton Head.

PEARL: Nap time.

SUSANNAH: Wait, telegram. From the other woman who works with the Library. I wrote her about your daughter and Hilton Head.—She's changed her plans. She sent this from Savannah; she's taking a boat to the island tomorrow. She'll look up your sister first thing.

PEARL: Hallelujah!

SUSANNAH: Who knows? Your daughter could have reached the island by now.

PEARL: That make it easier for me to get to sleep.

SUSANNAH: Huh. She says since she'll be there anyway, she might as well do some song collecting herself. Well thank you, Zora Neale Hurston.—Pearl, let's rehearse.

PEARL: We do that on the train.

SUSANNAH: Another time won't hurt.

PEARL: That telegram change things for you?

SUSANNAH: Nooo.

PEARL: Seem like it.

SUSANNAH: No, we got here first. But just in case, we need to be perfect. So we'll start with a slavery-time song from the island—

PEARL: "Little Sally Walker."

SUSANNAH: And then we'll talk about names. "Pearl, tell us how many of the people on Hilton Head got their names."

PEARL: (*Stiffly.*) "Lots of folks name their chillen after somethin' important to 'em. I had a auntie named after the biggest crop her father had: Okra."

SUSANNAH: "And so it is for people living close to nature."

PEARL: (*Breaking from the script.*) 'Course my husband hate that. He say, "Okra? How somebody name their child Okra?" I tell him it's the old ways. "The old ways are wrong. What if we have twins? What do you name 'em? Biscuit and Gravy?"

SUSANNAH: Let's stick to the script. "And tell us, Pearl, how did you decide to give your daughter a special name?"

PEARL: "We give her a name to remind her she unique. Uniqua."

SUSANNAH: "Oppressed people often have nothing *but* their name to remind them of who they are."

PEARL: Why is it if somebody colored name their chil' Uniqua it's folklore? Ain't your name folklore too? How come you never say why you Susannah 'stead of Susan?

SUSANNAH: It's not part of the show.

PEARL: Should be. What if we took the show to Africa? Maybe this guy (*She points to the African carving.*) want to know why white people name their chil' "Bob."

SUSANNAH: It's stupid. My mother named me for the song "Oh! Susannah."

PEARL: You think your life woulda been better you was Okra?

SUSANNAH: Pearl—

PEARL: My people name their chil' Okra after what help 'em survive. Maybe your mother name you for a song to help her survive.

SUSANNAH: Pearl—

PEARL: Maybe when she say "Susannah" that be her way of singin'. Ain't that folklore? Why don't you bring her to the show and we ask her?

SUSANNAH: Back to the script. Or else we will screw up the show. And everything we have worked for will be for nothing.

PEARL: You mean . . . if I don't do things right they don't like me?

SUSANNAH: There's a way to present things to people.

PEARL: So there *is* a chance they don't like me. We make a mistake comin' here.

SUSANNAH: No.

PEARL: But why should they like me? There's nobody in New York who sings?

SUSANNAH: Not the songs you know.

PEARL: But what about my trouble? They gonna be put off by prison.

SUSANNAH: They *love* that you were in prison. The program tonight is sponsored by the radical women at the historical society—they call it *herstorical*. "She sings authentic songs *and* she cut off a pecker? Perfect!"

PEARL: Cuttin' off a pecker is easy. There gotta be a woman somewhere in New York who can cut off a pecker and sing. Why ain't *she* perfect?

SUSANNAH: Because she's not authentic. Nothing in New York is. It used to be, but then it came here and became something else.

PEARL: No white people back in Texas cared 'bout this stuff. These people won't neither.

SUSANNAH: You're wrong.

PEARL: Don't you tell me I'm wrong. I know what white people think of colored people better than you do.

SUSANNAH: You're just having stage fright.

PEARL: You go tell those people we're not comin'.

SUSANNAH: No.

PEARL: Tell 'em I'm sick.

SUSANNAH: No.

PEARL: Tell 'em whatever—

SUSANNAH: No.

PEARL: —but you tell 'em we are canceling.

SUSANNAH: We are not canceling!!!

PEARL: . . . Yes, ma'am.

SUSANNAH: Don't "yes ma'am" me. I'm trying to help.

PEARL: So was Jesus, but He didn't shout the Sermon on the Mount.

SUSANNAH: His audience wasn't trying to cancel the show.

(*Silence.* SUSANNAH *gets out her autoharp.* SUSANNAH *starts to apologize.*)

SUSANNAH: Pearl . . .

PEARL: I don't care to hear you talk for a while, thank you.

SUSANNAH: You like fruit, right? You didn't see any for ten years, so here, dig in.

(*After a while, to break the silence,* PEARL *speaks.*)

PEARL: . . . It's coz of berries I meet the man I marry. Back on the island, when Thomas be a boy his father send him out to sell with a wagon. He use the fruit to flirt with all the females.

I GOT BLACKBERRIES, FRESH AND FINE.
I GOT BLACKBERRIES, LADY, FRESH FROM THE VINE.
I GOT BLACKBERRIES, LADY, TWO POUND FOR A
*   DIME.*
I GOT ANYTHING YOU NEED. I'M THE "I GOT 'EM
*   MAN."*

SUSANNAH: That's good. If I'm allowed to speak.

(PEARL *grunts if as she hasn't decided.*)

Tell me more about him.

PEARL: That man, even as a boy he'd brag: *AH'M GONNA JUMP DOWN, TURN AROUND, PICK A BALE OF COTTON.* I say, "Boy, you can't pick no bale a day. Nobody can. You just liiiiie." Then he tell me he not gonna be no cotton picker. He gonna run away and see the world, be a Pullman porter on the biggest train in the country. He say, "That train so big to make it took the biggest steel mill in the country two year workin' on a thirty-six-hour day and a nine-day week." I say, "Boy, you are lyin'." He say, "That train got seven *hunnerd* cars. It so long that when the conductor check tickets he gotta go up and down the aisle on a motorcycle. That train so fast when it come to a stop it still going sixty mile an hour." And he did leave. He did become a Pullman porter. I was sure he wasn't never comin' back. When I be churnin' butter there was a little song I sing: *THE MILK IN THE PITCHER, THE BUTTER IN THE BOWL YOU CAN'T CATCH A SWEETHEART TO SAVE YOUR SOUL.*

SUSANNAH: Let's put your husband in the show. His call, his story, and the song you sang about him when you churned butter.

PEARL: You'd do that for me?

SUSANNAH: We'll make a show that will become so famous, even if your daughter's not on the island? She'll hear about you and she'll find *you*.

PEARL: That sound good.

SUSANNAH: Pearl . . . sometimes I can be a little . . . overbearing.

PEARL: Um-hmm.

SUSANNAH: But I know what I'm doing. We didn't get here by accident. The show will go well. So can you just trust me?

PEARL: Yes, *Susannah*.

(*The actors step to the apron and bump right into the Cooper Union scene. The lights change and the sound of an audience applauding is heard.*)

SUSANNAH: (*To the live audience.*) Thank you. For the final song of the night, we've chosen one that was composed after the Civil War. Its author is lost to history, and the song was almost lost as well. But thanks to Pearl, the song and the people it is sung about live on. And thanks to the Carnegie Foundation's grant to the Library, it will live forever.

(SUSANNAH *starts to strum.*)

PEARL: (*Ad-libbing to the audience.*) So would you like to help out now on a song?

SUSANNAH: Uh, Pearl, some of us here are educated, stuffy folks who might not want to sing.

PEARL: Oh you'll do fine. I need you folks on this song. So when I point, you sing in a low voice *MANY THOUSAND GONE*. Try that.

(*She gets them to do it.*)

> That was pitiful. Let's try again . . . *MANY THOUSAND GONE*. Better. Here we go.—Miss Susannah.

(PEARL *points to her to play;* PEARL *takes over the show.* SUSANNAH *strums.*)

> *NO MORE AUCTION BLOCK FOR ME*
> *NO MORE, NO MORE.*
> *NO MORE AUCTION BLOCK FOR ME*

(*She points and sings with the audience.*)

> *MANY THOUSAND GONE. Again. MANY THOUSAND GONE.*
>
> *NO MORE DRIVER'S LASH FOR ME*
> *NO MORE, NO MORE.*
> *NO MORE DRIVER'S LASH FOR ME*

(*She points and sings with the audience, etc.*)

> *MANY THOUSAND GONE.*
> *MANY THOUSAND GONE.*
>
> *NO MORE MASTER'S CALL FOR ME*
> *NO MORE, NO MORE.*
> *NO MORE MASTER'S CALL FOR ME.*
> *MANY THOUSAND GONE.*
> *MANY THOUSAND GONE.*
>
> *NO MORE SLAVERY CHAINS FOR ME*
> *NO MORE, NO MORE.*
> *NO MORE SLAVERY CHAINS FOR ME.*
> *MANY THOUSAND GONE.*
> *MANY THOUSAND GONE.*

> One more, slower. *MANY THOUSAND GONE.*

SUSANNAH: Thank you for inviting us. And a final thank-you to
the Carnegie—

PEARL: Let's do one more.

SUSANNAH: Pearl. As my mother taught me, "When you go to a
party, leave too soon."

PEARL: Well, as my mother taught me, "Don't hide your light
under a bushel." Back on Hilton Head, we don't call the
church a *church*. It be a *praise house*. And your voices be good
enough to fit right in.

SUSANNAH: Maybe not everyone here is religious—

PEARL: Don't have to be. Just sing. If they don't sing in Heaven, I
don't wanna be there. And we got a hat we're passin' around.

SUSANNAH: No no, we don't need to pass a hat. It doesn't look
professional.

PEARL: But I not a professional. The point of me bein' here is I
be an amateur. 'Course, the Ark was built by amateurs; the
Titanic was built by professionals.

SUSANNAH: Pearl—

PEARL: You sing these words in a low voice going up like this:
KUM BA YAH.

(*She gets them to do it. This does NOT sound corny like the "Kum Ba
Ya" that contemporary audiences know.*)

And then you gonna go down: *KUM BA YAH.*

(*She gets them to do it.*)

These be island words that mean "come by here." And then
you add words for the ending: *OH LORD KUM BA YAH.*
Try that.

(*She gets them to do it and then sings, pointing for them to go up or
down.*)

> *IT'S KUM BA YAH, LORD.*
> *(KUM BA YAH)*
> *IT'S KUM BA YAH, LORD.*
> *(KUM BA YAH)*
> *IT'S KUM BA YAH, LORD.*
> *(KUM BA YAH)*
> *OH LORD KUM BA YAH.*

(SUSANNAH *stands by and tries to hide that she is annoyed.*)

> *ME MOTHER NEED YOU, LORD*
> *(KUM BA YAH)*
> *ME FATHER NEED YOU, LORD*
> *(KUM BA YAH)*
> *ME DAUGHTER NEED YOU, LORD*
> *(KUM BA YAH)*
> *OH LORD KUM BA YAH.*

> *WE NEEDS YOU OH WE NEEDS YOU, LORD*
> *(KUM BA YAH)*
> *WE NEEDS YOU OH WE NEEDS YOU, LORD*
> *(KUM BA YAH)*
> *WE NEEDS YOU OH WE NEEDS YOU, LORD*
> *(KUM BA YAH)*
> *OH LORD KUM BA YAH.*

(PEARL *starts stamping and points for them to sing.*)

Now chant *Kum Ba Yah.*

KUM BA YAH
(KUM BA YAH)
KUM BA YAH
(KUM BA YAH)
FATHER NEED YA
(KUM BA YAH)
MOTHER NEED YA
(KUM BA YAH)
DAUGHTER NEED YA
(KUM BA YAH)
WE NEED YA
(KUM BA YAH)
KUM BA YAH
(KUM BA YAH)
KUM BA YAH.
(KUM BA YAH)
KUM BA YAH
(KUM BA YAH)
KUM BA YAH.
(KUM BA YAH)

All together up.

KUM BA YAH

And the end.

OH LORD KUM BA YAH.

You good.

SCENE TWO

The next day. Noon. PEARL *enters from the bedroom with a hangover and in a flashy silk robe with exotic Chinese or Japanese markings.*

PEARL: You in the bathroom?—Oh.

(*She reacts to the hangover. She sings to the melody of "Raggedy."*)

> HUNGOVER, HUNGOVER, ARE WE.
> JUST AS HUNGOVER AS HUNGOVER CAN BE.
> WE GOTTA GET SOMETHIN' FOR OUR HEADACHE—

(*She pats the African head as she passes by it.*)

> Mornin'. COZ HUNGOVER, HUNGOVER ARE WE.

(PEARL *looks out the window at the house across the street.* SUSANNAH *enters unseen by* PEARL *with a sack and a newspaper but stops when she hears the song.* SUSANNAH *doesn't like the song.*)

> UNION UNION ARE WE
> JUST AS UNION AS UNION CAN BE
> WE'RE GONNA GET SOMETHIN' FOR OUR LABOR
> SO UNION UNION ARE WE.

SUSANNAH: Morning. Or actually, *afternoon.*

PEARL: Where you been?

SUSANNAH: Getting some things for tonight's show. So. The ladies of the historical society kept you out late last night.

PEARL: Those hysterical ladies get wild after midnight.

SUSANNAH: They promised me they'd bring you home after one more drink.

PEARL: Each one wanted to buy me one more drink. And there was five of 'em. I couldn't be rude.

SUSANNAH: So you had five drinks and left?

PEARL: And then they wanted me to sing for all the people there.

SUSANNAH: Sing?

PEARL: You know that young bandleader with the slick-back hair? Cab Calloway?

SUSANNAH: What songs did you sing?

PEARL: His shoes may be white as cotton, but him and all those people at that Cotton Club? They never picked cotton.

SUSANNAH: You didn't give any songs away, did you?

PEARL: I didn't sing no old songs. I wasn't gonna sing at all, but the drinks was talkin' to me.

SUSANNAH: So what exactly did you sing?

PEARL: *OH DON'T YOU FEEL MY LEG, DON'T YOU FEEL MY LEG*
COZ IF YOU FEEL MY LEG YOU'LL WANT TO FEEL
*   MY THIGH*
AND IF YOU FEEL MY THIGH YOU'LL WANT TO GO
*   UP HIGH*
SO DON'T YOU FEEL MY LEG.

Try it. It's like "Little Sally Walker" on gin.

SUSANNAH: Pearl, I left early last night because I thought you might want a break from me. But also, I needed a break from you.

PEARL: Why?

SUSANNAH: Let's not have any more surprises in the show, okay?

PEARL: People wanted to sing.

SUSANNAH: It's great that they sing. We'll make that part of the show. But we have to agree on things in advance. I would never have said yes to passing a hat.

PEARL: In church they pass a hat.

SUSANNAH: Forget the hat. Know why? You pass a hat, the best you can hope for is a hatful of money. Think Big. Our goal is to get you invited to a lot of places. And in some of these places passing a hat puts people off.

PEARL: I'm sorry. I won't make no more mistakes, I promise.

SUSANNAH: Really? So what about this union song? You didn't sing that in the Cotton Club, did you?

PEARL: No. I learned it after, over there, at the skinny house.

SUSANNAH: What'd they bring you there for?

PEARL: There was a load of folks there the ladies said couldn't afford the Cotton Club, but they wanted to meet me.

SUSANNAH: And the people there taught it to you?

PEARL: I like it. *RAGGEDY, RAGGEDY ARE WE.*
JUST AS RAGGEDY AS RAGGEDY CAN BE.
WE DON'T GET NOTHIN' FOR OUR LABOR
SO RAGGEDY, RAGGEDY ARE WE.

I think we should put it in the show.

SUSANNAH: Absolutely not.

PEARL: How come?

SUSANNAH: The program last night was paid for by the Carnegie Foundation. Carnegie is against unions.

PEARL: I heard 'bout that last night. Those people 'cross the street, they say this Carnegie man, he pay for a place called Carnegie Hall? And people proud to sing there?

SUSANNAH: Very proud.

PEARL: They proud this Carnegie man get rich runnin' non-union factories? When the workers go on strike to get a union, this Carnegie man have 'em beat up.

SUSANNAH: That's a bad thing, but—

PEARL: Some died. Do they sing 'bout that at Carnegie Hall?

SUSANNAH: We stay away from union songs. That's not who you are.

PEARL: But I said I like the song.

SUSANNAH: That's not enough.

PEARL: I like unions. Is that enough?

SUSANNAH: No. I like unions too. I'm *for* unions. You know how many widows of coal miners sang their songs to me? But we came to New York for you to sing old songs, of your people. That's what you're an expert on. Not unions.

PEARL: My husband didn't have no union. He serve meals in the meal car. You know you get fired if you have a hangnail?

SUSANNAH: Pearl—

PEARL: Rich people eatin' their food can't see a hangnail without it upset they's delicate stomach. My husband be an expert on that. My husband would want me to sing a union song in the show. Is that enough?

SUSANNAH: No! No union songs!

PEARL: ... I not gonna git mad you raise your voice again. Know why? Coz last night, after a few drinks, those herstorical ladies talk 'bout you.

SUSANNAH: Really.

PEARL: It wasn't all bad. They say there be a thousand college teachers inner-rested in the same stuff as you. They say any one of 'em coulda gone to all the prisons. But only you did. And only you woulda done what you done on the train: come all the way here 'cross the country, sittin' and singin' with me in the colored car. They say you a great woman. That's why they say your story, it be such a shame.

SUSANNAH: What's the point of this?

PEARL: Those women be worried 'bout you. They say you git- tin' older.

SUSANNAH: They should shut up.

PEARL: They say, What's gonna happen to you? They say the people who done pass you by ain't half the person you be. They say you bein' on the road so many years you become a hard, brittle woman. Miss Peanutbrittle. And Miss Peanut- brittle raise her voice sometimes coz you worried what's gonna happen to you too.

SUSANNAH: I'll show you what's going to happen. Here's what we got paid last night. Twenty, forty, sixty, eighty, a *hundred* dollars.

PEARL: Lemme hold that.

SUSANNAH: Feels good, right?

PEARL: This be more money that I ever hold in my life.

SUSANNAH: You'll hold a lot more than that. If we do things right. I told you Think Big? Tonight's show is for the convention of the Modern Language Association. A *thousand* college teachers, and they're all interested in folklore. They don't want to hear you sing a white union song from today. But they'll like the old song "Steal Away" about slaves slipping away from the slave owners. They'll like the idea of your people resisting the masters.

PEARL: How come you don't like it when I resist you?

SUSANNAH: If they like the program, then each of them will invite us to appear at their college. Now, which would you rather do? Sing the wrong song and ruin everything? Or go to a thousand colleges at a hundred dollars each? Do you think we can help your daughter if we've got a *hundred thousand* dollars?

PEARL: That's not possible.

SUSANNAH: Anything's possible.

(PEARL *starts to sing "Pay Me My Money Down."*)

PEARL: *PAY ME, PAY ME, PAY ME MY MONEY DOWN.*

PEARL AND SUSANNAH: *PAY ME OR GO TO JAIL.*
        PAY ME MY MONEY DOWN.

(*They dance together in a circle and/or parade around the room.*)

 YOU PAY ME, YOU OWE ME,
 PAY ME MY MONEY DOWN.
 PAY ME OR GO TO JAIL.
 PAY ME MY MONEY DOWN.

PEARL: Wait. What's the split? Fifty-fifty? Or you want more?

SUSANNAH: I don't care about the money. Take it all and help your daughter.

PEARL: Money matters.

SUSANNAH: If I had a million dollars right now, I couldn't do as much as I could if I had the right job.

PEARL: That Harvard again? I don't get this. You from the Liberry of—

SUSANNAH: The Library's got no budget. Us to Harvard is like a lightning bug to lightning.

PEARL: Then why ain't this Harvard helpin'?

SUSANNAH: They're all men. White men. They don't realize the importance yet of collecting songs from women, or anybody colored. They're like my parents. Know how I first got interested in old songs? My parents' Irish cook, who could only sing in Gaelic.

PEARL: What is Gaelic?

SUSANNAH: The old-world part of us that's been killed off. Anytime my parents heard anything Gaelic come out of her mouth, they shut her up. Now let's—

PEARL: Sing me something Gaelic.

SUSANNAH: We have things we should be doing—

PEARL: Just sing it.

SUSANNAH: I only remember a line or two.

(SUSANNAH *sings the first two lines of "Barbara Allen" in Gaelic.*)

> *CEN VAL THIMYAAAAAA SOME SEAL GUNDWA*
> *ISS BWA NA RAAAAA SE LEEDEN . . .*

If I can't make the people at the top see that the songs of people like you and that cook matter, then my whole life . . .

PEARL: Has been for nothin'? . . .

(*No reply.*)

PEARL: There gonna be people from this Harvard there tonight?

SUSANNAH: Front row.

PEARL: Then I gonna sing better tonight than I ever did.

SUSANNAH: And we're agreed on what to sing?

(PEARL *nods.*)

Thank you. And, Pearl, if we do this right, maybe— *maybe*—we can be even bigger than I thought. Listen to this. We're written up in the morning paper.

PEARL: A newspaper in New York has my name?

(SUSANNAH *opens the newspaper that she brought in. The sack is still in sight.*)

SUSANNAH: "Last night at Cooper Union we were treated to a miracle of near-Biblical proportions. Just as Paul and Silas were imprisoned but then sang and were set free, so has Pearl Johnson been set free. And this pearl is real; she's a black pearl, and this Black Pearl Sings!" Exclamation point.

PEARL: Black Pearl? My name is Pearl.

SUSANNAH: He thinks Black Pearl's catchy.

PEARL: How come you not White Susannah?

SUSANNAH: Some people can be ignorant and not know it. Ignore it.

PEARL: I gonna git dressed.

(PEARL *exits to the bedroom.*)

SUSANNAH: "Susannah Mullally—" Skip that.

PEARL: (*Offstage.*) No. I wanna hear 'bout you.

SUSANNAH: It's silly. "Susannah Mullally is a genius."—They call everybody a genius these days. "She discovered Black Pearl, who spent years in a Texas prison for taking a Neanderthal's manhood." So much for you having anything to worry about. This column is seen by *millions.* And it's got me to thinking—

PEARL: (*Offstage.*) Read some more.

SUSANNAH: Uh—"She has a scar on her neck that suggests she's a fighter. Your humble columnist could not tell—" That part's stupid.

PEARL: (*Offstage.*) Read it.

SUSANNAH: "—could not tell if the Homicidal Harmonizer carries a knife."

(PEARL *enters in a new dress.*)

PEARL: So now I'm the Homicidal Harmonizer?

SUSANNAH: He's trying to be clever. But he did say some things that give me ideas.

PEARL: If I meet him I'll give him an idea.

SUSANNAH: "I only have two criticisms. First, Black Pearl wore a piece of blue cloth. Your humble critic has heard that Negroes believe blue has magic power."

PEARL: I ain't talkin' 'bout hoodoo.

SUSANNAH: Hoodoo's got more pizzazz than Texas.

PEARL: You just said don't change the show with union songs. Why change it with hoodoo?

SUSANNAH: People are interested in the spirit world.

PEARL: It's foolish.

SUSANNAH: It's folklore. A lot of your people believe in hoodoo.

PEARL: A lot of your people believe this is a free country.

SUSANNAH: Showing off you and your culture is what the show is all about.

PEARL: Then why don't you wanna know the truth?

SUSANNAH: Everything in the show is truth.

PEARL: The whole truth. My husband—before he was my husband—he come back to the island for his mother's funeral. People come to the praise house all sick. He ask, why so many people sick? Minister say it be the will of God. Too many people not godly enough. But my husband say, "My mother was a godly woman. But she get sick and die.

You tellin' me God wanted that to happen?" Minister say, "Some people had conjure spirits and spells put on 'em." And my husband look around and say, "You want to know why people dyin'? Look where your church's outhouse is. It's dug too close to the well. It's leaking into your drinkin' water. You want a miracle to make people live? Dig your outhouse farther away." How you think people take that? The conjure woman, she was feelin' powerful: folks think people dyin' coz of her hoodoo, so she don't like it. The minister, he don't like it coz nobody foolish likes bein' told they's foolish. That night buncha rocks git throwed at Thomas's house. The holy people and the hoodoo people probly bump into each other runnin' away.

SUSANNAH: There's nothing wrong with reporting what people believe.

PEARL: There's somethin' wrong with foolishness. Thomas come to my house. He whistle me out. He say, "Pearl, I like you. You a good woman. Why don't you come with me to Texas? Texas will be the Garden of Eden." And then he say he goin' *now*. I got to decide *right then*. And I do. I turn my back on my family and all the foolishness you want to celebrate. Now do I tell people that every night?

SUSANNAH: No. We don't do our show and tell white people some colored people can be ignorant.

PEARL: Dumb come in all colors.

SUSANNAH: True, but these white people are college liberals. They're not ready to hear that yet. They're ready to hear some hoodoo.

PEARL: So no to union songs, but yes to hoodoo?

SUSANNAH: Right. And that leads me to the second big thing.

(*She reads from the newspaper again.*)

> "My bigger criticism is that Pearl is not dressed authenti-
> cally. Why costume her to look like a lady strolling Broad-
> way? Shouldn't Black Pearl be costumed like a cotton picker
> or a real-life Aunt Jemima?"

PEARL: What?

SUSANNAH: He's stupid; we're not doing that. But it did get me
to thinking . . . wouldn't it be more accurate—and bowl
people over more—to see you the way I first did?

(SUSANNAH *takes out a bright new black-and-white prison stripe outfit
purchased at a theatrical house.*)

PEARL: You want me to wear that tonight?

SUSANNAH: It's what you were wearing when we met.

PEARL: I don't want to be reminded of those times.

SUSANNAH: These people have never seen anyone in prison
stripes except in a picture.

PEARL: So show 'em a picture.

SUSANNAH: That's not real to them. They—

PEARL: I wear somethin' like that for ten year. That be the biggest thing I wanna forget.

SUSANNAH: No. A lot of these songs come from pain.

PEARL: My pain.

SUSANNAH: Not just *your* pain. Slavery isn't over; it continues
with the chain gang. The stripes make a powerful statement.

PEARL: Last night I wear the best dress I ever have. People clap for me. I sing at the Cotton Club, I sing with Cab Calloway, I sing better than Cab Calloway. That be who I wanna be.

SUSANNAH: You can be all of that. But this is who you were when we met. You can wear the prison stripes over the dress. And when we get to the point where you're set free, you pull the prison stripes off and throw them down. It'll make a great show.

PEARL: You want me to be a dancin' chicken.

SUSANNAH: No.

PEARL: Yes. Like in a carnival sideshow. The Dancin' Chicken dancin' for a few pieces of corn.

SUSANNAH: That's not what this is.

PEARL: People be real entertained by the Dancin' Chicken, but nobody stops to think that Dancin' Chicken got a heart full of hopes.

SUSANNAH: You're not a dancing chicken.

PEARL: Cluck cluck cluck.

SUSANNAH: Don't do that!

PEARL: Cluck cluck cluck!

SUSANNAH: Can't you understand? People want to see your journey so that they know you!

PEARL: You don't study me or my people for a *little while* and then *know* me.

SUSANNAH: This is what you've triumphed over.

PEARL: Would you be happier if I sang in blackface?

SUSANNAH: Don't you dare say that to me.

PEARL: *OH SUSANNY, DON'T YOU CRY FOR ME*
I COME FROM ALABAMY
WITH BULLSHIT ON MY KNEE.

(*The buzzer sounds.*)

SUSANNAH: I don't deserve that! Are you a fool? I got you out of prison. And whether you want to admit it or not, I am the best friend you've ever had. I am trying to help you and your daughter by putting on the most unforgettable show we can.

(*The buzzer sounds.*)

If we had a song that came here from Africa, then we could do without the stripes. And I notice you keep holding on to the money.

(SUSANNAH *exits.* PEARL *holds the blue kerchief.*)

PEARL: Help me, Grandfather. Let me know what to do. Wearin' prison stripes makes me stick in people's minds more. But I'd do anything to get out of wearin' that again.

(*She touches the head of the African carving.*)

What if I sing them our secret? What if I give them our song? Do I have your blessing? And if I don't have your blessing, but I give the song anyway, will you forgive me?

(PEARL *reaches her decision that she will tell the big secret.*)

(SUSANNAH *enters with a telegram.*)

SUSANNAH: Pearl—

PEARL: Susannah, I've decided.

SUSANNAH: There's . . . news. Your daughter was headed to the island. She gave birth prematurely on a train. It was difficult. The baby survived. But your daughter . . .

PEARL: My daughter's dead?

SUSANNAH: I'm so sorry.

(PEARL *reacts.*)

PEARL: When—when did she die? Did she die when I was drinkin' last night? Did she die when I was havin' a party?

SUSANNAH: I don't know.

PEARL: I didn't do enough.

SUSANNAH: You did all you could.

PEARL: I shoulda looked more places. I shoulda done more. I only looked three days. Three days is nothin'! My mother never woulda stopped lookin' for me! Instead I come here to New York. To do what? Sing?! If it'd save my daughter, I'd tear my throat out. I was singin' when I shoulda been searchin'! I shoulda been lookin'! I shoulda done more! Shame on me!

SUSANNAH: No.

PEARL: Shame on me! . . . And shame on you.

(PEARL *grabs her coat and exits the apartment.*)

SCENE THREE

The next morning. Lights up on SUSANNAH, *who has slept in her clothes, as she wakes on the couch. She checks to see if* PEARL *has returned. She folds up the prison stripes and puts them back in the sack. She tries to pray but cannot. Finally, she sings.*

SUSANNAH: *DO LORD, DO LORD, LORD, REMEMBER HER.*
    DO LORD, DO LORD, LORD, REMEMBER HER.
    DO LORD, DO LORD, LORD, REMEMBER HER.
    NOW DO, LORD, REMEMBER HER.

(PEARL *enters, having been out and up all night.*)

. . . I . . . I thought you might have gone to the train station. But you left with no money. I checked the parks. I just . . . wanted to make sure you were all right.

(*No answer.*)

Pearl, I am so sorry. I made some calls. Your daughter—Uniqua—gave birth on a train as it was coming into Atlanta. She died of an infection.

PEARL: What about her baby?

SUSANNAH: It's a girl, and she's fine. She's being kept at the hospital. The other woman who works for the Library is going with your sister. They'll bring her back to the island. Before Uniqua died, she named the baby . . . Pearl.

(SUSANNAH *gives* PEARL *the telegram.* PEARL *uses the blue kerchief if she needs it.*)

I'll buy the tickets. We can start South today.

PEARL: I missed the performance last night. Do they hate me now?

SUSANNAH: No. I explained everything. They were very sympathetic. Their meetings go on till tomorrow. They invited us to come back tonight. I told them we'd be on the train.

PEARL: Where be my daughter?

SUSANNAH: She's buried in Atlanta.

PEARL: In a potter's field. That mean she buried without no proper service. Buried by strangers.

SUSANNAH: We can arrange whatever you want.

PEARL: I don't need to be in no church to give her a service; God is everywhere. Her service is now.

(PEARL *and* SUSANNAH *take their places in an impromptu ceremony.*)

We are here to honor Uniqua Johnson. Mother of Pearl Johnson. Daughter of Thomas and Alberta Johnson. Granddaughter of William and Mary Watson. Great-granddaughter of Luke and Mpinduzi Davis. On this earth for twenty-two year. A strong woman. Brought down by a little germ. But nothing could bring down her spirit. When she be ten, she sing her first song alone at the praise house. An old island song I teach her. It be her favorite.

(PEARL *sings "Keys to the Kingdom" in the voice of her daughter when Uniqua was ten.*)

I GOT THE KEYS TO THE KINGDOM,
THE WORLD CAN'T DO ME NO HARM.

I GOT THE KEYS TO THE KINGDOM
AND THE WORLD CAN'T DO ME NO HARM.

TAKE OLD JOHN ON THE ISLAND,
PLACE HIM IN A KETTLE OF OIL.
ANGEL COME FROM A-HEAVEN DOWN
AND TOLD HIM THAT THE OIL WOULDN'T BOIL.

(PEARL *segues into her own voice.*)

I GOT THE KEYS TO THE KINGDOM,
THE WORLD CAN'T DO ME NO HARM.
I GOT THE KEYS TO THE KINGDOM
AND THE WORLD CAN'T DO ME NO HARM.
TAKE OLD PAUL AND SILAS,
PLACE 'EM IN JAIL BELOW.
ANGEL COME FROM HEAVEN DOWN,
UNLOCKED THE PRISON HOUSE DOOR.

I GOT THE KEYS IN MY BOSOM,
CARRY 'EM WHEREVER I GO.
I GOT THE KEYS TO THE KINGDOM
AND THE WORLD CAN'T DO ME NO HARM.

(PEARL *looks to* SUSANNAH *to indicate that it is her time to speak now.*)

SUSANNAH: I . . . never met Uniqua. I . . . I . . .

(SUSANNAH *can't speak. She sings "Six Feet of Earth" a capella. This is a song she learned in the Southern mountains.*)

IF A GIRL BE IN TATTERING RAGS
WE USUALLY REJECT OR DESPISE
BUT BENEATH IS A TRUE HONEST HEART
AND SIX FEET OF EARTH WILL MAKE US ALL OF
     ONE SIZE.

SOME PEOPLE GAIN FORTUNE AND FAME
WHILE OTHERS TRY HARD BUT CAN'T RISE

ABOVE DEGRADATION AND SHAME.
STILL SIX FEET OF EARTH WILL MAKE US ALL OF
  ONE SIZE.

A CUP OF COLD WATER IN CHARITY GIVEN
IS REMEMBERED WITH JOY IN THE SKY.
WE ALL ARE BUT HUMAN
AND WE ALL HAVE TO DIE
AND SIX FEET OF EARTH WILL MAKE US ALL OF
  ONE SIZE.

PEARL: Amen ... You say these people will let me sing tonight?

SUSANNAH: You don't want to go South?

PEARL: My daughter'll understand if we stay here one more day. If these professor people still want me.

SUSANNAH: Are you sure you're up to it?

PEARL: God will give me the strength. Just as God brought me to you, and you to me.

Think Big. That be what God meant me to learn from you. You find me barefoot poor in prison. But you Think Big and figure out a way to put me in front of powerful people in New York. I spent last night on a bench. By the Brooklyn Bridge. Man tell me when that bridge was built, it be higher than any building in New York.

Somebody can look at a wide river, and think big and imagine a bridge higher than any building. And somebody else can look at a swamp, and imagine a golf course. Someday somebody wanna build a bridge to my island. Make my island a golf course.

For fightin' for the Union, the goverment give my family the land they live on. Suppose to be forty acres and a mule.

But it usually turn out ten acres and no mule. And that was from the people who was grateful to us. Whoever build a bridge to Hilton Head and want to build golf courses, they won't be grateful to us. They try to get us out for nothin' and call it progress. This show, you really think you can get us invited to a thousand colleges?

SUSANNAH: Yes. But I don't want to do it in prison stripes.

PEARL: Prison stripes mean white professors will be more likely to invite us, right?

SUSANNAH: Pearl—

PEARL: Right?

SUSANNAH: Yes.

PEARL: Bring that thing back.

SUSANNAH: No. You told me why you don't want to wear it.

PEARL: That was yesterday.

SUSANNAH: Nobody's ever going to be a dancing chicken again because of me.

PEARL: Because of you I got a chance to save my people. I decided while lookin' at that Brooklyn Bridge. I gotta protect my people from "progress." And I got a new grandchile to support. Take money. So I gonna be the thing that make the most money.

SUSANNAH: I will not let you do something that hurts you.

PEARL: "Let" me? Susannah, from now on I choose what my life be.

SUSANNAH: What about your ancestors? What would they say?

PEARL: They'd say "Take care of the family." You think people who come here naked and in chains gonna care if I sing in stripes?

SUSANNAH: This will kill your soul.

PEARL: My soul gonna be fine. So hand me that sack.

(SUSANNAH *gives in and hands her the sack.*)

"When do-gooders wanna do you a favor, let 'em." We gonna wait another day before we leave.

(PEARL *takes the prison stripes out of the sack.*)

Tonight . . .

(PEARL *holds the stripes up to herself.*)

"Black Pearl Sings!"

SUSANNAH: I'll call to let them know.

PEARL: We done sung for my daughter. Now by tradition, we eat. Fresh food. Not somethin' from an icebox.

SUSANNAH: I'll go to the store and get something.

PEARL: Thank you. And call your parents. Ask 'em to come to the show again. And tell 'em their daughter be writ up in the New York papers. They be proud.

SUSANNAH: We'll see.

(SUSANNAH *exits.*)

PEARL: That thing about food prob'ly be somethin' you write down. It end up folklore. Forgive me, Susannah, but I gotta give somethin' to my daughter and you can't hear it. You don't get *this* song. Even though this song can get you that job at Harvard. When the time come, my new granddaughter gonna get that job. She gonna be the professor who knows about our songs, firsthand.

(PEARL *spreads the prison stripes out on the floor.*)

For you, daughter, a song from the birthplace of your old ones. From the people who give birth to the baby boy who one day fight in the War That Freed the Slaves wearin' this.

(*She spreads the blue kerchief out over the prison stripes.*)

From the people from the other side of the water.

(*She puts the African carving of the head at the top of the blue kerchief and the prison stripes.*)

A song they brung here on the slave ships. Sung in chains, in darkness, at the bottom of the boat. Sung when they didn't know where they was goin', only where they was from. Sung to help their spirits into the next world.

(*She kneels and speaks and sings from her knees as if by a graveside.*)

Even if there be only one person singin' this song, it be all of us in one mouth.

(PEARL *sings the African song as the lights change.*)

> *AH WAKUH MUH MONUH KAMBAY YA, LEE LUH,*
> *TAMBAY AH.*
> *WAKUH MUH MONUH KAMBAY YA, LEE LUH. KAH.*
> *HA SUH WILEEGO SEEHAI YUH GBANGAH LILLY*
> *HA SUH WILEEGO DWELIN DUH KWEN.*

HA SUH WILEEGO SEEHAI YUH KWENDAIYAH
HA SUH WILEEGO DWELIN DUH KWEN.

(*The sound of African drums begins, as if conjured by her singing. She repeats the verse and sings over the drums and moves rhythmically. She will finish with her arms outstretched to the heavens.*)

AH WAKUH MUH MONUH KAMBAY YA, LEE LUH,
    TAMBAY AH.
WAKUH MUH MONUH KAMBAY YA, LEE LUH. KAH.
HA SUH WILEEGO SEEHAI YUH GBANGAH LILLY
HA SUH WILEEGO DWELIN DUH KWEN.
HA SUH WILEEGO SEEHAI YUH KWENDAIYAH
HA SUH WILEEGO DWELIN DUH KWEN.

END OF PLAY

THE ART OF SACRIFICE

Anthony Clarvoe

The Art of Sacrifice was written with the support of a Playwrights Horizons / Amblin commission. Its writing was assisted by readings by Playwrights Horizons, Primary Stages, 78th Street Theatre Lab, and Merrimack Repertory Theatre.

The world premiere of *The Art of Sacrifice* was presented by Merrimack Repertory Theater (Charles Towers, artistic director), in Lowell, Massachusetts, on November 13, 2005. Set design was by David Evans Morris, lighting design by Juliet Chia, costumes by Jane Alois Stein, sound by Jamie Whoolery, props by Michaela Duffy; the stage managers were Emily McMullen and Adam Scarano. Charles Towers directed the following cast:

WILL	Nesbitt Blaisdell
ARON	Jeremiah Wiggins

CHARACTERS
ARON, thirties. An international grandmaster.
WILL, sixties. ARON's father.

SETTING
WILL's living/trophy room.

TIME
The present.

The beauty of a game of chess is usually assessed according to the sacrifices it contains.

—*Rudolf Spielmann,* The Art of Sacrifice in Chess

Sacrifices only prove that somebody has blundered.

—*Savielly Tartakower*

The way to refute a sacrifice is to accept it.

—*Wilhelm Steinitz*

SCENE ONE

WILL's *living room. Functionally furnished.*

On every available wall space, floor to ceiling, even in front of the window, hang the kind of inexpensive open shelves that you can buy at the hardware store. The shelves are filled with trophies, loving cups, plaques, ribbons, framed citations, certificates, clippings, and photographs. The trophies range from the few that are shining and fresh to the greater number that are coated in darkening shades of tarnish and dust.

Night.

ARON *is dressed for travel, with a dark coat over what from the fit and condition looks to be a good but secondhand suit. He has put down a battered briefcase that would hold a notebook computer.*

WILL *is dressed for bed, in a faded robe and pajamas.*

ARON *carries a grocery bag, out of which peeks a large and ornate trophy.*

They move, oblivious to each other.

WILL: Something wakes me up. He's standing at the door.

ARON: I drive up. No. I'm driven to the door. From—

WILL: He'll say—

ARON: The bus station. No, train station. Airport. Yes.

WILL: And I'll say—

ARON: I walk in.

WILL: And I'll say, what I meant.

ARON: I'm wearing . . . like when I was a kid. No.

WILL: All I meant.

ARON: No, I'll wear the suit. He'll like the suit.

WILL: No, first I have to . . .

ARON: I'll carry the trophy.

WILL: I'll invite him in.

ARON: In a box? In a bag?

WILL: Do I hug him? Shake his hand?

ARON: In my hand.

WILL: Nod?

ARON: (*Nodding.*) Yes. (*He takes the trophy out of the bag.*)

WILL: He kisses me on the cheek like when he was three years old. Before everything.

ARON: Nothing will be different.

WILL: Everything will be just like he remembers it.

ARON: But he'll see how I've changed. He has to.

WILL: He'll be his old self again.

ARON: I'll stand there.

WILL: He'll relax.

ARON: No matter how tired and hungry I am.

WILL: He'll make himself at home.

ARON: I won't sit down right away.

WILL: Don't get pissed off again. Don't.

ARON: I'm going to get there in the middle of the night.

WILL: (*Suddenly shouting.*) What were you doing? Why did you do that?

ARON: He'll open the door, and as soon as I'm inside he'll turn his back and go. Knowing I'll follow him. By the time I do, he'll be sitting in that room. His generation, they always put the king in the corner too soon.

WILL: And if I said . . .

ARON: And then he'll say . . . what?

WILL: So who died?

(*They look at each other for the first time.*)

   Quite the suit.

ARON: This is how I dress now. Didn't know if you'd be up.

WILL: I don't sleep much anymore.

ARON: You never slept much.

(*Both are aware of the trophy. Neither acknowledges it.*)

WILL: You haven't taken some money job, have you?

ARON: No.

WILL: The suit. You had me worried.

(*They watch each other.*)

Why aren't you at the Nationals?

ARON: I am at the Nationals.

WILL: What happened? They haven't posted today's results.

ARON: They're probably still playing.

WILL: Wait a minute.

ARON: It's fine.

WILL: Why aren't you playing? You didn't lose, did you?

ARON: No.

WILL: You did, you lost, you've lost, Jesus Christ, I don't see you since God knows when, and this is why you show up?

ARON: No. I had a rest day coming, I asked to take it early.

WILL: Why?

ARON: I told them I had a family emergency.

WILL: What family emergency?

ARON: Well, my father thought I lost and he fell down dead.

WILL: That's not funny.

ARON: It's a little funny.

WILL: No, because you're trying to make jokes. You only do that when you're worried.

(*They watch each other.*)

Do they know where you are? The tournament people?

ARON: They send their best.

WILL: They hate my guts. You told them you were coming to see me? I bet that put fear in their hearts.

ARON: I bet it did.

(*Beat.*)

WILL: (*Nodding to the trophy.*) So that's from last year?

ARON: Which? (*Looking at the trophy in his hand.*) Huh! What have we here?

WILL: Come on, come on—

ARON: Oh, this?

WILL: What have you got for me?

ARON: You want this?

WILL: Give it here, give it here.

(ARON *hands over the trophy.* WILL *sets it in his lap and dandles it like a grandchild.*)

Hello, shiny guy! Look at you! (*To* ARON.) It's beautiful.

ARON: Got your eyes.

WILL: You made me wait long enough! (*To the trophy.*) Oh, I've been thinking about you. You are even bigger than I expected. So much bigger than the last one.

ARON: The prize funds get smaller, the trophies get bigger.

WILL: It's gorgeous. Welcome! Come meet the family! I've been saving a special place for you. Right here. (*Setting the trophy in an empty spot on a shelf, rearranging some of the older trophies.*) Everybody bunch up a bit. Make room, make room. That looks great, doesn't it?

ARON: Sure.

WILL: (*Taking down the trophy again.*) Oh, but I've got to hold on to you for a while before you go to bed. Shiny guy, this makes my year, seeing you.

ARON: So, Dad. Hally called me.

WILL: Really.

ARON: About the last time you guys talked?

(WILL *is silent.*)

He was really upset. He paged me in the middle of the Nationals.

WILL: He paged you at the Nationals, he broke your focus to tell you that we talked on the phone? He calls me every week. What possessed him?

ARON: He said you weren't making any sense.

WILL: I have never made sense to Hally.

ARON: He said you were incoherent. You told him you were coming unglued.

WILL: Unglued? Unglued. Like I was glued before? And now I'm not, and that's a bad thing?

ARON: Then he said the line went dead. And he couldn't get through to you again.

WILL: I don't know what that's about.

ARON: I didn't know what I was going to find here.

(*They watch each other.*)

WILL: So when you face the unknown, this is what you wear?

ARON: I thought I might have to make funeral arrangements.

WILL: This is what you're going to wear to my funeral?

ARON: No, this is what I want to be buried in, I'm showing you 'cause you're going to outlast us all.

WILL: God forbid. So you want to call Hally, tell him false alarm?

ARON: I'll wait a little.

WILL: I'm fine.

ARON: Till I figure out what's going on.

WILL: Nothing's going on. False alarm.

ARON: Dad. Please. Move One, you scare Hally, and you know, Move Two, he's going to call me, and I'm not going to dismiss his feelings, what with everything, so Move Three, I'm going to do what he wants, drop what I'm doing and come here. It's a three-move sequence, a tactical shot. So what are you up to?

(*Beat.*)

WILL: You guys were worried. I'm . . . That's touching.

ARON: Call him.

WILL: Me? No, I'm incoherent. Let him stew.

ARON: You are, to this day, such an asshole.

WILL: Secret of our success. So you've reconciled, you and your brother. That's great.

ARON: We get along fine. Always did.

WILL: Always did? He hated you.

ARON: Oh, I know.

WILL: Hated your guts.

ARON: We got along. Is there anything to eat?

WILL: That depends.

ARON: Oh, could we not? I'm hungry, I've been traveling all day.

WILL: You want to eat?

ARON: Yes, Dad, I want to eat.

WILL: Have you done what you need to do?

ARON: As a matter of fact, can I tie up the phone line later, I need to go to the websites, work on tomorrow's game.

WILL: Do it now.

ARON: It'll keep, I'll work better with a little blood sugar.

WILL: What did I always teach you?

ARON: You always taught me the strongest person wins. May I please have some food?

WILL: Help yourself.

ARON: You know what? It's your house. When you want to offer me something to eat, I'll eat.

WILL: Up to you.

ARON: Dad. Why did you say that to Hally? That you'd come unglued?

WILL: I did not say I'd come unglued. I might have said I'd been feeling like I'd gotten a little unstuck. Not unglued. Unstuck.

ARON: I don't know what that means.

WILL: I don't either. I just remember saying it.

ARON: He said you were shouting it at him.

WILL: And that was my last call with him? They mush together, those calls, they're all the same, your grandson this, your granddaughter that, the milestones rolling by on a very flat landscape.

ARON: They are very nice children.

WILL: They are boring children.

ARON: No.

WILL: They are not champions.

ARON: No.

WILL: They will never be champions at this rate. Of anything.

ARON: Hally sounds like they are sweet, funny little people.

WILL: Eh.

ARON: God, you're awful. That man calls you every Sunday.

WILL: Like clockwork. But you! You're back!

ARON: Just for the night.

WILL: No, no, no, I mean you're number one again. The new magazine came, did you see it? Announcing the Nationals. There you are, on the cover again. The Defending Champion. Where is that, I was showing it to Dr. Rubinstein— the way they wrote about you! Swashbuckling, they said.

ARON: Swashbuckling?

WILL: Something like that. Cutting a swath, that was it, the defending champion cut a wide and deadly swath through the field last year. Did you do that?

ARON: Wide and deadly.

WILL: Recalling his youth, they said. His fabled youth. Was it fun winning it again after all these years? All on your own?

ARON: Yeah.

WILL: The champion of the United States. The spacious skies, the amber waves of grain. You're champion of that.

ARON: Yeah.

WILL: The fruited plain.

ARON: What are you up to?

WILL: God shed his grace on thee. I'm being nice.

ARON: The fruited plain?

WILL: Well, I started hearing myself. But I meant the other stuff. Is it fun? You get recognized?

ARON: At tournaments, sure, people know me. There are times—I was walking through the terminal here—God, it's stupid, walking along, thinking, I am the champion chess player of the United States! Make way! Make way for your champion!

WILL: That's how you should be thinking. The purple mountains' majesty. You're champion of that.

ARON: Yeah, right, shut up.

WILL: Did you see—the magazine, there was a piece about that kid, the one who came up about when you did, what was his name, real little nightmare for you.

ARON: Nick? Joel? John?

WILL: John.

ARON: What's he done now, playing in Europe or something?

WILL: He's retired!

ARON: He what?

WILL: Another one down!

ARON: He's retired? John's—what's he going to do?

WILL: Some money job. Executive assistant to some big financier or something.

ARON: John. Jesus.

WILL: Don't get grief-stricken, what's wrong with you?

ARON: Thirty years, a couple of times a year I have to play against John. And he's just gone? He was almost the only one I learned something from when we played.

WILL: You beat him in the final at the Nationals last year.

ARON: His clock ran out.

WILL: You beat him, I watched the moves online.

ARON: I could have beat him, I was a pawn up in a minor-piece endgame, but I didn't want to blunder, so I sat back and let him lose on time.

WILL: Good gamesmanship.

ARON: It's not my favorite way to win, it's like watching a man drown, frantic little futile . . . I can't get stronger if everyone who can beat me quits the game.

WILL: Aron. If everyone who can beat you quits the game, you
     don't need to get stronger. You'll be the best one left.

ARON: That's not the point.

WILL: Yeah. It is. Only a quitter would leave the game for a
     money job.

ARON: You had a money job.

WILL: I had to have a money job, I had kids to feed.

ARON: So do they, some of them.

WILL: They have kids? Chess people? Big mistake.

ARON: I'm sure.

WILL: Big, big mistake.

ARON: Heard you the first time, Dad. I take back what I said, I
     have got to get something to eat. (*He crosses away.*)

WILL: Hey! Where're the big guns playing this week?

ARON: Dad.

WILL: I know, I know, I'm sorry, it's just great to have somebody
     to talk chess with. Are they in Linares?

(ARON *stops.*)

ARON: Yeah.

WILL: Strong field this year?

ARON: Strongest ever, say the ratings.

WILL: The ratings are messed up.

ARON: Yeah.

WILL: You should be over there.

ARON: I wasn't invited.

WILL: You should be, you're strong enough. It's an unfair system. Hey, but who's this new kid?

ARON: Hally didn't mention you were manic, Dad—

WILL: I've been seeing online, this new kid, from Kazakhstan, Uzbekistan, someplace, he's thirteen or something, stomping everybody?

ARON: He's a novelty, you know how it is. We've been there.

WILL: Thirteen-year-olds are outranking you and you want to eat.

ARON: Well. Not so much now.

WILL: Good. Work, it'll give you an appetite.

ARON: I'll eat while I'm online. You want anything?

WILL: You think that kid from Uzbekistan eats before he works?

ARON: Oh, God damn it.

WILL: Well?

ARON: Dad. I cut a wide and deadly swath.

WILL: A year ago.

ARON: I'm the champion of the United States.

WILL: I hate to see you wasting your time.

ARON: Then why am I here with you?

WILL: Because you need a kick in the ass! Like you always did!

ARON: And here I thought it was because Dr. Rubinstein, in addition to congratulating me on the cover of the magazine, told me you were sleep-deprived and starving to death.

(*They watch each other.*)

WILL: You've been talking to my doctor?

ARON: You've been stalking me online. Now. Do you want anything from the kitchen?

(*Beat.*)

WILL: There's not too much in the kitchen. I need to shop.

ARON: There's nothing at all in the kitchen, is there.

WILL: I need to shop.

ARON: God damn it, Dad.

WILL: I am not starving. Do I look like I'm starving?

ARON: Malnutrition, that's what it means.

WILL: So you and Hally're thinking, what? Old man's going gaga?

ARON: No, that is not what I think.

WILL: And you're here to judge me? To judge if I'm competent to take care of myself? You?

ARON: We wanted to be sure you were okay.

WILL: And you figure you're a fit judge of that?

ARON: Dad. Heard you the first time. I get it. Have you been eating?

WILL: Of course I've been eating.

ARON: Every day?

WILL: Yes, every day. I get hungry, I eat.

ARON: Are you sure you always notice?

WILL: Yes.

ARON: If you didn't notice, would you know?

WILL: Yes I would know.

ARON: Because it's easy to miss those signals, when you've trained yourself not to care. Until it's too late.

(*Beat.*)

WILL: Have you been eating?

ARON: I know that when a person doesn't eat or sleep, he loses track of time. Is that what "unstuck" means?

WILL: Have you been having time trouble? In your games? That's not how I taught you.

ARON: I'm playing okay.

WILL: If you were playing really well, I'd have heard about it.

ARON: If I were champion of the world, you might hear about it.

WILL: If an American were champion of the world again, it would transform the game. It would be the salvation of the game.

ARON: I hear you.

WILL: Don't shut me up.

ARON: I said, I hear you! I hear what you're telling me!

(WILL *is silent.*)

ARON: Dad. The not eating. Because work comes first. Is that what this is? But . . . you're retired, your children are grown, you're done working. You can eat now, you can rest. You have nothing more to do.

WILL: And why should such a person deserve to be fed?

ARON: Because a person is worth more than what he can do.

WILL: No. He is not.

(*Beat.*)

ARON: Why aren't you sleeping?

WILL: Because my son has come home. And I never slept much.

ARON: You always said.

WILL: But lately, I don't know why, it's funny, you know what I started worrying about?

ARON: No, what.

WILL: It got in my head and I can't get it out, I have to get up,
you ever do that, hoping I can leave it there, in the bed,
and I'll stay out here till it decides to go bother somebody
else. But I guess it followed me out here, 'cause I'm talking
about it.

ARON: You're kind of talking about it.

WILL: Well, it's embarrassing. I keep thinking after I die . . .

ARON: Hey. That's not for long, long times yet.

WILL: No, I know.

ARON: You'll outlast us all.

WILL: Don't say—don't ever say that to me.

ARON: I didn't—

WILL: A son to a father. That is the last thing, the worst!

ARON: I hear you.

WILL: "I hear you," "I hear what you're saying," you say that a
lot, it's a very noncommittal move, is that what I taught you?
I keep thinking I'm going to die and you're going to turn
into somebody else.

(ARON *is silent.*)

In the magazine I also saw there was a column with your
name on the top.

ARON: Yes. That's my column, they gave me a column.

WILL: "Strategy Secrets of the Grandmasters?"

ARON: I know it's kind of . . . There's not a lot completely new to say about—

WILL: At the bottom of the column was the address of a website.

ARON: Yes.

WILL: You have a website.

ARON: I'm trying, yeah, game analysis, opening novelties—

WILL: I saw, I visited. It says you're taking private students.

ARON: Yeah. A few.

WILL: And there's a book.

ARON: Coming, yes, next month—

WILL: You wrote a book.

ARON: Collection of my best games, basically, with notes, you know, the usual kind of—

WILL: You're very busy.

ARON: Yes. That's—I haven't had a chance to come—

WILL: How do you have time to work on your game?

ARON: I do, I am, just in a different . . . I thought . . . winning, being champion again, I, the prize fund was pathetic, but the exposure, I was hoping, I could use the title, to piece together some kind of an, I don't know, a living. A life.

WILL: Sure. The years go by, you start to think, there's more to life than chess.

ARON: Yeah.

WILL: No. You're not missing a thing. People. You think they're happy? They're dead and their lives have no meaning. Believe me, I used to deal with them every day. No principles. Not like you. You live by a code. You're a warrior in the cause of logic and beauty. Who can say that anymore? Yours is a fine, lone life. A wandering knight, that's you.

(ARON *is silent*.)

Well? What's going to happen to all that, you think?

ARON: When?

WILL: After.

ARON: After what?

WILL: After me.

(*They watch each other*.)

ARON: I hear what you're . . . Your parents died, what did you do?

WILL: You don't—no, sure you don't remember, your grandma, you were too young, and your grandpa died, you were play-ing in a tournament, I didn't want it to mess you up. And I was right. Where is it? (*Peering at the trophies*.) Regional Under-12 Champion, where is it? There. See, you won.

ARON: I'm asking about you. He was your father. We're talking about the deaths of fathers now.

WILL: Well, you have to understand, with me . . . I was very angry at my father. So it was different.

(ARON *is silent.*)

And it was a different time, people expected different things from a father. But that man . . . I got nothing from him. Whatever I wanted to do, or to make of myself. Nothing. Which from a father is worse than nothing. So, I was really . . . I didn't even give him a decent burial. Oh, and . . . we had no money, I had to have him burned, I didn't want to give some vulture a lot of money for some ornate casket or urn or something.

ARON: (*A gesture toward the shelves.*) You could have used one of these.

WILL: What? No, I could not, he never earned such a thing in his life. But I swear I said just put him in something simple. I didn't say cheap. They gave him to me in a file box. His ashes. In a little sheet metal box like you'd keep three-by-five cards in. With the lid taped shut. They handed him to me at the cemetery and pointed to the plot. So your mother and Hally and I started walking across this big rolling swath of green. He'd been a veteran, he was entitled. But—have you ever been to a graveyard in Europe?

ARON: Whole place is a graveyard.

WILL: And the graveyards are like cities. Monuments. Little buildings. Family homes. All these bitty houses for the dead people to live. It's beautiful. An American veteran's cemetery, it's like a filing system. White slabs, green plots, green, white, green, white, to the horizon.

ARON: Like those roll-up vinyl chessboards.

WILL: Sure. They even give the plots a letter and number, like the squares in chess notation. Little flags stuck by some of the stones. Like the flags they put on the table next to you at international tournaments. No pieces, though. Just ... Funny to think every square on the board had its own little ghost, haunting it. And I'm walking over this, holding this box. And the box ... coating of ash on it. Coming off on my fingers. Found the right square on the grid. They'd dug a little hole. I put him in. My finger caught on a metal spur on the box. Cheap thing. Cut me.

ARON: Ow, I hate that.

WILL: Yeah, it was just a bad day all around. Put my finger in my mouth. And I'd touched those ashes.

ARON: God. What did it taste like?

WILL: What did it— Tasted like chicken. Asshole.

ARON: Sorry.

WILL: "Hey, Dad, what did Grandpa's ashes taste like?"

ARON: Sorry.

WILL: Tasted like ashes. You know that taste?

ARON: Yeah.

WILL: Yeah. Tasted like losing. Tasted just like losing.

(*Beat.*)

ARON: But what did you do? After?

WILL: Oh ... Did some thinking. Kept busy. Built this room.

(*Beat.*)

ARON: Are you still mad at him?

WILL: Sure.

ARON: Even though he's dead to you?

WILL: Dead to *me*?

ARON: Dead, I mean.

WILL: Funny way to put it, he's dead to everybody, he's dead.

ARON: You like saying that?

WILL: It has its charm. So why are you here?

ARON: I told you. Don't you remember? Dad—

WILL: Oh, I remember some tub of shit about how I laid a little non sequitur on Hally, the phone went dead—did you
call one of the neighbors? Did you call the cops? No, you
dropped everything and came running in the middle of the
Nationals. Sure. So what are you up to?

ARON: I told you.

WILL: You are here because you need something from me. And
I wish you would once in your life admit it! And tell me
what it is! So I can give it to you!

ARON: I told you something I want from you, I want something
to eat! Have you given it to me?

WILL: I told you to help yourself! Make yourself at home!

ARON: This is not my home! I have a home! I am a grown man, I have a home and this is not it!

(*They watch each other.*)

WILL: All right. The game tomorrow. What can you tell me about him?

ARON: Oh, for—

WILL: What! Champions have coaches. Why do you want to go it alone? What are you trying to prove?

ARON: Nothing!

WILL: Maybe that's the problem.

ARON: There's no problem, this is not why I'm . . . I haven't seen the pairings for tomorrow, I've been traveling. That's why I want to go online, find out who it is and get to work on him.

WILL: Done.

ARON: Done?

WILL: I looked it up earlier this evening, all the pairings.

ARON: I thought you didn't know I was coming.

WILL: I do it all the time.

ARON: So who am I playing tomorrow?

WILL: You sure you want to know?

ARON: You're dying to tell me.

WILL: Guess. Come on.

(ARON *is silent.*)

It's that kid from Uzbekistan!

ARON: No it's not.

WILL: Yes, it is. Don't you read the tournament bulletins?

ARON: Just who I'm playing next, but with this one-day bye, the schedule changed, the pairings changed—how can he be—

WILL: You knew he was there, didn't you?

ARON: God damn it!

WILL: What happened to Mister I Need People Who Can Beat Me So I Get Better for the Good of the Game?

ARON: I hate losing! Losing is the death tax on winning. What is he doing here! What is a kid from Uzbekistan doing in the American National Championship?

WILL: He emigrated.

ARON: What? When?

WILL: A week ago. He lives here now.

ARON: What kind of idiot moves to America to play chess?

WILL: His whole family came. His village put up the money for them all to come to America.

ARON: Oh, great. So he's a story. I've got to play against a fuck-ing story. The pride of Uzbekistan takes on the defending champion of the evil empire.

WILL: The evil empire? That was the Soviets. There's no evil empire.

ARON: I play against people from all over the world. Trust me.

WILL: They're trying to psyche you.

ARON: Maybe. But I know who they call the evil empire. I know what they think I'm the champion of.

WILL: They've got you tied in knots. Thank God you came to me. You've got to get another story in your head. You are esteemed. The world sends its best to test themselves against you. You teach them lessons and send them away, humbled and wiser. That sort of thing.

ARON: Dad. This is not . . . Okay. We're going to back up a few. Hally called me.

WILL: Said I was incoherent.

ARON: Said you guys were in the middle of a fight.

(WILL *is silent.*)

You have no memory of this? He says he shouted at you.

WILL: I don't remember your brother shouting at me.

ARON: Well, this is Hally. He might have thought he was shouting and you wouldn't necessarily know.

WILL: I might not necessarily hear.

ARON: Yeah. So he called me.

WILL: I admit it, he surprises me there.

ARON: He got back in touch a year ago, he heard I won the Nationals, called me up. Said it took having kids of his own to make him see.

WILL: Okay, see what?

ARON: That we were just children. That it wasn't my fault.

WILL: What wasn't your fault?

ARON: I don't know, his life?

WILL: What's wrong with his life, he has an easy life, far as I can tell, he's a lawyer, for God's sake.

ARON: He's a mediator, Dad.

WILL: Yeah, I know, that's just perfect.

ARON: Hey, how old are they now?

WILL: Hally's kids? Eight? Five?

ARON: Do they play, do you know?

(*They watch each other.*)

WILL: They're kids, of course they play.

ARON: You know what I mean.

WILL: Think about it, who's going to teach them, Hally?

ARON: You haven't taught them?

WILL: I want to! I keep offering to! First he said they were too young, now he changes the subject. Is your mother behind this, do you think?

ARON: Mom has not to my knowledge been part of this.

WILL: She's back there somewhere, you know she is. Why don't you teach them?

ARON: Because Hally said, the time we met and hashed things out, he said, one condition: never, ever teach them chess.

WILL: Why not? Why the hell not? To deprive them of all the—

ARON: Never going to happen.

WILL: I'm going to teach them. The next time they come, I'm going to sit them down, your old set is here, they're old enough, Kaylee's long since old enough, oh, this is going to be fun.

ARON: Dad. I don't—

WILL: I may not be able to give them much, maybe I've never been able to give anybody very much. But I sure know how to give somebody that. Oh, that'll be—

ARON: Dad? Don't.

WILL: What?

ARON: Don't teach the kids.

WILL: You're kidding.

ARON: I know it's hard.

WILL: If Hally feels like that, I mean if he feels that strongly, he can tell me so himself.

ARON: Dad. This is what he was shouting at you about.

(*Beat.*)

WILL: So that whole . . . "Do they play, do you know?" That
    was a trap.

ARON: Little trap, yeah.

WILL: You would think it was some weird old-world religion or
    something, like I was sneaking them off to some cult ritual
    or some shrine or some—

ARON: Dad? Look a-fuckin'-round.

WILL: Some form of abuse or something.

(ARON *is silent.*)

This is wrong. There might be some real talent there.

ARON: They wouldn't enjoy it.

WILL: How would you—

ARON: They couldn't sit still for it, they never sit still, it's amazing.

WILL: How would you know?

ARON: I've seen them.

WILL: The kids? When? Where?

ARON: Fourth of July. Hally invited me.

WILL: You don't do holidays.

ARON: Hally invited me.

WILL: You never do holidays, holidays are for the open tournaments, they get a crowd of patzers, patzers on their chess vacations, you clean up at those.

ARON: Well, this year I went to Hally's. We ate food outside. It's a funny day, the Fourth of July, it's everything-upside-down day. They cook the food outside the house. The men cook. I was dressed completely wrong.

WILL: You wore the suit, didn't you.

ARON: It's a holiday. I dressed up.

WILL: It's the Fourth of July.

ARON: I forgot! Sneakers and shorts and T-shirts, I forgot there was a holiday where you dress worse than usual? I guess 'cause, what, it's a day about being free? The whole day was like that, just . . . just absurd.

WILL: Was your mother there?

ARON: Yeah.

WILL: She is behind this. I knew it.

ARON: Why would she care?

WILL: Oh, life is a long, long grudge match, my son. You don't know. And who's the players and who's the pieces . . . People like chess 'cause it's simple. So do you see her?

ARON: No.

WILL: Do you?

ARON: What for? She abandoned me.

WILL: Abandoned you? Shared custody, you know that, she got Hally, I got you.

ARON: Please. That is not shared. That is divided.

WILL: Same thing.

ARON: No, it's not.

WILL: You were supposed to see her weekends and holidays.

ARON: But I don't do holidays, I've never done holidays, or weekends, that's when I play. She should have gotten me weekdays and you could have had the weekends and holidays.

WILL: That would have been a disaster. Weekends is when you play, but weekdays is when you work. Weekdays are for preparation. She never could have handled that.

ARON: Right. So she abandoned me.

WILL: She didn't abandon you. I'm the one she abandoned. You were not abandoned. She left you with me.

(*They watch each other.*)

Fine. I can't believe you felt you had to—and the Nationals—fine. So I'm supposed to promise not to teach my grandchildren—

ARON: Or their cousins.

WILL: Or their cousins! How to play chess.

ARON: That's right.

(WILL *is silent.*)

I know you need—everybody needs something to keep them ... to keep them ... going, but ... You just need to find something else. That's all.

WILL: Hm. You know what? No.

ARON: No?

WILL: That's right. No. This is stupid and I won't agree to it.

ARON: So I'm supposed to, what, persuade you or something?

WILL: You can try.

ARON: I don't know how to persuade people of things. I'm no good at that shit.

WILL: Well, then, that's—

ARON: I only know how to beat them and humiliate them.

WILL: What is that? A threat? Is that a threat?

ARON: Dad. Not at all. Of course not.

(*They watch each other.*)

WILL: This game tomorrow. You knew you were going to be playing this Uzbekistan kid, didn't you.

ARON: Sure, sooner or later—not tomorrow, I figured in the final, or ...

(*Beat.*)

WILL: You haven't faced something like this in a long time.

ARON: I am here to see how you are. I swear to you.

WILL: Sure, I know. And to tell me the thing about the grandkids.

ARON: I feel strongly about that, Dad.

WILL: Sure, okay. So you're leaving now?

(ARON *is silent.*)

> Remember the last time you came here? Before the Nationals last year? You picked a big fight with me, about, what was it?

ARON: I was thinking about taking a money job.

WILL: You slammed out of here. And had the tournament of your life. So. It's good we're having a talk.

ARON: I need to be gone in the morning.

WILL: So you're staying.

ARON: Just tonight.

WILL: Good. Good. We'll share some ideas. Because—I know I don't really know that much, not technically—but that's the point of the game, isn't it? A couple of guys bring their ideas to the table, their stories about how things ought to go. And they see who's right. Right?

(ARON *is silent.* WILL *exits.*)

ARON: Okay. So. He trapped me back. And now he's going to . . . And I can . . . And then . . . (*He looks at the trophies all around him.*)

(*The lights fade.*)

SCENE TWO

No one is in the room. Then WILL *enters, carrying an inlaid hard-wood Drueke chessboard and a polished mahogany box.*

WILL: Here we are. Aron? Aron? Where'd you go? Aron! (*Beat.*) He was here. He was here. (*Crossing to the new trophy, touching it.*) Aron?

ARON: (*Off.*) In a sec!

WILL: What are you doing? I'm setting up!

(*No answer.* WILL *wipes the table clean. He sets the chessboard on it and gazes at it. He opens the box. It holds a Jaques of London boxwood-and-ebony chess set, in the classic Staunton pattern, tournament scale, four-inch Kings. Top of the line, over the top, the most expensive thing in the room. Worn from years of use.* WILL *picks one up. He polishes it on his robe.*)

(ARON *enters. He is wearing jeans that are too short for him and an old chess tournament souvenir T-shirt.*)

WILL: Where'd you go?

ARON: I'm working, I'm working, see? (*He sits. He pretzels himself into the posture of someone half his age. He watches the empty chessboard.*)

WILL: Why are you wearing those?

ARON: They're my clothes?

WILL: They still fit you.

ARON: You don't eat much, you don't grow much.

WILL: Why are you dressed like you're seventeen?

ARON: That's all that's here. It's fine. I don't need new clothes all the time.

WILL: What happened to your suit?

ARON: I'll need it for tomorrow. Some chess people wear the same clothes for days on end. I try not to do that.

WILL: You're up to something.

ARON: I'm working. You want me to work, let me work. Jeez.

WILL: Why don't you set it up?

ARON: I think quicker without a set.

WILL: Just set it up?

(*Beat.* ARON *groans like a teenager and sets up the chess pieces.*)

Look at that. All he is.

ARON: Everywhere I go.

WILL: Parceled out into sixteen pieces of wood.

ARON: Every board I look at, it's this board.

WILL: The house has a chess kid again.

ARON: How are you there, Dad?

WILL: A little unstuck.

ARON: Get some sleep.

WILL: I don't sleep much.

(ARON *is setting up the set.* WILL *watches.*)

What pieces do you have tomorrow?

ARON: Black.

WILL: You've looked up his games? 'Cause I could—

ARON: Done.

WILL: Checked his openings?

ARON: Done.

WILL: Endgames?

ARON: He likes the endgame, he likes to trade the Queens early and simplify down, he's most at home when there's almost nothing to work with.

WILL: So?

ARON: So, duh, I've got to keep it complicated, make him deal with a lot of options. Welcome to America, shithead. (*Re: the chess set.*) There. Happy?

WILL: Yeah.

(ARON *looks at* WILL.)

Yeah! Ha! Bad move, kiddo. Look at this. The Prodigy Strategizes Amid the Spoils of Victory. And you tell me I don't want to have this again with my grandchildren? Ha!

ARON: I told you, I'm no good at persuading people of things.

WILL: That's what you had me for.

ARON: Let me work. (*He moves pieces, alternating white and black, strikingly fast, and stares at the resulting position.*)

WILL: Remember the time—where was that—they were going to make you play under that flickering fluorescent—

ARON: You always could spot the weakness.

WILL: They had paired you against an opponent rated a hundred points above you, three times your age, the pairing was unfair! I was just leveling the playing field.

ARON: You leveled it. Screaming over my table—"That lamp is strobing on and off over my son's board!"

WILL: Tournament director's, "Sir, I'm trying to start the clocks!"

ARON: The guy I'm playing—

WILL: "It's fine, I'm fine, it's fine with me"—

ARON: Everybody's staring up from their boards, nobody's playing their game—

WILL: Because they'd rather watch me beating on this guy under this flickering, strobing—

ARON: Remember you leaned down and said, "When I give the signal, start faking a seizure?"

WILL: I did! God I was good!

ARON: The tournament director shouting, "Rules are rules!"

WILL: Right! "Rules are rules!"

ARON: The call of the chess player.

WILL: "Rules are rules!"

ARON: I'm trying to work up a spit if you need me to froth at the mouth—

WILL: The director's begging—"Can we move the table?"

ARON: "No!"

WILL: "Can we change rooms?"

ARON: "No! How can you ask my little boy to play with all these distractions!" You're standing there screaming about distractions!

WILL: Finally he figures life's too short—

ARON: "Distractions! Distractions!"

WILL: So now two custodians—

ARON: Trying to get a twenty-foot ladder—

WILL: And a lightbulb—

ARON: Through two hundred chess sets!

WILL: "Coming through! Coming through!" Crash! Bang!

ARON: Guy I was playing—

WILL: "I'm fine! Really!"

ARON: He was a rat in a stress experiment. You cut his IQ in half.

WILL: He was ready to eat his own feet.

ARON: Well, the coup de grâce, the lamp was fixed, the clocks were started, you slam your fist on the table—

WILL AND ARON: "There! Now you can play!"

ARON: He blundered on move ten. Totally boring game.

WILL: You beat him. You won.

ARON: You beat him. That trophy should have your name on it. (*He picks up whatever pieces may have been scattered during the previous match and sets them back on the board in the opening position.*)

WILL: Great days, great days. Do they think—do you suppose they think you're bringing me back there with you? Wouldn't that be something? The hotel lobbies I've walked into, all over the world, and watched the chess people fall silent. Wouldn't that be something again?

ARON: Dad.

WILL: I know, I know.

ARON: A lifetime ban.

WILL: I know!

ARON: A lifetime ban.

WILL: I just—if I—

ARON: From all official chess events.

WILL: Yes! I've got it! The letter—you see it?

ARON: I see it.

WILL: I framed it!

ARON: I know.

WILL: With pride! That, there, that's my trophy!

(ARON *turns from* WILL *to look at the chessboard. He moves pieces fast, alternating white and black, in a standard sequence of game-opening moves.*)

What is that?

(ARON *moves the pieces with more deliberation as he reaches the limits of theory.*)

That's a great variation. They should name that variation after you.

(ARON *is silent.*)

How many times have you taken people out to that position and killed them?

ARON: Till John found the move that refutes my attack. Nobody plays it anymore. They all think it's unsound. (*He makes four more moves. He pauses and gazes at the board. The pieces are in a very sharp and theoretically unclear late-opening position.*)

WILL: You've got something, don't you.

ARON: A little thought. I've been saving it up.

WILL: What have you got? Show me.

ARON: I just like looking at it. Maybe today. God, let him play this today.

WILL: You think he might?

ARON: Well. He'd have to be willing to play my signature opening, this whole sequence of moves, against me, the American
champion.

WILL: But he's never played you before, maybe he doesn't know
what openings you prefer.

ARON: He knows. I'd know. He's young, he's new, looking to
make his name. What better way to do it? We've been there.

WILL: So you think he thinks he's the new fast draw in town—

ARON: And he thinks he knows my game better than I do. Or he
wouldn't be here. I bet he's got an idea of his own, waiting to
pull the pin. So we'll take each other all the way out to here,
nineteen moves each. This is the edge of theoretical praxis.

WILL: And then he'll walk into it.

ARON: And then we'll see who's right, and who's an asshole in
front of everyone.

WILL: But you found a new move.

ARON: Not just a move. A whole combination. A sacrifice.
Blows the whole position apart. And no one's found it but
me. No one's played it, anyway.

WILL: Show me.

ARON: You wouldn't get it.

WILL: This position? Sure I would.

ARON: Okay. Make yourself at home. You've seen all my games.

WILL: I haven't seen all your games.

ARON: You've read the moves.

WILL: Years since I've seen a real game.

ARON: Not my fault. Lifetime ban. So what happens now?

(*They stare at the board.*)

WILL: They still talk about me?

ARON: Sure. They still want to know your secret. How do you set out to raise a grandmaster.

WILL: Yeah? What do you tell them?

ARON: I tell them my father calculated, when I was four years old, how many things I would need to know. Openings, tactics, strategic positions, endgames. About a hundred thousand things.

WILL: I just did the math.

ARON: So every day, from age four, I learned a certain number of things. So many before I ate breakfast, so many before I ate lunch, before I ate dinner, before I could go to sleep . . . Adjusting for difficulty and increasing as I got older.

WILL: And that's all there is to it.

(*Beat.* ARON *looks up.*)

ARON: What?

WILL: Hm?

ARON: That last? What you said?

WILL: What you were saying, I said, that's all there is to it. Planning, application, discipline. And a finite number of things.

ARON: Hm. Hm.

WILL: You know, I'm getting up to speed here.

ARON: Yeah. Yeah. (*Re: the position.*) This is good. This deserves a snack.

WILL: I need to shop.

ARON: That's okay.

(ARON *takes down a trophy, undoes the top.*)

WILL: What are you doing? What is that?

ARON: Peanuts, cereal. Chex Mix. That was the snack we had around, remember, your favorite snack? Chex Mix.

WILL: You hid food?

ARON: I lived on this. You never knew? You never took any of these apart, looked inside them?

WILL: That's disgusting, give me that, I'll wash it out.

(ARON *puts a handful in his mouth.*)

    Stop that!

ARON: It's okay.

WILL: That's twenty-year-old cereal!

ARON: Twenty- . . . five, or I mistake my vintage. Found a move yet? (*He crunches loudly.*)

WILL: I thought you were in here working.

ARON: I was. I hid this stuff to stay alive on. Like a chipmunk.

WILL: You lied to me.

ARON: I was a kid sneaking food, calm down.

WILL: I was teaching you discipline. You ate, you slept. You didn't act hungry.

ARON: "Only a loser acts how he feels."

WILL: You worked through meals without noticing. You worked till the sun came up.

(ARON *swallows and eats some more.*)

Stop that!

ARON: Why, is this . . . distracting you?

WILL: Fine. Do what you want.

(WILL *stares at the board.* ARON *watches him, crunching loudly.*)

ARON: Well?

WILL: Is it . . .

ARON: No.

WILL: I didn't say anything!

ARON: I saw where your eyes were moving, that's not it. (*He swallows and eats some more.*)

WILL: That can't be edible.

ARON: It's edible. One thing you learn playing chess: a lot of
things turn out to be edible. (*Re: the board.*) Well?

WILL: I'm just . . . Wait . . .

ARON: Okay, maybe. Then what?

WILL: I'm not doing anything!

ARON: Yeah, you are. Here, here, here, right? But then what?

WILL: How do you do that!

ARON: Keep looking. (*He swallows and eats some more.*)

WILL: You can't be getting any nourishment out of that.

ARON: Oh, I'm getting plenty of nourishment out of this.

WILL: You're going to make yourself sick.

ARON: Can't be sick. Got a game. Remember that? "How can
you be hungry? You've got a game! How can you be tired?"
I was so dumb. You know, if I'd just done what you said,
if I'd eaten only when you said, and lived exactly like you
wanted, I would, at some tournament, I would have passed
out. Collapsed. It would have taken a few times. But you
know they had their eye on us, all I had to do . . . If I'd
showed up starving, they would have taken me away. And
I didn't. I didn't. I dreamed, no, let's be honest, I halluci-
nated sometimes, I was a passed pawn, every tournament
was another square up the board, and me, little Mister Pawn,
if I got through everything, and reached the last square, the
promotion square, I would be scooped away, right off the
board, and become any piece, something more powerful, a
Queen or a Knight. Lightheaded, it felt like that, I was lifting
up, to be set down somewhere else. But then I'd get scared,
dizzy, where would that other place be? What could I do

there? What good is a chess piece that isn't on a chessboard, it's nothing. So I'd eat from these, and keep going.

WILL: So all these have food in them?

ARON: No. Of course not. (*Strolling down the rows of trophies.*) There was one I used to piss in. Where is that?

WILL: Oh my God.

ARON: There we go.

WILL: The National Under-18 Championship Cup? You pissed in it?

ARON: You got suspicious of all the time I was taking in the bathroom, remember?

WILL: I knew you were just procrastinating in there! One sip of water, oops, got to go! You weren't getting anything done!

(*Beat.* ARON *keeps crunching.*)

Stop that now!

(WILL *grabs at the trophy.* ARON *lets him take it.*)

You were a prodigy! A phenomenon!

(*They watch each other.*)

ARON: Okay. Coach. Time's up. What's the right move here?

(*Beat.*)

WILL: How would I know.

ARON: Sorry, what?

WILL: I said, how would I know.

ARON: You mean you can't figure it out?

WILL: No!

ARON: It's right in front of you! You were so close! Look! Six candidate moves that I can see—boom boom boom boom boom boom—and branching off of those—ba-bing ba-bing ba-bing, or on the other hand ba-bing ba-bing . . . It's a beautiful position. The good moves don't simplify the situation. A beautiful position is not reducible to a finite number of things. It makes more things possible. You have to look far into the future to see what's right to do now. But if you do, you can push back this little bit of the unknown by a few more steps. A beautiful move shows every piece on the board what it was put in its place to do. Harmony. Sense. Mutual support. Of everything for everything. Beauty. You know? Everything that isn't just who beats who. Come on! Figure it out!

WILL: I can't!

ARON: Why not?

WILL: Because I'm not the fucking grandmaster, am I!

ARON: No. You are not. The fucking grandmaster. So. Before you say something like "That's all there is to it!"—

WILL: Oh, come on! That's—all I meant—that was a remark! A little—

ARON: Dad? It's the little moves, unconsidered, off the cuff, you didn't mean any big thing, right?

WILL: Right!

ARON: Blunders. Those moves we call blunders. (*Beat.*) Dad, look. Hally isn't going to be bringing his kids here.

WILL: What? Oh, we'll find a way. The holidays, we always—

ARON: Dad. Hally won't be bringing his children to this house anymore.

(*Beat.*)

WILL: Why would you say a thing like that?

ARON: Look at this room. Do you see Hally's name here anywhere? Do you see a trace of Hally here?

WILL: Whose fault is that?

ARON: Dad—

WILL: I'm asking you, whose fault is that? Mine or Hally's?

ARON: Dad. This is the kind of room where people ask that kind of question. Do you understand that? This room is all about who did better and who did worse. Hally's children shouldn't be here.

WILL: Well, good luck to Hally's children in America, because they're going to be walking into this room all their lives.

(ARON *is silent.*)

Fine. I can meet him halfway. More than halfway. He'll see. I'll come to them. It's better that way, there's only one of me, it's cheaper. I'll come to them.

ARON: Dad. Has he invited you?

(WILL *is silent.*)

You've always just announced you were coming. You assumed you were welcome. And he welcomed you.

(WILL *is silent.*)

Has he ever asked you to come to his home?

WILL: Of course he has. He has, of course he has.

(ARON *is silent.*)

Because of—what you were saying? Because of chess?

(ARON *is silent.*)

I don't understand.

(ARON *is silent.*)

Is this what he asked you to come here to tell me? And you've just been, what, been playing with me all this time?

ARON: No. This is one of the things I'm here to decide.

WILL: Well, it's not really up to you.

ARON: Yes, it is.

WILL: Maybe I'll drop by anyway. Yeah. Bring some presents for the kids. He's not going to bar the door. Not our Hally.

ARON: It'll be an uncomfortable scene.

(WILL *waits.*)

Of course you thrive on those.

WILL: Secret of our success.

ARON: No, Dad. The kids don't come here. You don't go there.

WILL: A lifetime ban, huh?

ARON: Yes.

WILL: Hally isn't a lifetime-banning sort of guy.

ARON: This isn't up to him.

WILL: Yeah, it is.

ARON: Do you want to see me again? Ever?

WILL: Is that your big threat?

(ARON *is silent.*)

You'll show up when you want something. Like always.

ARON: You think, to talk to you, I need to show up here? How many times have I had this conversation?

WILL: You don't have to tell me.

ARON: This is my set. This is the one I always see. I have this conversation with you a lot, okay? I put a lot of work into it.

WILL: Yeah, well, so do I.

ARON: Chess people, walking along, talking to themselves, I don't do that. People think I am, and I'm not, I don't talk to myself, I argue with you!

WILL: I sit here, like I'm sitting here now, every night—

ARON: You're sure? Lucky you. For all I know, I could be in a hotel room somewhere, having this conversation. I could be walking down the street on my way to the playing hall, having this conversation. The same one, again and again, did I have it already, could I ever really have it, am I remembering, am I imagining—

WILL: And you start to feel a little unstuck. Yeah. All night I've been thinking you're going to disappear. If I stop picturing you for one moment. And I wouldn't even notice, because I know what you're going to say, I've got my strategy ready. I sit here, every night—

ARON: Oh can we for God's sake not make a competition out of this? Can't we share anything? Do we always have to divide it up?

WILL: Oho! And that, that is your mother talking.

ARON: No it is not.

WILL: To the life, what she would say.

ARON: Maybe it's just what anybody would say back to you. Maybe that's just what you do to everyone!

WILL: I want to know who's behind this. This is their revenge, don't you see that? On both of us.

ARON: Whose revenge? Whose?

WILL: I don't know! I lie there thinking—who is doing this to us? Whose fault is this?

ARON: And?

WILL: I think you're still being coached. Just not by me.

ARON: No, I am not.

WILL: Are you sure? Is there a girl in this again?

(*Beat.*)

ARON: Cheap shot, Dad.

WILL: It's just—you talk about wanting a life, you've had a life—it wasn't—

ARON: All right, fair enough, I bring up your blunders, you bring up my blunders—

WILL: You were seventeen years old. The Champion of the United States of America. Who gets married at seventeen years old?

ARON: Somebody very tired and hungry.

(WILL *is silent.*)

> She liked chess. A girl who liked chess. That's what I thought anyway.

WILL: But no?

ARON: Took me years to figure out. At first, we talked about chess, all the time. But then I talked about chess and she would talk about us. Finally I would talk about chess and she wouldn't say anything. Nothing to offer. Pissed me off.

WILL: Well, whose fault was that?

ARON: It turns out, if a woman comes up to you, and she's asking you about chess, and she wants to talk with you about chess, and she wants to learn from you all about chess? She doesn't like chess.

WILL: No?

ARON: No, she likes you. I was so pissed off.

WILL: Yeah, well. I thought I could have a family and the game.

ARON: But no?

WILL: Some can. I couldn't. So it came down to choice. And there is no choice. One thing is better, one thing is worse.

ARON: I never knew you were ever that serious about your chess.

WILL: Not *my* chess.

ARON: So there I am. Seventeen years old. A freak show.

WILL: Seventeen, everybody's a freak show.

ARON: Seventeen years old. Divorced. Father banned from the game. Champion to laughingstock in one year. And here again, so dumb, I could have walked away, just . . . I could have gone to college. And I couldn't do it. I couldn't let them do it. No, I spend the next ten years learning to play all over again. None of your gamesmanship. Pure chess.

WILL: And to think you almost left for that money job. And then you won! You won! You did it!

ARON: Yeah. To this day, so dumb. I'd always thought, I'll show them, I'll win again, and then I will walk away. But now, it isn't about winning. It's never about winning, except when I'm here.

WILL: You love to win.

ARON: Nah, I just hate like hell to lose. But you've got to win, or you don't get to play against the best, and if you don't play against the best, you can't really learn what they have to teach you. And you can't keep seeing deeper in.

(ARON *watches the chessboard.* WILL *watches* ARON.)

WILL: So. What is the right move?

ARON: No, no. The first person who sees me make this sacrifice, he's going to have to pay dear.

WILL: Asshole!

(WILL *swings a slap at* ARON's *head, but* ARON *leans just out of range and the blow misses.*)

ARON: Hey! This is how chess people learn! Somebody makes you feel like shit, but he shows you something. Now, I told you, the combination to look for is the one with the sacrifice in it. This is what the kids don't get, they just try to take each other's pieces, like whoever has the most stuff wins. But the masters, we're always looking for what we can give up to break the game open. Because your pieces don't matter. Right? Only victory matters. That's what takes the beauty prizes, when you sacrifice everything, and leave yourself just enough to win.

WILL: You are a great player.

ARON: Oh, I can see as deep as anyone in the world now. Except the best. I hate this game, I hate this fucking game.

(*They are silent for a while.*)

WILL: Aron, I swear to you, you could not have achieved what you have—

ARON: You know you can play tunes on these? (*Walking to one wall of trophies.*) I worked it out one night. It's like a big xylophone. (*Using a small trophy, he starts tapping on the others.*)

WILL: You could not have achieved what you have if you did not love something here. It can't be done.

ARON: (*Singing along as he taps out a tune.*) *From the Halls of Montezuma to the shores of Tripoli—*

WILL: Aron.

ARON: (*Singing and tapping.*) *We will fight our country's battles on the land and on the sea.*

WILL: Aron.

ARON: (*Singing and pounding.*) *We will fight to dum dee dum dee dum*
And to dum dee dum dee deen
And we're proud to claim the title
Of United States Champeen.

WILL: I swear. If you have suffered, you have suffered out of love.

(*Beat.*)

ARON: Why did Mom leave?

WILL: Ask her. Have you asked her?

ARON: Not as such.

WILL: You've seen her, though, right? Fourth of July?

ARON: Yeah.

WILL: You talked.

ARON: Not really.

WILL: So you're asking me. You're asking me why she left.

ARON: No.

WILL: You did. Back up a few. You did.

ARON: Never mind.

WILL: No, no. You've never asked me that before. It's novel. Did
somebody suggest that you ask me that question?

ARON: No.

WILL: Look at me. Your mother, or Hally, or—

ARON: Why is it so hard for you to believe I'm here on my own?

WILL: Because you are full of this story about a poor sweet boy
forced into competition by his mean old dad. Who must be
stopped before he strikes again. That's the gist of it, right?

ARON: Something like.

WILL: Nothing like. Nothing. You were a hellion! Anybody
came close, whack! Smack! Your mother. You blacked her
eye one time with a Matchbox car. She thought you hated
her. Like raising a sea urchin, try to pick you up and ow ow
ow! You could be a sweet kid, I'm not . . . But with this, I
don't know, animal trapped inside.

ARON: This is weird. Why haven't I heard this before?

WILL: It's true! You came into this family like a panther or
something. Something little and fierce. A wolverine. We
tried everything. I play the piano a little, did you know that?

ARON: No.

WILL: You don't remember me showing you how to play the
piano a little?

ARON: No.

WILL: You were all thumbs. The baby dance classes your mother
took you to, remember those?

ARON: No.

WILL: You had two left feet. I taught you to throw a ball, you
remember that?

ARON: I still can't throw a ball very well.

WILL: You threw like a girl.

ARON: What's your point?

WILL: My point is, from the age of four, you played chess like a
man. A strong man. What you were asked to do—all you
were ever asked to do—was to learn how to make the most
of yourself. When did you ever get the idea that what I
loved was chess?

ARON: But when did it get to be this life-and-death thing?

WILL: Gee, I don't know. When it took over my house? When
it lost me one of my sons? When my wife left me over it?

ARON: I never asked for that.

WILL: You demanded it. You demanded it!

ARON: When! How!

WILL: By who you were! Just by being who you were! By seiz-
ing . . . you don't remember, why should you, your first
breath your first steps a child doesn't remember, the parent remembers. When you learned chess. You seized it.

You . . . "Play again, Dad! Play again! Play again!" We lay awake, your mother and I. What do we do? What is enough of a response to . . . who this is? Any parent. We were . . . how it started, we were doing what you do. And then . . . people will not take all the steps to their logical conclusion. They are ground to a halt by what's normal. And that's fine. But not in this case. To see a child seize on a thing. Devour it. Devouring. "More moves, Daddy! More traps, more tactics! More people to play!" We kept trying to keep up! Time, money, career, marriage, other children, having other children, having any more children, did that never register with you, you're the last, why that might be? Your mother thought it might be nice to have one more. Had always wanted a large family. I said, finally, I mean, how many conversations was this, how many years, I said, we have a large family. There he is. Oh, and your big brother. Him too.

ARON: I never asked for this.

WILL: You weren't a bad kid. But your talent. Your talent was a fucking animal. We threw everything in. It wasn't your fault. Everything, trying to feed this . . .

ARON: Is that true? About me hitting everybody?

WILL: Why do you think I drove you and drove you—drove us both—to all those places? Because I was afraid of what you might do if I stopped.

ARON: Because I threw tantrums or something?

WILL: Rages. Beatings! And all this time, the chess world thought . . . You think I liked walking into tournaments and acting like an asshole? I was, let's face it, a paper-pushing drone. What did I know about how to get my way? But you know who I learned from? You. You never let up! Everything I know about gamesmanship, I learned from you when you were three years old. But once you were in the circuit, I didn't want you doing that, it would have broken your focus. So I did it for you.

ARON: And chess, chess is what . . . it's my . . .

WILL: Medication.

ARON: Or my punishment or something.

WILL: It's a war game. A fine pastime for weak people who need to fight. Like the law, come to think of it. Thanks to chess, everyone you saw, you could beat them and beat them, and nobody came up to say, "Sir, there's a problem with your son." No one saying, "We don't want him playing with our children anymore." On the contrary! They offered their children up to you! You beat them and beat them.

ARON: I helped those children. They didn't care about the game. I beat 'em so quick, the parents would take pity on them. Take 'em home, saying—oh, and they'd say it just loud enough for me to hear, "Well, he plays a very strong game, of course, but if you have to raise a child to be that kind of freak . . . Well, I'm just glad ours is normal. Let's go home, munchkin."

WILL: Oh, they made sure I heard them, too.

ARON: I set more little kids free that way.

WILL: (*Pointing to a trophy.*) National Under-12 Champion. Nine years old.

ARON: Champion of the Children. Make way, make way.

WILL: Chess came along in the nick of time. Saved your life. Probably a few other lives along with. And then. And then. When it had turned you from this, this . . .

ARON: Sea urchin, wolverine . . . Monster, you can say it.

WILL: Into a grandmaster! Your mother. I'm here, she's sitting where you are—she goes, "Why can't we just raise him to be a regular person."

ARON: Really? She said that?

WILL: A regular person. An average person.

ARON: So somebody at some point actually said that.

WILL: And I go, "Why"—I mean—"why the hell would we want to do that?" And she goes, "It might be easier for him." I go, "What would?" She goes, "To find somebody to love him." And I go, "Why do you think somebody would be more likely to love a regular, an average—quote unquote—person," and she goes, "Well, honey, I love you."

ARON: Whoa.

WILL: Can you imagine?

ARON: Ow. I can see why you've never told me that one before. Ow, it burns.

WILL: All right now.

ARON: I can see why you'd spend your life nursing a grudge against someone who nailed you like that. "Well, honey, I love *you*." Go Mom.

WILL: Go Mom?

ARON: I just didn't think she had it in her.

WILL: She didn't. Not then. Finally it was too much for her.

ARON: It was? I was.

(WILL *is silent.*)

> So if chess was never that big a thing for you, why teach it to the children? What's the point of that?

WILL: It's an excellent pastime for young and old alike.

ARON: But, but, really, all it is—it isn't even about chess at all. Is it. You're just . . .

WILL: Planting the flag. In their turf. Yeah.

ARON: You don't even like them.

WILL: They're mine! Even if you hate something, it's hard to give it up. Isn't it? When it's all you've got?

(*Beat.*)

ARON: Dad. The kids. They have no strategy. It's beautiful, they just . . . Fourth of July. Oh my God, running all over, soaking each other with water, jumping in the pool, out of the pool, running with fiery things in their hands . . . I'm sitting on the sofa in my suit, watching the cars go round and round on TV. Just quiet. A pack of kids go screaming through. Walker comes barreling into my knees, he grabs my hand, he goes, "You wanna play with us? Come on, come play with us."

WILL: Is this what's behind all this? You want little friends, little childhood friends, you want—

ARON: I'm telling you about your grandchildren! People are supposed to love to hear about their grandchildren! The kids weren't playing anything. They were just . . . playing!

Like at one point one bunch of cousins took all the sofa cushions and dining room chairs and built this fort. And the other bunch of cousins got a bunch of pillows and stuffed animals. This was my team. And they were just going to all run in and attack this fort, but I said, I said if we send the littlest ones in first, like three toddlers, boom boom boom, then you guys slant in from the dining room and pile on, and then I'll charge in with the beanbag chair and wipe 'em out. We creamed 'em. I haven't had that much fun . . .

WILL: So they played the Sicilian Dragon Defense and you used a Yugoslav Attack.

ARON: What?

WILL: Black set up a fortress, right, on the kingside, and you, the white pieces, you sent a pawn storm up the kingside, that's the toddlers, then a Bishop exchange across the middle, slantways, and then you brought up the heavy pieces, Queen and Rooks, that's you. Classic attacking strategy. Way to go. You taught them chess.

ARON: No.

WILL: You taught them chess! Ha! Ha!! I'm proud of you, son. You haven't made me this proud in years and years.

ARON: I haven't—Dad. I just brought you the trophy—I'm the Champion of the United States of America.

WILL: Oh please.

ARON: What.

WILL: Do I have to say this to you? You won the U.S. Championship. And you're proud of that.

ARON: Shouldn't I be?

WILL: Oh please! While you were doing that, the cream of international chess was in Linares, and nobody even worried about the scheduling conflict because the championship of the United States is not considered by international chess to be a major tournament. And you know that. And still you walk in here bragging you're the American champion of something not even America gives a shit about!

ARON: I can't help it if Americans don't care about chess!

WILL: Of course you can! America doesn't care who the American champion of chess is because America doesn't care who the American champion of anything is. America only cares who the world champion is. Anything America cares about, we call the American champion the world champion: baseball, basketball, football. But anything where the rest of the world has something to teach us, we do not want to know. America cared about you when it looked like you might become the best in the world. But you're only the best in America, so nobody cares about you anymore. Except me, because God help me, I still believe you have it in you to be the champion of the world. But you will not make the commitment!

ARON: All the times—I told you—all the times I could have walked away—

WILL: But you didn't, because you knew I would know. You think I'm hungry and up nights because I'm ready to die? I'm afraid I'm going to die before you learn to be a winner! That's what is killing me! I am working, still working, trying to raise a winner!

(*They watch each other.*)

ARON: Okay. Okay. I was how old, I'd just won the States, or maybe the Regionals, I was eight. (*Looking around, pointing to a trophy.*) That one. I was holding that one. And I said, "Daddy, I might not want to play so much anymore. Okay?" And you said: "Over. My. Dead. Body."

WILL: That didn't happen. I don't remember that.

ARON: "Over my dead body."

WILL: I would remember.

ARON: You said it more than once.

WILL: I didn't mean it.

ARON: Of course you didn't. You were younger than me now, you couldn't imagine your dead body. But I could. A child imagines the scariest things. You were saying I had the scariest thing in my power. Just by stopping. My chess kept death away.

WILL: So that's why you're here. To see how soon till you're free. (*Beat.*) All my years. Devoted. And all you remember. A couple of offhand remarks.

ARON: Yeah. That's how it is, in this bitch of a game. (*He starts taking trophies off the shelves.*)

WILL: What are you doing? What, this is your big threat now, you're going to take your trophies and go? Is that what you're going to do?

ARON: Let's see, this is . . . National Under-10 Championship. (*He unscrews the top of a trophy. He overturns it. Out falls a pile of gray powder.*)

WILL: God, that stuff is rotten.

ARON: It's not food. (*Opening another.*) Hally did hate me, for a while. It was so clear who your favorite was. Late at night, in our room, I was scared he'd hurt me in my sleep, kill me even, so he'd have you to himself again. So one night I told him about "Over My Dead Body." He liked it. He had me tell it again. I told it a lot. It was our ghost story. "Over My Dead Body." It got to be a game we played, me and Hally, back and forth. Like when Hally first heard about heart attacks. We lay awake, so excited. Hally said a person can get so pissed off he dies, right there. Pissed off to death. We thought about that for a long time. We picked out music for your funeral.

WILL: What are those?

ARON: Hally told me about cremation, after Grandpa. It gave us a new idea. (*He pours out another pile of gray powder.*)

WILL: Those are ashes?

ARON: You and I would come home from a tournament, and you'd dance the trophy around, and put it up here, and I'd watch Hally watching this, and I'd whisper, tonight we'll put him in. It was our private award ceremony, Hally's and mine.

WILL: These are me?

(ARON *silently pours.*)

How did you . . . Where did you get ashes?

ARON: Different things. One time, Hally had done a report for school, on some kind of birds, with all these pictures of birds in colored pencil, he'd gotten an A+ on it, he was so proud.

WILL: And he burned it. And put it in here to be me.

ARON: The first time, we were like—I don't know who started first—crying, kind of. We were scared at what we'd done. We didn't know what would happen next. Then we were laughing because how ridiculous was that. We hadn't done anything, nothing had happened.

WILL: But it had. You'd killed me.

ARON: We hadn't killed you. See, to me, "Over My Dead Body" meant I could kill you by stopping. But Hally said that what you meant was that you *were* a dead body. Because Hally remembered a time when we had a dad who loved us. I was too young to remember. All I knew was, the man Hally was so sad about had gone away. In his place was this man who kept me locked up and starving and made me work and work and completely ignored Hally. And no one would admit that our dad was gone. That he had been killed, somehow, by chess.

WILL: All the years. Under this roof. The hate.

ARON: Dad. No. This is just how we could live with you. The dead can't lay a finger on us. Whatever you were doing, it wasn't real. It was being done by a dead body.

WILL: He calls me every week.

ARON: Every Sunday, yeah. He makes his little offering. He's got to act like a good son, what else can he do? There are things he likes to remember about you. From before everything.

WILL: From before you!

(ARON *is silent.*)

All these? They have ashes in them? My ashes?

ARON: The ones that aren't food, or dried piss, are ashes.

WILL: Is this . . . is this really true?

ARON: Look for yourself.

WILL: I don't believe you.

(ARON *pours ashes out of trophy after trophy.*)

ARON: My marriage license. Divorce papers. We made it you, and we burned it.

WILL: Your marriage license? Divorce—but—

ARON: The magazine with my picture on the cover. (*He picks up the trophy he brought with him.*)

WILL: Don't.

ARON: Hally calls you, I bring these, and that is supposed to keep you satisfied. Because Hally and me, we're . . . we are what we are. But you can't have the children. It's hard to tell you this, I'd hoped I wouldn't ever have to, it's the kind of thing you don't want to have to tell your parents. You hope if you wait long enough, they'll figure it out for themselves. You're dead.

WILL: To you.

ARON: To me, to Hally, to Mom . . . when you're dead to every-body, you're dead. (*He opens the trophy and pours ashes out.*) So stop losing sleep over what I'll do after you're gone! I buried you years ago and here I am. Still in the game. All right? All right? Why do I have to keep doing this?!?

(*Beat.*)

WILL: No. No. I don't believe any of this. These aren't even ashes.

ARON: Yes, they are.

WILL: No. See. These. These are old food. Just old food. Looks
like ashes, because, they're from so long ago. These aren't
burned at all. This is just what time does. So. See? You can
eat them. You can. (*Licking his fingers.*) Mm. Mm. You're
right. You could eat these. If you had to. So. Good try,
though. Nice try.

ARON: Dad. Stop.

WILL: Is this why you never come here?

ARON: I come here all the time.

WILL: You're not even here now. You're playing tomorrow's
game.

ARON: And when I'm playing, where am I?

WILL: Some, some hotel, some nothing place—

ARON: I'm here. Dad, I'm always here.

WILL: Fine! Yes! Great! You're always here! I hear you! You're
always here, and I can never help you.

ARON: Help me what?

WILL: Help you win! What have I ever done in my life but try
to help you win?

ARON: Every time I prepare for a game. Every time I'm tired and
hungry, I go to this room. I keep thinking, one of these times
you won't be here. But you always are.

WILL: I've been dead for years. Says you.

ARON: You will never be dead to me. You will outlast us all.

WILL: Good. Good! I told you these aren't ashes. I'm not dead.

ARON: So you're going to stay alive then?

WILL: Damn right.

(*Beat.*)

ARON: Good.

WILL: Good?

(ARON *seizes* WILL'*s head. Kisses his cheek. Holds him hard.*)

ARON: I better go. Got a game.

WILL: Glad you came?

ARON: It was worth it.

WILL: You're ready for it now?

(ARON *pulls away, still holding* WILL.)

ARON: Yeah, Dad. Yeah.

(ARON *exits.* WILL *holds the trophy.*)

WILL: My champion. My champion.

END OF PLAY

SHORT PLAYS

90 DAYS

Elizabeth Meriwether

90 Days received its world premiere on October 3, 2008, at the Cherry Lane Theatre, New York City, as part of SPIN, a series of short plays commissioned by stageFARM. The play was directed by Evan Cabnet and featured the following cast:

ELLIOT	Patch Darragh
ABBY	Rebecca Henderson

CHARACTERS
ELLIOT
ABBY

ELLIOT *sits in a simple bedroom. There's a phone on the table. And a plate of fried Tater Tots.*

ELLIOT: I've gained some weight.

(*A slight pause.* ABBY*'s voice comes from the phone.* ELLIOT *takes one of the Tots from the plate.*)

ABBY: That's okay. How much?

ELLIOT: Like. It's mostly in my face.

ABBY: Oh. What?

ELLIOT: Am I talking too loud?

ABBY: No. Am I on speaker?

ELLIOT: I'm just about to eat some Tater Tots.

ABBY: Is that a joke?

(ELLIOT *waits.*)

ELLIOT: Yes. It's a joke.

ABBY: I thought you were serious!

ELLIOT: No. It was a joke.

ABBY: Okay. Those are so bad for you.

(*A slight pause.* ELLIOT *puts one in his mouth and chews silently.*)

ELLIOT: I'm naked.

ABBY: What? I just took my contacts out.

ELLIOT: Where are you? Are you at home?

ABBY: I have astigmatism. I went to the eye doctor today. I'm glad we're doing this. It's so good to hear your voice. It's hard not to talk to you whenever—

ELLIOT: I know. I'm sorry. We're not supposed to—

ABBY: Yeah, I don't want you to break the rules. What are you doing now?

(ELLIOT *puts a Tater Tot in his mouth. He chews silently.*)

ELLIOT: Reading a book.

ABBY: I thought you'd be celebrating—I'm so proud of you. Ninety days is amazing. It's so great.

ELLIOT: Yeah.

ABBY: I mean. Come on! That's so great!

ELLIOT: Yeah. Yeah.

(*As she talks, he quietly chews more Tater Tots.*)

ABBY: My eye doctor told me not to get LASIK right now because I'm just going to have to get reading glasses when I get old.

(*A slight pause.*)

Do you want to have phone sex?

ELLIOT: I mean. Do you want to?

ABBY: Yeah, yeah, of course. Do you want to like—masturbate or something and then we can talk about it?

ELLIOT: Okay.

(*A slight pause.* ELLIOT *doesn't do anything. Keeps eating.*)

ABBY: Are you masturbating?

ELLIOT: Yeah. Ooo. Ooo.

ABBY: You can just put me on mute.

ELLIOT: Okay.

ABBY: Am I on mute?

(ELLIOT *doesn't say anything. He just keeps eating the Tater Tots.*)

How's it going? Oh, I forgot I'm on mute. Let me know when you're done.

(ELLIOT *finishes the plate of Tater Tots. As this is happening:*)

How's it going? That's great. You're doing great. Faster. No, I mean, do whatever you want to do. Yeah. Yeah. Cum on my tits.

ELLIOT: Okay, I'm done.

ABBY: That's great! That's awesome! Was it fun?

ELLIOT: Yeah.

ABBY: Do you have to clean up?

ELLIOT: Oh. Yeah. It's all over. Like. I better go get a lot of paper towels.

ABBY: Oh good! Good job! That's really hot.

ELLIOT: When does your flight get in?

ABBY: I think it's like two thirty-five. I can't wait to see you, it feels like it's been, it feels longer—oh. Look. It came out today.

ELLIOT: What?

ABBY: Brodie wrote something for Shouts and Murmurs.

ELLIOT: Are you reading *The New Yorker* right now?

ABBY: I was just packing—I was trying to figure out what to bring on the plane. Oh, did you build that shelf I sent you?

(ELLIOT *turns and looks at a box that's sitting unopened on the other side of the room.*)

ELLIOT: Yes. Thank you.

ABBY: You built it?

ELLIOT: Uh-huh.

ABBY: That's—that's so great—I'm so happy you built it. It's like—this is working. You know? I'm so proud of you.

ELLIOT: It's just a shelf.

ABBY: It's not just a shelf. It's—you taking responsibility. Can't I
be excited? I'm excited. Is it big? I couldn't tell if it was big.

ELLIOT: It's. It's fucking huge.

ABBY: Oh no, no—it's not supposed to be that big. How big
is it?

ELLIOT: It's like a—a midget. It's like a little person. With a
sword.

ABBY: (*Laughing.*) What?

ELLIOT: It's as tall as the prairie is high.

ABBY: (*Laughing.*) What did you say?

(ELLIOT *goes over to the box and tries to open it quietly.*)

It's Queen Anne style. They were almost sold out of it at
Crate and Barrel. I'm so glad you like it. That's so great. I
mean I can't remember the last time you actually did something like that. You put something together—

ELLIOT: Are you crying?

ABBY: No. No.

ELLIOT: It's okay if you—

ABBY: I'm not crying—I can't wait to see it tomorrow. I didn't
know what to tell them at Crate and Barrel, because they
asked me where to send it, and I had to whisper—

ELLIOT: Why did you whisper?

ABBY: I don't want everyone to know where you are.

ELLIOT: Why?

ABBY: Do you want everyone to know? I'll tell them. I'll tell everyone at Crate and Barrel that you were—if that's what you want, I'll tell them.

(ELLIOT *stares at the phone.*)

Hi.

ELLIOT: Hi.

ABBY: How are those mountains? Is it pretty up there? I should pack a raincoat or something. It's hot here.

ELLIOT: I don't know—I haven't really gone out—

ABBY: You just look out your window and it's like the whole thing, right? The trees.

ELLIOT: Thank you for—it's a great place.

ABBY: You don't have to thank me—

ELLIOT: I want to thank you—

ABBY: Elliot?

ELLIOT: Yeah.

ABBY: Tell me about the shelf.

ELLIOT: You want to hear about the shelf?

ABBY: What did you put on it?

ELLIOT: Like. A lot of books. All the books I've been reading. And. I put Yahtzee on it.

ABBY: Did you say Yahtzee?

ELLIOT: I've been playing Yahtzee.

ABBY: Okay. That's okay. Yahtzee! That's good for you to do things like that.

ELLIOT: What's wrong with Yahtzee?

ABBY: Nothing—I can't even remember what that is—dice or something—

ELLIOT: It's dice.

ABBY: Oh, dice. That sounds really fun. We can play.

ELLIOT: You don't want to play me, because I'm going to win every time. It's like the only thing I've been doing.

ABBY: Well, I don't care if I lose.

ELLIOT: I'm just saying—It's not going to be fun for you, because I'm amazing.

ABBY: We don't have to play—

ELLIOT: We can play if you want to—

ABBY: We don't have to play Yahtzee. We can do something else. What else do you do out there?

ELLIOT: I've been making pots.

ABBY: Oh that's great! That's amazing! What kind of pots?

(ELLIOT *holds up a weird ceramic thing that looks nothing like a teapot. He just stares at it.*)

ELLIOT: Like a. It's like a teapot.

ABBY: Oh, I'll bring some tea—

ELLIOT: No, you can't put tea in it—

ABBY: Then it's not a teapot—

ELLIOT: No, it's like shaped like a teapot, but you can't put tea in it—

ABBY: Oh, I'm sorry, of course it's a teapot—

ELLIOT: You don't have to call it a teapot—

ABBY: No, I'm sure it's a teapot—

ELLIOT: I don't want you to call it a teapot, Abby. Call it a pot. Just call it a pot.

(*A slight pause.*)

ABBY: I'm sorry. I'm just—

ELLIOT: No. Don't apologize. No.

(*A slight pause.*)

ABBY: So I'll just bring some tea out just in case.

(ELLIOT *makes a silent scream.*)

ABBY: I've been drinking chamomile. I haven't been sleeping, it's fine, but I just haven't been sleeping very well, so I've been drinking chamomile, so I'll just. I'll bring some. We don't have to put it in a pot, we can just put it in a mug or something.

(He picks up a bag of Cheetos from somewhere on his floor and starts eating whatever is left in the bag.)

What are you doing?

ELLIOT: *(Mouth full of Cheetos.)* I'm brushing my teeth.

ABBY: I love watching you brush your teeth. You're so bad at it.

(ELLIOT stops chewing and smiles.)

ELLIOT: I miss you.

ABBY: Yeah.

(A beat.)

Brodie says hi. I ran into him. He's working at *The Atlantic.* He said they'd love to hear ideas for freelance in a couple months or whenever you're ready. You should read the thing in *The New Yorker.* It's so Brodie. It's hilarious. It's a list of people you don't want to invite to your country house.

ELLIOT: Like—a werewolf.

ABBY: No, Republicans. It's political satire. It's like: Don't invite Republicans to your country house or they'll break all your chairs.

ELLIOT: Why do they break your chairs?

ABBY: Because they're Republicans. It's hilarious. It's so great for him.

ELLIOT: Didn't you used to date Brodie?

ABBY: Oh. Did I tell you that? No, we just fucked around.

(ELLIOT *rips the box open and the wood and the screws spill out over the ground.*)

Oh my god! What happened?

ELLIOT: I'm sorry, I was just—

ABBY: Were you still masturbating?

ELLIOT: (*A beat.*) Yes. Yes I was. I've been masturbating this whole time.

ABBY: That's okay, just put me on mute.

ELLIOT: You didn't tell me you used to fuck Brodie.

ABBY: Yeah. He liked me to lie really still like I was dead, because his father used to hit him. He wanted everything to be peaceful. Sometimes he would, like, read out loud to me. It was just a couple—

ELLIOT: He read to you during sex?

ABBY: Yeah.

ELLIOT: What did he read?

ABBY: I don't know. *The Great Gatsby.* He just didn't like— moving around that much.

ELLIOT: Do I move around too much?

ABBY: No—I was just saying there are other things to do—you can just let it, like, lie.

ELLIOT: My penis?

ABBY: Oh no. Are you upset? I didn't mean to—

ELLIOT: You want me to just lie on you with my penis out like a dead person?

ABBY: What? I can't understand what you're saying—

ELLIOT: I'm sorry I'm not Brodie. I don't have an article in *The New Yorker* and—and I don't fuck you like a dead person—

ABBY: Elliot—

ELLIOT: I'm sorry—

ABBY: I thought this was—

ELLIOT: This is—

ABBY: I thought we were trying to—

ELLIOT: We are! We are! I love you, I just.

ABBY: Everything's fine. Everything is totally fine. I don't want to talk about Brodie. He can only sleep with the lights on. He might be a sociopath. I don't know.

(*A beat.*)

What did you do today?

ELLIOT: I went to group therapy and I talked about my fucking dreams, Abby. I don't know. I made a fucking pot that can't hold any liquids.

ABBY: Why are you getting—

ELLIOT: Because, I don't know—

ABBY: Why did you talk about your dreams? Did you have a bad one?

ELLIOT: Yeah. I had a dream I killed a lot of butterflies. Someone told me not to get so many butterflies, but I bought them anyway and then they all suffocated to death. But they were on my pants.

ABBY: They suffocated on your pants?

ELLIOT: No. They grabbed onto my pants right when they died.

ABBY: What does that mean?

ELLIOT: I don't know.

ABBY: Well what did they say in group?

ELLIOT: They all thought it was about you.

ABBY: Why? No. That's not about me.

(*A slight pause.*)

I'm not a butterfly. Why would I be a butterfly?

ELLIOT: Do you want to just talk about—

ABBY: So group is good. I guess everyone is going through a lot. Hey. I'm proud of you. We got through it. I can't wait to see the shelf tomorrow. And then maybe, you know, we can have the big rescheduling conversation. Mom said we could rebook the room we liked. In the hotel. And get the same caterer. And the band is probably not doing anything, but I'm going to call and check. And I don't even think we need drinks. I think it'll be fun without a bar—we could get—we could take the money we were going to spend on alcohol and get, like, a karaoke machine. Or I don't know—

ELLIOT: Are you going to get a new dress?

ABBY: It's fine.

ELLIOT: It's not fine—

ABBY: It's fine. Oh my god. It's totally fine. I'll get a new—

ELLIOT: I'm a drug addict, Abby.

ABBY: And Mom was so happy that you sent her that letter—it really meant a lot and she sends her love, so. It's not a big deal, it's so not a big deal. I'll get a new one.

ELLIOT: I'm a drug addict.

ABBY: I don't need to—whatever you're doing—I don't want to do this, Elliot, okay? I forgive you.

ELLIOT: How?

ABBY: I just do. I love you and you're getting better and I forgive you and it's fine—

ELLIOT: How do you forgive me?

ABBY: It's a disease. You have a disease. You apologized.

ELLIOT: That's it? All I have to do is apologize? That's shit. It's shit. That's nothing.

ABBY: Well you're sorry, so it's fine—

ELLIOT: "Sorry." That's not—that's something you write on a note. It's not enough. There's nothing that's enough—I can't tell you how sorry—I can't tell you—

ABBY: It's going to be fine. We're going to start over. You know?

ELLIOT: Yeah. How?

ABBY: It's going to be great. We're going to be totally honest. We're just going to say everything—

ELLIOT: I didn't build the shelf. I didn't even start on it.

(*A slight pause.*)

I didn't build it. It's all over my floor.

(*A slight pause.*)

Say it. Say something real. Please.

(*A slight pause.*)

Say it.

(*A slight pause.*)

ABBY: I'm so angry at you. I'm angry at you. I'm angry.

(*A beat.*)

I slept with Brodie. We've been.

(*A slight pause. His whole body relaxes.*)

ELLIOT: Okay.

ABBY: Elliot?

ELLIOT: Okay.

(*A slight pause.* ABBY *doesn't hang up. We can hear her breathing on the phone.* ELLIOT *uses his plastic knife as a screwdriver and starts to put the shelf together.*)

Good.

END OF PLAY

BANK & TRUST

Kitt Lavoie

Bank & Trust premiered at the Transfjúz Company in Budapest, Hungary, on November 17, 2012. The cast included Ági Ábrahám, Olga Sára Kelenhegyi, and Gyuri Molnár. *Bank & Trust* was developed with the CRY HAVOC Company (www.cryhavoccompany.org).

CHARACTERS
MEL, mid-thirties
PAUL, mid-forties

A parking lot. Late afternoon. MEL, *mid-thirties, leans against a car. Waiting. She holds a plate of cookies. She sees someone coming from a distance. She straightens up.*

After a moment, PAUL, *mid-forties, enters, heading for the car. He sees* MEL *and stops at a distance. He takes a breath and slowly approaches.* MEL *lets him get close before speaking.*

MEL: Hey, Paul.

PAUL: Hi, Mel. How you doing?

MEL: You know . . .

(*A beat.*)

    I made you these.

(MEL *offers the plate of cookies.* PAUL *takes them. A long, uncomfortable moment.* PAUL *starts past* MEL *toward the car.*)

    Can you do anything?

PAUL: I'm sorry.

(PAUL *walks past* MEL.)

MEL: Just a couple more months. It would make all the difference.

PAUL: Mel, I'm sorry. I can't.

MEL: They're taking the land, too.

(PAUL *stops.*)

PAUL: Yeah.

MEL: That was a separate loan.

PAUL: Well . . . yeah. But it was used as equity on the construction. Three houses in— . . . It was an ambitious project, Mel. We knew that from the beginning. If the market hadn't gone soft, but— . . . I'm just sorry it didn't work out.

MEL: But it could, I'm saying.

PAUL: Mel—

MEL: There's nobody building, Paul. Just two more months. The amount of labor out there, we could have all three finished by then. Finished, on the market, and paid off. Two months. That's all we're asking.

PAUL: I can't, Mel.

MEL: *Two*—

PAUL: I already got him four, Mel. There's nothing more I can do.

MEL: What is the bank going to do with three half-finished houses, Paul? What are they going to do? What are they going to get, that they couldn't get more by letting us finish?

PAUL: I can't do any more. I'm sorry.

MEL: One month.

PAUL: I'm sorry.

MEL: *You're* sorry?

PAUL: I am.

MEL: Twelve years. Thirteen houses. Has he *ever* been late on a payment.

PAUL: I'm sorry, Mel.

MEL: Has he?

PAUL: No.

MEL: So . . .

PAUL: Yes, actually. A couple. Yes.

MEL: In twelve years.

PAUL: That's not what it's about. It isn't. It's— . . . I'm sorry. Times are tough. All around.

(PAUL *turns toward his car.*)

MEL: We had you over for dinner.

PAUL: This is inappropriate, Mel.

MEL: Don't "appropriate" me. We're going to lose our house.

PAUL: You won't.

MEL: I quit my job. When we started on the development, I quit my job so I could help him. We have *nothing* coming in, Paul.

PAUL: I'm sorry.

MEL: *Nothing.*

PAUL: I know. And that's why the bank called in the loan.

MEL: *You* called it in.

PAUL: No, I didn't.

MEL: You called him into your office. You told him— ...

(*A beat.*)

Our house, Paul.

(*A beat.*)

I thought you were a friend.

PAUL: You should go home.

(PAUL *heads for his car.*)

MEL: He cried. When he got home today, he fucking cried. In front of my fucking kid. In front of his son. He wouldn't like me telling you that—

PAUL: No, he wouldn't.

MEL: But he did. What about my kids, Paul?

PAUL: Good night, Mel.

MEL: *What about them?*

PAUL: They'll be fine.

MEL: They play with your kids.

PAUL: I know.

MEL: You want them to starve?

PAUL: They won't.

MEL: What am I going to feed them?

PAUL: I don't believe Derek is going to let that happen.

MEL: What is he supposed to do. You call in the loans. You shut down his business. The houses are two-thirds up. Two of them, and the third is on its way. That's money. That's money we spent. That you're taking away.

PAUL: I talked to him, Mel. It's going to be alright.

MEL: How?

PAUL: He has a plan.

MEL: What plan?

PAUL: There's a new Home Depot opening up in Leominster. They could use a man—

(MEL *smacks* PAUL. *Hard.*)

(*A beat.*)

You know, Barry foreclosed last week on Terry Morgan's property.

MEL: That was the subcontractor.

PAUL: Man pulls the drain in his Jacuzzi first night in his new home, he doesn't expect a hundred gallons of water to come crashing down through his dining room ceiling.

MEL: It was the subcontractor, Paul.

PAUL: And he sure doesn't expect to be on the hook for a hundred and fifty thousand dollars in repairs.

MEL: *You know it was the subcontractor.*

PAUL: I know. I'm just saying, sometimes things happen. Sometimes someone loses, and it's not always the fault of the person just 'cause they blame them. Sometimes it's the subcontractor. And sometimes it's the bank. And it always sucks, Mel. But there's nothing I can do. There were too many projects. Too many irons in the fire. It was the subcontractor, I know. But if he were on-site, Derek would have caught it. He's good. He would have. And if he wasn't trying to do three houses at once, he wouldn't have gotten behind like this.

MEL: He's not going to stock shelves at Home Depot.

PAUL: I'm not saying stock—

MEL: He is a businessman. Twelve years. He's not gonna do *anything* at Home Depot.

PAUL: He's gonna have to, Mel.

MEL: What does that mean?

PAUL: It means he's gonna have to. For a while. You've got nothing coming in. We're gonna see how the auction goes, but in this market— . . . The bank is strapped, Mel. If we don't recoup, we're going to have to pursue a deficiency judgment.

MEL: What does that mean?

PAUL: It means let's hope the auction goes well.

MEL: So, wait. They've recalled the loan. We've lost the new builds. We're going to lose our *house*? And *still* we're going to owe someone money.

PAUL: It was an ambitious project, Mel.

MEL: *Then why did you give us the money for it in the first place?*

PAUL: You should be talking to Derek about this. Not me.

MEL: No, I'm talking to you. If it was so damn "ambitious," why did you give us the money?

PAUL: It seemed like a reasonable risk—

MEL: Well, *clearly* it wasn't. You should have known that. That's your fucking job.

PAUL: For now, yeah.

MEL: What does that mean?

PAUL: You think you're the first person to point out that maybe I shouldn't have given you that loan? A construction loan is a "story loan"—and that means it's my job to know the story. It's my job to sit there and listen to your story and decide whether it looks like it's got a happy ending or not. And I guessed wrong. I guessed way the fuck wrong. And because of what's going on in the market right now, I guessed more wrong than right over the past year.

MEL: And we're supposed to be punished because you guessed wrong?

PAUL: Good night, Mel.

(PAUL *heads for his car.*)

MEL: Why am I the one losing my house when you're the one who guessed wrong?

PAUL: (*Wheeling on her.*) I didn't guess wrong. I *knew.* I knew Derek was taking on too much. He knew, too. The only one who didn't know was you. And you guys have Kara and I over for dinner and we have a nice time and great food and you just keep mentioning—*you*—just mentioning the great new lot Derek just bought on Woodside. "Perfect for three two-to-four bedrooms." I could see it, Mel. I could see it in his eyes. I could see it, he thought it was too much. But then the next week, first thing Monday morning, what do you know, he comes in and asks me to make it work. As a friend, to make it work. You talked him into it. And both of us knew better.

MEL: And women shouldn't get involved in men business?

PAUL: No, I'm saying *you. You* shouldn't get involved. Because look at what happened. He was a good man and a good businessman. And he's going to be working at Home Depot. And that's your fault. And I'm saying that as a friend.

MEL: A friend with a job, so . . .

(*A beat.*)

PAUL: You think I like coming to work here now?

MEL: Honestly, yeah. A little bit.

PAUL: Once I'm done mopping up this mess—

MEL: Our life savings isn't something that needs "mopping," Paul.

PAUL: All the same, once I'm done—once the foreclosures and the auctions are done—we're not making any more construction loans. Not until things start looking at least a little bit bullish. I make construction loans for a living, Mel. Things being what they are, how long do you think it's going to take them to notice I've got nothing to do here all day?

(*A beat.*)

MEL: It was my kids' college fund, Paul. The down payment. No problem, you said, we could make it work if we had the down payment. We trusted you.

(*A beat.*)

PAUL: You'll bounce back.

MEL: You think so?

PAUL: You and Derek are good people.

(*A beat.*)

(MEL *bats the plate of cookies from* PAUL*'s hand, sending them flying.*)

MEL: Go fuck yourself, Paul.

(MEL *turns and leaves.* PAUL *watches her go.*

Her car door slams, the engine starts, and the car pulls out of the lot.

PAUL *watches her drive off in the distance. He looks down and kicks a cookie across the lot. He heads for his car.*

Blackout.)

END OF PLAY

FUNNY VALENTINE

Ean Miles Kessler

Funny Valentine premiered as a part of Dei–GAH at Rutgers University in 2007. Kevin Kittle directed the following cast:

JOANNA	Sam Yim
CHARLIE	Ean Miles Kessler

CAST
CHARLIE, any ethnicity, age eighteen to twenty
JOANNA, Korean, age sixteen to twenty-two

For my grandmother, Rosalie Sklar
Special thanks to Sam Yim and Kevin Kittle

At rise: Korea, May of 1953, two months before the end of the war. A seedy back room at a gloomy brothel. JOANNA *(age sixteen to twenty-two), a Korean prostitute, looks for matches;* CHARLIE *(age eighteen to twenty) stands awkwardly.*

CHARLIE: This is a nice place—it—*Jo-wah*—Nice, it's . . . You live here, or—? You—?

(No answer. He meanders through the room, poking through her meager belongings. Finds a ratty edition of Mother Goose.*)*

This yours? Hey. This—this yours?

(Silence.)

Mother Goose?

JOANNA: Yes. English.

CHARLIE: Oh; yeah—yeah, English.

(She smiles, nods. CHARLIE *does the same. Puts down the book and looks through other things.)*

S'nice to be with a woman again, yanno?—feels good, feels—

(She comes back, having found the matches.)

JOANNA: Cigarette.

CHARLIE: Oh, yeah. Thanks.

(*He gives her a cigarette, lights it. She smiles her thanks; smokes.*)

There you go. Yeah, yanno—Korea six months already, ain't had any time to see any girls. Over in Kusong; fuckin' shithole.

JOANNA: Kusong?

CHARLIE: Yeah, you—

JOANNA: Ku—?

CHARLIE: Yeah.

JOANNA: (*Points at herself.*) Kusong.

CHARLIE: No shit.

JOANNA: Kusong.

CHARLIE: That's—wow, that's crazy. Wow.

JOANNA: Crazy.

CHARLIE: Yeah.

(*She points to him; smokes.*)

JOANNA: Marine.

CHARLIE: Yeah—hey; hell yeah.

JOANNA: (*She salutes.*) Semper fi.

CHARLIE: Yeah. Naw, good—real good. I didn't think you'd—I didn't think you'd know that. Huh. Yeah; naw, got a place to stay; food. Do pushups. Get paid. It's okay.

JOANNA: Okay.

CHARLIE: Yeah, it's all right.

JOANNA: Okay.

CHARLIE: Yeah, first time they cut my hair—clip it so short, run y'hand through it, it buzzes. Fresh, yanno?

(*He puts his hand through his hair a few times to show her—offers it to her. She does. They both smile.*)

JOANNA: Marine.

CHARLIE: Yeah. Oh—

(*He suddenly rolls up his sleeve to reveal a garish tattoo.*)

Y'see that?—got that, New Orleans at basic. Sixty bucks.

JOANNA: Nice.

CHARLIE: Yeah?

JOANNA: Very nice. Pretty.

CHARLIE: Pretty?

JOANNA: Very pretty.

(*He gives a breathless laugh.*)

CHARLIE: Jesus-fuck. Yeah. Pretty.

(*She reaches out and touches his tattoo, then his chest; leaves her hand there. An electric moment; he breaks it off with her, returns to looking through her things, feigning interest. She sits on the bed and regards him.*)

JOANNA: You—

CHARLIE: Naw, it's okay, it's—

(*He laughs nervously. She smiles to him. Offers him a drag on her cigarette.*)

JOANNA: Smoke?

CHARLIE: Oh; no. No, I don't really—I don't smoke. No, yanno, a couple a' the guys, they said you buy cigarettes for the women. Yanno. (*Laughs without breath.*) Bought two fuckin' cartons. The smell though—

(*She smiles and gives a slight laugh of understanding, despite her obliviousness. Awkward moment.*)

You live here; you—? Upstairs?

(*No answer.*)

Lotta girls here? Lotta—?

JOANNA: Girls!—yes.

CHARLIE: Yeah. You all live here, or—

JOANNA: Dancer.

CHARLIE: Yeah, no, I know—you were good; you're a good dancer down there. This a nice place; y'got a nice place, down there. Good bar.

JOANNA: Bar.

CHARLIE: Yeah, downstairs.

JOANNA: Yes. Dance.

CHARLIE: Yeah.

(*She begins to dance.*)

Oh, jeez; yeah, you don't gotta—

JOANNA: Dance.

CHARLIE: Yeah; naw, you—Yeah.

(JOANNA *continues to dance for him;* CHARLIE *is caught between enjoying this and being uncomfortable. While she dances for him:*)

You got nice hair. I, uh—I, I, I, I like your hair—Uh—

(*She takes up his hands, places them on her hips.*)

Soon as I get home, I'm'a get a, a grilled cheese sandwich, this place back home? Rudy's? S'a diner, s'a—Onion rings, soda, fries, pickle, ev-everything . . . You ever have grilled cheese . . . ?

(*He trails off. She doesn't respond, simply continues to dance.*)

You wanna go out later? There's a movie playing over at the base; you wanna go maybe see a movie—?

JOANNA: Burt Lancaster.

CHARLIE: Yeah!—yeah, right, Burt—

(*She touches his face.*)

Burt Lancaster; movies—I dunno what they got, but uh, yeah—

JOANNA: Movie. Burt Lancaster.

CHARLIE: Yes—great, we will—we'll find something with Burt Lancaster in it. Great.

JOANNA: Yes.

(*She begins to remove her dress.*)

CHARLIE: Great—

(*He realizes what she is doing; he stops her.*)

Oh; no—no, you—you don't gotta—no, it's all right—

(*He takes her by the hips and stops her motion.*)

JOANNA: Dance—

CHARLIE: No. No, not yet, not—

JOANNA: You—

CHARLIE: No, please. No. It's fine; I don't—I don't wanna see you dance.

(*She looks at him.*)

JOANNA: Half hour—

CHARLIE: Yeah, no, I know—

(*She stops; they look at each other.*)

JOANNA: No dancing.

CHARLIE: No.

(*Long awkward silence.*)

I'm from Jersey. New Jersey?—back in the States—?

(*Moment. She smiles.*)

Jersey . . . ? You—?

JOANNA: (*Pretending.*) *Oh!*

CHARLIE: Yeah; yeah, naw, it's all right.

JOANNA: *Jer-sey.*

CHARLIE: Yeah.

JOANNA: Nice.

CHARLIE: Yep.

JOANNA: Cigarette? Thank you—

CHARLIE: Oh; right—sure—Sorry—

(*He gives her a cigarette, lights it for her. She smiles, indicates the cigarette.*)

JOANNA: Luckies—

CHARLIE: Yeah; right— (*As if telling a light, upbeat, funny story.*) Yeah, naw, but—there's this guy I work with—back home— Lenny. Drives a truck; for the pound? Found some mutt over down at the slaughterhouse—thing all beat up.

We go back behind this diner, and the guys, they all, they held him down—the dog. Things goin' nuts, yanno—eyes all swelled up and screamin'; Lenny, everyone's just laughin.' I was just sittin,' back a' the alley, yanno. I mean, I just gave 'im a kick or somethin', just yanno once or—But I didn't—do anything else . . .

(*He laughs nervously.*)

Those guys—Lenny and them—

(*A short little laugh; it dies. She smiles, runs her hand through his hair again.*)

JOANNA: Marine.

(*She strokes his hair. Moment of something actually quite tender, soft, and vulnerable. She kisses him, full on the mouth. He draws back.*)

CHARLIE: Your—cigarettes—you, you taste—your mouth—like cigarettes . . .

JOANNA: Half hour—

CHARLIE: I know. I know.

(*Moment.*)

Just, just one second; just—

JOANNA: Semper fi—

(*He shakes his head "no"; she smokes. He looks at her.*)

CHARLIE: You're very pretty, very—I dunno—

(*He gives a little breathless laugh; he looks down at his hands in his lap. Slight moment. JOANNA moves her hands so that their palms are pressed together. Moment.*)

You have lovely hands; your hands—they're . . . lovely . . .

JOANNA: *Han*-ds.

CHARLIE: Hand—this; this is your hand—

JOANNA: Hand.

CHARLIE: Good—

(*He smiles. She smiles. He gently touches just below her eye.*)

Uh; eyes—?

JOANNA: Eyes.

(*He touches her nose.*)

CHARLIE: Nose—

JOANNA: Nose—

(*He touches by her mouth.*)

CHARLIE: Your mouth.

JOANNA: Your—mouth.

(*His fingers stay by her mouth. He looks closer at her face.*)

CHARLIE: How old are you? Hey. Hey, how old—how old are you?

(*Nothing.*)

You're very; you're small. Very little.

JOANNA: Dance.

CHARLIE: You were a lot taller in those shoes.

JOANNA: Nice shoes.

CHARLIE: Yeah, no, they were great; I really, I really liked them.

JOANNA: Nice.

CHARLIE: Yeah. Very nice shoes.

(*Moment.*)

Are you old enough for this?

(*Moment.*)

JOANNA: Money.

CHARLIE: Yeah.

JOANNA: First.

CHARLIE: No, I know.

(*He gets out his wallet and gives her a bill or two. She puts it in her dresser, turns to him, and puts out her hand.*)

JOANNA: Joanna.

CHARLIE: Oh, yeah. Yeah, no, I—Yeah. I'm Charlie.

(*They shake hands.*)

JOANNA: Charlie.

CHARLIE: Yeah.

JOANNA: Charlie.

CHARLIE: Yeah. Joanna.

JOANNA: Yes.

CHARLIE: Great.

(*Moment as she stands before him: silence.* JOANNA *touches his face. He laughs nervously, averts his eyes. She takes his hands, places them on her hips, drawing herself in close, and puts her arms around his shoulders. Moment.* JOANNA *kisses* CHARLIE.

Moment. CHARLIE *kisses* JOANNA. *Moment. She kisses him again—he does not draw away; she begins to run her hand along his leg, moving toward his belt. He stops her.*)

No—no, please; no—I. Please. Thank you. I just—no. Thank you. Not yet; just—

JOANNA: Half hour—

CHARLIE: I know; I just, I mean, yanno, I don't really, I don't do this much—I mean I uh, I'm—I'm not a cherry or a—or, or, or, or, or, or, or a sissy or somethin', I just, I mean—I, uh—

(*He laughs breathlessly at this.*)

Yanno?

(*Awkward moment. He sees the radio, then suddenly goes to it.*)

This is a nice—this is nice. Where'd you get this?

(*Moment.*)

Where'd you get this? The radio?

JOANNA: A boy.

CHARLIE: Oh. Yeah. Yeah; they, uh, they got a tower nearby; on the base—play some good songs—Can I, uh—?

(*He motions turning on the radio. She agrees; he turns it on. "My Funny Valentine" by Chet Baker plays. Moment, as they listen; he moves to the middle of the room, holds out his arms.*)

You wanna dance?

(*Moment; she does nothing.*)

You, uh, you . . .

(*He makes another gesture; she goes to him and just stands in front of him, very close. He takes her into his arms in a dancing stance and she slowly puts her arms on his shoulders. They begin to dance, rocking back and forth slowly.* CHARLIE *begins to sing, picking up somewhere in the middle of the song, out of tune, soft and guardedly.*

Their dancing slows with the end of the song. They stand, holding each other. Moment; she kisses him; he kisses back—he stops suddenly. CHARLIE *pulls back and studies her face; he begins again with all the more fervor. They go to the bed; they kiss,* CHARLIE *runs his hand through her hair. As the passion escalates, he buries himself in her neck, going lower and lower, until he is hugging her midsection, his eyes clenched shut. His hand wraps blindly through her hair, and clenches it into a knot.* CHARLIE *holds her tightly, in an awkward and confused embrace, desperate to keep their bodies together.* JOANNA *panics and begins screaming in Korean; eventually something clicks inside of* CHARLIE, *who opens his eyes and releases her immediately. She scrambles off the bed, as does he, his hands instantly up in surrender.*)

CHARLIE: I'm sorry, I'm—!

JOANNA: Leave!

CHARLIE: No, I'm—!

(*She moves to the door, and calls out.*)

JOANNA: *Jae Suk Ah!*

(CHARLIE *dumps a mess of crumpled dirty bills onto the bed, undoes his watch, takes off a ring, dumps his cigarettes—giving her everything.*)

CHARLIE: No, no, no, no, no! I'm sorry! I'm sorry. It's okay, it's okay—I'm sorry. I'm sorry—I'm . . .

(*He retreats to the opposite side of the room;* JOANNA *watches him cagily. They stare at each other—long tense moment; the radio plays . . . . But the lure of so much money is too much for her; she comes forward slowly with great trepidation, their eyes locked the entire time. She scoops up his money and valuables, puts them in the dresser.*

JOANNA *shuts off the radio. Silence; she turns to him, stares. He tries to meet her gaze.*)

JOANNA: You don't—no more.

CHARLIE: I'm sorry, I'm—

JOANNA: No *touch*; you—*no touch.*

CHARLIE: No, I know. I'm fine—I'll be okay. I promise—

(*She gestures with the money.*)

JOANNA: Mine.

CHARLIE: No, yeah, yours, all yours. You keep it.

(*Moment.*)

I'm sorry, I uh . . .

(*Silence. Long moment. Regarding the gum that he's left on her bed along with all of his possessions:*)

Could I get some gum? I had some gum—my pocket—? My mom—she always says, "Gum"—she always says—"it is always good to have a little gum, Charlie, 'cause y'never know if your breath smells . . ."

(*He trails off. Silence.*)

The—the gum?

(*She ignores him. Silence. He spots the edition of* Mother Goose *still on the bed. He picks it up, looking at it. She smokes, watching him, off to one side, still wary.*)

JOANNA: *Mother Goose.*

(CHARLIE *nods, puts the book down. Silence.*)

CHARLIE: Hey, uh, you mind—you put that cigarette out?

(*Nothing.*)

The cigarette. You put it out?

(*Moment.*)

The smell, it—I; it just it makes me—I was in Kusong; I don't—

JOANNA: (*Points at him.*) Kusong.

(*He gives a small nod, looks down at his hands. Slight moment.*)

CHARLIE: You got lovely eyes; dark, and—like . . . crow feathers, or . . . I dunno . . . They're lovely.

(*He gives a short breathless laugh, stopping himself.*)

You see a lotta guys? Lotta . . . ?

(*She points at him.*)

JOANNA: Marine.

CHARLIE: Yeah, no, but do you—do you see a lotta boys; lotta men?

JOANNA: Semper fi. Yes.

CHARLIE: No, I know, but how many guys? How many guys do you—? How many—?

JOANNA: Yes.

CHARLIE: I—

JOANNA: Marine—

CHARLIE: No; stop saying Marine! Stop, please—I don't wanna—I don't wanna hear Marine.

(JOANNA *stares at him simply.*)

I don't wanna hear Marine.

(*She continues to stare simply. Gestures to his tattoo.*)

JOANNA: Semper fi.

(*He looks down at the ground. Then:*)

CHARLIE: What's your real name? Joanna; I just—I just wanna know your real name.

(JOANNA *just nods.*)

JOANNA: Joanna.

(*He looks at her. A small, sad smile.*)

CHARLIE: You don't—none a' this, you—

(*Slight moment.*)

I am the president of the United States of America.

(*Sad little breathless laugh.*)

Yeah—I dunno; I dunno . . .

(*Another breathless laugh. He falls silent. Long moment. Suddenly:*)

I haven't been able to be with a woman in eight months. I haven't—my body, it don't work—I'm . . . Since we got here, since . . .

(*He regards her.*)

You not look at me? Please—you—?

(*She just stares at him, uncomprehending.*)

Please.

(*She doesn't understand and continues to stare. He fiddles with the covers on the bed.*)

She was fifteen—sixteen. Her village; two miles off from where we got stationed. Very pretty, very—tiny; really very small. Pretty eyes.

(*Moment.*)

I didn't do anything; I mean those guys, they—but, I didn't. I didn't.

(*Moment.*)

Her hair, I—I could smell her hair . . . and . . . —I felt her arms break—try'n' to get off that table. Just . . .

(*Moment.*)

Those guys, they left her a fuckin' pile.

(*Moment.*)

I stood up, they all laughed . . . I—I puked. All over myself.
I don't even remember.

(*Moment.*)

I didn't—I didn't touch—her; like that. I didn't . . .

(*Moment. He looks up at* JOANNA.)

They shot her.

(*Moment. He stares at her.*)

You kinda . . . the hair, yanno? The eyes.

(*He locks eyes with her and reaches out to touch her. She shies away.*)

No. No, I don't—I don't want that; I just . . . Just your skin.
That's all.

(*She hesitates, then lets him caress her face. He begins to cry and curls into
a ball on the bed; she sits down and places his head in her lap.* JOANNA
strokes his hair and smokes. Sings in a simple, dull near-monotone.)

JOANNA: *Jack and Jill went up the hill*
To fetch a pail of water.
Jack fell down and broke his crown,
And Jill came tumbling after.

(*Moment.*)

Jack and Jill went up the hill
To fetch a pail of water.
Jack fell down and broke his crown,
And Jill came tumbling after.

(Moment.)

Jack and Jill went up the hill . . .

(She sings the one line over and over as he cries. Lights fade to black.)

END OF PLAY

THE GIFT

Simon Fill

The Gift was first presented by Skeleton Key Theatre Company (Simon Fill, Julie Hamberg, Robert V. Hannsman, Shawn Hirabayashi, Frank Pisco, founding members) at the Nada Theater, New York City, on April 18, 1996. Julie Hamberg directed the following cast:

JONES	Andrea Maulella
JOHN	Ernesto Barrios

The play was later produced by the Lab Theater Company (Michael Warren Powell, artistic director) in residence at the West Bank Cafe, New York City, on April 30, 1997. Emily Tetzlaff directed the following cast:

JONES	Carrena Lukas
JOHN	Brad Newman

CHARACTERS
JONES, a sixteen-year-old girl
JOHN, a seventeen-year-old boy

TIME
The present.

LOCATION
A concrete park in Manhattan.

Darkness. A loud crush of hard-core punk music. Lights up. A teenage boy and girl sit in a small concrete park, somewhere in Manhattan. The boy wears glasses. JONES *looks at* JOHN *as he takes out a stick of beef jerky. Silence.*

JONES: Like, that sucks.

JOHN: Tell me about it. The whole world is some kind of tortured experience. I mean, look at Sophie. She's beautiful. Her dad's CEO of some corporation, like, it doesn't even do anything. It exists to own other corporations. She's got honors. Every guy in the school wants to go out with her. She's been with Rick since ninth grade. He never cheated on her. I know. I played handball with him. He, like, loves her. Fuck. She's a good person. *I* even like her. So. What does she do? She ODs on pills.

(Pause.)

What's up with that?

JONES: Why would anyone do that?

(Silence.)

Is her sister okay?

JOHN: Phoebe? I don't know. Her parents got her a horse or something.

(*Beat.*)

JONES: I can't believe I never met you before today.

JOHN: Do you always cut school?

JONES: Sometimes.

JOHN: Me, too. If I hadn't seen you outsida Jerry's Bagel's . . .

JONES: How'd you know I went to St. Joe's?

JOHN: You looked uptight.

JONES: Oh.

JOHN: But you aren't.

JONES: Oh.

JOHN: Like, have you got a boyfriend?

(*Pause.*)

JONES: Not in over a year.

JOHN: Nothing happens.

JONES: Jerry's Bagel's. With an apostrophe on the "bagel's."

JOHN: Didya ever understand why?

JONES: Like, it's definitely disturbing. Jerry's bagel's what? I mean, duh.

JOHN: Duh.

JONES: Duh.

JOHN: Duh.

JONES: Duh.

JOHN: Duh.

(*They crack up.*)

JONES: You're funny.

(*Pause.*)

And . . . gentle.

(*Silence.*)

JOHN: Wow. Is it hot or something? Wow. This jerky bites.

(*He throws the jerky down, takes a tissue from his wallet.*)

JONES: You bit it.

JOHN: What?

JONES: The jerky.

JOHN: I did.

JONES: Yeah.

(*Silence. She grabs his wallet, dances around, looks at a card from it.*)

Oooo! J. E. Filbert. Big man with a driver's license.

JOHN: Know what they gave my test in? A Ford Aspire. I drove
    perfect. At the end, I go, "What's the exam in next year, a
    Mitsubishi Envy?" The tester failed me!

JONES: No!

JOHN: Yeah! She made me take it again a month later!

JONES: That is the *worst* thing I ever heard!

JOHN: I know!

(*She hands the wallet back. Silence.*)

JONES: I can't wait till I'm seventeen.

JOHN: It's not too different from sixteen.

JONES: No. I mean, time. That saying. 'Bout time. How it gets rid of all wounds.

JOHN: Maybe. I don't know.

JONES: Oh.

(*Pause.*)

   John?

JOHN: Yeah?

JONES: Like, do you think I'm . . . like . . . pretty?

JOHN: (*Softly, about her.*) This morning I was up at five a.m. I sat on my brother's roof. It was just light out. I saw a blue heron. I thought, what's a blue heron doing flying over Manhattan? It must be lost. It was alone. It looked so beautiful.

(*Silence.*)

JONES: You okay?

JOHN: Yeah.

JONES: Sure?

JOHN: Yeah. It'll be winter soon.

JONES: I'm cold.

(*Pause. To self.*)

  As in, "I'm a leaf that drops in autumn."

JOHN: Like, "The smallest sorrow is the longest breath, and each
    room I walk through is an absence."

JONES: Wow. Did you write that?

JOHN: Yeah. Whatever.

(*Pause.*)

  Jones. Why don't you have a boyfriend?

JONES: Why don't you have a girlfriend?

JOHN: I wear glasses.

JONES: I don't get it.

JOHN: Wow. It's so cold, but the sky is so clear. Everything is,
    like, up close and far away.

JONES: John?

(*Pause.*)

  The last boyfriend I had . . . like, it was . . . Jon Crispin.

(*Silence.*)

JOHN: Wow. That's so heavy.

(*Pause.*)

    Were you sad when he died?

JONES: Your boyfriend jumps off a highway overpass into oncoming traffic? Yeah, I think I was sad when he died?

JOHN: Did you know he was gonna do it?

JONES: Actually, we sat down together the night before and planned it carefully so it would go off smoothly. What! Are you retarded or something!

JOHN: I'm sorry. I'm kinda still a little buzzed . . . from that joint we had in fronta the museum.

(*Pause.*)

JONES: I like dinosaurs.

JOHN: Yeah.

(*She cracks up.*)

JONES: I can't believe you almost got us busted.

JOHN: What?

JONES: A *Tyrannosaurus rex* does not have a wishbone.

JOHN: I had to see up close.

JONES: WHY?

JOHN: I wanted to make a wish.

(*They crack up.*)

So. Like, what was up with Jon Crispin?

JONES: Oh.

JOHN: I mean, are you okay?

JONES: You're the first person I ever told.

JOHN: I am?

(*Pause.*)

That's so dope.

JONES: Really?

JOHN: For sure. I'm, like, honored.

(*Pause.*)

JONES: Really?

JOHN: Definitely. It's, like, you trust me.

JONES: Maybe I do!

JOHN: You shouldn't . . .

JONES: John?

JOHN: . . . trust me.

(*Silence.*)

JONES: John?

(*Pause.*)

Do you want to tell me something?

JOHN: What was Jon like before he died?

(*Pause.*)

JONES: I'm . . . not sure.

JOHN: I think it's gonna rain pretty soon.

JONES: Maybe it'll snow.

JOHN: Maybe.

JONES: I gotta buy a hat.

JOHN: Sure.

JONES: For the snow.

(*Silence.*)

JOHN: Jones.

JONES: He wasn't like anything.

JOHN: It's chill.

JONES: We'd only known each other, like, three weeks. And we'd just started like, you know, like, doing it. He was quiet. But he said he loved me. Then, you know, like, we started doing it more, he got more and more intense about it, and my whole body was . . . air. Every moment we had we'd be doing it. I loved him, he loved me. And I was . . . air. Then the air blew away. He was gone.

(*Pause.*)

I thought he was lovin' me more. I thought he was happy. That's why he wanted to so much. But he was usin' me to hold on to life. And the string broke with no sound.

(*Silence.*)

I'm sorry. I oughta go.

JOHN: Don't.

JONES: Know what I wrote in my diary? "I walked on the edges
of someone else's sadness." But I should've known something, don't you see? His laugh sounded to me just . . . like
a laugh.

(*Silence.*)

JOHN: Know what my brother would say if I told him that story?

JONES: What?

JOHN: Yo, man. You bringin' me down.

(*They crack up.*)

JONES: As in, what's his name?

JOHN: Who?

JONES: Your brother.

JOHN: Delbert.

JONES: Delbert Filbert.

JOHN: It's not the greatest name. His whole life has been an
attempt to compensate.

JONES: What does he do?

JOHN: He's an investment banker.

(*Pause.*)

I live with him, but he's never home. Our parents . . . I didn't even know what they were doing . . . they died, like, two years ago, in a car.

JONES: No shit! Me, too. Like, my mom died when I was five. Then my father ran away when I was seven.

JOHN: Gee. That's terrific.

(*Pause.*)

This is like, if the Little Rascals were totally depressed.

(*Beat.*)

JONES: John. How do you learn to love someone when you think they could just disappear, like that. When you're scared you don't know what's going on in their head. How do you *know* someone?

JOHN: Wait a second. Hello? Do I look like someone who would have the answer to that? Like, am I a talk show? I don't think so.

JONES: Jon was the only boyfriend I ever had.

(*Pause.*)

JOHN: I'm sorry, Jones. I really am.

JONES: I really like you.

(*Silence.*)

JOHN: It isn't a good idea.

JONES: Why?

JOHN: You wouldn't if you knew me.

JONES: You look so . . . vacant.

JOHN: Who do you live with?

JONES: My aunt.

JOHN: Oh.

JONES: John?

JOHN: I'm sorry, Jones. Like, I gotta go. Take good care of yourself, 'kay? This bites. I'm so sorry.

(*Pause.*)

It isn't your fault.

(*Pause.*)

People aren't responsible for what other people do.

JONES: What, are you gonna throw yourself in front of a Toyota? (*Beat. A slow realization.*) Oh my God.

JOHN: . . . If I'd known . . .

JONES: Why?

JOHN: . . . I swear . . .

JONES: You don't got any parents either.

JOHN: . . . Oh, it doesn't matter . . .

JONES: This is not hilarious.

(*Pause.*)

JOHN: It never was.

(*Silence.*)

JONES: It isn't serious if you don't know how.

JOHN: Tonight. The Empire State Building. After everyone's gone. A mop closet I can hide in. One in the morning.

JONES: As in, "Do you want me to compliment your organizational skills!"

JOHN: Not even. You're not supposed to be here.

JONES: You told me you don't believe in God. Doesn't the idea of nothing . . . scare you?

JOHN: Whatever.

(*Pause.*)

    Right?

(*Silence.*)

JONES: Boy, if this gets out, no guy's ever gonna wanna go out with me.

JOHN: Maybe they will. It's a challenge. Like the drummer always dying in a great rock band.

JONES: I never even kissed you.

(*She does.*)

    Wow. Like, I always thought everyone I knew was gonna live until they were old, like forty.

(*Pause.*)

John, why're you gonna do it?

JOHN: Lookit life. It's like, every day I come to school the prin-
cipal's like, "What's up, John?" He's a good guy. He hits me
in the arm. This means something to him, like we're buds.
He's been doin' it two years, since my parents died. Like, my
arm's gonna fuckin' fall off.

JONES: This is a reason to kill yourself?

JOHN: It's part of a bigger picture. Nothing happens. Fuck. Look.
You know. It's like, "our lives."

JONES: That's bullshit.

JOHN: It is, isn't it?

JONES: I mean, you.

(*Pause.*)

JOHN: I don't get it.

JONES: The sky is so gray now. (*To self.*) I guess I'll be watching
it alone tomorrow morning.

JOHN: Look. Up there. There's a patch of clear.

JONES: It's gone. (*Beat.*) 'Cause you don't control what occurs to
you, it doesn't make the sky mean any more or less.

(*Pause.*)

Even if it did, it's only the sky.

(*Silence.*)

JOHN: We can't hear Columbus Avenue from this park.

JONES: I've never been here before.

JOHN: Oh.

(*Pause.*)

I'd say you could think of this as "our place," but I guess that's kind of a bummer.

(*Pause.*)

My father used to smoke cigarettes here. When I was a kid. For sure. He'd drop butts all over.

JONES: Like, he sounds "excessive." Don't you love that word? I've adopted it. As in, "He touched her arm. Did he know what he was getting into? She was so exquisitely . . . *excessive.*"

(*They crack up.*)

You were close to him.

(*Silence.*)

John?

JOHN: . . . No.

(*Silence.*)

He was an engineer. He invented a new needle for sewing machines. He had an office at Eighty-Sixth and Columbus.

JONES: He must've loved your mother.

JOHN: How come?

JONES: I don't know. I just like to think it.

(*Pause.*)

What's up?

(*Pause.*)

The sky is so still.

JOHN: Nothing happens.

JONES: I'm tired of people telling me when I get older I'll understand. I understand enough. Everything sucks.

JOHN: Like, sometimes I think that's what the newspaper should be. One sheet of paper, notebook size, blank. Except on top, in print so tiny it hurts you to read it, it says . . . "Bite me."

(*Pause. They laugh.*)

JONES: John?

(*Pause.*)

You ever in love with someone?

JOHN: . . . No.

(*Silence.*)

JONES: Best friend?

(*Silence.*)

JOHN: Sure. Before I came to St. Joe's. At Brickly. Seventh grade.

JONES: What happened?

JOHN: He got messed up . . . He found a diary.

(*Pause.*)

Edward. I used to hang at his apartment a lot. In Chelsea—I
could board there from Delbert's. Like, it was a fucked-up
situation. So. It's in some books his mom asks him to toss.
She owned a used bookstore when he was born—and kept
a lot of the shit after it closed. Sometimes people'd leave
their private stuff in what they sold her. So. I open this old
diary—and the first thing I read is, "January twelfth. Boiled
an egg for breakfast." Like, it's the whole entry for January twelfth. It's, like, hilarious. We crack up. Then, "January eighteenth. A catastrophe of onions." A catastrophe of
onions? I mean, please. What does that mean? We're, like,
totally losing it. Then, "January twenty-first. I could never
love this boy. I wish it'd never been born." We're, like, "Not
only is this writer unbalanced, he or she's an asshole, too."
He's laughing, I'm laughing. Then he's, like, looking to see
who wrote this, if there's a name inside.

(*Pause.*)

His mom wrote it when he was four years old.

(*Silence.*)

JONES: (*Stunned.*) Time to give the babysitter some credit, eh?

JOHN: It explained why his mother'd always been cold to him,
though he didn't really know why. After that, he didn't want
to hang out with me so much. It's, like, he associated me
with something he never wanted to know. But we did have
coffee once. It was hilarious. I thought, "We're about to have
coffee, like grown-ups." Then I was like, "Wow. Coffee tastes
like shit. What is up with older people?" He told me he was
trying to see his father, his parents split when he was two.
You see, his father'd stopped seeing him when he was, like,

eleven. The mother said the dad was busy, and it sort of just trickled out. I thought, "This is tragic, I should pay for the coffees." So. It's four years since he's seen his father, and he's trying to hang in his father's neighborhood. One day, he walks into someone. He looks up. It's his father. He thinks, "This is great." Then his father looks worried and goes, "Are you lost?"

(*Pause.*)

He didn't even know who Edward was.

(*Silence.*)

JONES: Sometimes you're an orphan and your parents are still alive.

(*Silence.*)

Did you ever feel you knew someone before, but you never met them?

(*Little pause.*)

It's like, I looked at your eyes this morning, and I could see my eyes looking at your eyes. It's not like that with most people.

(*Pause.*)

That's the thing I don't get. Was I, like, responsible for Jon Crispin or not? I mean, it's not like people are alone or something.

(*Pause.*)

You cared about your friend, didn't you?

JOHN: It got boring.

JONES: That's mean.

JOHN: Why do you put a judgment on everything!

JONES: 'Cause the world has got a lot of judging coming to it!

JOHN: (*Beat. Understands.*) Oh.

(*Pause.*)

JONES: I mean, you don't say that about someone you love!

JOHN: I'm sorry, okay!

JONES: It's like, he needed you and you split!

JOHN: He was a downer!

JONES: Oh, that's nice!

JOHN: Maybe he wasn't lovable!

JONES: What, did he have braces or something!

JOHN: He had glasses!

(*Silence.*)

JONES: (*To self.*) He had glasses.

(*Silence.*)

    John?

(*Silence.*)

John? Could I ask you something?

JOHN: I don't know.

(*Silence.*)

JONES: What's your middle name?

(*Silence.*)

What is it, John?

(*Silence.*)

JOHN: Edward.

(*Silence.*)

Oh.

(*Silence.*)

How could you love someone when you've never been loved?

(*Silence.*)

JONES: (*To self.*) We're all alone, aren't we? Each of us is by ourselves.

(*Silence.*)

JOHN: Do you think things are different in Sweden?

JONES: They're worse.

(*Pause.*)

It's getting colder.

JOHN: I know.

JONES: Could you be next to someone and miss them?

(*Silence.*)

John? John?

JOHN: Yeah?

JONES: (*Beat.*) Will you watch the day begin with me tomorrow?

JOHN: Sure.

(*Pause. They smile, move closer to each other.*)

JOHN: The sky. Nothing's happening.

JONES: It's beautiful, John.

JOHN: Nothing's happening.

JONES: It's beautiful.

(*Fade lights.*)

END OF PLAY

HAIL CAESAR!

Michael Mitnick

Hail Caesar! premiered on January 20, 2010, at the Yale School of Drama. The cast was as follows:

WILL	Will Connolly
TALI	Rachel Spencer

SETTING
A white-tablecloth restaurant.
Dinnertime.

TALI: Are you still waiting for someone?

WILL: Waiting for someone?

TALI: I mean. Are you dining alone tonight?

WILL: I can't come to an expensive restaurant and eat a meal by myself?

TALI: No—you can. You are. You will be.

WILL: Sometimes my food and I like to be alone with each other.

(*Pause.*)

TALI: So . . . I'm Tali. I'll be your waiter this evening.

WILL: I'm Will and I'll be the guy ordering.

That's kind of funny.

Ordering.

Isn't a very polite term, is it?

I *order* you to bring me . . . ah . . . bring me a thick piece of lamb! I *order* you to bring it to me! Did you not hear my *order*?! I *ordered* lamb, this is fish!

(*Pause.*)

THAT IS MY ORDER!

(*Pause.*)

TALI: So . . . you want lamb?

WILL: No, I'm a vegetarian. I was just riffing.

TALI: So . . . what would you like?

WILL: What do you recommend?

TALI: Well, for vegetarians, you gotta get the Artichoke Risotto—very popular. Meat eaters even order it as their entrée. It's my personal favorite too. Really delicious, very filling, but you don't leave feeling like, *weighed down*, you know? It is just a satisfying full-ness. Yeah, I'd definitely say the Risotto, by far.

WILL: I'll have the Caesar salad.

And bring some bread. Lots of bread.

TALI: Right away.

(*She walks away.*)

WILL: Yes—Bring Caesar his Salad! The Great Caesar has ordered his Salad! You know, that Caesar guy—he really had it all figured out.

(*She pauses when she hears him—awkwardly caught between his lingering conversation and the kitchen.*)

That's probably why they put him in charge, don't you think? Because he had it all figured out.

(*She walks a bit back toward him.*)

TALI: Wait.

Are you still talking to me?

WILL: Unless there's someone else in this empty chair. So, yeah, that Caesar guy. Totally amazing. Look—

(*Starts counting on his fingers.*)

He got a *salad* named after him.

A *Caesar* salad?

TALI: Yes.

WILL: He got the whole month of July.

Named after his first name.

Julius.

TALI: Right.

WILL: Not to mention Orange Julius, a national chain of fruit beverages.

Also—oh! oh! oh! oh! oh! oh! oh!—Caesarean SECTIONS.

When you cut open a woman's belly and pull out a baby.

TALI: Yes, I know what a Caesarean section is.

WILL: Man, what a lucky guy.

TALI: Right.

And he also was surrounded by sixty Roman men who stabbed him twenty-three times until he bled to death.

WILL: So I'm gonna go with the *Greek* salad.

TALI: And a lot of the free bread, right?

WILL: *Exactly.*

You're a fantastic listener.

Wait!

And, also, in movies whenever the king wants to capture a woman who has wronged him, he cries out to his guards, "Guards . . . *Caeeeeesar!*"

TALI: What?

WILL: You know . . . "Caeeeeesar!"

Even the British kings respected him.

TALI: They were saying, "Seize her."

"Seize."

"*Seize* her."

WILL: Oh.

Well.

That makes a little more sense.

TALI: I'm gonna go put in your order.

WILL: Wait!

Listen. I think I owe you an apology.

I feel like there's all this weird baggage between us.

TALI: Weird baggage?

WILL: —Between us. Yeah. You feel it too. Right.

I'm kind of . . . well . . . I've had a heck of a day.

So I want to apologize if I seem, I dunno, like, a little looney. A little *off.*

TALI: No. It's fine. I'm gonna go put in your—

WILL: Do you want to know what happened to me, Tali?

TALI: Oh good, you remember my name.

WILL: Of course I remembered it. I remember everything you ever said to me.

Oh crud—that's not supposed to be creepy. I just have a photographic memory.

So, don't take that the wrong way.

I will remember even what you LOOK LIKE, exactly, precisely, each little detail.

Like, tonight, when I'm lying in bed—

TALI: Jesus Christ—

WILL: Trying to fall asleep, I'll remember you.

Perfectly.

Anyway, my girlfriend and I . . . man . . . what's the best way to put this . . .

TALI: Broke up?

WILL: *Broke up.* That's . . . yeah . . . that's awesome. That's a great metaphor for it. *Broke up.*

Like we were once one solid thing and then it broke up into pieces. Namely, two.

Broke into *two pieces.*

(*Long pause.*)

TALI: Are . . . are you okay?

WILL: Hm?

TALI: I said.

I wondered.

Are you okay?

WILL: Yeah. I just. I really loved her.

TALI: That's really sweet.

WILL: Thanks.

TALI: What was her name?

WILL: *Was?* She's not *dead*. She just broke up with me, to use your nice metaphor.

TALI: Fine. What is her name?

WILL: I mean. She *could* be dead right now. I don't know. We haven't spoken since lunch.

Though when you die, you still have a name. Your name doesn't go away once you die. So why would you say,

"My dead husband's name was Louis." His name is STILL Louis.

TALI: I guess that's true. I mean, the First President of the United States IS George Washington. Not, the First President *was* George Washington. That hasn't changed.

WILL: Oh, I see what you're saying.

You think that Beth is dead.

You think that my ex-girlfriend is now dead.

TALI: No, of course not.

WILL: Me neither.

I mean, it's unlikely.

Unless she put the key in the ignition of her car already, but she doesn't drive it, except on Sundays.

(*Silence.*)

Would you go out with me?

TALI: Would I go out with you?

WILL: Yeah. Would you go out with me?

(*Silence. Then,* TALI *smiles.*)

TALI: Well.

Sure, I guess.

You talk a lot, but it's sort of funny.

Yeah, I'm sure I'll regret this but . . .

Yeah. Yes, I'll go out with you.

WILL: What?

No, I just wanted to know if you *would*. See—that's what's so crazy about *Beth*. She was all like, "I don't know why I ever went out with you. No one in her right mind would ever go out with you." But you're obviously not nuts, I don't think, I mean, that's a weird hair thing you've got going on, but it's not an indication that you're . . . like . . . clinically INSANE. Just misguided. Fashion-challenged.

TALI: I'm gonna go get your salad.

(*She marches off.*)

WILL: Yes!

For that is what I have ordered!

A Greek Salad!

Oh, and can you wrap it up to go?

With the bread.

Man.

I can't believe Beth is dead.

END OF PLAY

HEARING AID

Pete Barry

CHARACTERS
OLD WOMAN, seventies
OLD MAN, seventies

For
Andrew,
James,
Meem,
and my mother
(who would hear this dedication as "ankle-chain meat thermometer")

In the darkness, two loud, competing noises: a drippingly melodra-matic TV show and Bach's Goldberg Variations.

Lights. OLD WOMAN *and* OLD MAN, *in easy chairs. She listens to the radio, her ear up against the speaker. He watches TV, squinting.*

OLD WOMAN *turns the music down a little. She removes her hearing aid and checks it.*

OLD WOMAN: Battery's dead.

OLD MAN: Is he? I knew he'd come to no good.

OLD WOMAN: What?

OLD MAN: What'd they do, shoot him?

OLD WOMAN: (*Indicating the radio.*) It's not Schubert, it's Bach.

OLD MAN: Who's back?

OLD WOMAN: Whose back? Your back?

OLD MAN: (*Indicating the TV.*) Jerry Orbach hasn't been on for years. This is *CSI.*

OLD WOMAN: See whose eye?

OLD MAN: No, I haven't seen José. I thought you were talking about Barry.

OLD WOMAN: I was what?

OLD MAN: You said "Barry's dead."

OLD WOMAN: It's nothing to be embarrassed about, your back.

OLD MAN: I'm not harassing you about it. I'm just asking.

OLD WOMAN: You get old, things don't work so well anymore.

(*The* OLD WOMAN *turns off the radio.*)

OLD MAN: Ah, come on, now, I missed half of what this girl was talking about. I can't figure this show out.

OLD WOMAN: I'd better go make dinner.

(*She starts off toward the kitchen.*)

OLD MAN: If you're going in the kitchen, bring me a cold Heineken.

(*She shoots him a quizzical look.*)

OLD WOMAN: What?

OLD MAN: Wouldja just bring me a Heineken?

OLD WOMAN: What for?

OLD MAN: Not four! Just one!

OLD WOMAN: I'm going as fast as I can.

OLD MAN: What d'ya think I am, some kind of alcoholic?

(*She goes. He yells at the TV.*)

I can't watch this garbage anymore. I'm gonna do the crossword.

(*He switches off the TV and procures the newspaper and a pencil. He counts.*)

Thirteen? Hey! Thirteen letters! What's a thirteen-letter word for "nearly deaf"?

OLD WOMAN: (*Off.*) What's the question?

OLD MAN: NEARLY DEAF!

OLD WOMAN: (*Off.*) "BANK OF AMERICA"!

(*Pause.*)

OLD MAN: Well, it's thirteen letters.

(*She returns, empty-handed.*)

OLD WOMAN: You shouldn't sit there watching TV all day if it's gonna make you this cranky.

OLD MAN: What happened to my beer?

OLD WOMAN: You shaved it off six months ago.

OLD MAN: You don't have to save beers. It's not like there's a shortage or something.

OLD WOMAN: It was never very long. You weren't like a Nazarene.

OLD MAN: What?

OLD WOMAN: You know, like Jesus grew it.

OLD MAN: (*Sarcastic, indignant.*) That's a real nice thing to say!

OLD WOMAN: It's historical.

OLD MAN: I'm not getting hysterical!

OLD WOMAN: What's the matter?

OLD MAN: You're crazy, that's what!

OLD WOMAN: Then turn up the thermostat!

OLD MAN: I'm like a big joke.

(*The* OLD WOMAN *seems surprised at this, but considers it. She sniffs the air.*)

A target for stray insults. A waste of space doing the crossword. Nobody even listens to a word I say. Like I'm talking to the wind.

(*The* OLD WOMAN *continues to sniff around the room. She shrugs.*)

OLD WOMAN: I don't smell anything. But I can't hear anything, either, I guess. Are you sure?

(*He stares at her, blankly. She sniffs again.*)

OLD MAN: What are you doing?

OLD WOMAN: You smelled cigar smoke?

OLD MAN: What about cigar smoke?

OLD WOMAN: You said you smell cigar smoke?

OLD MAN: WHAT ABOUT CIGAR SMOKE?

OLD WOMAN: YOU SMELL CIGAR SMOKE?

OLD MAN: I DON'T SMELL CIGAR SMOKE.

OLD WOMAN: YOU SAID YOU SMELL CIGAR SMOKE.

OLD MAN: I SAID I *DON'T* SMELL CIGAR SMOKE!

OLD WOMAN: YOU SAID YOU *DO* SMELL CIGAR SMOKE!

OLD MAN: *I SAID I DON'T SMELL CIGAR SMOKE!*

OLD WOMAN: Why are you yelling?

OLD MAN: If I don't yell you don't listen to me!

OLD WOMAN: I can't listen if you don't talk to me!

OLD MAN: I'm talking to you right now!

OLD WOMAN: You're not talking, you're yelling!

OLD MAN: What do you want me to do?

OLD WOMAN: Stop yelling and say something!

OLD MAN: Say what?

OLD WOMAN: Say anything!

OLD MAN: HOW MUCH WOOD COULD A WOOD-CHUCK CHUCK IF A WOODCHUCK COULD CHUCK WOOD!

OLD WOMAN: You don't have to be vulgar.

OLD MAN: Are you ever gonna get me a Heineken?

OLD WOMAN: Were you serious?

OLD MAN: Why would I want cereal with a Heineken? Do you mean poured over the cereal?

OLD WOMAN: Whatever you want.

OLD MAN: That's the worst thing I've ever heard of. Never mind. I'll take my cold comfort in the crossword puzzle.

(*She goes. He tries the crossword again.*)

Four down. "One-eyed Rat Packer." "Sammy." What? Seven letters. Uh. "Davis"?

No. "Junior"? What? Four down. "One-eyed Rat Packer." That's "Sammy"! What's wrong with this puzzle? Four down, "One-eyed Rat Packer"! Seven letters! Am I insane? FOUR DOWN, "ONE-EYED RAT PACKER"! Oh, four across.

(*He fills it in.*)

(OLD WOMAN *rolls in a gold-painted shop window mannequin.* OLD MAN *stares blankly at it.*)

OLD WOMAN: Were you saying you were going to design and build a four-man juice squeezer?

OLD MAN: What the hell is that?

OLD WOMAN: You asked for it.

OLD MAN: Are we opening a boutique?

OLD WOMAN: What about Little Bo Peep? Is that a clue in the crossword?

OLD MAN: So I'm doing the crossword! Is that a crime?

OLD WOMAN: You're yelling again!

OLD MAN: Does that give you the right to make a mockery of me?

OLD WOMAN: "The right maid to muck around with"? What does that mean?

OLD MAN: I'm not here for your entertainment, for your merriment!

OLD WOMAN: You made a mistake . . . marrying me?

OLD MAN: No, I don't need a steak marinade!

OLD WOMAN: 'Cause you know, I coulda done better!

OLD MAN: Oh, I'm a dumbbell, am I?

OLD WOMAN: You don't appreciate what you've got!

OLD MAN: Oh, I'm a breezy-eight used car, am I?

OLD WOMAN: You'd be lost without me! You'd destroy the closets, burn the laundry, shatter the glasses, let mold grow everywhere! You'd call strange people at all hours of the night! You'd spin out of control! You wouldn't get a nice dinner, I'll tell you that! You can't even make a fried egg!

OLD MAN: Shows what you know! It's not Friday! It's Thursday!

OLD WOMAN: If you're thirsty, then go get yourself a Heineken!

(*She collapses in tears.*)

OLD MAN: Hey. Hey now. What's wrong?

OLD WOMAN: This marriage is not working anymore. After forty-two years, it breaks my heart to say it. We don't communicate. I'm leaving.

OLD MAN: If you're freezing, then turn up the thermostat.

(*She gets up to leave.*)

Wait! Wait a minute.

(*She stops.*)

There's something wrong here and I just don't understand what.

OLD WOMAN: Well I can't stand it either.

OLD MAN: We talk and the sentences don't fit together.

OLD WOMAN: It has become like a prison sentence.

OLD MAN: Everything I say gets all twisted around. Either I'm not saying what I mean or you're not hearing what I say. And I can't figure it out and it makes me hate everything.

OLD WOMAN: I can't hear what you're saying, I'm too upset.

OLD MAN: What'd you say? I didn't hear you.

(*She points to the radio.*)

OLD WOMAN: I used to love music so much. I can't hear it anymore. I hear sounds, but they're not distinct. There's no rhythm or pitch. It's all noise. It was such a joyous part of my life and now it's gone. It's infuriating. And it just makes it worse when you yell at me for something I can't help. So why should I stay, just to get yelled at?

(*He looks from her to the radio, really trying to understand, but clearly lost.*)

You can't hear a word I'm saying. Forget it.

(*She turns to leave.*)

OLD MAN: Wait!

(*She turns back. He turns on the radio.*)

OLD WOMAN: I just told you I can't hear it.

OLD MAN: What?

OLD WOMAN: I CAN'T HEAR IT!

OLD MAN: NEITHER CAN I!

(*He begins to dance. He is awkward, totally off the rhythm, but he commits to it wholeheartedly. She manages an unenthusiastic smile. He beckons to her.*)

OLD WOMAN: I can't dance to it. I can't hear it.

OLD MAN: Come on. C'mere.

(*She goes, reluctantly. They sway together. He puts his lips up to her ear. Softly.*)

Can you hear this?

OLD WOMAN: Yes.

OLD MAN: How about—

(*He whispers in her ear. She smiles.*)

OLD WOMAN: Yes.

(*He whispers again. She giggles. She whispers in his ear. He laughs, a loud hearty belly laugh.*

They engage in a merry whispering conversation while dancing to a beat totally separate from the music.

The lights drop slowly to black.)

END OF PLAY

THE KISS

Mark Harvey Levine

The Kiss was first produced as part of "Combo Platter: An Evening of Plays by Mark Harvey Levine" at ZJU Theatre in North Hollywood, California, on June 21, 2002. It was directed by Jordan Cole with the following cast:

ALLISON	Heidi Fecht
DENNIS	Jim Eshom

The Kiss received its first Equity production as part of "Cabfare for the Common Man: An Evening of Plays by Mark Harvey Levine" at the Phoenix Theatre in Indianapolis, Indiana, on May 12, 2005. It was directed by Bryan Fonseca with the following cast:

ALLISON	Megan McKinney
DENNIS	Michael Shelton

The Kiss won the People's Choice Award at the Fifth Annual InspiraTO Festival, Toronto, Ontario, Canada.

CHARACTERS

ALLISON, twenties to forties. Sweet, strong-willed, whimsical.
DENNIS, twenties to forties. A little neurotic.

ALLISON's *apartment, early evening. She is doing laundry and listening to music, and after a few seconds begins to dance and sing (loudly and badly). There's a knock at the door.* ALLISON *quickly stops singing and dancing.*

ALLISON: Hello?

DENNIS: *(O.S.)* Allison, it's me . . .

(She opens the door.)

ALLISON: Dennis? What are you doing here?

DENNIS: *(Entering.)* Do you have a second? I need your help . . .

ALLISON: Don't you have a date with Printer Lady?

DENNIS: Yeah, I'm on my way. But first I have to ask you something . . .

ALLISON: What?

DENNIS: Well . . . I don't want you to take this the wrong way, but— Can I kiss you?

ALLISON: What?!

DENNIS: . . . I need to know if I'm a good kisser.

ALLISON: *(Pause.)* . . . WHAT?!

DENNIS: I need to know if I'm a good kisser! Look, you remember Sharon . . .

ALLISON: The one who did the thing with—

DENNIS: With the bird, yes. Well, when we were breaking up . . . in the middle of everything . . . she told me I was a lousy kisser.

ALLISON: Dennis.

DENNIS: I know, we were breaking up, and she probably just said that to— But maybe it's true!

ALLISON: Dennis, this is Sharon we're talking about here.

DENNIS: I know . . . but I think I'm going to kiss Anne tonight, and I want to know if I'm doing it correctly.

ALLISON: You're using lips, right?

DENNIS: You know what I mean. Can you help me out here?

ALLISON: You want to kiss me.

DENNIS: If it's not too weird. (*She gives him a look.*) I mean, I know it's weird, but—

ALLISON: You want to kiss me?!

DENNIS: And then I want a critique. I really like Anne. If I'm a bad smoocher, I need to know before tonight.

ALLISON: Well, how would I—I mean, it's not—for God's sake, Dennis!

DENNIS: Look, have you ever been kissed . . . really kissed, long and hard and by someone who knows how?

ALLISON: (*Smiling.*) Well . . . yes, actually.

DENNIS: And have you ever been kissed badly?

ALLISON: Yeah, sure.

DENNIS: Then you can tell the difference.

ALLISON: Is this some sort of strange romantic overture?

DENNIS: Allison . . .

ALLISON: I mean, really.

DENNIS: I just need—

ALLISON: (*Tenderly.*) Dennis . . . we've been friends for what . . . five years now? If you have some feelings for me . . . it would be natural. But you've got to tell me. Be honest now.

DENNIS: (*Tentatively, heartfelt.*) Alright . . . well . . . we HAVE been friends for a long time . . . and you know I . . . care about you a lot . . . and I enjoy . . . being with you . . . and I was just thinking about you—

ALLISON: Okay. I thought something like this was coming. I think it's been coming for a long time. But as much as I care about you—and I do, Dennis, you know I do—I just don't . . . think about you in that way. You're such a good friend; I don't know what I would do without you. You were there for me during the whole James fiasco, and getting laid off . . . but I just don't . . . I really just want to stay friends.

(*Pause.*)

DENNIS: Yeah, me too. Now can you tell me how I kiss?

ALLISON: Oh my God.

DENNIS: I can't believe you made me say all that just so you could give me the "Let's Be Friends" speech.

ALLISON: You're a terrible person.

DENNIS: I know. Kiss me.

ALLISON: Are you sure you—?

DENNIS: No, darling, I just like you as a friend, too. Now kiss me, you fool.

ALLISON: (*Pause. Exhales.*) Alright, fine. So what are we looking for, here?

DENNIS: I simply want an honest, sober appraisal of how I kiss. That's all.

(*With a "what the hell" sound, she moves to him. He leans in, they start to kiss, and she is shaking up and down. They part; she is laughing hysterically.*)

ALLISON: (*Still laughing.*) Okay, okay . . . I'm sorry . . . I think it was the phrase "sober appraisal."

(*He moves to kiss her; she starts laughing again.*)

   (*Calming down.*) Okay. Here we go. Really kissing now.

(*But as soon as he leans in to her she collapses in giggles. She falls face first into the couch.*)

DENNIS: Look, I'm going to take my lips and go elsewhere.

ALLISON: No, I can do this, I can do this.

(*She shakes out her hands. After a few false starts, they kiss. They part.*)

Wet your lips more.

(*He does. They kiss. They part.*)

DENNIS: Well?

ALLISON: Well ... hmmm ... it's like technically you're okay ... lips firm, yet yielding ... making solid contact ...

DENNIS: But?

ALLISON: But ... there *is* something missing ...

DENNIS: What?

ALLISON: I'm not sure ... try it again.

(*They kiss.*)

It's fine, it's lovely, an amusing after-dinner kiss with a top note of peppermint ...

DENNIS: I brushed my teeth about twelve times before coming over.

ALLISON: Yet it lacks ...

DENNIS: What? Tell me! This is what I came here for!

ALLISON: ... passion.

DENNIS: No passion?

ALLISON: Mmmmm ... no. Sorry.

DENNIS: Okay, okay, great, now we're getting somewhere. This is what I want. Okay. Let me try to add a little more passion in the mix.

(*He grabs her face and kisses her hard. He pulls away.*)

ALLISON: . . . Ow.

DENNIS: Ow?

ALLISON: That wasn't passion, that was velocity.

DENNIS: Okay, lemme try again.

(*He kisses her again, his hand slipping to her side.*)

ALLISON: Hey, whoa, what was that?

DENNIS: What was what?

ALLISON: That was a grab.

DENNIS: That was *not* a grab.

ALLISON: You were trying for second base.

DENNIS: Oh my God, we're in junior high.

ALLISON: You totally grabbed for my boob.

DENNIS: I wasn't in the same time zone.

ALLISON: Just stay away from the whole breastal area.

DENNIS: I'm trying to add passion here.

ALLISON: Well do it with your lips, not with your hands!

DENNIS: Look, I'm ready to bag this whole thing.

ALLISON: Oh, don't be a baby. Now kiss me like you mean it.

DENNIS: Sure you don't wanna spin a bottle first?

ALLISON: I'm going to *hit* you with a bottle if you don't—

(*He kisses her, very passionately. He pulls away.*)

(*Flustered.*) Whoo . . . now we're talking . . .

DENNIS: No, that was angry kissing.

ALLISON: Well . . . You might be onto something. Can you get pissed off at Anne tonight?

DENNIS: Sure, I'll have her give me the "Let's Be Friends" speech.

ALLISON: Dennis—

DENNIS: Seriously, how is it every woman in the world knows that exact same speech?

ALLISON: They hand it to us in health class. Are you mad at me now?

DENNIS: I think you *wanted* me to be in love with you, just so you can have the thrill of rejecting me.

ALLISON: Oh, yes, I really enjoyed breaking your heart.

DENNIS: My heart's fine. Sorry to disappoint you.

ALLISON: Why would I be—?

DENNIS: You want me to be madly in love with you! Just like every woman wants her male friends to be in love with them, without, of course, having to actually love them back.

ALLISON: Oh, please!

DENNIS: It's true!

ALLISON: Excuse me, who came over wanting to kiss whom?

DENNIS: That's got nothing to do with—

ALLISON: I think *you're* angry because I'm not in love with you!

DENNIS: Oh, yeah, right.

ALLISON: Think about it. It's an inherent rejection! Here I am, warm, funny, beautiful! Why don't I love you?

DENNIS: You're not that warm.

ALLISON: Why don't I love you?!

DENNIS: (*Deflating.*) I don't know . . .

ALLISON: Why don't you love me?

DENNIS: Oh, Allison . . .

(*He hugs her.*)

ALLISON: Why don't we love each other?

DENNIS: I don't know . . .

ALLISON: We're nice people. We're kind. We're fun. Aren't we fun?

DENNIS: We're huge ten-pound sacks of fun.

ALLISON: Why don't we love each other?

DENNIS: We do . . . We just—

ALLISON: —Don't love each other.

DENNIS: Like you said . . . there's no passion.

ALLISON: We're too comfy.

DENNIS: No fear of rejection.

ALLISON: Oh my God . . . Romance actually needs fear of rejection?

DENNIS: Maybe.

ALLISON: I must be the most romantical person in the world.

DENNIS: That's why I love you. (*Pause.*) Well. I'm going to go meet Anne now.

ALLISON: Okay.

DENNIS: Say something discouraging . . .

ALLISON: She'll hate you.

DENNIS: Thanks.

(*He starts to leave.*)

ALLISON: But I never will.

(*He pauses a moment. He goes and kisses her gently on the top of the head, and then exits.* ALLISON *stays and stares after him.*

Lights fade.)

END OF PLAY

LADY LIBERTY AND THE DONUT GIRL

Eric Lane

Lady Liberty and the Donut Girl was first performed as a reading at the Lark Play Development Center (John Clinton Eisner, artistic director; Suzy Fay, associate program director) in New York City in January 2011. Victor Maog directed the following cast:

ERIN	Molly Carden
WES	Gio Perez

The same cast performed the play in the Eighteenth Annual 15-Minute Play Festival, presented by the American Globe Theatre and Turnip Theatre Company in April 2012.

Lady Liberty and the Donut Girl also was named finalist for the Heideman Award in the Actors Theatre of Louisville's National Ten-Minute Play Contest.

CHARACTERS
WES, seventeen years old. Dressed in a simple, ill-fitting Statue of Liberty costume.
ERIN, eighteen years old. Works at the local Jolly Shop supermarket making donuts.

SETTING
Main Street. The storefront for "Liberty Tax & Go." It is simply indicated by either a sign or a sandwich board with Lady Liberty plus red, white, and blue balloons. There is an outdoor bench. Early April. Afternoon.

Main Street. The storefront for "Liberty Tax & Go." Early April. Afternoon.

WES, seventeen years old, wears an inexpensive, ill-fitting Statue of Liberty costume. It includes a foam crown (askew), a torch, a dress over his regular clothes, and high-tops. He stands in front of the store, waving as cars pass to drum up business. His wave is continuous, deliberate, and in the style of royalty.

ERIN, eighteen years old, enters. She is on break from the local Jolly Shop supermarket, where she works making donuts. She wears a combination of street clothes and her work outfit, including a Jolly Shop smock top.

She sees WES, who continues to wave. After a moment:

ERIN: Hey.

(*He ignores her.*)

    I said, hey.

WES: I heard you.

ERIN: So—

WES: Why don't you go away?

(*She remains.*)

Go away.

ERIN: It's a free country.

WES: Maybe.

ERIN: What's that supposed to mean?

WES: For some people it's free. For some, not so much.

ERIN: Which are you?

WES: Take a guess.

(*He looks at her briefly.*)

Nice outfit.

ERIN: Like you should talk.

WES: What are you, on a break?

(*She nods.*)

I hate Jolly Shop anyway. With their stupid Big Can Sale.

ERIN: I love the Big Can Sale.

WES: With all those smiley faces hanging around the super-market. And that commercial they play with all these like French women dancing and their cartoon skirts all ruffly and stuff.

ERIN: So.

WES: So when was the last time you saw some French lady dancing in the aisles over a giant can of kidney beans? Huh?

ERIN: It makes people happy.

WES: (*Continuing.*) . . . Not once.

ERIN: Knowing they're getting all these big bargains. Cans of tuna and beans flying off the shelves. It makes the day go fast.

WES: Don't you have to get back to your donut station?

ERIN: How'd you know I make donuts?

WES: 'Cause I can smell it on you, like from over here. You're like one big walking plastic box of fried dough and cinnamon.

ERIN: Shut up.

WES: You could always leave.

ERIN: I don't smell bad.

WES: Go back to your land of powdered sugar and yeast.

ERIN: Don't say that.

WES: Hot oil seeping into your skin.

ERIN: No.

WES: Into your pores.

ERIN: Like you'd know.

WES: Like one giant overripe dough ball that's sprouted legs and odors.

ERIN: Don't say I smell bad 'cause I don't!

WES: Okay. You don't.

(*A beat.*)

I saw you there. At Jolly Shop. Making donuts. Chopping them up and giving out free samples. You looked kinda—I don't know—happy.

ERIN: It doesn't suck.

WES: Better than this.

ERIN: I guess.

WES: At least people like what you're doing. It may make them fat and clog their arteries and contribute to the national obesity epidemic but at least they like it.

ERIN: Thanks.

WES: (*Mumbles.*) You smell nice. Kinda sweet.

ERIN: Whatever.

(*She looks at the store sign.*)

Liberty Tax & Go. My mom went here.

WES: They suck.

ERIN: She got a refund.

WES: They still suck. Just 'cause I owe him some money—

ERIN: Who?

WES: My stepdad. Just 'cause I charged a few things on his credit card. So now I gotta stand in front of his stupid store dressed like the Statue of Liberty. I wish I could just disappear. Like everybody else. Just gone.

ERIN: I used to.

WES: What?

ERIN: Disappear.

WES: (*Skeptical.*) Yeah, right.

ERIN: When I was a kid. This magic trick. I must've been like what? Five years old.

WES: Get out.

ERIN: We had these curtains in front of the window. And my dad, he'd introduce me. "Presenting the Amazing Erin." This is when he was still around. And I'd come out—like—

WES: What?

ERIN: I don't know. Forget it.

WES: Like what?

ERIN: (*Annoyed.*) Like I don't know—happy, okay. Like all happy. I stand in the middle of the living room. "And now I will make myself disappear. Close your eyes."

WES: (*Laughs slightly.*) Get outta here.

ERIN: Then I'd run behind the curtains. (*Calls.*) "You may now open your eyes."

Amazing, right.

WES: Ten.

(*She looks at him.*)

What I borrowed.

ERIN: That doesn't seem so bad. So you borrowed ten dollars from him. Big deal.

WES: Not ten.

ERIN: Didn't you just say—

WES: More.

ERIN: How much more?

(*He points up.*)

Like how much?

WES: Ten thousand.

ERIN: Ten thousand. You stole ten thousand dollars off your dad's credit card.

WES: Stepdad. And I didn't steal it.

ERIN: No?

WES: I was gonna pay it back. Eventually.

ERIN: Eventually?

WES: And I would've, too, but—

ERIN: But—

WES: Just forget it.

ERIN: How were you gonna pay back ten thousand dollars?

WES: Stop saying that.

ERIN: What?

WES: Ten thousand dollars. Ten thousand dollars. Ten thousand
dollars.

ERIN: That's what you said, isn't it?

WES: Around ten thousand dollars.

ERIN: You mean like less.

(*He says nothing.*)

Less, right?

(*He points his thumb up.*)

Jesus.

WES: What?

ERIN: Like how much?

WES: Just more, okay?

ERIN: Eleven.

(*Shakes his head no.*)

Twelve.

(*No.*)

Thirteen.

WES: You're getting closer.

ERIN: Fifteen.

(*He nods.*)

Fifteen thousand dollars on your stepdad's credit card.

WES: I said I was gonna pay it back.

ERIN: Yeah, right.

WES: And I would've, too, except the minimum payments kept getting higher and, well, forget it.

ERIN: How could he not notice an extra fifteen thousand dollars on his credit card?

WES: It was a separate card I took out. Platinum.

ERIN: In his name.

WES: Yeah. And I'd get home from school and get the mail before he did. It worked for a couple of months—

ERIN: What could you possibly buy for fifteen thousand dollars?

WES: Stuff.

ERIN: Like . . .

WES: Meals.

ERIN: What kinda meals?

WES: Expensive meals. Like for friends.

ERIN: And . . . ?

WES: Gifts. It wasn't stuff for me. It's just like—

ERIN: What?

WES: I had friends, okay. And they liked me, so I just, I don't know. I just figured—

ERIN: What?

WES: They'd like me more.

ERIN: Right.

WES: Only now—

ERIN: What?

WES: You don't see them, do you?

(*She shakes her head no.*)

It's just me on Main Street in this stupid outfit. I may as well have a big scarlet letter A on my chest. I feel like Hester Prynne.

ERIN: What grade's she in?

WES: Tenth.

(*A beat. He laughs.*)

ERIN: What . . . ?

(*He shakes his head at the ridiculousness of it all. A beat.*)

WES: (*Quietly.*) Twenty-five.

ERIN: Thousand. Dollars.

(WES *nods.*)

You owe your stepdad twenty-five thousand dollars.

WES: Well, closer to twenty-nine.

(*She laughs. So does he.*)

ERIN: You're gonna be standing out here the next thirty years.

WES: At least.

You better go.

ERIN: I still got a few minutes.

WES: You're gonna get in trouble.

(*She shakes her head no.*)

ERIN: I noticed you, too. At the store yesterday. You took a free donut sample, went around the store. Then came back for another free sample like it was your first one.

Close your eyes.

(*He looks at her.*)

Just close 'em.

(*He does.*)

Now open them.

(*He does. Looks at her.*)

WES: Still here.

ERIN: Magic.

(*They look at each other. Then out at the street. They both wave.*

Lights fade.)

END OF PLAY

MY HUSBAND

Paul Rudnick

My Husband received its premiere on November 13, 2011, at the Minetta Lane Theatre in New York City as part of the evening "Standing on Ceremony: The Gay Marriage Plays." The show's contributing writers included Mo Gaffney, Jordan Harrison, Moisés Kaufman, Neil LaBute, Wendy MacLeod, José Rivera, Paul Rudnick, and Doug Wright. Stuart Ross directed the following cast:

GABRIELLE	Harriet Harris
MICHAEL	Mark Consuelos

TIME
3 P.M.

PLACE
The Upper East Side living room of Gabrielle Finklestein.

The front door opens and MICHAEL FINKLESTEIN *runs in, frantic.*

MICHAEL *is nice-looking, in jeans and a sports jacket. He's a dedicated New York City public school teacher.*

MICHAEL: Mom? Mom? Where are you? Are you okay? Mom?

(GABRIELLE FINKLESTEIN *enters, from the kitchen or an interior hallway. She looks great; she's an NYU professor, a deeply loving mom, and a passionate advocate for liberal causes. At the moment, she's moaning and staggering, as if she's very near death. She can barely speak.*)

GABRIELLE: Michael . . .

MICHAEL: Mom!

(MICHAEL *runs to his mother and helps her into a chair.*)

GABRIELLE: Michael . . .

MICHAEL: Mom, what is it, I ran all the way here, should I call someone, should I call 911 . . .

GABRIELLE: Michael . . .

MICHAEL: Mom, talk to me, what's happening, is it your heart, is it, oh my God, do you have a fever, are you nauseous, okay . . .

(*He holds up his hand, in front of her face.*)

... how many fingers?

GABRIELLE: (*Even closer to death.*) One ... two ... three ...

(*She pauses.*)

MICHAEL: Oh my God—only three?

GABRIELLE: ... four ... five ... five fingers ...

MICHAEL: That's right, thank God, five fingers ...

GABRIELLE: But I still don't see a ring ...

MICHAEL: Mom?

GABRIELLE: Did you hear?

MICHAEL: Hear what?

GABRIELLE: (*Thrilled beyond belief.*) This afternoon! Gay marriage! It passed the state legislature! Now you can get married!

MICHAEL: Mom ...

GABRIELLE: Isn't that spectacular news? Isn't that the best?

MICHAEL: Mom, you phoned me at work and said that you were having a dizzy spell and that it might be a stroke. I was in a meeting, which I left to run thirty-eight blocks to make sure you were okay ...

GABRIELLE: I'm *fabulous*!

MICHAEL: But I don't even have a boyfriend!

GABRIELLE: Is that my fault?

MICHAEL: Mom . . .

GABRIELLE: God knows I've tried. I introduced you to Carolyn Kramer's son, who was very hot . . .

MICHAEL: He was eighty-seven!

GABRIELLE: And I fixed you up with my stockbroker, Billy Berman, who's so cute . . .

MICHAEL: He's in jail!

GABRIELLE: And I set you up with my doorman, who's six foot four with shoulders and a jawline and biceps . . .

MICHAEL: And he's straight!

GABRIELLE: Who cares—do you know how much we tip him?

MICHAEL: Mom!

GABRIELLE: Do you know what it's like for me? Do you have any idea? I'm a liberal Jewish Democrat, I teach Political Science at NYU, and all of my friends, when they heard the news, about the vote, everyone called, and they all wanted to know—so when is Michael getting married?

MICHAEL: Why would they call? Everyone knows I'm single.

GABRIELLE: Not everyone.

MICHAEL: What did you do?

GABRIELLE: Nothing!

MICHAEL: *What did you tell them?*

GABRIELLE: I was embarrassed, for both of us! I mean, fine, you're gay, but it's not enough, not anymore! You know

Karen Calhoun, who teaches English Lit? Last week her son got married in the Grand Ballroom at the Plaza, with a fifty-eight-piece orchestra and thirty-seven ushers, all dressed as angels, and the rabbi was flown in from the ceiling in a golden chariot, which burst into flames.

MICHAEL: Who was their wedding planner?

GABRIELLE: Julie Taymor. And you know Madeline Melman, with the identical-twin lesbian daughters? Last month in New Hampshire, they had a double ring ceremony, because they met another pair of identical-twin lesbians!

MICHAEL: Another pair of identical-twin lesbians?

GABRIELLE: *African-American* identical-twin lesbians! How am I supposed to compete with that? It was so moving! You should've seen the wedding cake—it looked like an ad for *The Help*!

MICHAEL: Mom!

GABRIELLE: Every Sunday, when I read the wedding announcements in the *Times*, I look for your picture.

MICHAEL: Mom, I have been trying to meet someone forever. I've spent thousands of dollars, on the gay versions of eHarmony and JDate and Match.com.

GABRIELLE: Me too.

MICHAEL: You? Why?

GARBRIELLE: I pretended I was you. "Michael Finkelstein, public school teacher, loves his mom, hot, hard-bodied and hung."

MICHAEL: Did you get any responses?

GABRIELLE: Only other moms.

MICHAEL: Exactly! Look, someday, like in a million years, maybe I'll find someone and maybe we'll get married, or maybe not. But you have to stop pressuring me.

GABRIELLE: Fine. I understand.

MICHAEL: Thank you.

GABRIELLE: I only have one minor, tiny little request.

MICHAEL: Name it.

GABRIELLE: This weekend, please do me a favor, and don't read the Sunday *Times*.

MICHAEL: Mom . . .

GABRIELLE: At least not the wedding announcements . . .

MICHAEL: Oh my God, *Mom* . . .

GABRIELLE: Just aim right for the Book Review . . .

MICHAEL: I swear I will kill you. Mom, Mother, what did you do?

GABRIELLE: Nothing! Not a thing! It's just, okay, please, I'm begging you, please try to understand, I was in Starbucks, minding my own business, and Eleanor Markowitz comes in, you know the one, she teaches Queer Cinema.

MICHAEL: Even though she's not gay.

GABRIELLE: Exactly. She just does it to show off, to prove that she's got the gayest life ever. She calls her husband, Sidney, she calls him her partner. And she's always showing me pictures of the two of them, both dressed as sailors, she says it's very homoerotic, in the tradition of Jean Genet. And I told her, no, it's ridiculous, in the tradition of *Anything Goes*.

MICHAEL: That's right!

GABRIELLE: But Tuesday was the last straw. Because she shows me pictures of her son Oscar's honeymoon. And you know, they named him Oscar Wilde, just to make sure he'd be gay.

MICHAEL: So his name is Oscar Wilde Markowitz?

GABRIELLE: Oscar Wilde Walt Whitman Michelangelo Markowitz.

MICHAEL: Oh my God . . .

GABRIELLE: And so she shows me one picture after another, here's Oscar and his husband in front of Stonewall, here's Oscar and his husband at the revival of *The Normal Heart*, here's Oscar and his husband making one of those "It Gets Better" videos. They were surrounded by all of their hundreds of wedding gifts, and Oscar looks right into the camera and he says, "If you're being bullied in middle school, don't worry, because it gets better." And his husband says, "And you get stemware."

MICHAEL: Oh my God . . .

GABRIELLE: And the two of them, they're hyphenating their last names . . .

MICHAEL: Oh no, please no . . .

GABRIELLE: So he's gonna be Oscar Wilde Walt Whitman Michelangelo Markowitz-Waldbaum!

MICHAEL: Stop!

GABRIELLE: And they just adopted a Ukrainian baby, and do you know what they're calling it?

MICHAEL: What?

GABRIELLE: Christopher.

MICHAEL: Well, that's not so bad . . .

GABRIELLE: Christopher Street Marcel Proust Rosie O'Donnell Markowitz-Waldbaum!

MICHAEL: That's insane!

GABRIELLE: I cracked! I couldn't help myself! Eleanor just made me so angry, so I told her, I said, you know—my son Michael is getting married too!

MICHAEL: You didn't!

GABRIELLE: To a cardiac surgeon who operates exclusively on gay children in third-world countries.

MICHAEL: Wait—how does he know the children are gay?

GABRIELLE: Because their hearts are so big.

MICHAEL: Oh my God . . .

GABRIELLE: And your husband, I wanted him to be even gayer than Eleanor's son and his husband put together, so I told her that his name was—Dr. Todd Williams-Sonoma-Outlet.

MICHAEL: Of course.

GABRIELLE: And you're getting married next weekend, and you're registered everywhere, and I sent the announcement to the *Times*.

MICHAEL: I can't believe this! I can't believe that you have so little faith in me! I can't believe that my own mother would stoop so low!

GABRIELLE: I'm sorry, I was out of my mind! I'll call Eleanor, I'll tell her it was all a lie, and then I'll call the *Times* and I'll have them cancel the announcement.

MICHAEL: Wait.

GABRIELLE: What?

MICHAEL: Did you . . . did you send in a picture? Of the happy couple?

GABRIELLE: Of course. Because when Eleanor's son got married the two men both had matching trendy haircuts and matching trendy eyeglass frames and they both looked so smug. So, for Todd, I found this picture of a male model and I Photoshopped the two of you.

MICHAEL: Which male model?

GABRIELLE: He's gorgeous, from the Dolce & Gabbana ads . . .

MICHAEL: Oh my God, the guy with the chest and the abs and the tiny white bathing suit?

GABRIELLE: Of course.

MICHAEL: In the photo, in our wedding picture, is he—is he wearing the tiny white bathing suit?

GABRIELLE: You both are.

MICHAEL: Really?

GABRIELLE: For the picture of you, I used your head, but I Photoshopped Superman's legs, Captain America's arms, and the Green Lantern's shoulders.

MICHAEL: What about my waistline?

GABRIELLE: Wonder Woman.

MICHAEL: I love that!

GABRIELLE: I got an advance copy of the announcement. (*She takes out a copy of the* Times *and reads aloud.*) "Michael Finklestein and Dr. Todd Williams-Sonoma-Outlet were married earlier today onstage at Radio City Music Hall, during the Tony Awards, by the Pope. His Holiness told Mr. Finklestein, 'Your mother has convinced me that gay marriage is great.' The Pope concluded the ceremony by announcing, *'Fuck Eleanor Markowitz.'*"

Is that okay?

MICHAEL: (*Sincerely.*) Mom, it's beautiful.

GABRIELLE: Mazel tov!

(*They embrace joyously.*

Blackout.)

END OF PLAY

SADDAM'S LIONS

Jacob Juntunen

Saddam's Lions is based, in part, on interviews with Sergeant Shizuko Jackson. An early draft, entitled *The Woods*, was given a workshop production by the 2009 Vet Art Project Chicago (Lisa Rosenthal, artistic director; Jessa Carlstrom, lead artist). It was directed by Jacob Juntunen, with the following cast:

RASHIDA	Noelle Hardy
JON	Curtis Jackson

Saddam's Lions had its premiere at CulturalDC's 2010 Source Festival (Jenny McConnell Frederick, director of performing arts) in Washington, DC, on June 13, 2010. It was directed by Danielle Drakes; the lighting design was by Cory Ryan Frank; the sound design was by Matt Otto; the costume design was by Janet Minichiello. The cast was as follows:

RASHIDA	Zenzele Cooper
JON	Jamell Carter

CHARACTERS

RASHIDA, an African-American Iraq War veteran in her early twenties who has recently returned home. She wears nice but informal clothes for a family get-together.

JON, Rashida's younger brother, late teens. He also wears nice but informal clothes.

SETTING

The tree-filled backyard of a suburban house outside of Milwaukee, Wisconsin. It's late afternoon in the spring. A bare stage with lighting suggesting spring would be fine.

RASHIDA *enters, extremely agitated, throwing on a light jacket. She tries to shake off her mood and relax. She embraces the cold, the solitude, the afternoon sun, and the trees.* JON *enters, also throwing on a light jacket.*

JON: I've been looking everywhere for you! Do you need something? A drink? More chicken teriyaki?

RASHIDA: I might take a walk through the woods.

JON: Come on, you can't skip out on your own homecoming party.

RASHIDA: I told Mom I didn't want a party.

JON: Mom's asking for you. Didn't you love what she did when she saw you?

RASHIDA: I guess.

JON: She was like, jumping up and down and bawling, like: (JON *imitates their mother.*) She didn't act like that when she saw me.

RASHIDA: You're one state away, not in a combat zone.

JON: Well, at Christmas, when you weren't here, Mom was like, "Rashida's not here. Grr." Like actually saying "Grr!" Joking, I guess, but, you know, 'cause she was sad. You sure I can't get you something?

RASHIDA: So how's University of Chicago? You rich yet?

JON: I wish. I miss Milwaukee.

RASHIDA: It's your first year; you get used to being away from home.

JON: Do you want to move to the front yard where there's sun?

RASHIDA: It's nice finally seeing real trees.

JON: Baghdad didn't have trees?

RASHIDA: Not real ones. Coupland talked about missing these conifers, these oaks. We were in a kind of palace area, in a huge beautiful building right on the river, but half blown up, you know? So we made quarters in the rubble. And Baghdad's sort of tropical with palm trees and stuff, but in the summer it would be like, probably 130-something, 140, so it's hot, and everything just turns brown, gets wilted and burnt up.

JON: 140 degrees?

RASHIDA: And you still have to keep on all your gear.

JON: Damn. Doesn't spring here feel cold?

RASHIDA: It feels good. Coupland and I used to talk about getting back here and sleeping in the woods, smelling the leaves, catching a cool breeze. The guys would sleep inside, but she and I would sleep on the roof, try to cool off in the wind, but it's like someone blowing a hair dryer in your face, so it doesn't really help.

JON: You sure you don't want more chicken teriyaki or something? You're skinny.

RASHIDA: Yeah, nothing I left here fits me anymore.

JON: I thought you'd build up muscle carrying that stuff around.

RASHIDA: I lost weight 'cause I didn't want to eat those freakin' MREs.

JON: That's all you had?

RASHIDA: Sometimes we got Iraqi food, but yeah. Mostly MREs. Some had Combos or pretzels, but they also had this meat loaf thing . . . or ravioli in a tube that you squeeze into your mouth. Ick.

JON: So why aren't you eating more of Mom's chicken teriyaki?

RASHIDA: I don't know.

JON: You wrote about it all the time.

RASHIDA: All we did was talk about food. I don't know.

JON: What?

RASHIDA: It's just, like, I don't know. It's just chicken teriyaki.

JON: Well, you need to put some of the weight back on. I bet none of your bras fit right, either!

RASHIDA: Shut up!

JON: Damn—and what did you do to your hair?

RASHIDA: Everyone's hair got messed up! The heat, sweat, stress, Kevlar. I'm going to see Tina tomorrow.

JON: I sent you all that relaxer and stuff.

RASHIDA: Yeah, and me and the two other black females in our company used it. Give it a rest.

JON: Couldn't you just put it in a ponytail or something?

RASHIDA: Why don't you go back inside and see if Mom needs help?

JON: What did the Iraqi women use?

RASHIDA: How many black Iraqi women do you think there were?

JON: Couldn't you just go to an Iraqi store and see—?

RASHIDA: Okay, for one, I don't speak to Iraqi women because I'm in full battle rattle and look like a dude, and they don't come up to the Humvees. And for two, they don't have deodorant half the time, they don't relax their hair, and I can't go shopping!

JON: Why couldn't you go shopping?

RASHIDA: Like I'm going to get a squad of Humvees just to go down the street to get hair products? What are you talking about?

JON: Why do you need a squad of Humvees to go out? You just said you got Iraqi food.

RASHIDA: Yeah, if we were coming back from a mission or something—

JON: Well, how am I supposed to know that?

RASHIDA: We couldn't even drive down the street without maybe getting blown up, you know? Always swiveling, scanning, looking for IEDs, just these piles of garbage that'll explode, but the thing is, there's garbage everywhere, it's like driving through a landfill, a third-world country, you know, so, I mean, it's kinda hard. I'm not going to just go get hair supplies.

JON: Is that why you drove around the block this morning?

RASHIDA: When?

JON: On the way to Benji's for breakfast, you, like, made a U-turn and went all the way around the block instead of parking in that space.

RASHIDA: I don't know.

JON: Wasn't there, like, a box or something by the spot?

RASHIDA: Who cares?

JON: I don't know. It was just weird.

RASHIDA: Yeah, there was a box. So what? I just didn't like that spot.

JON: Did you like eating at Benji's this morning?

RASHIDA: It was okay.

JON: I thought it was great. Man, you can't get a breakfast like that in Chicago.

RASHIDA: Coupland never had it. We were going to get it when we got back.

JON: Oh.

RASHIDA: So, you know. It was all right. I'm sweating. Are you hot?

JON: It's pretty chilly out, still. Do you want want to go in and—

RASHIDA: What are they doing in there?

JON: Looking at your pictures.

RASHIDA: Oh, God.

JON: There's, like, one of you and Coupland in bikinis.

RASHIDA: That was after we got the hajjis—uh, Iraqis—to clean up the palace pool. Pool day! Man, that was awesome. We had that pool for months. And you all laughed when I packed that bikini, you were like, "It's the desert," and I was like, "You never know." All the other girls had to wear T-shirts, except Coupland. She brought a bikini, too. We were the only ones. I can't believe we didn't meet until we got there. Drilling together for years, but.

JON: Just how the National Guard is, I guess. It'll be different when you're a cop.

RASHIDA: I had enough being an MP.

JON: I thought the whole reason you joined was to get the police training?

RASHIDA: Is Coupland's mom still in there?

JON: Yeah.

RASHIDA: Is she coming out to dinner with us, too?

JON: I guess.

(*Pause.*)

Hey, what's the deal with the lions?

RASHIDA: What lions?

JON: In your pictures.

RASHIDA: Oh, they're just Saddam's lions.

JON: What do you mean, "they're just Saddam's lions"?

RASHIDA: Oh ... (*Laughing.*) It's not funny, but those are the lions that Saddam fed people to.

JON: What?

RASHIDA: Yeah (*Laughing.*), it's not funny, but he killed people with those lions—

JON: (*Laughing.*) That's not funny.

RASHIDA: And we were like, "What are we supposed to do with these?" Nobody knew. So we just kept them, and they were just like behind a chain-link fence. You know, a high one, but it wasn't secure, and— It was so funny: there was this sign, I should of took a picture, this sign said, "Please don't feed the lions. Don't throw over MREs, garbage, food . . . dogs, cats!" (*Laughs.*) So you know people did it. There were lots of stray dogs and cats and some stupid soldier would just pick one up and watch the lions tear it apart. (*Laughs.*) It's not funny. Coupland got scratched by a lion.

JON: (*Laughing.*) What kind of shit is that? My friend got scratched by a lion?

RASHIDA: It was a small one.

JON: Oh, it was a small one.

RASHIDA: I have a picture of her somewhere with her face like she's pretending to be afraid, you know, like (*Mugging fake fear for the camera.*), because the lion's right behind her—and then she for real got scratched!

JON: It's a lion! Leave it alone!

RASHIDA: She didn't think it could fit its paw through the chain-link fence.

JON: There was also, uh, this picture of a car, the inside of a car, and the car was kinda messed up, there were like specks of something, like, I think we were looking at, I don't know. What was that?

RASHIDA: That was my picture?

JON: It's not my picture.

RASHIDA: I don't think I took it.

JON: I don't know, it was with—

RASHIDA: Guys would borrow the camera, you know? Get shots of different gruesome, disgusting things, "cool stuff," "must of blew through a checkpoint," so I might have some of that, but . . .

(*Pause.*)

JON: Don't tell Mom that guys fed dogs to the lions.

RASHIDA: What were we supposed to do for those lions, you know? Just let them go? Take care of them? How could we help them? Like, what was the point? I think for me, just not knowing the point was . . . you know? We had these lions, but they were getting annoyed with us and we were getting annoyed by them. So I don't know why we were still there. And I don't know what to say to Coupland's mom.

JON: I've been thinking about taking this semester off school and coming home.

RASHIDA: Why?

JON: To be with you.

RASHIDA: Why would you do that?

JON: I don't know. You come home all skinny and just spend all this time up in your room alone, don't even want to talk to Mom, and maybe you got messed up—

RASHIDA: I'm fine.

JON: I thought maybe when you guys got attacked and Coupland—

RASHIDA: I was in my rack when that happened! Asleep! The BC pounded on the door until someone let him in and he was like, "We lost someone." And I'm thinking somebody's lost in Baghdad, like maybe their vehicle drove off without them, and I'm like, "That's messed up! We gotta go find them!" Shit.

JON: But I could take a semester off, just spend—

RASHIDA: No, look, I just want to go back to school. Get back into routine. No welcome-home parties. No ceremonies. Maybe that's good for some people, but I just want things to be normal. That means you in Chicago. So don't even—

JON: Okay, I get it.

RASHIDA: If you even think about—

JON: I said I get it.

RASHIDA: Sorry, I—

JON: You just want to be out here with the real trees.

RASHIDA: And go back to school on Monday, and not get annoyed when people complain about their crappy cell phones, or the dirty bathrooms— At least you have a phone. At least there is a bathroom.

(*Pause.*)

JON: You sure you're okay out here?

RASHIDA: The breeze feels great.

JON: I guess I should get back inside, then.

RASHIDA: Tell them I'll be inside in a little bit.

JON: Okay.

(JON *exits.* RASHIDA *looks at the trees.*)

END OF PLAY

SKIN

Naveen Bahar Choudhury

Skin premiered at the Ensemble Studio Theatre (William Carden, artistic director; Paul Slee, managing director) in New York City on September 17, 2011. *Skin* was directed by Jamie Richards. The cast was as follows:

ANGIE	Nitya Vidyasagar
ROBBY	Vandit Bhatt

CHARACTERS
ANGIE, early twenties, Bangladeshi-American.
ROBBY, early twenties, Bangladeshi-American.

TIME
The present.

PLACE
College campus health clinic waiting area.

(*The waiting area of a college campus health clinic. Several chairs made of decomposing plastic.* ANGIE, *wearing whatever a disenchanted poet wears, sits in a corner alone, typing furiously on her iPhone. It is clear that she has been crying.* ROBBY, *wearing whatever a wannabe hip-hop guy wears, sits on the other side of the room. He is pretending to read a copy of Henry David Thoreau's* Walden, *but actually he is observing* ANGIE. ROBBY *gets up, approaches* ANGIE *cautiously, and sits in the empty seat next to her.*)

ROBBY: (*Looking at his book.*) *Quiet desperation, my ass.* I livin' a lifa *loud* desperation up in here.

(ANGIE *pretends to not notice* ROBBY *and continues typing on her iPhone.*)

My hair ain't usually like this. I don't even usually leave the house in humidity like this. But this was the only time I had to get my flu shot.

(ANGIE *continues to type.* ROBBY *tries a different approach.*)

Dass a long text message.

ANGIE: What?

ROBBY: You've been (*Makes texting gesture.*) for like, twenty minutes. What are you writing?

ANGIE: None of your business.

ROBBY: It's not a text message, you only get a hundred sixty characters.

ANGIE: I'm busy.

ROBBY: It's not a Twitter, you only get a hundred forty characters.

ANGIE: Fuck off.

ROBBY: Nope, not a "Fuck off," dass only eight characters. You writin' somethin' long.

(ANGIE *switches seats and continues typing.*)

I'm sorry. You was cryin' for like thirty-seven minutes, and I just thought it woulda been rude to talk to you *then*, but then you *stopped* cryin', went into the ladies' room, you musta washed your face in there, 'cause you look a lot fresha now, and then you sat down and started tappin' out this epic email to somebody—

ANGIE: I'm not tapping out an epic anything. I am playing the Bubble Wrap game.

ROBBY: The Bubble Wrap game? Ohhh, no, you goin' waaaaay too slow for the Bubble Wrap game! You can't press the buttons all deliberate like that, you gotta (*Miming the actions with his fingers.*) POP POP POP POP POP POP POP POP POP POP POPOPOPOPOP—

ANGIE: I get it. Thank you.

(ANGIE *gets up and moves.* ROBBY *follows her.*)

ROBBY: I seen you around campus. But you never talk to nobody.

ANGIE: People are shit.

ROBBY: Hehe, yeah, I figga'd you kinda the angry type. You all intense. I like that. I'm Robby.

ANGIE: Angie.

ROBBY: Angie? What kinda Bengali name is Angie? It's short for something? Anjana? Anjali?

ANGIE: I'm not Bengali.

ROBBY: Okay, what are you?

ANGIE: I'm just like . . . like . . . like a regular Indian.

ROBBY: Yeah, okay.

(ROBBY *tries a different approach and starts to sing a cheesy Bengali love song.*)

> (*Singing.*) *Chirodini! Tumi je amar, juge juge ami tomari. Chirodini! Tumi je amar, juge juge ami tomari . . .*

(ANGIE, *recognizing the song, cracks up.*)

> Yeah, dass what I thought! You got that look. That Bengali look. Like that intellectual, pretentious kinda look . . . Like you read Tagore while drinking chai, and listening to sitar music or somethin'.

ANGIE: (*Laughing.*) Why, is that what you do? Angie is short for Gitanjali.

ROBBY: *Gitanjali?* You must write poetry?

ANGIE: (*Defensive.*) No. Well. Maybe.

ROBBY: I *knew* it! I feel like I know you already, like I known you my whole life. You prolly writin' a poem on your iPhone!

ANGIE: (*Uncomfortable.*) Whatever.

ROBBY: I like you.

ANGIE: You don't know me.

ROBBY: You are different from anybody I've ever met in my whole life!

ANGIE: Everybody is different from everyone else you've met in your whole life.

ROBBY: Not true. Some people completely indistinguishable from the next dude. No *color.* No *flava.* They personality is like watchin' somebody drink tap water on a black-and-white television set.

(ANGIE *laughs.*)

You got a pretty laugh. Your laugh is like . . . rose-colored.

ANGIE: (*Intrigued.*) So . . . I don't really get you . . . are you like . . . a hip-hop guy? Or a guy who watches Bangla movies? Or a guy who reads Thoreau? You can't be all three.

ROBBY: I versatile. I got all the colors goin' on. I'm like what you see when you look through a prism.

ANGIE: I'm gonna go back to the Bubble Wrap game now.

ROBBY: Why you say you not Bengali?

ANGIE: I don't want you to think we have anything in common.

ROBBY: We already got somethin' in common—

ANGIE: Why is it that if one Bengali sees another Bengali somewhere in public, they *insist* on making conversation? My dad, everywhere he goes, manages to find another Bengali and then it starts: *Where are you from? Bangali nake?? Ohhh, do you know Noor Bhai?* We have to add like twenty minutes to our travel time everywhere we go to account for possible Bengali sightings. Nobody *else* does this. Do you ever see Jewish people stopping each other on the street to ask, *Oh, you're Jewish, too! Which of the twelve tribes of Israel are your ancestors from?* NO! Why can't you people just be cool? I get it. We're both Bengali. Big fucking deal.

(*Beat.*)

ROBBY: I was juss gonna say I like poetry, too, but. Whateva.

(ROBBY, *frustrated, gets up and moves to a different seat and opens up his book.*)

ANGIE: I don't feel like talking. I just want to be left alone. So I don't want you to make small talk with me, and I don't want you to make me laugh, and I don't want you to be charming.

ROBBY: Dass gonna be really difficult. I'm not like a charm robot that you can clap on and clap off. My charm is like . . . organic. It's like the wind.

(ANGIE *starts crying.*)

Oh shit. I'm sorry—I'll stop being charming—I promise— what's wrong?

ANGIE: It's bad enough that I had to have all these blood tests alone today—I just see a needle and I pass out—

ROBBY: I scareda needles, too! Why do they put the people waiting to see the doctor in the same room as the people waiting for results? It's like two totally different levels of anxiety. Half the people shakin' 'cause they scared of a needle, the other half scared they sick—

ANGIE: I'm not scared I'm sick. I'm scared I'm pregnant.

(*Beat.*)

ROBBY: But then like . . . what about the dad?

ANGIE: He . . . doesn't know. He's . . . He's this sculptor. I mean, who's a sculptor anymore? I met him at one of his exhibits and—

ROBBY: You fell in love?

ANGIE: No. More like hero worship. I'd never met anyone so completely self-defined. But . . . he turned out to be a little bit of a sociopath. Like ninety-seven percent sociopath and three percent amazing sculptor. I haven't spoken to him since. (*Starts to sob.*) And now I might be pregnant with a baby who's fifty percent Bengali, and forty-eight-point-five percent sociopath, and one-point-five percent amazing sculptor . . .

ROBBY: What kind of sociopath was he?

ANGIE: I don't know. More stupid than scary. Like he stole my earrings and gave them back to me as gifts. He would follow me everywhere, and tell me all these weird lies. He had some kind of . . . klepto–stalker–compulsive liar disorder.

ROBBY: So he was like . . . a *white* sociopath.

ANGIE: Excuse me?

ROBBY: I was just checkin'. Because you were makin' all kindsa calculations before, fifty percent Bengali, and—

ANGIE: Do you have a point?

ROBBY: Nono, I don't got no point, I juss glad white sociopath is outta the picture, because you a picture I'd like to be a part of.

ANGIE: Um, did you hear the part where I might be pregnant?

ROBBY: So what? You're like . . . you're like something a caterpillar turns into.

(NURSE): (*Offstage.*) Angie? Dr. Kelley is ready for you.

(ANGIE *gathers her things.*)

ROBBY: Listen, if I'm not here when you get out, it just means I'm in there with the doctor. Wait for me. I wanna know that you okay.

(ANGIE *exits.* ROBBY *notices* ANGIE *has left her iPhone behind.*)

   Wait, you left your—

(ANGIE *has already left.* ROBBY *hesitates for a moment, and then looks at her iPhone. He starts pressing buttons.*)

   "Molting." Huh.

(ROBBY *looks around to be sure no one is watching, then continues to read what he finds on* ANGIE's *phone.*)

"You've got it all wrong
They screwed up my packaging
Outside, I am human
But inside, I'm a reptile
I am ectothermic and highly adaptable
I am meant to creep, slither, slither, the hell out of my skin . . ."

(ANGIE *returns, but* ROBBY *does not immediately notice. To himself.*)
Damn. This a lot deeper than the Bubble Wrap game.

(ROBBY *notices* ANGIE *has returned;* ANGIE *realizes* ROBBY *has her phone.*)

This is beautiful.

ANGIE: This is *private*! What the fuck are you doing, looking through my phone!

ROBBY: No, wait! I get this, okay? I get you. (*Reading.*)

"I want to rub my face against a rock
That tears my outer layer
So I can creep, slither, slither out of my skin—"

ANGIE: Stop. Talking.

ROBBY: But. Are you . . . what did they say?

ANGIE: Just give me my phone.

ROBBY: Listen, I love the poem. We got more in common than you think. I was right—you are like something a caterpiller turns into—but you even somethin' deeper than that. You're like . . . a butterfly *within* a butterfly—

(NURSE): (*Offstage.*) Robby? The doctor is ready for you.

ROBBY: I juss wanna know you okay. Are you?

ANGIE: (*Indicating she is pregnant.*) No.

ROBBY: Please wait for me. It'll take five minutes. Please.

ANGIE: I really need someone to talk to *now.*

(NURSE): (*Offstage.*) Robby, the doctor's waiting.

ROBBY: I can't. I gotta . . . I ain't here for no flu shot. I gotta get my results, you know.

ANGIE: Never mind. Give me my phone.

(ROBBY *gives* ANGIE *her phone and she begins to exit, but stops when* ROBBY *calls after her.*)

ROBBY: Okay, I lied, so what? You not the only one with some *complexities.* You want that everybody see you as your own unique person, not just another member of a category, but you too blinded to see me that way! I like *you.* Like, *specifically.* I can see who you actually are. You could see me, too, if you wanted. I'm a whole 'nother kind of animal from everybody else.

(ROBBY *exits to see the doctor.* ANGIE *considers whether to wait or leave. After a moment, she takes a seat to wait for* ROBBY. *She sees that he has left his copy of* Walden *behind, and she picks it up. Lights fade.*)

END OF PLAY

WILDWOOD PARK

Doug Wright

Wildwood Park received its world premiere as part of the evening "Unwrap Your Candy" at the Vineyard Theatre (Douglas Aibel, artistic director) in New York City on October 8, 2001. The cast of *Wildwood Park* was as follows:

MS. HAVILAND	Leslie Lyles
DR. SIMIAN	Reg Rogers

CHARACTERS
MS. HAVILAND, a Realtor. She is middle-aged, a working mother. She wears an attractive quilted jacket, a navy skirt, and cloisonné jewelry. Her shoes are sensible, for walking.
DR. SIMIAN, a prospective buyer. He is of indeterminate age and wears an expensive suit. He is disarmingly handsome.

TIME
Now.

PLACE
The stage is bare. The architecture, the furnishings, and the props of the play are all invisible, and are indicated by the actors through gesture—not in an overly demonstrative or "mime" fashion, but simply and clearly, with minimal movement. Even when specific mention is made in the text of nightstands, vanities, or fireplaces, these things are not seen; they are created through inference and the power of suggestion.

> *Repulsion is the sentry that guards the gate*
> *to all that we most desire.*
> *—Salvador Dalí*

A stark, sunny day. In the distance, the sound of suburban children at play. Both MS. HAVILAND *and* DR. SIMIAN *wear dark glasses to shield their eyes from the offending light. They stand side by side, in front of the "house," gazing up at its exterior.*

DR. SIMIAN: The neighborhood. It exceeds my expectations. The trees are symmetrical. The mailboxes have tiny flags. Along the alley, the trash cans all have matching lids.

MS. HAVILAND: It's well-tended.

DR. SIMIAN: It's *almost* perfection, isn't it? (DR. SIMIAN *smiles at* MS. HAVILAND. *She does not return the gesture. There is a stiff pause.*)

MS. HAVILAND: How did you hear about this listing?

DR. SIMIAN: The newspaper.

MS. HAVILAND: The *real-estate* section?

DR. SIMIAN: Yes.

MS. HAVILAND: That's not possible. Boulevard Realty . . . in the interest of discretion . . . in the interest of *taste* . . . opted not to publish this particular address. So when you called, when you called with your *specific* request . . .

DR. SIMIAN: The . . . ah . . . front page, Ms. Haviland. That is how I knew. I realized . . . I *surmised* . . . the house would be for sale.

MS. HAVILAND: Did you?

DR. SIMIAN: And your firm . . . your size, your reputation . . . what other firm, I asked myself . . .

MS. HAVILAND: Well. What other firm *in this area* . . .

DR. SIMIAN: Surely I am not alone. You must admit, public pre-occupation with . . . *this house* . . . I am not the first prospective buyer whose interest was initially piqued by reports of an altogether different nature . . .

MS. HAVILAND: No. You're not. *You most certainly are not.* (*A tense pause.*) Where have you been living?

DR. SIMIAN: Glen Ridge.

MS. HAVILAND: I'm not familiar with Glen Ridge.

DR. SIMIAN: No?

MS. HAVILAND: I have never even *heard* of Glen Ridge.

DR. SIMIAN: Beyond Ridge Falls. Near Beacon Ridge. Before Ridge Dale.

MS. HAVILAND: Suddenly you've decided to move?

DR. SIMIAN: Yes.

MS. HAVILAND: More room? Better schools? A sound investment strategy?

DR. SIMIAN: It's *time.*

MS. HAVILAND: Why *now*?

DR. SIMIAN: I've weathered a change in status.

MS. HAVILAND: Marital? Professional?

DR. SIMIAN: Both.

MS. HAVILAND: I hope it works out. For the best.

DR. SIMIAN: I hope. (*Another stilted pause.*)

MS. HAVILAND: I'd like to point out some of the exterior features of the house, if I may. It's a Colonial, of course. The portico dates back to the Revolutionary War. Wildwood Park's own Monticello. Of course, the drainage system, the storm windows, the pool, the carport—that's all contemporary.

DR. SIMIAN: Conservative, isn't it?

MS. HAVILAND: Classic. Beyond faddish. A constant. (MS. HAVILAND *points.*) Notice the weathercock.

DR. SIMIAN: Where? I don't see . . . I can't quite . . .

MS. HAVILAND: The rooster.

DR. SIMIAN: The glare . . .

MS. HAVILAND: The *silhouette.*

DR. SIMIAN: The sun's so *white* . . .

MS. HAVILAND: Left of the chimney.

(DR. SIMIAN *uses his hands like a visor, shielding his eyes. He spots the weather vane.*)

DR. SIMIAN: Ah! Yes!

MS. HAVILAND: It wasn't bought; it was commissioned.

DR. SIMIAN: Impressive.

MS. HAVILAND: This house belongs on the dollar bill. (*Another pause.*) What sort of work do you do?

DR. SIMIAN: Medical.

MS. HAVILAND: You're not a journalist?

DR. SIMIAN: Should I be?

(MS. HAVILAND *glances from left to right. She speaks in a low, confidential tone.*)

MS. HAVILAND: I have to ask . . .

DR. SIMIAN: Yes?

MS. HAVILAND: You're not *undercover*, are you?

DR. SIMIAN: Under what?

MS. HAVILAND: You're not *wearing a wire*?

DR. SIMIAN: Excuse me?

MS. HAVILAND: You are not an *opportunist*, are you?

DR. SIMIAN: I rather expected I'd be asking the questions this afternoon.

MS. HAVILAND: I've learned the hard way, Dr. Simian. I can't be too careful. A few weeks ago, a man came, requesting to see the house. He brought a camcorder. He told me that his wife was back home, in Terre Haute, and that he intended to mail the tape back to her, before deciding. Well. You can imagine my surprise when, a few days later, I turned on the television, one of those alarmist news programs, and there it was. Edited. With an ominous sound track.

DR. SIMIAN: He'd sold the tape?

MS. HAVILAND: So forgive me if I exert caution.

DR. SIMIAN: My sole interest, Ms. Haviland, is in purchasing a home.

MS. HAVILAND: Thank goodness.

DR. SIMIAN: I am far more invested in a firm foundation, a basement which does not leak, a patio for summer parties, than I am in . . . *the unsavory.*

MS. HAVILAND: Count yourself among a rarefied few.

DR. SIMIAN: If you distrust my *sincerity* . . .

MS. HAVILAND: I didn't say that.

DR. SIMIAN: I am *eager* to relocate. I have an *approved loan.* My intentions could not be more *serious.*

MS. HAVILAND: I am *relieved.*

DR. SIMIAN: Would you care to see my correspondence with the bank? A copy of my current mortgage?

MS. HAVILAND: Please. I—

DR. SIMIAN: Proof positive. The listing for my own home in *The Town Tattler.*

MS. HAVILAND: That isn't necessary.

(DR. SIMIAN *pulls a folded newspaper from his inner breast pocket.*)

DR. SIMIAN: (*Reading.*) "Glen Ridge Charmer: Raised ranch, designed with family in mind. Three bedroom, two and a half bath, breakfast nook with skylight, basement rec room—"

MS. HAVILAND: I *apologize.*

(DR. SIMIAN *slaps the paper against his hand twice, to flatten it. He refolds it and returns it to his pocket. Another short pause.*)

DR. SIMIAN: I would be less than honest—

MS. HAVILAND: (*Quickly.*) Yes?

DR. SIMIAN: —if I didn't confess to an ulterior motive.

MS. HAVILAND: I suspected as much.

DR. SIMIAN: The reason I chose this house . . . this *particular* house . . . with its rather . . . *notorious* . . . history . . .

MS. HAVILAND: Mm-hm?

DR. SIMIAN: I am . . . I am . . . I am a *bargain hunter.*

MS. HAVILAND: Oh. Well.

DR. SIMIAN: Correct me if I'm wrong, but I would assume, by-in-large, your average buyer would have, well . . . *trepidation.* A fear that the house had somehow been . . . *besmirched.* That it had absorbed its own history, and that it had somehow become . . . *a hard sell.* But I am not a superstitious person. Karma, aura. These things mean nothing to me.

MS. HAVILAND: (*With significance.*) I have an unhappy surprise for you, Doctor. (MS. HAVILAND *makes a thumbs-up gesture, which suggests that the asking price has soared.*)

DR. SIMIAN: No.

MS. HAVILAND: (*Nodding.*) *Oh yes.*

DR. SIMIAN: That's shocking.

MS. HAVILAND: Through the roof.

DR. SIMIAN: Is that the culture? The culture-at-large? Is that what we've become?

MS. HAVILAND: (*As a vulture.*) Caaw! Caaw!

DR. SIMIAN: You'll make me a cynical man, Ms. Haviland.

MS. HAVILAND: 1120 Sycamore Avenue has made me a cynical woman.

DR. SIMIAN: And the property values. In the neighborhood. They are—

MS. HAVILAND: Holding their own.

DR. SIMIAN: My, my.

MS. HAVILAND: Wildwood Park has not changed. It is the same enclave it always was. The traffic, of course, is heavier.

DR. SIMIAN: People ignore the blockades.

MS. HAVILAND: It's a constant battle.

DR. SIMIAN: License plates from Iowa. From California.

MS. HAVILAND: The furor will die down. By the time you're ready to take occupancy . . . should you decide to pursue the house . . . the traffic will taper, I assure you . . .

DR. SIMIAN: Naturally.

MS. HAVILAND: We still boast excellent schools. And I don't have to tell you, Doctor, the shopping in our little town is world-class. We have our own library. Our own post office. Our own women's auxiliary, and our own police force.

DR. SIMIAN: I couldn't help noticing. At the curb. The squad car.

MS. HAVILAND: A precaution against vandalism. A few weeks ago—a rock, some spray paint. *Eggs.*

DR. SIMIAN: I see.

MS. HAVILAND: An isolated incident.

DR. SIMIAN: It's to be expected.

MS. HAVILAND: It gives me great civic pride, Dr. Simian, to tell you that—for weeks—the front porch was teeming with candles. Bouquets. My own daughter made a wreath from sapling twigs. I was moved. (*A pause.*) Shall we go inside?

DR. SIMIAN: Please.

(MS. HAVILAND *begins the complicated process of opening the door.*)

MS. HAVILAND: You'll notice there are two double bolts, with pick-proof cylinders. In addition, the house has a twenty-four-hour, fully computerized security system with built-in alarm, automatic police and fire notification, and an electronic fence.

DR. SIMIAN: These precautions. They are . . . recent?

MS. HAVILAND: Yes. They are *new.* They were not here *before.* (*Another brief pause.*) Shall we? (*They "enter" the house. As* MS.

HAVILAND *and* DR. SIMIAN *move from room to room throughout the house, it's as though they are tokens on a board game, moving through implied three-dimensional space.*) Eight thousand square feet, Doctor. Five bedrooms, four and a half baths. (MS. HAVILAND *makes an extravagant gesture, indicating the vast expanse of the front hall.*) Notice the upward sweep of the foyer. The walls rise the full height of the house. The candelabra; that's brass. And look at the sunlight streaming down. We're flooded, aren't we? We're drowning in light. (MS. HAVILAND *removes her sunglasses.*) Dr. Simian. Your glasses. The color scheme.

DR. SIMIAN: Safe now, isn't it? (DR. SIMIAN *removes his glasses and slips them into his breast pocket.*) And that?

MS. HAVILAND: Where?

DR. SIMIAN: Above the arch.

MS. HAVILAND: Ah, yes. *That.* It's Pennsylvania Dutch. A touch of *whimsy.*

DR. SIMIAN: What is it?

MS. HAVILAND: *Oh, dear.*

DR. SIMIAN: You're blushing.

MS. HAVILAND: It's a hex sign. *That is a hex sign.*

DR. SIMIAN: No.

MS. HAVILAND: For *good* luck.

DR. SIMIAN: One can't help thinking—

MS. HAVILAND: Please. Don't.

(DR. SIMIAN *wanders ahead.*)

DR. SIMIAN: Is this the living room?

MS. HAVILAND: I must ask you, *don't barrel through.*

DR. SIMIAN: Forgive me.

MS. HAVILAND: I am conducting the tour.

DR. SIMIAN: Of course.

MS. HAVILAND: "Follow the Leader." *Indulge me.* Watch your step.

DR. SIMIAN: Thank you.

(*They "enter" the living room.*)

MS. HAVILAND: An exquisite space, Doctor. Floor-length windows. On the ceiling, rosettes. And the fireplace. You'll note its size. Its grandeur. Quarried marble, Venetian, I think.

(DR. SIMIAN *runs his hand along the mantelpiece.*)

DR. SIMIAN: A substantial mantel.

MS. HAVILAND: Yes.

DR. SIMIAN: Can it support sculpture? Can it support objets d'art?

MS. HAVILAND: (*Curtly.*) I think you can *gauge,* Doctor.

DR. SIMIAN: The house is still furnished.

MS. HAVILAND: Not for long.

DR. SIMIAN: It looks . . . *inhabited.*

MS. HAVILAND: Things happened so quickly. The house was placed on the market so soon.

DR. SIMIAN: This room reminds me, Ms. Haviland, of an exhibit in a museum. The stillness. Its past hanging heavy in the air, unspoken.

MS. HAVILAND: There was of course, a will, provisions were naturally made, but in the absence of any ... *beneficiaries* ... the furniture will be sold at auction.

DR. SIMIAN: Aha.

MS. HAVILAND: The proceeds will benefit the Children's Legal Defense Fund.

DR. SIMIAN: An appropriate gesture.

MS. HAVILAND: If ... *when* it is recovered ... after its release from evidence . . . the Nubian statuette is expected to fetch a startling sum.

DR. SIMIAN: Surprise, surprise.

MS. HAVILAND: "Who," I ask myself. "Who would buy—"

DR. SIMIAN: Our society is predatory.

MS. HAVILAND: I'd almost bid on it myself. So I could take it home. So I could take it home with me, and with my husband's hammer—

DR. SIMIAN: *Yes.*

MS. HAVILAND: I'd pay a hefty sum, just for the pleasure of seeing it *destroyed*.

DR. SIMIAN: Do you know, Ms. Haviland, the totems of our time?

MS. HAVILAND: The "totems"?

DR. SIMIAN: In Milwaukee, a stockpot on the stove. In Brent-
wood, an errant glove.

MS. HAVILAND: And among them . . .

DR. SIMIAN: . . . yes . . .

MS. HAVILAND: . . . in Wildwood Park . . .

DR. SIMIAN: . . . exactly . . .

MS. HAVILAND: A Nubian statuette. (*They "enter" the dining room.*)
You'll notice how the living room segues into the dining
room. Dignified, isn't it? *Vintage.* You can comfortably seat
up to twenty-four. Those sconces are from a tavern in the
Hudson River Valley, circa 1890. You'd never guess . . . (MS.
HAVILAND *toys with a light switch.*) . . . they're on a dimmer.

DR. SIMIAN: The kitchen can't be far behind.

MS. HAVILAND: Careful; that door swings. (*They "enter" the
kitchen.*) A rustic look, but with every modern convenience.
An electric oven, an industrial range, a microwave, and—for
"old world" effect, a touch of antique romance—a wood-
burning stove. Charming, yes? The cabinets are cherrywood,
and the countertops are Mexican tile. And you'll note,
there's an island . . . cherry, too, with a granite top, pull-out
shelves below, and of course . . . a . . . you see it, there . . . with
a . . . a . . . *oh, dear* . . .

DR. SIMIAN: A what?

MS. HAVILAND: A *block*.

DR. SIMIAN: A block?

MS. HAVILAND: A *butcher* block. (MS. HAVILAND *smiles a guilty smile.*)

DR. SIMIAN: Why, Ms. Haviland.

MS. HAVILAND: I'm horrible.

DR. SIMIAN: You've made a pun.

MS. HAVILAND: I'm a monster.

DR. SIMIAN: A pun, that's all.

MS. HAVILAND: I should have my tongue *cut out.* (MS. HAVILAND *suppresses a giggle.*) Oh, there. I've done it again.

DR. SIMIAN: You're *giddy.*

MS. HAVILAND: Shame on me. Shame on us both.

DR. SIMIAN: Humor, Ms. Haviland, fortifies.

(MS. HAVILAND *wipes tears from her eyes, composing herself.*)

MS. HAVILAND: This house, all day, every day. Dodging past the news vans. Those rapacious tourists. I fight my way past. *I have business here.* If it's made me loopy, Doctor, then I have every right to be.

DR. SIMIAN: Bravo.

MS. HAVILAND: My husband says it's nerves. My husband says all those infernal shutterbugs, all those flashbulbs, they've *seared* my *brain.*

DR. SIMIAN: A fanciful thought, Ms. Haviland.

MS. HAVILAND: My husband tells me that I take things to *heart*. That I should go on *automatic*. That is easy, Doctor, for *my* husband to *say*. It is, after all, his *forte*. (MS. HAVILAND *snorts a laugh, a little bark, which afterward makes her cheeks burn red.*)

DR. SIMIAN: I'd like to see the master bedroom.

MS. HAVILAND: (*Sadly.*) I'm exhausted. Frayed. That's the *truth*.

DR. SIMIAN: The bedroom, please.

MS. HAVILAND: But you haven't seen the den. You haven't seen the home office, the playroom, the maid's suite—(DR. SIMIAN *leaves the kitchen.* MS. HAVILAND *follows, suddenly strident.*) *Don't charge ahead!*

DR. SIMIAN: I'm overeager.

MS. HAVILAND: I can't have people *wander*. I can't have people *traipsing through*.

DR. SIMIAN: I might go nosing in the linen cupboards.

MS. HAVILAND: Don't be absurd; it's not that.

DR. SIMIAN: I might empty the medicine chest.

MS. HAVILAND: *It's not that at all.*

DR. SIMIAN: I might pirate away knickknacks, and open a souvenir stand on the corner.

MS. HAVILAND: I am responsible for the house, and its contents. I have *police* on my back. There are *attorneys*. A *battalion* of *lawyers*. Under the circumstances, it is an *overwhelming* duty.

DR. SIMIAN: I was insensitive.

MS. HAVILAND: My psychiatrist is *worried*. She *fears* for my *safety*. I am on *tranquilizers*.

DR. SIMIAN: It must be a strain. (*They "enter" the master bedroom.*)

MS. HAVILAND: There are ceiling fans in all the bedrooms. You'll find that saves a fortune in cooling costs during the summer. A walk-in closet, which I daresay is larger than my living room.

DR. SIMIAN: Poignant, isn't it?

MS. HAVILAND: What?

DR. SIMIAN: There. On the floor, by the bed. (DR. SIMIAN *points:*) Empty shoes. (*A palpable chill descends in the room.*)

DR. SIMIAN: This is where it began, yes?

MS. HAVILAND: (*Alarmed.*) *I beg your pardon?*

(*The following dialogue is rapid-fire, accelerating in speed, a crescendo.*)

DR. SIMIAN: The balcony doors.

MS. HAVILAND: I'd rather not.

DR. SIMIAN: They were left ajar? They were pried open?

MS. HAVILAND: You know I don't *approve* . . . I don't *appreciate* . . .

DR. SIMIAN: Around the lock, scuffs. Gouges.

MS. HAVILAND: I'm here to show the house. I'm not a *detective*. I am not a *talk show host*.

DR. SIMIAN: Forgive me. But I couldn't help noticing—there—on the wainscoting—

MS. HAVILAND: The paint has been retouched.

DR. SIMIAN: Along the molding—

MS. HAVILAND: The carpets have all been shampooed.

DR. SIMIAN: Traces exist.

MS. HAVILAND: No. Where?

DR. SIMIAN: *Splotches.*

MS. HAVILAND: *There is nothing to notice.*

DR. SIMIAN: There. On the edge. Rimming the baseboards . . .

MS. HAVILAND: *I don't see a thing.*

DR. SIMIAN: The electrical outlets. Where are they?

MS. HAVILAND: (*Frightened.*) What?

DR. SIMIAN: It's a fair question.

MS. HAVILAND: It's a *taunt.* It's a *jibe.*

DR. SIMIAN: For *lamps.* For *clock-radios.* A *laptop.* These things require *voltage.*

MS. HAVILAND: All sorts of *appliances* require voltage, Dr. Simian. ALL SORTS.

DR. SIMIAN: A heating pad, perhaps! An electric blanket! Nothing menacing, nothing *pneumatic.*

MS. HAVILAND: Don't be *facetious,* Doctor.

DR. SIMIAN: SHOW ME.

MS. HAVILAND: *Please!*

DR. SIMIAN: *WHERE?*

MS. HAVILAND: Behind the headboard. And there. Under the vanity.

(*A short rest.* DR. SIMIAN *goes to the vanity table. He gets down on his hands and knees and looks beneath it.*)

DR. SIMIAN: The wall plate. It's scorched.

MS. HAVILAND: What did you expect? It was *overburdened*, it was profoundly *misused*.

DR. SIMIAN: Hidden down here. Out of sight, out of mind?

MS. HAVILAND: There are still a few details . . .

DR. SIMIAN: A few *vestiges*?

MS. HAVILAND: A few REPAIRS.

(DR. SIMIAN *stands up. He looks in the mirror of the vanity, back at* MS. HAVILAND'*s reflection.*)

DR. SIMIAN: She was a singer for a while, wasn't she? She was on television in New York.

MS. HAVILAND: Dr. Simian, if you have inquiries about the house, about its *architecture*, its *design*, its *upkeep*—

DR. SIMIAN: She sold thigh cream, and overcame personal problems. And he made a fortune in junk bonds.

MS. HAVILAND: I'm sure I don't know.

DR. SIMIAN: Of course you know. *Everybody knows.*

MS. HAVILAND: I'm not *interested*.

DR. SIMIAN: You can't flip on the radio, you can't watch the news—

MS. HAVILAND: I *mute*, Doctor.

DR. SIMIAN: Even pick up a paper—

MS. HAVILAND: Because of my *professional obligations* . . . my *necessary involvement* . . . there are certain things. I'd rather *not* know . . .

(DR. SIMIAN *notices something on the wall. He points.*)

DR. SIMIAN: The little one. The youngest. The girl.

MS. HAVILAND: I have recommended to my employer that we remove these photographs. They're unnerving. Prospective buyers are unhinged.

(DR. SIMIAN *traces the shape of the frame on the wall with his finger.*)

DR. SIMIAN: Freckles. A gap tooth.

MS. HAVILAND: Their eyes follow you. No matter where you turn.

DR. SIMIAN: What was her name?

MS. HAVILAND: All day, every day, they stare me down. Here at work. In *this* room. Outside, too. In line at the grocery store, the tabloids. On *T-shirts*, for God's sake, they've even been *silk-screened* . . .

(DR. SIMIAN *notices another picture, this one on the nightstand. He approaches it and picks it up.*)

DR. SIMIAN: Here she is again, in a pageant of some kind.

MS. HAVILAND: *Put that down!*

DR. SIMIAN: Look at her. She's dressed as a radish. She's singing.

MS. HAVILAND: *You're not supposed to touch things!*

DR. SIMIAN: Oh, and look. Washing the family dog. (DR. SIMIAN *puts the picture back in its place.*) Is it true? *Even the dog?*

MS. HAVILAND: *You are disturbing things . . . me . . .*

DR. SIMIAN: The police posit that, sometime after three, she . . . the girl . . . heard a sound. If only she'd opted to hide under the bed, they said, if only she'd run out the back door, they said, if only her little legs—

MS. HAVILAND: (*Relents, and cuts him off.*) Heather. (*A pause.*) Her name was Heather.

DR. SIMIAN: Take me to the nursery. (*Another pause.*)

MS. HAVILAND: Do you have *children*, Dr. Simian?

DR. SIMIAN: More questions, Ms. Haviland?

MS. HAVILAND: Because if you don't have children . . . if you don't have *young* children . . . then the nursery is *irrelevant.*

DR. SIMIAN: Surely you are not offering the house on a room-by-room basis.

MS. HAVILAND: Don't insult me, Doctor.

DR. SIMIAN: I am interested in the entire structure. Not a portion thereof.

MS. HAVILAND: It's just, you've hardly inspected the house. The living room, the kitchen, the dining room, and nary a remark. "He's bound to have questions about the plumbing," I say to myself, "and radon, and chimney flues. He'll want to know about the new roof, about winter insulation." *But no!*

DR. SIMIAN: Ms. Haviland, I—

MS. HAVILAND: *Oh, no!* With you it's all ... hex signs ... and hollow shoes ... and *little girls.*

DR. SIMIAN: There are still whole rooms—

MS. HAVILAND: The tour is over.

DR. SIMIAN: *Entire wings—*

MS. HAVILAND: It's half-past-five.

DR. SIMIAN: The backyard. The guest house.

MS. HAVILAND: The workday has come to a close.

DR. SIMIAN: I've driven a great distance—

MS. HAVILAND: Please leave.

DR. SIMIAN: I can't readily arrange a second visit—

MS. HAVILAND: Wildwood Park is a private community. A discreet community. It is not some sordid *theme park,* Doctor. It is not a *freak show,* with its tent flaps spread—no, *torn*—open for the nation's *amusement.* It is not some *dime store, penny-dreadful, Stephen King—*

DR. SIMIAN: A daughter, six, and a son, eight. (*A pause.* MS. HAVILAND *blushes. Slowly and definitively—like a lawyer giving a summation of evidence—*DR. SIMIAN *continues.*) My daughter's name is Sarah. She has a widow's peak, hazel eyes and what at first might seem like an extra appendage but which, upon closer examination, reveals itself to be a very old, very odorous stuffed bear, a veteran of her bouts with the flu, the washing machine and even a long, torturous night spent, abandoned, in the supermarket. He has one eye, and leaves an unmistakable trail of fleece wherever he goes. His name, should you require it for the record, is Mister Pete. My son is Joshua. Because he was slow to walk, he was misdiagnosed with cerebral palsy, and it gave us quite a scare. Now he is graceful and long of limb. He is obsessed with choo-choo trains. The court—at the recommendation of my wife's psychologist—has granted custody solely to me.

MS. HAVILAND: (*A long pause.* MS. HAVILAND *swallows, hard. Her face is pinched. Finally:*) It's upstairs. (*They climb in silence up an invisible flight of stairs to the nursery. Finally, they enter. The sound of children playing in the street wafts through an open window.*) The wallpaper is a pale green candy stripe, suitable for a boy or girl. The border is Beatrix Potter. Window guards, of course. An intercom, so wherever you are in the house, you never feel far away. The children have their own bath. The basin is low, and the tub has a rail. As you can see, the emphasis here ... the design ensures ... *attempts* to ensure ... a child's *safety*. (MS. HAVILAND *sighs, heavily.*) I want *desperately* to sell this house. I like fretting over parquet, and measuring square feet, and judging closet space. I do not like being a *sentinel*. I do not like standing by quietly as people *gape* and *mock* and *jeer*. It's a disease, Doctor, and it is contagious, and some days, it's true, I fear *I am catching it*. This is not a *movie*. This is not *television*. (MS. HAVILAND *cries, softly.*) What I do is necessary. Houses are bought and sold. But sometimes ... because it is so recent ... because it is so far *beyond* tragedy ... what I do here feels like *desecration*. Walking in their tracks. Sifting through their things. *Oh, God, forgive me.*

DR. SIMIAN: Did you know the victims, Ms. Haviland?

MS. HAVILAND: No.

DR. SIMIAN: Even a passing acquaintance?

MS. HAVILAND: No.

DR. SIMIAN: Then permit me to suggest . . . this unfortunate event wields far greater power over you than perhaps it should.

MS. HAVILAND: *It's all I think about.* I have my own husband, my own children, we're remodeling our place on the Eastern shore, my mother has *cancer*—these things, they are *the substance of my life*—and now they are merely *distractions* to keep me from *obsessing* . . . *Why that night? Why those children? The parents, were they spared the sight, were they taken first, or were they forced to witness . . . And . . . this, Doctor, haunts me the most . . . what sort of man . . . what kind of brute creature . . .*

DR. SIMIAN: Anyone, I suppose, would wonder.

MS. HAVILAND: It's worse than *wondering.* Far more *extreme.* (MS. HAVILAND *cannot continue. She musters strength, and then:*) Once . . . a canceled appointment . . . I barricaded the front door . . . reset the alarm . . . drew the blinds . . . from her closet, a robe, blue with pink piping . . . and I sat in the study . . . swathed in her smell . . . poring through family albums. Birthdays. Christmases. The first day at school, afternoons at the fair, anniversary notes, private, still perfumed . . . They were not mine, but they *could've* been mine, they *might as well have been* mine . . . I am such a *hypocrite,* Doctor.

DR. SIMIAN: (*Soothing.*) It's all right.

MS. HAVILAND: I sat, alone in this house, with the lights out, and I waited.

DR. SIMIAN: For what?

MS. HAVILAND: The balcony door to open. The soft, almost noiseless crunch of rubber soles on white shag . . .

DR. SIMIAN: Why?

MS. HAVILAND: *If God gave me the chance to see evil, Doctor, then I would look. And that's a terrible thing to know about oneself.*

(MS. HAVILAND *looks at* DR. SIMIAN *pleadingly. He responds in a tender voice.*)

DR. SIMIAN: You are . . .

MS. HAVILAND: Go ahead. Say it.

DR. SIMIAN: (*Enigmatic now.*) You are a *very bad* little monkey.

MS. HAVILAND: I want my own life *back.* My own *concerns.*

(DR. SIMIAN *takes her hand.* MS. HAVILAND *takes a moment to calm herself.*)

DR. SIMIAN: Take a breath. We don't have to move.

MS. HAVILAND: A new family. Here. That would be nice. An *antidote,* yes, Doctor? Isn't that the word? I hope that you will contemplate this house. I hope that with all my heart.

DR. SIMIAN: I intend to.

MS. HAVILAND: I would like . . . I would like to be free of this. And I would like you . . .

DR. SIMIAN: Yes?

MS. HAVILAND: You . . . and your children . . . a fresh start.

DR. SIMIAN: Remember, Ms. Haviland, that you have your *own* home. Your own *retreat.*

MS. HAVILAND: (*Consoled.*) Yes.

(DR. SIMIAN *slips his dark glasses out of his pocket. He puts them back on.*)

DR. SIMIAN: Would you see me to the porch?

MS. HAVILAND: My pleasure, Doctor. (*Again, they backtrack in silence, this time without any obvious tension. They leave the house and step outside onto the porch.*) I'm embarrassed. My employer.

DR. SIMIAN: The robe, the snapshots.

MS. HAVILAND: If they knew . . .

DR. SIMIAN: Not a word.

MS. HAVILAND: Here's my card. If you have any question, don't hesitate.

DR. SIMIAN: (*Taking the card.*) I won't.

MS. HAVILAND: I'm sorry. My *display.*

DR. SIMIAN: Don't mention it.

MS. HAVILAND: I've shown you quite an afternoon, haven't I?

DR. SIMIAN: Quite.

MS. HAVILAND: You. A *stranger.*

DR. SIMIAN: I did wonder—

MS. HAVILAND: Yes?

DR. SIMIAN: A musing. A curiosity. Nothing pragmatic. Nothing "nuts and bolts."

MS. HAVILAND: Please.

DR. SIMIAN: One thing concerns me.

MS. HAVILAND: Oh?

DR. SIMIAN: No arrest. No conviction.

MS. HAVILAND: Sadly enough.

DR. SIMIAN: No substantive leads.

MS. HAVILAND: Every day, we pray.

DR. SIMIAN: As you suggest . . . there exists the possibility of . . . well, the perpetrator . . . he might return.

MS. HAVILAND: I see my paranoia has spread.

DR. SIMIAN: No, no. Your *prescience*. It's often been documented. Many a criminal—in spite of the immense risk—will return to the scene of the crime.

MS. HAVILAND: I can't *imagine* . . .

DR. SIMIAN: Regardless of the alarms. The reversible bolts. The electronic fences. Even the squad car at the curb.

MS. HAVILAND: But *why*?

DR. SIMIAN: All in pursuit of the covert thrill that comes with the successful commission of a wrongful act.

MS. HAVILAND: Is that *true*? Is that what they *say*?

DR. SIMIAN: It would not shock me to learn, Ms. Haviland, that you yourself had escorted the culprit through these halls.

MS. HAVILAND: It is a good thing that I am so *thorough,* Doctor. So *vigilant.*

DR. SIMIAN: He feigns interest in the housing market. Comes well-armed, perhaps, with the *classifieds.* You interrogate him, and for every question, he has a ready quip. He is from an obscure town. He is a banker. No. A lawyer. No. *A doctor.*

(MS. HAVILAND *freezes. Her whole body seems to clench.* DR. SIMIAN *takes a step closer to her.*)

MS. HAVILAND: *Yes.*

DR. SIMIAN: (*Takes another step, even closer.*) He is newly married. No. Expecting a baby.

MS. HAVILAND: No. *Separated.*

DR. SIMIAN: (*And another step closer.*) He has grown daughters. No. Adopted sons. No—

(DR. SIMIAN *is so near, she can feel his breath.*)

MS. HAVILAND: *A boy and a girl. One of each. Her name, it begins with an "S" . . . she has a toy, an old . . . a very beloved . . . it's plush . . . Mister Somebody . . .*

(DR. SIMIAN *cocks an eyebrow and waits for* MS. HAVILAND *to finish.*)

I can't . . . I don't . . . oh, God . . .

(DR. SIMIAN *reaches down and takes her hand. He separates her fingers with his own, and intertwines them. He speaks in a sensuous, hypnotic tone. Deep within* MS. HAVILAND, *continental plates begin to shift.*)

DR. SIMIAN: You usher him over the threshold. As you patter on—stucco and mini-blinds and Formica and chintz—with each step he's reliving, with a kind of salacious glee, the very night he thwarted every fragile notion of civilized behavior. The very night he let loose the constraints of his own base nature, and made the very darkest kind of history. (*With his free hand, gently,* DR. SIMIAN *takes* MS. HAVILAND *by the chin. He raises her face to meet his. They stare at each other.*) Tell me. *Do you ever consider that possibility?*

MS. HAVILAND: No. I do not.

DR. SIMIAN: Perhaps you should.

MS. HAVILAND: *I emphatically do not.* I can't . . . *afford* . . . to entertain such . . . *notions.* It would render my job untenable.

DR. SIMIAN: Yes.

MS. HAVILAND: It would induce paralysis. It would hold me captive.

DR. SIMIAN: Precisely.

MS. HAVILAND: *I cannot live my life that way.*

DR. SIMIAN: You're a wise woman.

MS. HAVILAND: (*Speaks with a very slight, almost imperceptible tremor.*) I hope that you will consider this house. I hope that you are in the market, and I hope that you will buy.

DR. SIMIAN: (*Nods in the direction of the squad car.*) Perhaps, when I leave, you'll offer the policeman a cup of coffee.

MS. HAVILAND: No.

DR. SIMIAN: Perhaps you'll have a conversation.

MS. HAVILAND: We've never met. I see him every morning, but we've never met.

DR. SIMIAN: Perhaps today is the day.

MS. HAVILAND: I do not know him.

DR. SIMIAN: That doesn't preclude a polite introduction.

MS. HAVILAND: I know *you*, Doctor.

DR. SIMIAN: Thank you.

MS. HAVILAND: You are the man whom I know.

DR. SIMIAN: Thank you *so much*. (DR. SIMIAN *lets her hand go. He takes a step back.* MS. HAVILAND *wavers, starts to melt into him. She holds herself back.*) It's been a lovely afternoon. And the house. The house is beautiful.

(DR. SIMIAN *turns to leave.* MS. HAVILAND *calls him back.*)

MS. HAVILAND: You're interested, then?

DR. SIMIAN: Yes.

(*Again,* DR. SIMIAN *turns to go. Again,* MS. HAVILAND *stops him.*)

MS. HAVILAND: (*Impulsively.*) Dr. Simian?

DR. SIMIAN: Ms. Haviland?

MS. HAVILAND: (*Darkly; almost seductively.*) You *are* interested? (DR. SIMIAN *smiles an enigmatic smile. He holds up* MS. HAVILAND'*s business card. With deliberate slowness, he slips it into his breast pocket. He pats his heart three times. They stare at one another a long time. Finally,* DR. SIMIAN *leaves.* MS. HAVILAND *lingers after him for a moment. Slowly, she turns back to gaze at the house. Slow fade to black.*)

END OF PLAY

BEA AND MAY

Edwin Sánchez

Bea and May premiered in 2007, as part of the UMass Play-in-a-Day Festival.

BEA *enters. She looks at* MAY, *dressed as a bride.* BEA *is fifty;* MAY *is thirty. Ish. Emphasis on the* ish.

BEA: May.

MAY: Bea.

(*They kiss. The kiss suddenly grows in passion until* MAY *breaks it off. They separate and stare at each other.*)

BEA: It wasn't so much what I could have, it was all about what I couldn't have. That is what keeps me up at night. Looking at you, knowing you don't care. Knowing you'd just as soon set me on fire as look at me, well, baby, that's just candy. That's just chocolate.

MAY: You missed the bridal shower.

BEA: Did I? I'll catch the next one.

MAY: There's not going to be a next one.

BEA: Uh-huh. Let's go with that for now. So.

MAY: So.

BEA: We doing it?

(*Silence.*)

Okay. We're not. But we'll still see each other?

MAY: In passing.

BEA: That's always been the best way with you.

MAY: You said you'd play nice.

BEA: You want me to play nice?

(MAY *checks herself in the mirror.*)

MAY: I knew I shouldn't have hired you as the caterer.

BEA: You needed at least one person you loved at your wedding.

MAY: You know, my mother once told me—

BEA: Oh God—

MAY: She told me that with age comes wisdom.

BEA: What was she, a hundred and five?

MAY: No. But she said the best thing, and you have to realize that I never listened to my mother, I mean, I'd rather chew glass than listen to her.

BEA: I would glaze over when my mother talked to me.

MAY: Color me surprised. Anyway, my mother said the best thing, she said, later in life, someone will ask you, "Who was the great love of your life?" and you'll be able to answer. Without remorse. Just a sort of "Oh yeah, that was them." So-and-so was the love of my life. And somehow, you missed it.

BEA: And that would be me.

MAY: No, that would be the man I'm about to marry. But, you would be in the top ten.

BEA: Do you have anything to drink?

MAY: How's that?

BEA: Alcohol. A drink. A cocktail.

MAY: No. It's a dry wedding. Good Lord, woman, you're the caterer, you must know we're driving this thing dry.

BEA: Vicks Formula 44? In a flask. On your thigh.

(*Pause.* MAY *retrieves a flask from under her dress.*)

MAY: Ice?

BEA: Straight up.

MAY: I can do that.

BEA: He doesn't know you drink, does he? God knows you're of age.

MAY: So sayeth the AARP cardholder.

BEA: Ouch. That's gonna leave a mark. And so uncalled-for.

MAY: I calls 'em like I sees 'em.

BEA: And how do you see me?

MAY: Lonely.

BEA: Can't be sued for libel on that one.

MAY: I've seen you in love, in heartbreak, in total despair.

BEA: Yeah, well.

MAY: You know why, don't you?

BEA: Sweet Lord, she's going to tell me.

MAY: Because you're obsessed with me. You're obsessed with me because I'm unattainable.

BEA: Egomaniac, your table is ready.

MAY: You've watched me fall in love, you've seen me marry a man.

BEA: Or two.

MAY: George didn't count.

BEA: Why, 'cause you caught him in your wedding dress?

MAY: Well, yeah. That should count as a deal breaker.

BEA: And who did you run to when it was all over?

MAY: To you. Where else would I run? Don't you know that some people are not meant to last a lifetime?

BEA: So, the new man in your life?

MAY: Jerry. Very sweet. Very rich.

BEA: And you love him?

MAY: I love the fact that he's grateful. And generous. That he makes no demands.

BEA: So, who does he look like?

MAY: The truth? Rosie O'Donnell.

(BEA *laughs.*)

He looks like an old woman. You know how some men look genderless when they get to a certain age? That's Jerry.

BEA: And he's rich?

MAY: Comfortable. (*Pause.*) Okay, rich. Filthy rich. Disgustingly rich.

BEA: Money trumps love.

(MAY *shrugs.*)

MAY: Tell me what money doesn't trump. I'll wait.

BEA: Your son is going to give you away? He doesn't know about us, does he?

MAY: If you ever tell him—

BEA: I won't.

MAY: I would never talk to you again.

BEA: I wish you well.

MAY: Yeah, right.

BEA: No, I do.

(*The Wedding March starts.*)

BEA: Ah, they're playing your song. It belongs to you. To a man and a woman.

MAY: Bea—

BEA: I swore I'd play nice.

MAY: I'm not going to fight with you.

BEA: I'm tired of fighting. For all the good times we've had, there have been too many battle scars. Every time we've kissed I felt as if my head were being held underwater. As if I were dying from a lack of oxygen.

MAY: Get the door.

BEA: Thirty seconds. A bride's supposed to make an entrance. I'm dying.

(MAY *stops.*)

Bouquet up. . . . I will be dead in under a year. It's irreversible.

MAY: What? Don't do this to me.

BEA: And oddly enough it's still about you. I swear, it's a gift. I'm releasing you, May. Letting you go. But I had to tell you.

MAY: To ruin my day.

BEA: To make sure when you heard about it, it would be from me, so you wouldn't feel guilty. That's not the right word. You wouldn't feel . . . guilty, I don't know if you'd feel any-thing. God forbid you should feel something. They're starting the wedding march again. They can start it up to three times before they send someone back here. Three times is cute. It's "Isn't the bride nervous?" as opposed to, "Did she open a window and make a break for it?"

MAY: Why didn't you tell me anything?

BEA: I'm telling you now. I hear some nervous twitters out there. I'm getting married myself. Tomorrow.

MAY: Don't joke.

BEA: Lovely girl. Woman. Older than the hills. Unattractive. Humorless. And loves me without measure. Has already promised to be there during the worst of it.

MAY: (*Looking at the door.*) Tell me you're lying. Tell me you're not dying.

BEA: And she'll do all this knowing she's my second choice.

(MAY *embraces* BEA.)

Don't make me slap you on your wedding day. The music stopped.

MAY: Oh crap, Jerry's coming up the aisle.

BEA: Tell him it's bad luck to see the bride before the wedding.

MAY: (*Calling out through a crack in the door.*) Don't you dare come in here. Zipper problem. I'll be right out.

BEA: And he believed you.

MAY: I'll cancel the honeymoon. I'll just stay in town, and take care of you.

BEA: No, that's Sheila's job. That's her name. She would do anything for me.

MAY: But you don't love her.

BEA: A minor detail. They're playing your song again. A little more tentatively this time. Those little pauses between the dum-dum-dah-dum.

(MAY *gets to the door, stops.*)

MAY: Jerry's rich. I can take care of you. I marry him, and I promise to take care of you. The best of everything. I swear.

(*Silence.*)

Don't be stupid. You won't want for anything. Everything you need. Please. Let me do this for you.

BEA: And if I told you the one thing I needed, the one thing I wanted, was for you to walk out of here. With me. Could you do that?

(MAY *hesitates, takes* BEA*'s hand. Goes toward the door that* BEA *came in through at the beginning.* BEA *stops her.*)

No. Through the other door. Through the door where all your family is waiting for you to come through. Take my hand and walk me through that door.

(MAY *stops. She begins to cry. She can't do it.* BEA *covers* MAY*'s face with her veil.*)

Go. Get married. I was lying.

MAY: No, you weren't.

BEA: No. I wasn't. But, if you don't have the strength to love me, how would you have the strength to help me die? This is going to be the last image I see of you. Be a pretty bride for Bea.

(MAY *takes a flower from her bouquet, gives it to* BEA. MAY *exits.* BEA *holds the flower, kisses it.*)

That's. Gonna leave a mark.

(BEA *exits.*)

END OF PLAY

DEEP JERSEY

Nina Shengold

Deep Jersey was performed as a staged reading by Actors & Writers at Saugerties Performing Arts Factory, Saugerties, New York, on October 6, 2012, as part of the evening "Spanking New Shorts," produced by Sarah Chodoff and Katherine Burger. The play was directed by Nina Shengold. The cast was as follows:

ANGIE SPIOTTO	Dannah Chaifetz
LAUREN BLAIR	Mary Gallagher

CHARACTERS

ANGIE SPIOTTO, former cheerleader whose looks have begun to calcify, with an unmistakable Jersey accent, stiff hair, and manicure.
LAUREN BLAIR, a semisuccessful novelist, dressed for stress: expensive but untended haircut, no makeup, tossed-on baggy sweats. No Jersey accent at first, but it sneaks in like crabgrass. They're both pushing fifty.

SETTING

Checkout lane in a twenty-four-hour supermarket in Bayonne, New Jersey, 3:30 A.M. Fluorescent lights, Muzak. No one in line. ANGIE, in pastel cashier's smock, talks on a cell phone.

ANGIE: . . . *Totally* dead, yeah. Hadda coupla stoners hittin the bulk bins around three ayem, then some toad bought a twelve of Bud Light. Now it's just me an the geek with the mop . . . Yeah, well, maybe slow is good news when you work the E.R., but I am like climbin the *walls*. It's dead beyond deadness.

(*Beat.*)

. . . Graveyard shift, yeah, I *know* why it's called that, Louise. You think you're the first person thought a that?

(*Beat.*)

Don' go get pissed at me, I was just . . . Yo, Louise! Whattaya, fuckin hang *up*? Are you shittin me? Really?

(*Beat.*)

Loser . . . . Oh, ya there? . . . Hold for what, like some nursey emergency?

(*Looks over her shoulder.*)

Gotta go, I gotta customer.

(LAUREN *pushes a grocery cart into the aisle, child seat piled high with mac 'n' cheese boxes, ice cream, potato chips, package of cupcakes. She starts loading them on the conveyor without making eye contact. * ANGIE *peers closer at her.*)

Lauren? Lauren *Blair*?

(LAUREN*'s wary, not pleased to be recognized.* ANGIE *points at herself.*)

Angie Spiotto, from Bayonne High.

(LAUREN *stares. Clearly wouldn't have known her.*)

LAUREN: . . . Angela?

ANGIE: Yeah! We had, what did we have togetha?

LAUREN: Gym.

ANGIE: Riiiight, gym class! Coach Fedda. You cut your hair.

LAUREN: Well, it's been thirty years.

ANGIE: (*Shakes her head.*) I didn mean gym. You look diff'rent from that photo, the one on ya book cover.

LAUREN: Oh. Yes, I'm in black-and-white.

ANGIE: I meant, yanno, hair, makeup . . .

LAUREN: Younger.

ANGIE: I didn say—

LAUREN: Younger. That photo was taken eight years ago. But thanks. Thanks for reading it.

ANGIE: I didn read it. I saw it on Lifetime.

LAUREN: So sorry.

ANGIE: It rocked. Tori Spelling was killa!

LAUREN: The novel is . . . different.

ANGIE: What, they made up a new ending or something?

LAUREN: Not really, well yes, but that's not what . . . The book is just . . . mine.

(ANGIE *nods, doesn't get it.*)

The movie belongs to the people who made it.

ANGIE: Like . . . it was adopted?

LAUREN: By parents with radically different values.

ANGIE: Whateva. I gotta huge bang outta seeing your name, Story by Lauren Blair. I was all like, I *know* her!

LAUREN: (*Hoping to leave.*) Well. Thanks.

ANGIE: Are ya writin anotha?

LAUREN: I've written two others. They weren't on Lifetime. In fact, they weren't published.

ANGIE: That sucks.

LAUREN: Yes it does. Well . . .

(*She takes out her wallet.*)

ANGIE: So what brings you back to Bayonne?

LAUREN: I'm just here for the weekend.

ANGIE: We don' get many writers from Lifetime at three thirty fuckin ayem.

(*Looks over her groceries.*)

Cupcakes, Ben, Jerry . . . You havin a party?

LAUREN: . . . Oh. Kids.

ANGIE: Yeah? How many?

LAUREN: Two boys and a girl.

(*Beat.*)

They're my sister's kids. I'm the weird aunt.

(*Beat.*)

Could you ring me up?

ANGIE: Are you in a hurry or somethin?

LAUREN: I . . . don't want to take up your time.

ANGIE: Whattaya, kiddin? This place is the crypt. Wait'll Louise hears I saw youze. She'll have a cow.

LAUREN: (*Beat.*) Louise Amicucci?

ANGIE: Yuh-huh, you remember her?

LAUREN: (*Dark.*) I remember *everything.* You used to strut down the hall in this pastel pink bomber jacket, cut up to . . .

(*Hand at waist.*)

Pink rabbit fur, with the shoulder pads?

ANGIE: Whoa. You remember my fuh?

LAUREN: With the Farrah hair. Platforms. The overdye jeans.

ANGIE: Uck, were those hideous!

LAUREN: Not at the time. You looked like Olivia Neutron Bomb.

ANGIE: The hell you say. Laura Branigan!

LAUREN: Gloria, right.

ANGIE: GLAW-ri-ya!

LAUREN: You used to go out with Gerard diCandido.

ANGIE: Ger-rod, what a pig.

LAUREN: What happened to him after high school?

ANGIE: Got married.

LAUREN: That figures.

ANGIE: To me.

LAUREN: Oh.

ANGIE: Knocked up, yanno? Happens. Divorced me right after, the turd.

LAUREN: That sucks.

ANGIE: He's an asswipe, good riddance.

LAUREN: So you've got a—daughter, son?

ANGIE: Both. I got four a my own, plus my third husband's daughter, she's livin with us while her mother's in rehab. Good times. Oh, and two grandkids, twins.

LAUREN: *Grandkids??*

ANGIE: You asked. Don't ask and don't tell, right? I wouldn'a told. But you asked, so. Hey, you're not a lesbian, are you?

LAUREN: What?

ANGIE: It's cool, I like Ellen. And whatsername, Linsey Lohane.

LAUREN: I'm not a lesbian. Not that it matters.

ANGIE: I just thought, no makeup, no kids, yanno, famous—

LAUREN: I'm not famous either.

ANGIE: You're famous for here.

LAUREN: You know, that might be true.

ANGIE: Swear to god. There's like *nobody* came from here, ever. Bruce, Bon Jovi, Danny DeVito, they're all like South Jersey, yanno? Jersey shore.

LAUREN: Snooki.

ANGIE: Snooki?? *Snooki's* from fuckin Poughkeepsie! Don't get me started on Snooki. Lab rat with a tan.

(LAUREN *laughs.*)

Nobody comes from deep Jersey. Nobody.

LAUREN: We do.

ANGIE: Right. Us.

LAUREN: You were so mean to me.

ANGIE: Geddouttatown, I was not.

LAUREN: Are you fucking kidding me? You and Louise used to call me the Exorcist Girl. You poured pea soup in my locker.

ANGIE: That was Louise.

LAUREN: Stole my books. Tore up my homework. Sprayed me with Cheez Whiz, poured nail polish onto my gym suit . . .

ANGIE: Kids, yanno? Kid stuff.

LAUREN: You told all the boys I had hair on my chest. And wore falsies, and shaved every morning.

ANGIE: Okay, yeah okay, I was a bitch.

LAUREN: Total bitch. *Thank* you.

ANGIE: . . . Because you were leaving.

LAUREN: What?

ANGIE: You had one foot out the door. We could smell it on you. Eau duh Ivy League.

LAUREN: Vassar.

ANGIE: Same difference. You left.

LAUREN: I came back.

ANGIE: Yeah, right. For the weekend. Big whoop.

(*Points at her groceries.*)

That ice cream's gotta be melted by now. Better go swap it, the kids'll be pissed.

LAUREN: The . . .

ANGIE: Your sister's kids?

LAUREN: Right. They're at home.

ANGIE: You were sayin.

LAUREN: At home. In L.A.

ANGIE: (*Gets it, nods.*) . . . Yeah, okay, right. I was wonderin what kinda kid would eat Chubby Hubby and Dulce de Letch.

LAUREN: I will put it back, though.

(*She doesn't.*)

Sometimes it seems better than nothing. And then it seems worse.

ANGIE: Been there, done that.

(*Pats her hips.*)

So whattaya, pukin it?

LAUREN: Treadmill. I live at the gym. It beats writing.

(*Beat.*)

You look good, Angela.

ANGIE: I look old.

LAUREN: We *are* old.

ANGIE: Yeah, fuck you too.

LAUREN: Listen, at least you have kids.

ANGIE: And grandkids, and stepkids. Two asswipe ex-husbands. My family's a regular dog pound. I'd kill to be single.

LAUREN: My mother, she's sick.

ANGIE: Oh. Is it, like—

LAUREN: It is, yes. Stage four.

ANGIE: So you . . . might be here more than the weekend.

LAUREN: As long as she knows who I am.

ANGIE: If you need any . . .

LAUREN: Thanks. I'm okay.

ANGIE: Louise works at All-County. If you need like a doctor or something.

LAUREN: We've got plenty of doctors. Doctors we got. I better get back.

(ANGIE *nods, picks up the package of cupcakes.*)

Oh, I'm gonna leave those. In the writing biz we call that editing.

ANGIE: One fuckin day at a time, right?

(*Sets package aside.*)

Hey, I'm sorry I . . . Like, with Louise?

LAUREN: (*Shrugs.*) Gave me something to write about. Life's a bitch.

ANGIE: If you wanna hear more, I could cry you a river.

LAUREN: I bet.

ANGIE: I got stories right out the kazoo. If you wanna, I'm here every weekend. The graveyard shift. You could come visit.

LAUREN: Right.

(*They look at each other, both feeling the distance, volumes unsaid.*)

ANGIE: Paper or plastic?

END OF PLAY

HEADS AND TAILS

Kelly Rhodes

Heads and Tails was first performed on December 8, 2011, at the Mildred Dunnock Theatre at Goucher College, where it was produced by Kelsa Dine and Aubrey Clinedinst through Goucher's Playworks. The director was Allie Moss, and the cast was as follows:

SHAWNA   Lindsay Carbonneau
LILLIAN   Diana Vogel

Stage is set as a dorm room with two beds. LILLIAN*'s side is a little bit messier. There is a large cage with two small animals in it near* SHAWNA*'s.*

Lights low, both girls enter together, having a silent argument. They get to the center of the stage. A bright spotlight comes on and they stop arguing, blinking against the light.

SHAWNA: Oh look, an audience . . .

LILLIAN: Good, you all can settle this bullshit for us. We'll both tell you our sides and you can decide which of us is the crazy one.

(SHAWNA *glares at her.*)

SHAWNA: Fine. But I get to go first.

LILLIAN: Oh, hell no.

SHAWNA: I said it first!

LILLIAN: (*Removes a quarter from her pocket and flips it.*) Call it.

SHAWNA: Heads!

(*Coin lands.*)

Ha! I get to go first! (*Grabs the coin and runs offstage.* LILLIAN *sighs angrily, puts on her headphones, and lies down on her bed, doodling in her notebook.*)

(*Lights come up.* SHAWNA *enters, drops her bag on her bed, then sits down, watching* LILLIAN.)

SHAWNA: Lil. (LILLIAN *doesn't hear her. Louder.*) Lil! (*Louder.*) Lillian!

(LILLIAN *takes off her headphones and turns to face* SHAWNA, *mimes talking.*)

I need to talk to you about something.

(*Looking concerned,* LILLIAN *sits up, mimes talking.*)

I feel like we've become pretty good friends this semester.

(LILLIAN *mimes talking.*)

I'm not done, babe. We've become pretty good friends, but I feel like we should talk about our whole roommate situation.

(LILLIAN *mimes talking.*)

I'll start. I feel like our room is kind of a mess, and that's something we could fix really easily. We just need to work together on it.

(LILLIAN *mimes talking.*)

Oh, I'm over that now.

(LILLIAN *mimes talking.*)

Yeah, it was just a twenty-four-hour thing.

(LILLIAN *mimes talking.*)

No, it is. I've read about it. Don't worry about it.

(LILLIAN *mimes talking.*)

(*Waves dismissively.*) Forget about it. Moving on. About that guy who comes over sometimes.

(LILLIAN *mimes talking.*)

(*Friendly sarcasm.*) No, that other guy you spend all that time alone with in here. Yes, him.

(LILLIAN *mimes talking.*)

No, of course not. I'm just asking that you let me know when he's going to be here so I don't walk in on you guys . . . well, you know . . .

(LILLIAN *mimes talking.*)

Call it what you will, just warn me.

(LILLIAN *mimes talking.*)

Well, there's no need to put it like that . . . but yeah.

(LILLIAN *mimes talking.*)

(*Goes over to the cage.*) Are they bothering you? I thought you said you would be okay with them.

(LILLIAN *mimes talking.*)

I bought them from a breeder . . .

(LILLIAN *mimes talking.*)

Okay, so maybe they're not purebred or whatever, why does that bother you?

(LILLIAN *mimes speaking.*)

Well, they're nocturnal.

(LILLIAN *mimes an angry rant.*)

(*Raising her voice.*) That's completely uncalled-for! This is my room too, you don't get to decide what's okay in here and what isn't without talking to me about it!

(LILLIAN *mimes yelling more.*)

Is that really so much to ask?

(LILLIAN *mimes yelling and then storms out.*)

(*Walks back over to her bed and flops down on it.*) What a bitch.

(*Lights go low, like they were in the beginning.* LILLIAN *storms on stage and holds out her hand.* SHAWNA *places the quarter in her waiting hand.* LILLIAN *goes to her bed, puts on the headphones, and starts to doodle.* SHAWNA *stays on her bed, arms crossed angrily.* LILLIAN *turns, sees she's still there, clears her throat, and shoos her away.* SHAWNA *grabs her bag and stomps offstage.* LILLIAN *resumes doodling.*

Lights come up. SHAWNA *enters, drops her bag on her bed, then sits down, watching* LILLIAN. *She mimes speaking.*)

LILLIAN: (*Takes off headphones.*) Yeah. What's up?

(SHAWNA *mimes speaking.*)

(*Sits up.*) Of course.

(SHAWNA *mimes speaking.*)

I mean, I don't know if I'd say that. We—

(SHAWNA *mimes interrupting her, then speaking.*)

> You know, I'm glad you brought that up. I've been wanting to talk to you about some stuff.

(SHAWNA *mimes speaking.*)

> I said that last week. You told me you couldn't clean because of your asthma.

(SHAWNA *mimes speaking.*)

> You're over your asthma?

(SHAWNA *mimes speaking.*)

> Shawna, asthma isn't like the flu. You don't just catch it and then wait for it to go away.

(SHAWNA *mimes speaking.*)

> That doesn't make any sense.

(SHAWNA *waves dismissively while miming speaking.*)

> Who? Jason? The guy who helps me with math?

(SHAWNA *mimes speaking.*)

> You have a problem with him helping me with statistics in our room?

(SHAWNA *mimes speaking.*)

> Doing statistics?

(SHAWNA *mimes speaking.*)

Sexile you when I'm doing statistics?

(SHAWNA *mimes speaking.*)

Fine, whatever. But also, I wanted to talk to you about your . . . umm, hamsters.

(SHAWNA *walks over to the cage, mimes speaking.*)

I would be totally okay with hamsters. Those are not hamsters.

(SHAWNA *mimes speaking.*)

Shawna. I did some research. Those things are called aye-ayes.

(SHAWNA *mimes speaking.*)

They're on the endangered species list! It's illegal to have them as pets! And you let them out of the cage at night!

(SHAWNA *mimes speaking*)

(*Getting really angry.*) So!? They can be nocturnal in their fucking cage! Or better yet, they can be nocturnal in their natural environment or a zoo or something, somewhere that there's no risk of me getting arrested just because my batshit insane roommate can't tell they're not hamsters!

(SHAWNA *mimes yelling.*)

So what you're saying is that I need to help you clean this hellhole because you're convinced your twenty-four-hour asthma is gone, I need to warn you when Jason will be here because clearly sex and statistics are the same thing, and that I should be totally okay with you allowing endangered animals to wander around my room at night, poking me in the goddamn ear looking for bugs, until PETA shows up?!

(SHAWNA *mimes exasperated yelling.*)

You are completely insane! (*Storms out, slamming door.*)

(SHAWNA *walks back to her bed, flops down on it, and mimes speaking.*

Lights dim again and spotlight comes up in center of stage. Both girls step into it, pushing each other to be the first there.)

LILLIAN AND SHAWNA: WELL?!

(*Blackout.*)

END OF PLAY

LESSONS FOR AN UNACCUSTOMED BRIDE

José Rivera

Lessons for an Unaccustomed Bride received its world premiere on August 4, 2011, as part of Summer Shorts 5 (J. J. Kandel and John McCormack, producing directors) at 59E59 Theaters, 59 East Fifty-Ninth Street, New York, NY 10022. The play was directed by Jen Wineman. The cast was as follows:

MAYRA	Shirley A. Rumierk
YESSENIA	Socorro Santiago

Miraflores, Puerto Rico, 1953.

A small old one-room house filled with dolls, candles, incense, statues of saints and West African gods, lucky bamboo, folk medicine, oils, amulets, esoteric books, fortune-telling cards.

A small coal-burning stove is the kitchen. A hammock is the bedroom.

MAYRA, *sixteen, in a plain dress, holds a large old cast-iron pot. She wears a small gold cross on a chain.*

YESSENIA, *thirties, covered in amulets and charms, stares at* MAYRA.

MAYRA: I wasn't going to come.

YESSENIA: Your eyes are lighter than I remember them. I like the way you wear your hair.

MAYRA: It was just my mother—*insisted* that I—

YESSENIA: I remember you throwing up all over my shoulder. You were about a year old. I don't think you ever apologized for that.

MAYRA: And, you know, with all due respect, I don't really believe in any of this . . .

YESSENIA: And you didn't apologize for the time, when you were six years old and your adult teeth were growing in, and you bit me on the leg. You remember?

MAYRA: I don't believe in—I mean, I'm a good Catholic—

YESSENIA: You don't remember. You treat me like a stranger. Like I'm someone to be afraid of.

MAYRA: I'm not afraid. I'm not afraid of you.

YESSENIA: Good! We're making progress! That's the first time you actually responded to something I said since you walked into my house.

MAYRA: I'm sorry, I know I'm being rude—

YESSENIA: But you don't want to be here.

MAYRA: I don't want to be here.

YESSENIA: And you're afraid.

MAYRA: And I'm afraid.

YESSENIA: You see? There's a lot we agree on. And you brought payment! Very, very good! Just put them right down here.

MAYRA: I don't believe in getting something for nothing . . .

YESSENIA: Why don't you put them down?

MAYRA: No, I'll hold on to them, thank you. I don't mind.

YESSENIA: Okay. Hold on to them. Why don't you sit?

MAYRA: I think I'll stand. Thank you.

YESSENIA: Some coffee? I just made coffee. It's nice and hot.

MAYRA: No thank you. I don't want any coffee.

YESSENIA: Some water?

MAYRA: No thank you.

YESSENIA: Rum?

MAYRA: No. No rum, please.

YESSENIA: No liquids of any kind. You're not going to put anything in your mouth while you're here. Why? Do you think
I'm going to poison you or put some nasty mojo in your
drink?

MAYRA: I had a full meal before coming to your house, Doña.

YESSENIA: Yeah, a full meal? Then explain to me why you're so
skinny. When you were a baby, you were fat. You ate everything in sight.

MAYRA: I really don't remember my childhood.

YESSENIA: That's why you've forgotten that you threw up on
me. And you never apologized.

MAYRA: Would you feel better if I apologized right now? Is that
what you want?

YESSENIA: Actually—yes. Apologize. And for biting my leg. I
still have the teeth marks. Look, I'll show you—

MAYRA: Oh, you don't have to—

YESSENIA: I'm sorry for throwing up on you and biting your leg,
Doña—say it!

MAYRA: I'm sorry for throwing up on you and biting your leg, Doña. It won't happen again.

YESSENIA: I should say not! You're sixteen years old! Imagine a girl your age throwing up on a woman my age? And biting her leg?

MAYRA: Maybe I should go. Maybe this was a bad idea.

YESSENIA: No. Stay. It's a good idea. You're doing exactly the right thing by seeing me.

MAYRA: Am I? I don't know anymore.

YESSENIA: Of course you don't. You're confused.

MAYRA: I'm not accustomed to . . . navigating the roads of love . . . my feelings are so . . .

YESSENIA: Of course! How could you be? It's a terrible situation.

MAYRA: You know the situation? You know what's going on?

YESSENIA: Of course I do. I know everything that happens in every barrio from here to Arecibo. Every time someone falls in love, I know about it. Fullano is cheating on Fullana? I have the details. Old Don So-and-So has cancer in his balls? His oldest son just impregnated his first cousin? Some idiot sold his horse for a handful of dust? Another idiot is worshipping the bottle? A hurricane is coming next week? My love, I am the island's newspaper! I have the facts at my fingertips!

MAYRA: That's quite a, a talent.

YESSENIA: Tell me about it. It's a burden. A cross to bear. My gift? Well, it's like purgatory itself.

MAYRA: Then why do you do it? Why not just turn your back on all this and come back to the church? It's not too late—

YESSENIA: You think I have a choice? You think my gifts are optional? My love, I don't control this. I don't ask it to come and go. It controls me. It tells me what to do. It is completely in charge!

MAYRA: How do you live like this? I just can't understand it.

YESSENIA: Well, it has its perks. Its rewards. I mean, look at me, right?

MAYRA: I know. You don't look like a woman who is old enough to be my mother.

YESSENIA: So, there is a bright side even to the slavery these gifts force on me. You're shaking with fear.

MAYRA: I'm sorry. I'm very sorry . . . I'm not accustomed . . .

YESSENIA: Well, I told you to stop being afraid. I told you, didn't I? Now stop it right now!

MAYRA: I'm trying . . .

YESSENIA: Look me in the eye. Nothing can happen in here unless we look each other in the eye.

MAYRA: Okay.

YESSENIA: Good. Settle down and breathe. Let your fear and negativity just fall off you. From the top of your head, your fear is just going to flow down like water. Through your shoulders and down your arms. Out across your hands and down—drip, drip, drip—off your fingers. Okay? Better?

MAYRA: I guess so.

YESSENIA: Good. Your fiancé is seeing another woman. She's someone he's known all his life. He's always been attracted to her. But she has a terrible reputation and no one wants to marry her.

MAYRA: Why does he want to see her so much?

YESSENIA: Because she's not you, my dear. Because your fiancé loves you but since you are so devoted to your virginity, he can't have you yet. So in his frustration and lust he does what all men do—he follows the course of least resistance and finds his way to the bed of a woman he wants to love but doesn't want to marry.

MAYRA: What—glad you brought that up—what do they do in that bed . . . ?

YESSENIA: Ay! What *don't* they do?!

MAYRA: It's—whatever it is—it's so wrong for him to be with her. He's mine. He made promises!

YESSENIA: Yes, it's wrong. And sinful. And very very common. Boring, even!

MAYRA: I loved him because I thought he was un-common.

YESSENIA: That was mistake number one, I'd say! My love, they are all the same. They are all sinners and cheaters and the faster you learn that little lesson the better you will be.

MAYRA: I can't believe that . . . I don't want to believe that . . .

YESSENIA: Believe it or not, it's your choice. If you *choose* to be a fool, there's nothing I can do for you—

MAYRA: I feel like a fool now!

YESSENIA: No, actually, coming to me was the smartest thing you've ever done. You could have gone to any witch in the barrio—but you came to the best. You came to me.

MAYRA: No, it's all weird and . . .

YESSENIA: Because *my* spells don't fail. My spells are potent. Ask anyone. To date, I have rescued fifty-six marriages. I have been responsible for the birth of four hundred and nineteen children. I've cured seven cancers. I've given good luck to countless.

MAYRA: . . . ay, how can I even believe what you're telling me . . . ?

YESSENIA: When I put this spell on your fiancé—*guaranteed*—he'll be a hundred percent faithful to you for the rest of his life. Every time he looks at another woman he'll see nothing but a hairy abomination and he'll vomit on the spot!

MAYRA: No. No. I can't. I'm sorry. Have a good day, Doña.

YESSENIA: Only if you leave your payment are you allowed to go home!

Go home and be a fool the rest of your life!

MAYRA: Payment? For what? Insulting my intelligence? Offending my Christian principles?

YESSENIA: Consulting fee! My time is valuable!

MAYRA: It's all a *scam* . . .

YESSENIA: Tell me you're not going to be like everyone else in this barrio! Use my services then refuse to pay me!

MAYRA: . . . it's all nonsense . . .

YESSENIA: Without these payments, I don't *eat*, you understand that?

MAYRA: . . . anathema to, to morality itself . . .

YESSENIA: Your mind is closed. Your mind is a coffin.

MAYRA: My mind and my heart are open to the truth. To the words written in divine fire by our Father Almighty. Those things are real. The objects of idolatry in your house? Straw, wood, rocks, paint, smoke—*nothing.*

YESSENIA: Okay, for coming into my house to insult me, you owe me *double* payment for that!

MAYRA: You want real magic? Open the Bible. There's magic on every page. There's power in every single syllable on those pages.

YESSENIA: *Stories*, that's all those are, myths and stories you tell a stupid and gullible child.

MAYRA: You really are as bad as everyone says you are.

YESSENIA: Parables and riddles and poems and legends that are so old no one knows where they started. And *you* people, you *hicks*—

MAYRA: I was a fool to come here and spend a moment of my time with you!

YESSENIA: You people swallow it whole and think it's all true, all literally true. The words in that book are clouds, my dear. And when you look at a cloud you see exactly what you want to see.

MAYRA: Look at all this shit in your house. Rubbish and nonsense.

YESSENIA: The virgin birth? The immaculate conception?

Transubstantiation? The trinity? The resurrection? Can we talk *bullshit*?

MAYRA: Voodoo dolls and chicken blood and love potions and wisps of hair and dream interpretation and playing cards and dice? Rubbish and nonsense!

YESSENIA: Well, then, get out. Take your ignorance and your Biblical superstitions with you. Oh, and while you're at it, ponder something for me. Ponder the goddamn sadistic killing of a young man whose death machine you wear around your neck—

MAYRA: This is a symbol of love and hope, lady, not death! This is where life *starts*. In the redemption he offered for our sins! This is the beginning of life!

YESSENIA: Out I said!

MAYRA: Look at it. Why don't you want to look at it? What are you afraid of?

YESSENIA: Take that pornography out of my house.

MAYRA: You can't, can you? You can't look at it. You'd rather worship the horns of a goat than look at this beautiful—

YESSENIA: Look, young lady, don't make me curse you! I like your mother and she respects me and right now she's the only thing keeping me from zapping some really nasty shit on you!

MAYRA: Look at it, touch it, feel the magic in this tiny, sad, human and completely divine little man—

YESSENIA: I'm so close to cursing you and your seed—

MAYRA: What are you afraid of? Why won't you even look at it? Huh? Come on—*look*!

YESSENIA: I've looked at it! I've looked at it all my life! I've done nothing but look at it! For Chrissakes! What is wrong with you? You come here and insult me and then you stab my heart with your fucking crucifix and treat me like I've never known the damn thing my whole life long! But you don't know, young lady, you don't know . . .

MAYRA: Know what?

YESSENIA: The hours. The days and months. Spent in this room. This house of wood and straw and rock that you love to insult. Sixteen years old and completely alone . . . a dead-drunk husband vomiting under a ceiba tree . . . and me, kneeling until my knees were bleeding, praying to God, invoking the mercy of the Holy Ghost and begging for a sign from your little metal man.

MAYRA: Doña, don't cry . . . I didn't mean to make you . . .

YESSENIA: Don't you worry about that. You haven't earned the right to see me cry.

MAYRA: But I see your tears, Doña. I'm sorry, I'll leave the payment and I'll go home and I'm sorry for . . .

YESSENIA: Hours and days and months, on my sixteen-year-old knees, right here, not eating, not sleeping. The twins were sick. It happened so fast. Their stomachs were so hard and round. Their fevers were burning. They couldn't open their eyes. I prayed to your friends in your book for their relief. I didn't even want salvation, I just wanted their fever to go down. And your little book with its little selfish God wouldn't even give me that. Two babies in the same week, dead and gone and the emptiness in this old house nearly choked me to death.

MAYRA: My God, Jesus, how could that happen . . . ?

YESSENIA: You think love is all about making life? Love is the place where death's worst work is done. A cow dies, a tree falls and you don't mourn because you don't love. But love—love as hard as I did—and death is magnified until it's stronger than the sun.

MAYRA: Tonight I will pray for you, I will.

YESSENIA: Oh, thanks! That'll help! My girl, this house was *full* of Christ! Christ up to the ceiling! I threw it all out. Right in the trash in the back of the house where the pigs eat— and I burned the rosary beads and the pretty painted smiles of the Virgin and the Last Supper flickered in the twilight and the ashes flew straight up in the air.

MAYRA: Listen, Doña, I . . . I can heat some of this up for you . . . would you like me to do that?

YESSENIA: I turned away, after that little holocaust. Yes, I turned away. I heard the twins crying at night, long after they were buried. I heard the sobs and their pleas for mercy, and, yes, I turned away. And found a different path and made a different choice and opened myself up to the secret gifts I always suspected I had—the power I ignored because I was afraid of it—and I came to *this*—all of THIS—I found something here—and it brings me some escape and, when I'm lucky, a few *pasteles* and chickens as payment, and, when I'm even luckier, some coins to spend on something foolish. Do you understand?

MAYRA: I . . . I understand your choice, Doña, even if I don't approve of it.

YESSENIA: Holy fucking Christ, you are a stubborn one.

MAYRA: Yes, they all tell me that. The way I was raised, I guess.

YESSENIA: You were raised well. Unlike me. I can see it.

MAYRA: My parents were very strict . . . but they never told me anything about . . . *life*, and . . .

YESSENIA: They did *something* right. Your head is full of trash but you know right from wrong, I can see that.

MAYRA: Don't you want to sit down? I really will heat this up for you.

YESSENIA: I sit all day. My ass hurts from sitting all the time. But, yes, if you want, you can heat that up for me.

MAYRA: I think you'll like these *pasteles*. Mami worked all day on them and the pork is fresh.

YESSENIA: It smells good.

MAYRA: Mami doesn't do anything half way. She taught me that. I guess that's why I'm here. I've loved this man so much, Doña, with everything in my being. I've been honest with him. I've told him everything about me. Told him about the childish things I've done and even about having rickets and worms when I was young . . .

YESSENIA: That explains the vomiting . . .

MAYRA: Even about my terrible temper . . .

YESSENIA: The teeth marks on my legs!

MAYRA: He inspires me, Doña. He tells me a story and suddenly I'm not here anymore. I'm not poor, living in a barrio, wearing the same dress day after day and wondering where the next meal is going to come from. I'm flying. I'm drifting into the sky on the soft carpet made of words. His words. And then . . . his touch, Doña . . . the few secret times I've held his hand or put my head on his chest . . . it's the opposite of flying . . . it's a little like dying . . . a warm, satisfying and gentle little death.

YESSENIA: I have to meet this man!

MAYRA: No, I don't think I'll let you do that, Doña! I have enough trouble with him already!

YESSENIA: So . . . do you want my help or do you not want my help?

MAYRA: I don't know. I really don't.

YESSENIA: Okay, I'll be honest, there are limits to what I can or cannot do. I can't perform miracles. I can't turn a pig into a horse. I can't stop a hurricane.

MAYRA: I didn't think you could . . . not even my prayers could do those things . . .

YESSENIA: So here we are. Two women. A pretty young woman and a slightly older woman who has kept her beauty and youth, not by magic, but by being careful . . . being careful never to love a man again . . . being careful never to attach myself to any living thing again . . . to never let anyone see me cry . . .

MAYRA: Ay, Doña, I'm so sorry for your loss . . .

YESSENIA: But here we are! Two women with a man-problem. A cheating man we love and can't get out of our minds. A man we can't just expel out of our lives like an olive pit. What do we do? Shall we kill the son-of-a-bitch?

MAYRA: No! We can't do that! We can't kill the man!

YESSENIA: Shall we change him through magic? That's a serious
question.

MAYRA: I . . . don't want it that way, Doña. I don't want any other
force working on him. No force of any kind . . . not your
candles and dolls . . . not the force of Christ and the cross . . .
only . . . the force of his own morality and decency and the
force of my love . . .

YESSENIA: Yes, okay . . .

MAYRA: But how do we do that? How do we start that process?

YESSENIA: Eat with me. I'll put out the candles and hide the
dolls in the back of the house and you'll close your little
Bible and take off your crucifix. Not for the rest of your
life, but just for tonight. And we'll sit down and we'll eat
and we'll talk about men and how they really are and how
we really are, and what mistakes *we* made, and how *we* can
change. And we'll figure this out together, young lady. Like
two smart country girls, we'll figure this out.

MAYRA: Yes. It's just a man-problem, isn't it?

YESSENIA: Men are idiots! It's so easy to figure them out!

MAYRA: You really think so?

YESSENIA: God bless me, that smells so good! Your mother made
it, you said?

MAYRA: All of it. I don't cook. I hate to cook.

YESSENIA: Well, girl, that's mistake number two, I'd say!

MAYRA: That's nonsense! *He* can learn to cook for me! The
nerve! I'm no one's slave, you know!

YESSENIA: No you're not! What else are you not?

MAYRA: I'm not a fool!

YESSENIA: You're not a fool. I see that now. I see you're going to be okay.

MAYRA: You see that? Through your dolls and cards?

YESSENIA: Through your eyes. I see you're strong and very teachable and I think you're going to be okay.

MAYRA: Thank you. It's good to hear that for a change. My parents say I'm an idiot. My father hits me on the head all the time. My mother laughs at my questions. They make me feel so stupid! That's why they sent me here!

YESSENIA: I'm sorry to hear that. You deserve better.

MAYRA: Thank you.

YESSENIA: Look, well, as long as you're ready for the wedding night, that's all you really need to know.

MAYRA: Why?

YESSENIA: What do you mean, why?

MAYRA: What happens on the wedding night?

YESSENIA: Don't you know?

MAYRA: No one will goddamn *tell* me, for the love of God!

YESSENIA: Oh, girl. Pull up a chair. We have a lot to talk about, oh yes we do . . . I see that now!

MAYRA: Oh. Now I'm *really* scared!

(YESSENIA *laughs.*)

(*Confused, concerned, scared, and a little excited,* MAYRA *serves the* pasteles.)

(*They sit to eat.* YESSENIA *prepares to teach her about the facts of life.*)

(*Fade to black.*)

END OF PLAY

THAT FIRST FALL

Daria Polatin

That First Fall premiered at Actors Theatre of Louisville in January 2011, in an evening of short plays entitled "The Tens." The play starred Ellen Haun and Martina Bonolis, and was directed by Lila Neugebauer.

CHARACTERS
SKYLER, around eighteen
ZOE, around eighteen

SKYLER *and* ZOE, *two girls around eighteen, sit on the stoop of a brownstone in Brooklyn.* ZOE *is dressed in preppy clothes, and* SKYLER *is a hippy-hipster blend. It's dusk.*

SKYLER *is rummaging through her bag.*

SKYLER: I mean it was just like, so lame, you know? Like, we read *Wuthering Heights* in high school, right? And no one there had even heard of it.

(*Rummaging.*)

Where are they . . . Oh, and also? No one there speaks English. So that's super fun.

(SKYLER *finds what she was looking for: a small silver case.*)

Thank God.

(SKYLER *opens the silver case and takes out a clove cigarette. She lights it and takes a long drag.*)

I'm so over college . . .

(SKYLER *passes the clove to* ZOE, *who hesitates a moment, then takes a drag. They continue to pass the clove back and forth throughout the play.*)

ZOE: It'll get better.

SKYLER: I hope so. Do you have to take stupid high school–level English classes too?

ZOE: Kind of. We have these—they call them foundational classes, so there's a lot of remedial stuff.

SKYLER: I don't get it: We already learned that shit, you know? That's *why* we went to high school.

ZOE: I know, but they just want to make sure everyone knows the basics.

SKYLER: I guess.

(*After a moment.*)

So is your mom making a turkey or is she doing duck again?

ZOE: We're going to my uncle's in Westchester.

SKYLER: Is your cute cousin gonna be there?

ZOE: Dan?

SKYLER: Amanda.

(*A tense pause.*)

ZOE: I don't know. My parents haven't really told me much. They're just so excited that I'm home. They won't stop trying to feed me. I've gained, like, two pounds already and I've only been home for a day.

SKYLER: I thought you just got back.

ZOE: Oh, I got in last night.

SKYLER: Why didn't you tell me?

ZOE: It was late, and I had a ton of stuff to do today . . .

SKYLER: I was up last night. You should have told me. I streamed this really crazy ninja movie from this Japanese website with the most amazing subtitles. It was so funny.

ZOE: Cool . . . How's your mom?

SKYLER: She's good. She's selling at a bunch more stores now, so she's busy, which is good.

ZOE: That's great! . . . Have you talked to your dad?

SKYLER: You know, if he did even call? I'd be like, I don't even wanna talk to you, okay? So don't bother. Hope you're having fun in *Jersey.*

(ZOE *doesn't know what to say.*)

He and whatever-her-name-is can take their twins and shove 'em back up her hoo-ha. I was over there last month and he barely even said a word to me. All he did was fawn over those stupid kids, and he kept being like, "Aren't they cute? Aren't they cute?" Of course they're cute—they're fucking babies.

ZOE: I'm sorry, Sky.

SKYLER: Oh! Okay, so Friday night, 'member JD? You know, "Rasta-Man"?

ZOE: JD "The Black White Guy"?

SKYLER: He finally got dreads.

ZOE: Blond dreads? That must look weird.

SKYLER: They actually look kinda cute on him.

(*Beat.*)

So, okay: He's having everyone over on Friday, and we're gonna, like, party and eat leftover turkey and shit. He's inviting our whole class.

ZOE: Everyone came back?

SKYLER: Pretty much. I think everyone's home except for Devon—her family went to, like, Haiti to build houses or something. I think they're Pagan . . . So JD's is gonna be awesome. And his friend Trina has this sweet ganja hookup.

ZOE: I'm not sure if I'll be back.

SKYLER: You have to! Everyone's gonna be there. Stella and Todd are back from Vassar, and Evangeline's home from Smith. You're not gonna stay at your uncle's the whole weekend, are you?

ZOE: No . . .

SKYLER: So come back Friday afternoon. Take the train or something.

ZOE: (*Beat.*) On Friday I'm actually going to stay with another friend.

SKYLER: So bring them.

ZOE: In Connecticut.

SKYLER: Who lives in Connecticut?

ZOE: A friend from school.

SKYLER: Oh ... What's her name?

ZOE: His name is Chandler.

SKYLER: Chandler? Zoe, "Chandler"? Seriously?

ZOE: He's nice.

SKYLER: He must be if your parents are letting you stay with a guy they don't even know.

ZOE: They—do know him.

SKYLER: Your parents met him?

ZOE: A couple of times.

SKYLER: When?

ZOE: At parents' weekend. And ...

SKYLER: And what, Zoe?

ZOE: ... He came over for dinner.

SKYLER: You came home? Why didn't you tell me?!

ZOE: It was a really short visit. And I didn't want to bother you 'cause I knew you were busy with schoolwork and stuff.

SKYLER: Um, first of all, if you read any of my emails, Facebook updates, or tweets, or looked at my Instagram, you would know that I happen to be very un-busy with schoolwork. Second of all, this "Chandler" must be a very good friend if you brought him home and you were so busy you didn't even have time to call me.

ZOE: Sky—

SKYLER: So you're gonna, like, go hang out in Connecticut for the weekend at some Ivy League guy's house instead of chilling with your real friends? What are you gonna do, play golf? Cricket?

ZOE: Don't be a snob.

SKYLER: I'm not the one going to Connecticut. Where does he live, Greenwich?

ZOE: Westport. His family is having us over for dinner on Friday, then I'm staying for the weekend.

SKYLER: And your parents are letting you do that? I mean, I know my mom wouldn't care—she might not even notice if I was gone for a whole weekend, and my dad—please. But your parents? Letting you stay at a strange boy's house? This guy must be really special.

ZOE: Come on, Skyler.

SKYLER: So you're seriously going to hang out with some book-smart, preppy jock rather than hang out with your best friend?

ZOE: . . . It's not like that.

SKYLER: Zoe, we played in Prospect Park before it was safe. We hung out on Fifth Avenue before there were boutiques. We bought weed from the kids in the projects.

ZOE: I know, it's just . . .

SKYLER: What, Zoe? Now that you go to an Ivy League school and I go to state college, I'm not good enough for you?

ZOE: No.

SKYLER: But Chandler's your boyfriend, right? Which you didn't even tell me. And you've known him for what, two months? We've known each other since we were born. I can't believe you didn't tell me!

ZOE: I knew you were going to get mad.

SKYLER: I'm mad 'cause you don't tell me anything anymore.

ZOE: I wanted to wait until the right time.

SKYLER: Like, during the two seconds you have to see me before you go back to Connecticut?

ZOE: I'm sorry, Sky.

SKYLER: You know what? Whatever. It's fine. If that's the way you want to be, that's fine.

ZOE: Sky, look, it's not what you think. I still . . . You're still my best friend.

SKYLER: Why thank you, your Yale-ness.

(ZOE *gets up.*)

ZOE: I have to get home.

SKYLER: I was kidding. God . . . Don't go . . .

(*Re: the clove.*)

You have to help me finish this.

(ZOE *takes a moment, then slowly sits back down.*)

If you don't want to come to JD's, that's your deal.

ZOE: It's not that I don't want to. I'm just doing something else instead.

SKYLER: Chandler.

ZOE: Skyler!

SKYLER: What!

(*They stare at each other for a few moments. Then, slowly:*)

ZOE: . . . What happened in August isn't going to happen again.

SKYLER: What?

ZOE: You know . . .

(*Long silence.*)

It's not. Going. To happen. Again . . . Ever.

SKYLER: Whatever, we were drunk.

ZOE: I'm not going to do that again . . . I'm not that kind of person.

SKYLER: And what exactly is "that kind of person"? A person like me? You're saying you're not a person like me?

ZOE: No, Sky, it's . . .

SKYLER: What, Zoe, don't they teach you how to speak full sentences at Yale?

ZOE: Stop it.

(SKYLER *is quiet.* ZOE *takes a moment.*)

We're friends, Skyler.

SKYLER: I know.

ZOE: That's all.

SKYLER: I get it . . .

(*Beat.*)

I've been dating a bunch of guys, BTW.

ZOE: That's great.

SKYLER: So . . .

(*Quiet.* SKYLER *stubs out the clove.*)

I have to go. My mom's making vegan chili for tomorrow and I have to chop a million vegetables.

ZOE: That sounds good.

SKYLER: It's *vegan chili.*

(SKYLER *gets ready to go.*)

ZOE: Do you wanna have one more?

SKYLER: What?

ZOE: Clove? . . . Before you go?

SKYLER: Oh . . . Okay.

(SKYLER *sits back down. She takes another clove out of the case and lights it. She takes a drag, then passes it to* ZOE.)

I do really have to go soon, though.

ZOE: Okay.

SKYLER: Okay . . .

(SKYLER *and* ZOE *share the cigarette in silence as the lights fade.*)

END OF PLAY

WAKING UP

Cori Thomas

Waking Up was first performed as part of the evening "The River Crosses Rivers II" (Elizabeth Van Dyke and Jamie Richards, coartistic directors) at Ensemble Studio Theatre (William Carden, artistic director; Paul Slee, executive director) in New York City on September 17, 2011. Set design was by Rebecca Lord-Surratt, sound design by Bill Toles, lighting design by Greg MacPherson, costume design by Erica Evans; the production stage manager was Kevin Clutz. It was directed by Tea Alagić, with the following cast:

AMERICAN WOMAN	Amy Staats
AFRICAN WOMAN	Lynnette Freeman

Lights up on two women. One is an AMERICAN WOMAN. *She could be any race. The other is an* AFRICAN WOMAN *about the same age. She wears a* lapa *and sandals. During the course of the play, they do not speak to each other, they exist in their own space in a parallel universe.*

AMERICAN WOMAN: I found a lump.

AFRICAN WOMAN: I found a bump in my left breast.

AMERICAN WOMAN: In my right breast.

(*Beat.*)

While I was in the shower. I called my best friend who called her therapist who referred me to an internist who knows one of the best breast surgeons in New York. I googled him and he looked great. Everyone said, "He's the best!" I called his office. They told me to come in the next day. I cancelled a meeting I had with a new client who wants me to decorate her office. My assistant got her on the phone, "I'm so sorry," I said. "I found this lump." She said, "Don't worry, go and get a massage and for God's sake, take a Valium or a Xanax for your nerves. This happened to me. It was nothing, but oh my God, someone should complain. What they put you through. I'm telling you, take something!"

AFRICAN WOMAN: I went to the clinic. It is two hours walk from my village. I stood on a long line and waited and waited. It was raining. I found a big leaf from a banana tree and I held it over my head, but no use. And they turned us away. "Too many people. Too much HIV. Too much typhoid and malaria. Go and come back another day." I turned and walked back to my village. Two hours. When I almost reached home, the rain stops falling. Near my house, the chickens and the goats greet me and we all walk together.

AMERICAN WOMAN: They put my breast between two plates and squeeze hard. And squeeze hard. They squeeze and squeeze and squeeze . . . and squeeze. They squeeze until they get what they want. Then they send me in for the sonogram. The lady squirts cold gel all over my breast. She guides the wand over the gel. She stares at the screen. You look up at her. Looking for a clue. She refuses to meet your eyes. "Is it okay?" you ask, and she says, "You'll have to wait for the doctor to speak to you." "But can't YOU just tell me what you think?" you ask. She says, "Sorry, no."

AFRICAN WOMAN: That evening I pluck a newly killed chicken, season it, and put it in the pot. I sit on the wooden stool my husband made me. I feel the stupid bump inside of me. It is small. Like a small pea. Like the bead in my daughter's hair. I begin to pray. I say, "Please God, don't let this small bump kill me. I have two boys and a girl, and a husband, and these chickens and a goat. My husband has promised me I can begin high school in a year. Please don't let this small bump kill me. *Ase!*" (*Pronounced* a-shay.)

AMERICAN WOMAN: The doctor tells me eighty percent of these things are benign. "Do you have a family history?" "No," I say. "Good," he says. "And also, you're young." "I don't feel that young," I say, kind of to myself. Kind of in a low voice. He doesn't look into my eyes. "You'll have a biopsy tomorrow. The pathology report will tell us what we need to know. For what it's worth, I don't think it's anything." My heart does this little jump. I try to think positive. I try to remember what this thing I read in a magazine said about manifesting your wish by seeing it. My wish right now is that this is nothing. I erase everything from inside my head so that I see . . . nothing . . . nothing . . . just nothing.

AFRICAN WOMAN: After supper, I say, "I must walk to my mother's home." My eldest son wants to come. "No," I say, "stay and study your lessons. Do you want to be like me? I don't know book." My Mum sends my cousin to get some of the ladies of the village to come right away because this might be the same breast sickness my grandmother died from.

AMERICAN WOMAN: That night before I go to bed, I pray. I never pray. I try to remember this prayer my mother used to make me say when I was a little girl, "Now I lay me down to sleep. I pray the Lord my soul to keep. If I should die before I wake, I pray the Lord my soul to take."

(*Beat.*)

Why would I die before I wake? . . . Why would I want someone to take my soul? . . . Instead of trying to figure this prayer out, I take an Ambien. And I sleep.

AFRICAN WOMAN: The ladies stand around me in a circle. Nobody speaks. They put their hands on me. They all put their hands . . . on me and I feel . . . safe.

AMERICAN WOMAN: I dream about my first night in college. My mother, made my bed, "for the last time," she said. She put my clothes away in the narrow dresser. "I'm retired from motherhood now, you're on your own, kid."

AFRICAN WOMAN: I do not want to die. If a snake appears and poisons me, so be it. If the rebels come and shoot me, or cut my throat with a knife, so be it. I cannot control that. But for my own body to turn on me, and kill me, no, I cannot accept that. *Ehenh!*

AMERICAN WOMAN: For the biopsy, you get undressed. You lay facedown on a table. They put your breast in a hole which squeezes. A doctor gets under the table and sticks a big needle into your breast, it's the painkiller, but it hurts. Then she inserts another needle for the biopsy. She says, "Don't worry, I do these all day. They find something in maybe one patient . . . every three days . . . and don't move . . . and don't cry." A nurse holds my hand. She dries my tears with a tissue, I squeeze her hand as if to say, "Thank you." They send me home with an ice pack.

AFRICAN WOMAN: My Aunty makes a paste of hot pepper, mud, and crushed leaves. She says, "Rub this paste over the bump and bind your chest tightly with a cloth so that the medicine can enter your skin."

AMERICAN WOMAN: I lay on my purple chaise lounge with an ice pack on my chest and an ice pack over my eyes. And I keep telling myself, "If he says it's nothing, it must be nothing, nothing, nothing . . ."

AFRICAN WOMAN: I tell my husband, "I cannot raise my legs for you tonight because it is my time of the month." But it was really because of the paste. He is annoyed, but then he says, "You are a good wife." He has never said something like that to me. It gives my heart hope. But in the morning, the bump feels as if it has grown a little.

AMERICAN WOMAN: I go to meet with the doctor for results. My friend Julie, the lawyer, is with me. They say you should have someone with you. I have not even told my Mom. I'll call her with the good news. After this is over, I'll call her. With good news.

AFRICAN WOMAN: Finally, I enter the clinic. A white man, who is a doctor, will examine me. A lady says, "My name is Comfort. I will stay in the room with you." The doctor asks me if

I have children, if anyone from my family has had the breast sickness, if they died from it, if I am married, and I say, "Yes. Yes. Yes. Yes." Comfort says, "Undress, then lie down and lift your left arm so he can feel the bump." As his fingers mash around my skin, he closes his eyes as if he is listening to a very quiet sound. When he comes to the spot where the bump is, he stops, and then he mashes there again. And again. And again. As if he is making sure he really feels what he feels. He does not open his eyes. He is hearing something only he can hear. A secret. "Does it hurt?" he says, and his voice is deep, and I do not want to speak. Because while he is pressing and listening to the bump, I prefer that it is his hand feeling it instead of mine. I prefer that he is listening to its quiet music. He asks again, "Does it hurt?" I say, "No. It does not hurt."

AMERICAN WOMAN: "The test is positive, you have cancer." That is what he says. That. Is. What. He. Says. "You have cancer. You have cancer." I try to rewind. The word "positive." "Isn't positive a good thing?" In fact, I smiled when I heard it, because at first I thought it was a good thing. I wish I could go back to yesterday. To last week. But I'm here now. And this is now.

(*Beat.*)

This is now.

AFRICAN WOMAN: When I get home, I pretend as if nothing is wrong. I cook dinner. Greens and crawfish, rice, hot pepper. Mango plum. Every time I rub my fingers over my flesh I wish that I will not feel something under there. But every single time, I do.

AMERICAN WOMAN: He tells me that in a week I will have a lumpectomy. "Then you'll start chemotherapy and you will lose your hair." I google everything he says. There's other stuff too, I find out. I'll feel tired. I'll lose my hair, yes. I may get sick but they have medicines for that so probably not. My hands and feet may get numb. And after that . . . Well . . . after that . . .

AFRICAN WOMAN: My Aunty says, "They must cut your whole breast off!" "Eh?! The whole thing?" "Yes," "Can't they just remove the bump?" "That is what they do. Be brave! Get to the hospital early, so you are in the front of the line. That way the doctors will be fresh. Here is some money from the village women for your journey." When I arrive, there are already five people in front of me. We all sleep outside together. Thankfully the rain does not fall during the night and when we hear the cock crow and when we open our eyes and when we see the sun come up, the day is bright.

AMERICAN WOMAN: My best friend Julie, the lawyer, has found a lump now. Oh my God! Is this an epidemic? I go with her to her appointments.

AFRICAN WOMAN: My chest pains me, because they have removed my breast. The wound is awful to see. I try to touch it gently for it is the me I am now.

AMERICAN WOMAN: Julie's case is worse than mine was. I am surprised that I can have cancer and feel lucky. That is a new feeling, feeling lucky. I used to only care about my client base, and making money, and finding a successful man. Now, I think about laughter and flowers and hugs. My apartment is beautiful but it's empty. I walk from room to room and I think about finding someone to sit in my house with me. So silly! but really . . .

AFRICAN WOMAN: My husband has left me, although I begged him not to take my children. I begged him. And . . . he has relented! He has left them with me! He said, "If the sickness returns, I will come back to take them away from you." I rub their soft cheeks every morning. I am so happy that they are here with me. And touching them and feeling their skin makes me laugh. (*She laughs.*)

AMERICAN WOMAN: (*She laughs.*) I laugh because I realize I'm breathing in and out. I am breathing /

AFRICAN WOMAN: And knowing I am breathing makes me feel strong /

AMERICAN WOMAN: And I feel hope because /

AFRICAN WOMAN: And I feel hope because /

(*Slightly overlapping.*)

AMERICAN WOMAN: I'm alive!

AFRICAN WOMAN: I'm alive!

END OF PLAY

3:59am

a drag race for two actors

Marco Ramirez

3:59am: a drag race for two actors premiered at the Actors Theatre of Louisville's Humana Festival of New American Plays in March 2009. The scenic design was by Paul Owen, costume design by Emily Ganfield, lighting design by Nick Dent, sound design by Benjamin Marcum, and properties design by Mark Walston. The stage manager was Paul Mills Holmes and the dramaturg was Julie Felise Dubiner. Amy Attaway directed the following cast:

LAZ	Daniel Reyes
HECTOR	Matthew Baldiga

Black. Then a pinspot on LAZ, *nineteen. Direct address.*

LAZ: It's like a hundred degrees outside,
    The asshole downstairs is watching porn again with the vol-
    ume all the way up,
    And every time I close my eyes I feel the walls *closing* in on
    me in my room,
    'Cause even though it's just *me* in there now,
    (My sister moved out like two weeks ago
    And we don't know where she is
    And we don't talk about it),
    Even though it's just *me*,
    I swear to god the place is getting smaller.
    . . .
    And my aunt is coloring her hair,
    And my mom is smoking cigarettes in the kitchen,
    Screaming some shit about how I'm just like my father
    But I just *go*.
    . . .
    I leave the apartment in my flip-flops and my gym shorts
    and my Field Day T-shirt from the sixth grade that still fits
    me 'cause I was a fat little shit,.
    . . .
    I just *go*.
    . . .
    And even though it's a hundred degrees outside I still gotta
    warm up my Civic,
    'Cause it's old-school like Hammerpants and I bought it off
    a guy works at Chicken Kitchen,
    But I get in,

Keys in ignition.

. . .

And for a minute or two I just listen to that Honda engine
put-put some shit in Japanese

. . .

And it comes to life,.

. . .

The trunk smells like Chop-Chop curry mustard and Mr.
Pibb but that doesn't matter,
'Cause with the volume all the way up,
I sink into the driver's seat like shit was
Custom-made for my ass.

. . .

And I start driving,
In my flip-flops and gym shorts and Field Day T-shirt from
the sixth grade that still fits 'cause I was a fat little shit.

. . .

And I don't remember putting my foot to the pedal
Or first gear
Or second gear
Or stoplights
But I'm gone.

. . .

I fly.

. . .

And next thing I know I'm down a half a tank of gas
And I look at the clock,
And bro,

HECTOR AND LAZ: It's two o'clock—

LAZ: —In the fucking morning.

(*Pinspot on* HECTOR,
Late twenties,
A name tag,
Direct address as well.)

HECTOR: And my manager's being a dick.

And not just because all managers are dicks pretty much always,

I mean, tonight he's being like a *remarkable* dick,

So I wave to him all nice on my way out of my job

And I take out my keys and I take out my cell phone on my way to the car—

And I am SO tired

And I am SO hungry

And I didn't wanna work a second shift today but my wife's three months pregnant

So that means I'm working a third and a fourth shift if I have to,

And I *just* wanna go home.

. . .

I know it's two o'clock in the morning but I call her anyway just to let her know I'm on my way,

. . .

And she picks up fast like the phone was already in her hand.

. . .

And the first thing she says is "How was work."

But she's not asking,

. . .

She's stalling.

. . .

And there's this silence.

. . .

There's this silence but I hear monitors and machines in the background.

And she's with her mom and my mom

And I'm like "What?"

And she tells me she didn't want me to worry.

. . .

Three months pregnant,

She didn't see the *point* in bothering me at work.

LAZ: But that doesn't even matter,—

HECTOR: —And that's when she tells me we lost him.
> . . .
> . . .
> And ten minutes later my sleeves are covered with tears and snot.
> Twenty minutes later my knuckles are scraped and dented from punching the dashboard.
> Window's fogged.
> Empty parking lot.

LAZ: (*Quiet.*) It's just *me* in there now.

HECTOR: And I'm getting calls from the hospital but I can't pick up.

LAZ: (*Quiet.*) . . . Just *me.*

HECTOR: And this is the point where I realize I've memorized the geography of my Subaru:
(*He takes a quick inventory,*)
> Dashboard,
> Turn-signal,
> Scooby Doo steering wheel.
> . . .
> It was familiar before, but now I got all of it memorized.

LAZ: Keys in ignition—

HECTOR: —It's *my* car,
> Yeah,
> But at this point these things've all been staring quietly at snot dripping outta my nose
> And we've become friends.
> And I know I *should,*
> I know it should be the first thing I do,
> But something tells me I can't see her.
> I can't.

. . .
Not 'cause of *her.*
. . .
'Cause of *me.*
. . .
. . .
'Cause I'm just not strong enough.

LAZ: Keys in ignition,

HECTOR: So I start the car—

LAZ: —And I don't remember putting my foot to the pedal—

HECTOR: —I start that car—

LAZ: —I don't remember first gear or second gear
      But by now I've driven *past* the places I know—

HECTOR: —And I just go—

LAZ: —And I'm *not* thinking about my sister,
      Or the look on her face when she left,
      Or how weird it is to sleep in that room,
      Or the fact that I prayed
      —Me: the fucking loser of all losers—
      To make sure she was all right.
      And I'm *not* thinking about how I should call her
      Even though my mom told me if I did I'd be a traitor and
      an embarrassment to the family
      And I'm like "The Family"?—

HECTOR: —The seat belt light is still on with this annoying
        chime thing that goes ding if you don't put it on and I'm
        normally real safe about everything but not tonight,—

LAZ: —And I turn on the radio—

HECTOR: —Tonight I don't—

LAZ: —And it's the shitty late-night DJs that are like not good enough for regular radio so let's give them their own shitty late-night programs,—

HECTOR: —And the streetlights are getting dimmer,—

LAZ: —And it's one—

HECTOR: —After another—

LAZ: —After another—

HECTOR: —Streetlights—

LAZ: —And eventually I just settle on static—

HECTOR: —I don't even know where I'm going—

LAZ: —Static—

HECTOR: —I'm the kinda guy who makes his parents recycle and here I am just eating up gas streetlight after streetlight 'cause driving is just—

LAZ: —*Nice* with the static all up and—

HECTOR: —Loud—

LAZ: —So—

HECTOR: —LOUD—

LAZ: —Yeah—

HECTOR: —Clean—

LAZ: —Fuck yeah—

HECTOR: —*Blinding*—

LAZ: —And every streetlight is like something I never seen before!—

HECTOR: —And for no reason in particular at one point in my driving,
In my whatever-I'm-doing,
I slam on the brakes,
. . .
Put it in park.

(*A beat.*)

LAZ: And I put the car in park.

HECTOR: And I look at my watch.
And—

LAZ: —Jesus bro—

HECTOR: —At this point—

LAZ: —It's three fifty-eight AM and I dunno where the hell I am.

HECTOR: But I don't care.

(*A beat.*)

LAZ: Wherever it *is* I've driven, everything looks like—

HECTOR: —pitch-black—

LAZ: —Except a thin trail of moonlight tracing over—

HECTOR: —A couple buildings in the background,—

LAZ: —Like in the movie *TRON*.

HECTOR: . . .
>And normally there's someone on the street
>Even this late, right?
>Normally there's at least a cop car or a crackhead
>But right now there's—

LAZ: —Nothing.
>Bro.
>. . .
>*TRON*.

HECTOR: And I hear this stupid put-put sound coming from a car next to me.

LAZ: And in the middle of all the dark I look up and there's this fucker I never seen before.

HECTOR: And it's just us and our steering wheels.

LAZ: And he looks me in the eyes like we're friends or some shit—

HECTOR: —Cowboys—

LAZ: —In the eyes—

HECTOR: —Showdown—

LAZ: —Like we're friends.

HECTOR: . . . And I rev the engine—

LAZ: —Oh yeah?—

HECTOR: —And, you have to understand:
>I've never "revved" the engine before,
>I don't even know how you spell that—

LAZ: —Like he's some kinda hot shit in his Subaru—

HECTOR: —CarMax—

LAZ: —So I do the same—

(—*Building*—)

HECTOR: —And it's just me and this guy I don't know—

LAZ: —And everything is pitch-black except his headlights—

HECTOR: —And I have NO idea where we are,
    We're in some part of the city they don't even put on maps—

LAZ: —Come on—

HECTOR: —And am I really about to race someone?—

LAZ: —Come on, yo,—

HECTOR: —Ohmygod—

LAZ: —COME ON—

HECTOR: —And I dunno what the hell got into me but I just go—

LAZ: —And I don't even remember putting my foot to the pedal—

HECTOR: —Or first gear—

LAZ: —Or second gear—

HECTOR: —Or third gear—

LAZ: —Or fourth—

HECTOR: —Or stoplights—

LAZ: —But it's three fifty-nine AM and we're gone—

(—*Building*—)

HECTOR: —Holy shit—

LAZ: —And next thing I know I'm going eighty—

HECTOR: —Ninety—

LAZ: —Ninety-five miles an hour down a stretch of road that's empty, that nobody's been on for like a hundred years—

HECTOR: —I fly—

LAZ: —Hundred miles an hour, the road curves—

HECTOR: —I curve with it—

LAZ: —Hundred-ten he catches up—

HECTOR: —What the fuck am I doing—

LAZ: —And at a hundred-twenty I'm about to max out but I don't even care—

HECTOR: —I'm going a hundred-thirty miles an hour like some kind of *moron*—

LAZ: —And the speedometer isn't even doing nothing no more—

HECTOR: —It's not registering—

LAZ: —COME ON DAWG—

HECTOR: —FIFTH GEAR SIXTH SEVENTH EIGHTH GEAR
HOW MANY GEARS DO I HAVE?—

LAZ: —HOLY SHIT—

HECTOR: —THE SPEEDOMETER ISN'T EVEN CLOCKING HOW FAST I'M GOING ANYMORE WHAT THE HELL AM I DOING—

LAZ: —AND I AM *NOT* THINKING ABOUT MY SISTER—

HECTOR: —NINTH GEAR TENTH GEAR HOW FAST AM I GOING—

LAZ: —FLYING—

HECTOR: —AND SUDDENLY ALL THE DARKNESS AROUND US BECOMES LIKE SOMETHING ELSE—

LAZ: —WHAT?!—

HECTOR: —SOMETHING *ELSE*—

LAZ: —AND OUTTA NOWHERE THERE'S MAD *STREAKS* OF LIGHT JUST STREAMING ACROSS THE WINDSHIELD LIKE LIGHT WAS MADE INTO WATER AND IT'S RAINING BRO—

HECTOR: —I HAVE NO IDEA WHAT'S GOING ON—

LAZ: —LIKE *HYPERSPEED*—

HECTOR: —IT'S RAINING LIGHT BUT AT THIS POINT I'M EVEN SCARED TO SLOW DOWN—

LAZ: —HYPERSPEED   HAN   SOLO   MILLENIUM
FALCON-STYLE—

HECTOR: —AND   OUTTA   NOWHERE   THERE   ARE
THESE—

LAZ: —STARS SCRAPING AGAINST MY WINDSHIELD
AND I MOVE TO PUT THE WIPERS BUT I CAN'T
'CAUSE—

HECTOR: —THERE'S LIKE A G-FORCE HOLDING ME
BACK AND I CAN'T MOVE—

LAZ: —LIKE ON A ROLLERCOASTER—

HECTOR: —LIKE IN SPACE—

LAZ: —*APOLLO THIRTEEN* DAWG!—

HECTOR: —AND AT THIS POINT WE'RE NOT EVEN
RACING AGAINST EACH OTHER—

LAZ: —AT THIS POINT I'M LOOKIN' THROUGH THE
WINDOW AND I COULD SEE THE SIDES OF THIS
DUDE'S SUBARU ON FIRE BRO—

HECTOR: —WHAT?!—

LAZ: —ON *FIRE* BRO—

HECTOR: —AND THE STEERING WHEEL AND THE
SCOOBY DOO COVER AND EVERYTHING START
TO RATTLE—

LAZ: —AND   MY   "PUT-PUT"   BECOMES   LIKE
SHAKING—

HECTOR: —AND EVERY HINGE AND EVERY SCREW IN MY CAR FEELS LIKE IT'S ABOUT TO COME APART—

LAZ: —BUT JUST BEFORE IT DOES—

HECTOR: (*To himself.*)—EVERYTHING'S ABOUT TO COME APART—

LAZ: —AAAAGH!—

HECTOR: —WHAT AM I DOING?!—

LAZ: —JUST BEFORE IT DOES—

HECTOR: (*To himself.*)—GROW UP—

LAZ: —JUST JUST JUST—

HECTOR: —*MAN THE FUCK UP!!*—

LAZ: —JUST BEFORE LIKE *ALL* OF IT—

HECTOR: —EXPLODES, I HEAR—

LAZ: —NOTHING.

(*A beat. Silence.*)

(*Just.*)

(*Silence.*)

HECTOR: And there's this moment.
This moment of . . .

LAZ: . . . nothing.

(*A beat. Then softer,*)

HECTOR: And through the flames and the light and the dark and
the shaking and the speed I see—

LAZ: —This fucker's face I never even seen before—

HECTOR: —And wherever it is I've driven,
Everything looks pretty much—

LAZ: —Pitch-black.

(*Silence.*)

HECTOR: And when I wake up, my car is in the middle of an
intersection.

LAZ: Streetlight, puddle, garbage cans, payphone, just . . .

HECTOR: An intersection.
. . .
And I'm in one piece.

LAZ: Yup.

HECTOR: And so's *he.*

LAZ: (*Shock.*) Whatthefuck, yo.

HECTOR: And somewhere a gutter drips,

LAZ: And you could hear a car a block or two away.

HECTOR: And now,
Everything's—

LAZ: —Normal.

HECTOR: ...
My tank's almost empty,

LAZ: And my engine's back to put-putting,

HECTOR: And I lean out my window and I can see there's a
streak like a burn-mark on the side of my car, but other than
that—

LAZ: —We're *alive.*

(*For the first time, they look at each other.*
A beat.)

HECTOR: And I look at this guy and I dunno what to say—

LAZ: —And neither does he,—

HECTOR: —But he shoots me this little head-nod like—

(—LAZ *shoots him an alpha-male head-nod.*
A beat.)

And that's enough.

(*A beat.*
Something's changed.)

And I turn the key in the ignition,

LAZ: Put-put. Put-put.

HECTOR: Dashboard,
Turn-signal,
Scooby Doo steering wheel.

LAZ: Like normal.

HECTOR: And I put my seatbelt on.

LAZ: It's 3:59 in the morning.
    Still.
    And I don't know where the hell I am,—

HECTOR: —But I got somewhere I need to go.

(*Light out on* HECTOR. LAZ *looks around, taking inventory,*)

LAZ: Chop-Chop smell.
    Streetlight.
    Puddle.
    Garbage can.
    Payphone.
    . . .
    Payphone.
    . . .
    . . .
    And now I'm outta my car.
    And now I'm picking up the headset.
    . . .
    Now I'm outta my car,
    . . .
    And my sister gets a call.

(*Blackout.*)

END OF PLAY

FINALS, TOUCHDOWNS, AND BARREL KICKS

Jacqueline E. Lawton

Finals, Touchdowns, and Barrel Kicks was produced by Active Cultures Theatre (Mary Resing, artistic director; James Hesla, producer) in Riverdale, Maryland, on May 2, 2009. It was directed by Colin Grube; the set designer was Marie-Audrey Desy; the costume designer was Alli Lidie; the lighting designer was James Hesla; the sound designer was Ian Armstrong; the dramaturg was Mary Resing; and the stage manager was Karen Mixon. The cast was as follows:

EVAN	Brandon White
BOBBY	Christopher Herring
COACH	Gregory Burgess

Note: *Finals, Touchdowns, and Barrel Kicks* was originally commissioned, developed, and produced by Active Cultures Theatre's 2009 Sportaculture festival.

CHARACTERS
EVAN, University of Maryland football player, free safety
BOBBY, University of Maryland football tutor

TIME
Present.

SETTING
University of Maryland campus. Terps Football Team Study Hall.

At rise:

BOBBY *sits ready to work, but* EVAN *paces back and forth, annoyed as all get-out.*

EVAN: Come on, Bobby, seriously? Four hours? Cut me some slack. I've been up since five a.m.

BOBBY: I know, I know. I've got your training schedule. I don't know how you guys do it.

EVAN: What other choice do I have? I want to be the best. The best free safety the Terps have ever had. Do you know how hard my job is? I've got to be a wide receiver, with the speed. A linebacker, with the rough aggressive drive. I've got to be able to see the entire field at once, you know? Peripheral vision. Zoom, zoom, zoom! And never lose sight of the ball.

BOBBY: I hear ya, man. I'm a big fan of yours. You're good. Really good.

EVAN: Thanks man. I'm here for the team, you know? So we're straight? I'm outta here.

BOBBY: Not so fast. You've got to clock in four hours Monday, Wednesday, and Friday. Have a seat.

EVAN: Come on, I've gotta work out and go meet my girl.

BOBBY: First, you need to write this paper and practice your speech.

EVAN: Look it. All my other tutors just did my work for me.

BOBBY: Yeah, and they were fired.

EVAN: But not until after my work was done.

BOBBY: That's great for you, but I need this job. Come on, it's my first day. I can't mess this up.

EVAN: Alright, I'll make a deal with you.

BOBBY: I'm not writing your paper.

EVAN: Just hear me out.

BOBBY: Evan, come on, you're wasting valuable time here.

EVAN: Seriously, Bobby, stop being so uptight.

BOBBY: Fine. Say what you gotta say, but you should know it's not going to change anything.

EVAN: Let's just see about that. You know my girl, Jessica? Come on, you know, Jessica.

(*He shows her picture.*)

BOBBY: She's hot.

EVAN: I know. We've been together since high school. Junior year. We went to Eleanor Roosevelt.

BOBBY: Yeah, I know. I went to Thomas Jefferson Science.

EVAN: Figures. Anyway, everybody thought we were going to break up after graduation, but no way. I chased her for two years. Had to prove myself. Not just on the field either. In school too. She wouldn't date anyone who didn't get straight A's. Never fought so hard for anything in my life. Until now.

BOBBY: Is she a Terp?

EVAN: Yeah, English major.

BOBBY: Really? And she won't help you with your paper?

EVAN: No way. I mean, she would if I asked her, but I want her to think, you know, that I can do it on my own. Anyway, she's also captain of the dance team. Well, co-captain. Caitlin's her co-captain. They're best friends. Since middle school. They were on Prom Squad together.

(*He shows a picture.*)

BOBBY: They're both hot.

EVAN: Yeah and they're good too. They can do everything perfect. (EVAN *demonstrates each move to the best of his ability.*) Front Leaps. Side Leaps. Barrel Turn. Single, Double, and Triple Pirouettes. Front, Side, and Back Kicks. Splits. Um. Yeah, no. And they can dance! (EVAN *dances.*)

BOBBY: Um, two questions.

EVAN: Go for it, man. What you need to know?

BOBBY: One: how do you know how to do all of that?

EVAN: Come on, man, she's my girl. I've got to be all interested in what she's doing and everything. It can't just be all about

me all the time. This is a relationship. I'm not just biding my
time with her, you know? I'm in love.

BOBBY: Okay. Fair enough. Two: what does this have to do with
the fact that you need to finish your paper and practice your
speech?

EVAN: Alright. Get this. Caitlin broke up with her boyfriend,
Scott. You know Scott Arlen, right?

BOBBY: Is he on the team?

EVAN: Come on! Scott's the best basketball player the Terps have
ever seen. He was the Cavs' top choice, but decided to play
for the Wizards.

BOBBY: Why?

EVAN: Wanted to stay close to home.

BOBBY: But the Cavs, man.

EVAN: Naw, I'm feeling him. I don't care who picks me up, I'm
only playing for the Ravens.

BOBBY: That's cool.

EVAN: Anyway, Scott'll make more money and spend less time
on the bench on a losing team than he would on a winning
team.

BOBBY: Makes sense.

EVAN: Alright, so the dance team had tryouts this afternoon.
Jessica texted me, Caitlin's all broken up and crying, could
barely focus or anything.

BOBBY: But I thought she broke up with him.

EVAN: Yeah, he was cheating.

BOBBY: But she's hot.

EVAN: Yeah, but sometimes, you know, someone hotter comes along.

BOBBY: True.

EVAN: I mean, not for me. Jessica, she's my one and only.

BOBBY: She must really appreciate that.

EVAN: My grandma raised me right. Anyway, Caitlin's heart is hurting. So I gotta work out and then take her and my girl out to the club.

BOBBY: Where you going?

EVAN: The Fey, where else? I mean, Caitlin's gotta dance out her heartache.

BOBBY: That's really nice of you. You're a sensitive guy. Very considerate.

EVAN: Thank you. Can I go?

BOBBY: No. These are finals, man. We've got to keep you eligible.

EVAN: Hell, I'll be alright. Even if I make D's, I'll still pass.

BOBBY: Don't think that way. You just said you wanted to be the best.

EVAN: Yeah, that's what I'm saying. I need to work out.

BOBBY: But why stop at football, man? As your tutor, I can help you set some goals.

EVAN: Hey, I've got goals. I'm gonna be a better safety than Taylor Mays. He played for USC and was scary. His size and speed were freakish: six-three, two hundred twenty-six pounds, six percent body fat and could run an electronically timed forty in 4.32 seconds. 4.32! Just you wait, by the end of the summer, I'm going to top him!

BOBBY: Okay, that's great, but it won't mean anything if you're not eligible to play.

EVAN: I hear ya. Seriously. And here's what I'm willing to do to show just you how dedicated I am. If you write my paper for me, I'll let you come along tonight.

BOBBY: What? Seriously?

EVAN: Yeah, you can be Caitlin's date. You can dance, right?

BOBBY: Um. Yeah.

EVAN: Let me see.

BOBBY: What?

EVAN: Let me see your moves.

BOBBY: Come on, we don't have time for this.

EVAN: Look it, a fine girl like Caitlin won't date just anybody. And, I mean, you're not built.

BOBBY: But I know how to dress.

EVAN: Sure. I can plainly see that *GQ* has taught you a lot.

BOBBY: And I'm not ugly.

EVAN: I mean, you're not . . . ugly.

BOBBY: Alright then.

EVAN: Still. I need to see your moves.

BOBBY: Alright, but don't laugh.

EVAN: I can't promise I won't laugh.

BOBBY: Come on.

EVAN: Naw, man, if you throw out some lame ass white boy, lip biting, knee jerking, hands all up in the air dance moves, I'm gonna laugh.

BOBBY: Fair enough.

(BOBBY *dances; he's good.*)

EVAN: Alright, alright. Very good! Tonight's your lucky night, my friend. We got a deal or what?

BOBBY: I don't think so.

EVAN: What? Come on, why not?

BOBBY: Seriously, Evan, I need this job. I'm on scholarship with the Business School, but it doesn't cover everything. Besides what would your girlfriend think if she knew you were cheating your way through college?

EVAN: Come on, man, why you gotta bring my heart all into this?

BOBBY: I'm just saying. Think about how hard you worked to get her. You want to just throw it all away like that?

EVAN: But what about Caitlin?

BOBBY: Take her and Jessica to brunch tomorrow. Girls like brunch. Buy them some mimosas and eggs Chesapeake with some soft-shell Maryland crabs. Trust me, you can't go wrong.

(EVAN *steams for a bit and paces.*)

EVAN: Fine. You're hired.

BOBBY: What? I thought I already had the job.

EVAN: Kind of. You were on probation until now. Coach puts all of our tutors though a test like this.

BOBBY: So all of that was an act?

EVAN: Yep, I'm a theater major. Acting is my plan B.

BOBBY: What about Caitlin?

EVAN: Not tonight, I've got a paper to write. But I'll introduce you. That brunch idea was great and you can dance. Now, let's get to work.

(EVAN *sits down to study.* BOBBY, *still a little dazed, joins him.*)

END OF PLAY

FRANK AMENDS

Halley Feiffer

Frank Amends was first produced as part of "Dear Darkness . . . : Plays That Go Bump in the Night" in October 2012 at the New Ohio Theatre in New York City. It was produced by Michael Puzzo and Jade Lane, with set design by Jason Simms, costume design by Alexis Forte, and lighting design by Greg Goff. The composer and sound designer was Andre Fratto; prop master, Jamie Bressler; stage manager, Jeanne Travis. Brian Roff directed the following cast:

DOCTOR	Robert Sella
FRANKENSTEIN	Matt Stadelmann

Darkness. Then—a CRASHING THUNDERBOLT! *Then—*

Billie Holiday's "I'll Be Seeing You" plays as lights creep up on a hermetic cottage in the woods. A nebbishy middle-aged gentleman in a white lab coat putters about the house.

He readies a platter of deviled eggs on a service tray, meticulously squeezing yolky filling into each egg-white crescent with a pastry squeeze bag.

Suddenly, there is a THUNDEROUS KNOCK *at the door. The man* JUMPS!

MAN: (*To himself.*) Dear *god . . . !* Does he always have to be so . . . loud . . . ?!

(*He searches around the house for something, and then finds on his coffee table a remote control, which he uses to turn off the Billie Holiday.*

Then, he goes to the door, takes a deep breath, wipes his sweaty palms on his apron, and then opens the door.

Another piercing BOLT OF THUNDER, *accompanied by a powerful* FLASH OF LIGHTNING, *as the door swings open to reveal a figure shrouded in a rollicking sea of fog.*)

FIGURE IN DOORWAY: (*Awkwardly.*) Hey . . .

DOCTOR: (*Cold.*) Hey.

FIGURE IN DOORWAY: It's . . . me.

DOCTOR: I know—

(*As the fog clears we see the figure is . . .*)

FRANKENSTEIN: Frankenstein . . .

DOCTOR: I know . . . !

FRANKENSTEIN: From the . . . lab—

DOCTOR: I *know!* I know who you are, I know where I *know* you from, I

DOCTOR:—just—	FRANKENSTEIN: . . . Okay. . . .
(*Flustered, turning away back into the house.*) —just, never mind—come in, come in.	
	(*Awkward.*) Cool, cool . . . Thanks . . .

(FRANKENSTEIN *enters the house, closes the door behind him. We see he is wearing a really hip, hipster-y outfit: skinny jeans, bright neon oversized high-tops, and a bright red American Apparel hoodie.*

He jams his hands into his skinny jeans and looks around, anxious.

The DOCTOR, *his back to his guest, puts the finishing touches on his platter of hors d'oeuvres, perhaps sprinkling paprika on the deviled eggs.*)

FRANKENSTEIN: Your place looks—	DOCTOR: And your *name* isn't "Frankenstein," by the way—that's *my*

name—*"Doctor
Frankenstein."*

FRANKENSTEIN: (*Abashed.*) . . . I know . . .

DOCTOR: *Your* name, as I *know* you already know, is "Frankenstein's MONSTER," or you can go by *"Frank"* if you
really want to, but *"Franken*stein" is *my* name, which I don't
understand why that is so frikkin' *complic*—

FRANKENSTEIN: Okay—okay! I'm sorry, I'm sorry . . .

DOCTOR: O*kay.*

(*A beat. The* DOCTOR *looks at him. Pointedly.*)

Huh.

(*A beat. They stare at each other.*)

FRANKENSTEIN: (*Suddenly self-conscious.*) What . . . ?

DOCTOR: You seem . . .

FRANKENSTEIN: What . . . ??

DOCTOR: Different.

FRANKENSTEIN: Oh . . . ?

DOCTOR: You look more . . . put together . . .

FRANKENSTEIN: (*Modest.*) Oh . . . thanks . . .

DOCTOR: Did you zip that hoodie yourself?

FRANKENSTEIN: (*Nods.*) Uh-huh!

DOCTOR: Huh.

(*Beat.*)

Yeah.

(*Beat.*)

DOCTOR: And you're . . .   FRANKENSTEIN:
speaking . . . more clearly . . .   (*With real pride.*)
                                        Oh . . . yeah.
                                        Thanks . . . !

DOCTOR: Not so much of, uh . . .

(*He imitates* FRANKENSTEIN *stalking about with his arms out and groaning. Then he stops.*

An awkward beat.)

Yeah. Not so much of that.

(*The* DOCTOR *looks* FRANKENSTEIN *up and down once more, then returns to his deviled eggs, now topping them off with precut slices of chive.*

FRANKENSTEIN *sits on the couch and unzips his hoodie to reveal an ironic T-shirt.*

An awkward moment of tense silence.

The DOCTOR *wheels the service tray into the living room and places the hors d'oeuvres on the coffee table.*

Then—)

DOCTOR: Can I get you something to drink?

FRANKENSTEIN: (*A little unnerved; popping a deviled egg into his mouth.*) Um, do you have . . . like a . . . ginger beer?

(*Beat.*)

DOCTOR: (*His voice dripping with contempt.*) No, I don't have a "*ginger beer.*"

(*Beat.*)

FRANKENSTEIN: Oh cool, then just—

DOCTOR: What do I look like, an artisanal organic East Brooklyn soda shoppe?

FRANKENSTEIN: Um, no, I'm sorry, I just—

DOCTOR: I mean, I could make you a *seltzer,* if you want . . .

FRANKENSTEIN: Oh, *yeah,* actually—that'd be gr—

(*The* DOCTOR *lifts a sheet off a contraption on the bottom level of his service cart, revealing a glimmering Soda Stream seltzer maker.*)

FRANKENSTEIN: (*His mind blown.*) Whooaaa . . . You *make* the seltzer???

DOCTOR: Yes. You've never seen one of these before?

FRANKENSTEIN: No . . .

DOCTOR: It's a Soda Stream.

FRANKENSTEIN: No.

DOCTOR: (*Retrieving a Soda Stream bottle of water from his service cart.*) Oh. Well, it's not complicated. It's just chemistry.

(*He puts the bottle in the seltzer maker. He pumps on the CO2 pump. It makes a loud sound.*)

FRANKENSTEIN: (*Terrified, covering his ears and bringing his knees to his chest.*) AAAAHHHH!!!!

DOCTOR: (*Alarmed.*) What?!

FRANKENSTEIN: What *is* that?!

DOCTOR: It's the ... It's the CO2 ...! That's how the ... the ... bubbles ...

(FRANKENSTEIN *looks like he might cry.*)

FRANKENSTEIN: It's ... scary ...!

DOCTOR: (*Taken aback.*) Well ... *I'm* sorry, but that's how seltzer is *made,* Frank—jesus ...

(*The* DOCTOR *pumps two more times, with* FRANK *covering his ears and twitching a bit. The* DOCTOR *then unscrews the bottle and pours fizzy seltzer into two glasses.* FRANKENSTEIN *starts to giggle a bit.*)

DOCTOR: (*Cold.*) What.

FRANKENSTEIN: (*Lighter.*) It kind of ... It kind of sounds like ...

DOCTOR: What?

FRANKENSTEIN: (*Giggling a bit.*) It kind of sounds like a ... fart ...

(*Beat. The* DOCTOR *stares at him. Then—*)

DOCTOR: (*Handing a glass to* FRANKENSTEIN.) Well, science isn't *silent,* Frank.

(*They both sit on the couch and sip seltzer, awkwardly.*

Beat.)

FRANKENSTEIN: This is super . . .

DOCTOR: —I know—

FRANKENSTEIN: . . . bubbly . . .

DOCTOR: I know.

(*Beat.*)

FRANKENSTEIN: Okay. Well, I guess I'll just . . . cut to the . . . I mean, I came here tonight, to, uh—to—

(*He mops his brow.*)

God, I'm nervous all of a sudden . . .

DOCTOR: Okay, well, I don't really have all day, so . . . .

FRANKENSTEIN: Okay, sorry. I'm here because, after I left you— your lab, I mean—well, and you—I just—

(*A bit emotional.*)

Well, um, as I'm sure you know, when I was living with you, I was, um, I was . . . drinking . . . ? Really heavily . . . ?

DOCTOR: You were . . . ??

FRANKENSTEIN: You didn't know???

DOCTOR: (*Trying to remember.*) Not . . . *really*—I mean, we would have a glass of *pinot* sometimes, if it complemented the lean *protein* we were eating . . .

FRANKENSTEIN: Oh, yeah, but then—but then, like, after you'd go to bed . . . ? It'd be like, off to the races . . . for me . . .

DOCTOR: (*Incredulous.*) *Really . . . ??*

FRANKENSTEIN: Well, *yeah* . . . And then the next day . . . ? The hangovers . . . ?!

DOCTOR: God, I had *no idea . . . !*

FRANKENSTEIN: Yeah, I mean, like, why did you think I was always, like, you know, like—

(*He imitates himself the same way the* DOCTOR *imitated him earlier—stalking about with his arms out and groaning.*)

DOCTOR: Well, I thought it was just 'cause . . . like . . . you're a monster.

FRANKENSTEIN: No . . . ! It's 'cause I was *wasted*.

DOCTOR: Wow. I—wow . . .

FRANKENSTEIN: Yeah, I think I was just, like . . . *created* . . . ? Like that?—and I'm not blaming you!—I mean, just, like, ever since I was . . . ever since I can remember, I just—I always felt separate, apart, different . . . from everybody else . . .

DOCTOR: Huh.

FRANKENSTEIN: And I thought it was, like, 'cause, you know . . .

DOCTOR: You're a monster.

FRANKENSTEIN:
I'm a monster, right.
And that's definitely
a *part* of it. But there
was a part I wasn't
understanding, yet.

DOCTOR: Huh.

FRANKENSTEIN: Yeah. And after I left you, I just—well, let's just say, it got . . . things got . . . worse. Like, a *lot*. Worse.

DOCTOR: . . . Okay . . .

FRANKENSTEIN: Yeah. Like cheap motel rooms. Blacking out, remembering nothing. Waking up with gashes in my head that I didn't remember getting. That weren't from being a living corpse—

DOCTOR: Right.

FRANKENSTEIN: They were from drinking.

DOCTOR: I got it.

FRANKENSTEIN: But the good news is . . .

DOCTOR: . . . Yes . . . ?

FRANKENSTEIN: (*Straightening himself up; with a lot of conviction.*) I am now a sober member of Alcoholics Anonymous.

(*Beat.*)

DOCTOR: Wow.

FRANKENSTEIN: And I'm here to make my formal Ninth Step Amends.

(FRANKENSTEIN *takes a folded-up piece of paper out of his pocket.*)

DOCTOR: Wait.

FRANKENSTEIN: What.

DOCTOR: I don't know ... about this ...

FRANKENSTEIN: Oh ... Oh, okay ...

DOCTOR: I mean, you did some really *bad* things, Frank ...

FRANKENSTEIN: I know.

DOCTOR: I mean, like, you *strangled* that little girl ...

FRANKENSTEIN: I know.

DOCTOR: And you caused all those villagers to show up here with, like, *pitchforks*, and burning *torches*, and stuff ...

FRANKENSTEIN: I know ...

DOCTOR:
That was really *embarrassing* ... for me ...

FRANKENSTEIN: I *know* ... !

DOCTOR: AND you killed my *wife*—

FRANKENSTEIN: I *know*!

DOCTOR: Like, that's not the kind of thing that you can just show up here and be, like—

(*Mockingly.*)

"Oh, I have a hoodie, and I zipped it up myself, so I'm all better now and will you please"—

FRANKENSTEIN: (*Cutting him off.*) I *know*! That's why I'm *here*! 'Cause I *know*! And I feel ... *bad*! And I wanna say ...

(*Beat; he becomes emotional again.*)

I wanna say . . .

(*Fighting emotion.*)

I'm sorry. And I'm not like that anymore. I've changed. And I wanna show you how I've changed.

(*A beat. The* DOCTOR *considers.*)

(*With all the sincerity in his heart.*) Please.

(*Then—*)

DOCTOR: (*Relenting.*) Okay.

FRANKENSTEIN: *Thank you.*

(FRANKENSTEIN *unfolds the piece of paper.*)

(*Reading from letter, woodenly; trying not to get too emotional.*) "Doctor Frankenstein: Thank you for meeting me here today. I was looking back on past behaviors and wanted to set right some wrongs . . ."

DOCTOR: (*Cold.*) Okay.

FRANKENSTEIN: (*Pushing through; this is very hard for him.*) I was: hard, abrupt, inconsiderate, selfish, unkind, and a murderer. I may have caused you harm while we were cohabitating because I was self-involved and reckless. And a murderer. I regret this behavior.

DOCTOR: (*Abrupt.*) All right.

FRANKENSTEIN: (*Ignoring him; pressing on.*) I appreciate how dedicated you are to your work, and what a good creator you were to me . . .

(*We see that the* DOCTOR *is, in spite of himself, becoming ever so slightly emotional . . .*)

FRANKENSTEIN: (*Emotional also.*) I love—

(*Choking back tears.*)

> I love how you always remembered to change the bolts in my neck when they got rusty . . .

DOCTOR: (*A wistful memory.*) . . . I *forgot* about that . . . !

FRANKENSTEIN: (*With deep nostalgia.*) How you would always try to trim my unibrow—

DOCTOR: (*Remembering, fondly.*) . . . It got so *bushy* . . . !

FRANKENSTEIN: (*Laughing.*)—and I wouldn't let you—

DOCTOR: (*Tittering.*)—You *hated* it!—

FRANKENSTEIN: (*Cracking up.*)—and you'd be like—"Frank—Frank! You *have* to prune that thing! You look like the—"

DOCTOR: (*Giggling.*)—No I *didn't!*—

FRANKENSTEIN: (*Cracking up.*)—"You look like the walking *dead*, Frank!"

DOCTOR: (*Cracking up too.*) I *never* said that!

FRANKENSTEIN: Oh em GEE you said it *so* many times!

DOCTOR: I just wanted you to look more . . . *normal!*

FRANKENSTEIN: Yeah, as if *that* would ever happen!

DOCTOR: I know, I know!!

FRANKENSTEIN: "Paging Doctor Delusional!"

DOCTOR: (*Conceding.*) Touché, touché . . .

(*They laugh.*

They calm down.)

FRANKENSTEIN: (*Returning to his letter.*) "Is there anything you would like to say to me?"

DOCTOR: Um . . . .

FRANKENSTEIN: (*Still reading from letter.*) "Is there any way I can right these wrongs? The End."

(*Beat.*)

DOCTOR: Wait. Are those two questions or one?

(*Beat.*)

FRANKENSTEIN: Um.

(*Beat. He thinks.*)

Shit.

(*Beat. He looks at the letter. He starts to giggle again.*)

I have no idea!

(*They both start to really giggle.*)

I guess I should call my sponsor!

(*They both laugh.*)

DOCTOR: (*Impressed. Then, earnestly:*) Buddy, you have a sponsor? That's so great . . .

FRANKENSTEIN: Oh, yeah, you might know him—his name is Dracula?

(*Beat.*)

No, just kidding, he's this dude from Bay Ridge named Vince.

(*Beat.*)

DOCTOR: (*Flatly.*) Oh. Ha-ha.

FRANKENSTEIN: Yeah.

(*Beat.*)

DOCTOR: I was confused for a second.

FRANKENSTEIN: Yeah. Sorry, I—

DOCTOR: 'Cause I was like . . . why would *Dracula* be—

FRANKENSTEIN: No, I know—I was trying to make a joke. It wasn't great.

DOCTOR: Oh. Okay. Well, you can work on it and try it out again . . .

FRANKENSTEIN: Thanks. But seriously, though: Is there anything you'd like to say to me?

(*A beat. The* DOCTOR *thinks.*)

DOCTOR: Eh . . . not really.

FRANKENSTEIN: (*Disappointed.*) Oh.

DOCTOR: (*Ominously.*) But there is something you can do to right your wrongs.

FRANKENSTEIN: (*Intimidated.*) Oh ... okay ...

DOCTOR: (*Threateningly.*) And you better goddamn do it.

FRANKENSTEIN: (*Getting kind of terrified; trying not to show it.*) Uh-huh ... ?

(*A beat. The* DOCTOR *stares* FRANKENSTEIN *up and down. Then:*)

DOCTOR: You can give your creator a hug.

(*A beat. Then,* FRANKENSTEIN *grabs his former master in a tight, squeezy, desperately loving bear hug.*)

FRANKENSTEIN: (*His voice slightly muffled from the hug.*) I love you, man.

DOCTOR: I love you too, buddy.

(*They separate.*

An awkward beat, both unsure what to do next.)

DOCTOR: So ...

FRANKENSTEIN: So ...

DOCTOR: What now?

(*Beat.*)

FRANKENSTEIN: You wanna get a drink?

(*Beat. Then—the* DOCTOR *cracks up.*)

DOCTOR: Oh! Hahahahaha!!

FRANKENSTEIN: It was a JOKE!

DOCTOR: HAHAHAHA! I know!! HAHAHAHA!!!

FRANKENSTEIN: You *got* it!!

DOCTOR: Well, 'cause that joke was actually *good*!

FRANKENSTEIN: (*Fake defensive.*) Hey! My other joke was—

DOCTOR: (*Affectionately teasing.*) Your other joke was *terrible*!

(*They laugh. A beat. They look at each other; take each other in; smile. Then—*)

You wanna make some seltzer?

FRANKENSTEIN: You mean . . . *I* make it . . . ?

DOCTOR: C'mon! I'll show you how. It's simple as pie.

FRANKENSTEIN: (*Apprehensive.*) Okay . . .

(*They stand and approach the Soda Stream seltzer maker. The* DOCTOR *retrieves a new Soda Stream bottle from the service tray. He hands it to* FRANKENSTEIN.)

DOCTOR: Okay, so you screw it in here . . .

FRANKENSTEIN: (*Does so.*) Uh-huh . . . ?

DOCTOR: And then you pump, here—*hard*.

FRANKENSTEIN: (*Really nervous.*) Uh-huh . . . ?

DOCTOR: Do it.

FRANKENSTEIN: I'm scared.

DOCTOR: You can do it!

FRANKENSTEIN: Okay . . .

(*He closes his eyes and pumps it.*)

AHH!!

DOCTOR: Good! Again!

(*He pumps it again.*)

FRANKENSTEIN: (*Excited now.*) AAAAHHH!!

DOCTOR: Good!! Again!!

(*He pumps it one more time.*)

FRANKENSTEIN: (*Mirthfully and joyously.*) AAAAAHHHHH!!!!

DOCTOR: Good! Good!! Good!!!

(*A beat.*)

You just made seltzer. Now unscrew it.

(FRANKENSTEIN *does so. It fizzes, loudly. He smiles with pride. He looks at his creator.*)

FRANKENSTEIN: That felt good. Scary but good.

DOCTOR: I'm proud of you.

(They look at each other. They smile. They look at the seltzer. They smile. Then—)

It *does* kind of sound like a fart.

(BLACKOUT.)

END OF PLAY

STRANGE FRUIT

Neil LaBute

Strange Fruit by Neil LaBute received its premiere on November 13, 2011, at the Minetta Lane Theatre in New York City as part of the evening "Standing on Ceremony: The Gay Marriage Plays." The show's contributing writers included Mo Gaffney, Jordan Harrison, Moisés Kaufman, Neil LaBute, Wendy MacLeod, José Rivera, Paul Rudnick, and Doug Wright. Stuart Ross directed the following cast:

TOM — Craig Bierko
JERRY — Mark Consuelos

SILENCE. DARKNESS. A man, TOM, *standing in a bright light. Wearing a tux. He talks to us. Another man,* JERRY, *in a tux, stands next to him. Smiling.*

TOM: . . . I love cock. I do. I'm really sort of just into it, you know? Cock. And that's what got all this started, I mean, how I ended up here in the first place. Because of that. The "cock" situation. (*Beat.*) And I had, like, no idea when I was younger, I really didn't! None. I wasn't secretly putting on my mom's dresses or makeup at night or, or, reading the Hardy Boys and getting a boner . . . nothing like that.

JERRY: I loved the Hardy Boys, are you kidding me?! They were so cute, with all their . . . or maybe I'm thinking of the show. With Parker Stevenson. Yeah, that's it! That's the Hardy Boys I know. The TV ones. God, he was good-looking . . . *Parker* . . .

TOM: Funny thing is, I was *totally* into girls when I was younger— seriously, I was!

JERRY: I grew up in Oregon. Beautiful part of the country . . .

TOM: So I did the whole "marriage and kids" thing when I was *nineteen* . . . I did. Yeah! Why I don't know, because I was supposed to? Maybe. It was expected of me and so that's what I did. I did that . . . made it through sixteen years. *Sixteen.* (*Beat.*) No, "made it through" sounds so—accurate. I don't wanna be like that, dump on her or be all— Well that's what I did. I *just* made it through. *Barely.*

JERRY: I met him when he was living in Chicago, divorced and just starting to dip his toe into the scene a little bit—totally not sure about what he wanted, how he saw his life going in the next however long . . . but he did like cock. That part was a given. Oh yeah!

TOM: I already said that, didn't I? And it's true—second I did that, it was like a light went off in my head and all these, like, *fireworks* and stuff . . . big letters up in the sky saying "YES! WE'RE HOME!!" (*Beat.*) It was pretty awesome . . .

JERRY: He couldn't get enough and I was, you know what it's like—hey, I've always been a very giving person! Who am I to stop a guy who wants to learn? And this dude just couldn't get enough . . .

TOM: I just like the whole—the shape of the thing and how it's . . . the taste of it, I mean—not *taste,* really, it's only skin after all, how does that taste? But it's true, there's a certain— anyway, I'll shut up now! But you know what I'm saying . . . that shit is good! Cock.

JERRY: Wow. I mean, yeah . . . he got really good at it. All of it. Sex.

TOM: And somehow we sorta just stayed together and became, I dunno, a couple, I guess . . . I mean, pretty soon he was moved into my place and there we were. Him and me. This . . . *couple.* In a relationship.

JERRY: I had always been looking for someone. I mean, a guy . . . Someone special, who gets me.

TOM: Anyway! Enough about us and the whole . . . trust me, it was working and if it does, *when* it does—in life, I'm saying—you shouldn't question happiness. Not ever.

JERRY: He was just a funny guy, really. That's what I liked about him. (*Beat.*) And great with his kids—on the phone, anyway.

He's not allowed to have them out to see him; they're in Orlando so he has to fly there if he wants to be around 'em at all, and that's . . . (*Beat.*) Did I mention that he's good in bed?

TOM: I do like sex!—I found that out pretty early on. Like, immediately.

JERRY: And that's how it went and suddenly, you know how it is . . . like, five years go by! We're looking in the mirror one morning—we love to shave at the same time, share the water and, and the, you know, use the same little brush thingie with the soap—and, my god, I'm looking at myself and I say to him, "Jesus Christ, look at me. I'm thirty-*nine* years old." (*Beat.*) He leans over—doesn't say a word—just sort of lowers his head toward me, this little peck on my cheek. Then he whispers to me, "Wait'll next year. Forty's a bitch . . ."

TOM: He had a drop of foam on his nose, like a little puppy. Really fucking cute, if you wanna know the truth . . .

JERRY: And we just stood there, bare-chested and with these towels on and started kissing. It was *so* good. Just—anyway, that's when he asked me. Said "Let's get married."

TOM: Which was a big deal, right? I mean, like I said, I'd already done it before and it was, well, whatever . . . it was what it was. My kids are terrific. (*Beat.*) Anyway, we'd even talked about marriage before but living in Chicago it was always about *civil unions* and *domestic partnerships*, all this shit that wants to be the same, to give us a little hope that people are about to stop being so goddamn idiotic about something so basic, *so* simple if they'd just let it be but it's . . . anyway, he told me that he had this dream. About it. Like, a wish.

JERRY: I just wanted it to be the same as anyone else, you know? Except two guys on top of the cake, in tuxes—really cute and both of us looking . . . it's stupid, I know, but I had *actual* dreams about it! Since I was a kid.

TOM: We kinda just watched and waited, without saying too much about it and yet nothing at all was changing so we thought maybe we could move to another state or, or, you know—but years go by and finally I say it as we stand there in the bathroom shaving. I'm the one to say it but we're both thinking it. Let's make this thing real! Marriage.

JERRY: Boom! Next day we've got tickets, we're off to California—there's a window out there for us, I mean, we're two active, informed, vibrant people, right? We see what's going on in the world and it turns out there's, like, this five-month period in 2008 where that golden state near the ocean comes to its senses and says, "Yes, it's okay to be who you are" and we run out there like everyone else. Do this thing before anybody can say "no" to us again. And they do, they close that thing down like a book snapping shut, a few months later. Bam! But we do it. We get married.

TOM: We looked amazing—I mean, yes, it was just the court-house and all, but we did the whole deal he'd been wanting. Tuxes and, and just the entire—we were pretty much awe-some. Standing there in the hall and . . . well, people were staring. That's all I'm gonna say. They were. *Staring.*

JERRY: Just like I'd dreamed about. Seriously.

TOM: And we were just giddy the rest of the day. We snuck off to San Diego to be at that hotel that was in the movie with Marilyn Monroe and the guys dressing up like two women . . . you know the one! It's, ummmmm . . .

JERRY: I'd never been to the Hotel del Coronado. Just gorgeous, this big ol' place propped up on the beach there . . . just very . . .

TOM: I took my tux off but I could not get my husband—or *wife* or whatever the hell I was gonna call him now—he wouldn't take his off! Said he was gonna go downstairs and get some cigarettes . . .

JERRY: My one vice.

TOM: He'd been a smoker for years—works out *religiously* but wouldn't think of giving up his nicotine! (*Smiles.*) He was standing there, at the door to the room, smiling at me, this big grin on his face. Asking me if I wanted anything. Some Twinkies or whatever.

JERRY: Somebody loves "Hostess."

TOM: I said "No thank you, I'm a married man now . . ." and we laughed and I blew him a kiss. Out he went.

JERRY: They didn't have any Marlboros there in the little gift shop so I went out into the streets. Looking for a 7-Eleven.

TOM: And . . . apparently . . . he ran into three guys who were coming up from a swim. Just some college kids from what the news said . . . and the police report.

JERRY: I was walking along in my tux, carrying a bag of *mangoes* and one of those stupid roses that you buy—the single ones with a bit of plastic around the petals—they keep 'em right up there by the checkstand so I got one for my fella . . .

TOM: And they must've said something because I know that . . . he could never let shit go . . . you know? *Ever.* Some guy two feet taller than him and ten years younger and he'd go after 'em like a little *rooster* if it was about us or being gay or, like, any of the stuff he believed in. Those kids in *Africa* or, or Amnesty International—he'd be up in your face and telling you that you're full of shit! (*Laughs.*) That was just him. You know?

JERRY: I remember these surfer boys passing . . .

TOM: He wasn't found until the next morning. Down by the rocks, where the water's . . .

JERRY: It's just funny . . . one day I'm standing in Chicago, the next thing you know I'm walking down a street with palm trees on it! I mean, *palm* trees!! With a rose in my hand and a paper bag full of strange fruit and, I dunno, this . . . love, I guess. Yeah, *love* in my heart for him and everybody else. Right? Even these three guys who are moving toward me now . . .

TOM: The story made the papers and was kind of a big deal, especially after all the . . . anyway. Yeah.

JERRY: Three boys who are getting louder as they come . . .

TOM: One day, few months later, somebody sent me a picture of us, before all that, standing on the courthouse steps as we waited in line to go in—and I keep it out where I can see it now; I'll give it a glance when I head off to work or out for a run, that kinda thing—it's of the two of us, both in our suits and smiling and from a distance or, if you stand back from it just a bit, you know what?

JERRY: I couldn't see their faces but they were laughing and yelling and the sun was just behind them as they came closer . . .

TOM: We're like that couple you see on top of a cake. That little plastic couple, only it's two guys. *Us.* Vibrant and young and frozen for a moment. I mean . . . well, you get what I mean, right?

JERRY: They were laughing . . .

TOM: Us standing there and smiling, as if all was right with our lives and not anything could possibly go wrong. You know?

JERRY: And they were getting louder and rowdier but to me, on this day and how I was feeling . . . it sounded like little birds singing.

TOM: As if nothing in the whole wide world was able to scare us or hurt us . . .

JERRY: These beautiful little birds . . . singing just to me from up in Heaven above . . .

TOM: . . . or frighten us. No. Not us. Not ever again . . .

(*Suddenly a light over* JERRY *blinks off and out. He is now lost in the darkness. Hands unlock.* TOM *stands alone in the fading light.*

TOM *tries to smile but this too fades away.*

SILENCE. DARKNESS.)

END OF PLAY

AN UPSET

David Auburn

An Upset was produced by Ensemble Studio Theatre (William Carden, artistic director; Paul Slee, executive director) as part of the 2008 Marathon of One-Act Plays on May 13, 2008. It was directed by Harris Yulin; set design by Maiko Chii, lighting design by Evan Purcell, costumes by Danielle Schembre, sound by Shane Rettig; production stage manager, Jeff Davolt. The cast was as follows:

1	Matt Lauria
2	Darren Goldstein

CHARACTERS
1, a tennis player, nineteen years old
2, a tennis player in his late thirties

SETTING
A locker room.
Several months separate each of the three scenes.

ONE

2 changing, furious. 1 enters.

1: Good match.

2: Fuck you.

1: I just want to say . . . is an honor to be on court with you.

2: "Is an honor." Can you fucking speak English?

1: I only learn English last year.

   I see you are not very happy right now. I leave you alone.

2: Well thank you very much.

(*Beat.*)

   It's just . . . you fucking QUALIFIERS.

1: Excuse me?

2: You play in your little qualifying tournament. You beat a bunch of granddads, and juniors on Ritalin, and country club teaching pros diddling around on the circuit for a lark, for the groupies, they're AMATEURS. But congratulations, cheers, you WON it . . . So you come into the main draw all nice and warm, feeling confident, your pecker's UP . . . meanwhile I come in after a week and a half in NEW HAVEN busting my ass against TOP TEN PLAYERS, vicious . . . Plus I'm ME . . . I've got to walk out on that stadium court with everyone praying I'll lose. "Let's see something NEW." "Let's see what the Czech kid can do"—

1: I am Romanian.

2: Romania. You actually have tennis courts there?

Christ, the crowd. They're bored. They're so bored, they're jaded, they'd root for anything as long as it was "different." They're like Romans in the Colosseum: they'd root for a GIRAFFE against me, or a pair of DWARVES—of course they get on your side. You're the "underdog." "This crowd in New York sure loves an underdog." I watch the tape tonight—I gave you a nickel every time the TV guys say that you'd walk away with ninety-five bucks. Of course the first bad call they're on your side.

1: The ball was in.

2: (*Explodes.*) It was NOT in! It was out by a country mile! You couldn't possibly have seen it! You were sprawled on your ass twenty-five feet away! I was standing right next to it!

1: It was called in. I'm sorry you do not like it.

2: You're goddamn right I do not like it. A bad call at break point in the third and you're fucked. You're fucked.

1: Excuse me. You are not fucked.

2: Excuse ME—

1: I had still to win three sets.

2: Have you ever heard of MOMENTUM? It's ALL ABOUT momentum! I go down a break in the third and the crowd goes all giddy 'cause they think they're "seeing something." An Upset! An Upset "in the making"! And suddenly they're screaming your name every time you knock in a bloopy forehand—a passing shot I could make in my sleep when I was fifteen brings down the house—guys in the stands, "hard-core" fans who think they're seeing something "new," being "mavericks" because they spin on a dime and start worshipping a "new face"—God, I can see the two-faced fuckers with their white shorts and their visors—why the FUCK do tennis fans wear fucking tennis CLOTHES when they go to WATCH a fucking tennis MATCH? You don't see Giants fans at the fucking Meadowlands in shoulder pads, for fuck's sake. I just know those assholes were calling their asshole friends on their cell phones, saying, "Yeah, I'm in the stadium! Where are you? The food court? Hey, you gotta come over! Yeah, put down your fifteen-dollar roasted-vegetable-and-hummus wrap and come see this, I'm watching an UPSET!" All because you make a little diving volley at the net on break point that goes OUT, but everyone is too dazzled by the Romanian no-name qualifier doing his little flouncy gymnastics routine on a shot that you could have made VERTICALLY like a normal man if you'd MOVED YOUR SILLY FUCKING FEET—and there goes the set. And the next two sets. And the match goes down the fucking toilet.

1: I suppose you did not lose them.

2: Oh, I lost them all right. And don't think I can't stomach it. I've lost matches before. I've even lost matches on cocksucking calls before. The thing is, what I've never done is lost a FIRST ROUND MATCH IN A MAJOR on a cocksucking call to a nineteen-year old ROMANIAN QUALIFIER ranked 164 IN THE WORLD with a BACKHAND like a postmenopausal mom playing Sunday DOUBLES in the PARK with the GIRLS FROM THE BOOK GROUP.

(*Beat.*)

1: You know my ranking.

2: What?

1: I did not think a man like you would know my ranking. Or my age.

2: Don't get all misty. I do my homework. What do you think?

1: My backhand is not strong, I realize this.

2: You're not turning your shoulder.

1: I am working on this.

2: You ought to be looking over your shoulder at the ball.

1: This is what my coach says.

2: You should listen to him.

1: I do. But he's in Romania.

2: Your coach didn't see your big U.S. upset because he's in Romania?

1: Yes. He is . . . very sick.

(*Beat.*)

2: Well that's a real heartbreaker. Congratulations. The press will gobble that.

1: I think he will die soon.

2: What a shame.

(*Beat.*)

1: You play him once.

2: I did?

1: Oh yes. A great match.

2: Remind me.

1: The 2004 Australian Open. The Fourth Round.

2: Fourth Round, 2004, Australia . . .

   Not the bow-legged lefty with the metal racquet.

1: He used metal racquet.

2: That was FREAKISH. The last guy on the tour playing with metal! This hilarious aluminum Eastern Bloc piece of crap! It was—Yeah, yeah.

1: Yes, metal.

2: (*Remembers.*) And I got a cocksucking call THEN! You miserable Romanians! He was up a break in the fourth when I doubled at 30–40 on a FOOT FAULT! They call a foot fault RANDOMLY once a tournament just to show they remember the fucking rules and I got it, so this rubber-legged Romanian metal-wielding FREAK ranked seventy-fifth in the world took a second set off me!

1: He often talks of it.

2: I won the Fifth, though, 7–5.

1: He talks of it as the great match of his life.

He has picture of you and he together at the net shaking hands after the match. He keeps it above the, how do you say, the fire-piece?

2: The mantelpiece.

1: The mantelpiece. In the main room, the living room of his apartment.

2: Or you could say "fireplace." Same thing.

(*Beat.*)

1: The racket from the match is there too. He never used it again. It's up on the wall next to the picture in a frame.

2: Well that's where it belongs.

    (*Beat.* 1 *is finished dressing. He picks up his bag to go.*)

2: So what's he got?

1: Cancer.

2: Too bad.

1: I should call him now.

(1 *goes to exit.*)

2: Hey.

(1 *turns.*)

    Tell him Fuck you from me.

(*BLACKOUT.*)

TWO

     1 *dressing after a match.* 2 *enters, dressed in street clothes.*

2: Very nice.

1: Thank you.

2: I watched the last set from the stands.

1: I saw you.

2: What is that now. Twenty-three straight? Twenty-four?

1: Oh no no no no. Nothing like that. Twenty-one.

2: It get so you can't remember losing?

1: I remember a little bit.

2: But it stops feeling like it can happen to you.

1: It can always happen to you.

2: Is it going to happen to you tomorrow?

1: I don't believe so. No.

2: You see? That's when you got to be careful.

1: The man tomorrow is unseeded.

2: You were unseeded a few tournaments ago. Now look at you.

1: A few tournaments from now he will be still. You can see it.
   In his shoulders.

(*Beat.*)

2: You managed to tart up your backhand a little.

1: Yes. Is much better. Thank you for the advice.

2: Don't give me any credit for it, please. It's no longer an embarrassment, now it's merely pitiable.

1: It feels much better. Like everything.

2: Here.

(*He tosses* 1 *a tennis ball.*)

1: What?

2: Sign it?

1: You're joking.

2: No. I would like your autograph please.

1: I don't understand this joke.

2: It's not a joke, sadly. It's for my sister's kid. He made me promise. Evidently he's a fan.

1: You did not tell him to "fuck off"?

2: He's eleven.

1: The way you say all the time to everybody, "Fuck off, fuck you, fucking fuck"?

2: I'm not saying that wasn't the initial impulse. For a second there. Then I took a deep breath and choked down my pride, in the name of benevolent uncle-hood and for the good of the game. Need a pen?

1: No. What is his name?

2: Nate.

(1 *takes out a Sharpie and signs. He tosses the ball back.*)

Thank you.

1: I never want to disappoint a fan.

2: Attaboy.

You're getting a lot of new fans.

1: Yes.

2: How are the girls treating you?

1: I have a girlfriend.

2: She on tour with you?

1: No.

2: Ah. Back in the old country.

1: In Bucharest, yes. She is studying.

2: A scholar.

1: Sports medicine.

2: Ah.

1: It is a very demanding course.

2: Sure sure.

1: She works very hard.

2: Couldn't cut it as a player, figured she could stay close to you taping your knee and giving you back rubs.

1: We . . . haven't decided if she will tour with me.

2: Pretty girl?

1: I think she is very pretty, yes.

2: Good. So how many have you fucked on the tour?

Yours is back in Romania, you can't tell me you haven't made a few selections from the buffet outside the players' lounge. Come on, I can see it in your shoulders.

1: You are wrong.

2: Come off it. There are too many of them. The lovely spoiled little slags from all across the globe. Brazilian and Greek and Dutch and Italian and American trust-fund honeypots, couldn't decide which would piss off Daddy more—moving to Paris to work on their drug habit while they "try modeling," or spending a year on the circuit fucking tennis pros. You double up yet?

1: I'm sorry?

2: Two at once. Or three? Better do it while you can, it gets much harder after you fall out of the top fifty. Come on. You can tell me.

(*Beat.*)

1: Yes I do this.

2: Attaboy. And?

1: I'm afraid I disappoint them.

2: Oh they don't care. Get that straight in your mind and you'll
   be okay. They don't care about you. Once, this girl knocked
   on my hotel room door—I was getting ready to go to the
   airport—and she says, Can I come in? I was number three
   in the world. I said, I've got to leave in fifteen minutes. She
   says—are you ready? She says, That's okay, I only need ten.
   They don't care. It's a notch on their belt, or, today, an entry
   in their, what is it, blog or something. You can have fun with
   it. Once, at a party, this girl comes right up to me—no pre-
   liminaries, no name, nothing, says, Come into the bathroom,
   I want to suck your cock.

1: What did you do?

2: I said, What's in it for me?

1: (*Laughs.*) What did she say?

2: She loved it. She laughed.

1: Then she suck your cock.

2: Right. Don't worry. You didn't disappoint them. Maybe
   YOU were disappointed. Were you disappointed?

1: A little.

2: Yeah, I felt the same way. I'd rather be inadequate with one
   woman at a time.

1: I was not "inadequate."

2: Oh no, no. But it's nicer with your girlfriend.

1: Yes.

2: That's sweet.

You'll try it again, though.

1: Yes.

2: That's the spirit. Keep at it. Keep trying.

1: (*Shrugs.*) I am an athlete.

(*Beat.*)

Can I ask you something? Something . . . personal?

2: Sure.

1: Who is your art dealer?

2: Uh, I don't have just one, there are a couple of guys I've worked with over the— Why?

1: I'm thinking of buying a painting.

2: Yeah? What?

1: I don't know yet. But I like always this idea of buying art. And now one day I know I'll buy a house and I will need art to put up on the walls.

2: One day? Buy a house now, the year you're having.

1: I'm not ready yet. I don't know where it should be. Florida? Spain? Monte Carlo, for the taxes?

2: Bucharest?

1: Not Bucharest. Have you been to Bucharest?

2: In and out.

1: This is the way to go.

So, I read how you are famous for your art collection. You know all the artists. Who is good?

2: Well what sort of stuff do you like?

1: I don't know. I don't know anything about what makes a good artist, a good painting.

2: A good painting is a painting you enjoy looking at.

1: Well, I don't know what I enjoy.

2: Then you're not ready to buy.

1: I wanted to buy a painting with the money I win from this tournament.

2: Whoa. Take it easy. You're not over the finish line yet.

1: I will be.

2: Look. Forget about dealers. Take some time, go to the museums, go to the galleries—whenever you're in a new city take an afternoon—buy yourself a little notebook, write down the names of what you like. Buy some books, educate yourself a little bit. Then we can start talking dealers. Okay?

1: Okay. (*Beat.*) I just like the idea . . . I respect that you have this hobby. That you have knowledge of an area outside the game, that you—

2: (*Suddenly angry.*) You don't need a fucking HOBBY right now, all right? Jesus Christ you ignorant little hayseed! You need to WIN.

(*Beat.*)

1: Yes. You're right.

(*Beat. He finishes dressing.*)

I'm sorry you were eliminated.

2: Guy slapped me around like a bitch. Ran my legs right off. I had to call for a trainer in the fourth set just to catch my breath. I'm lucky there WAS a fourth set. The first two were like those nightmares where you can't wake up. At least they were over fast.

You'll face the fucker in the final, probably.

1: He is good, I agree. He is going all the way this time. I will play him there.

(*Beat.*)

If your nephew would like a ticket, please tell him I will be happy to—

2: Yeah okay. Thanks.

(*Beat.*)

1: Any advice?

2: For you?

1: As you say. I'm not over the finishing line yet.

(*Beat.*)

2: I don't think you have anything to worry about.

(*BLACKOUT.*)

THREE

> 1 *changing.* 2 *enters.*

2: Well! What do you know.

1: Yes. What do you know.

2: The "old dog" . . .

1: Yes.

2: Thanks for what you said out there.

1: Of course.

2: You memorize that?

1: No.

2: 'Cause it was eloquent. I mean your English has improved a lot in a short time.

1: Well.

2: And hey, this is the last one. Don't worry.

1: The last one what?

2: I'm announcing I'm retiring at the end of the season.

1: Oh.

2: Tomorrow. We'll do a press conference, whole bit.

1: I see.

2: Feels right. I'd rather go out like this. I'm not operating under any illusions here. I don't think this is, you know, the beginning of the "second act," or—

1: Yes, fine.

2: I mean, yes, I always thought about, you know, "Go around one more time." But it has to be the right way. The last thing you want is to seem desperate or pathetic, crap out in the first round—or worse, the second: pull some kid in the first who's nervous and starstruck and green so you take him down easy, then get my clock cleaned by some cold-eyed Russian or Swede, never broke the top ten but a veteran, makes a career getting into the third round of every fucking tournament he enters, he's not about to let me stand in the way of his twenty-four grand, he needs it to pay his coach and his trainer and his nutritionist and his brother who carries his rackets . . .

Listen to me. Babbling away. I guess I'm keyed up. Can you blame me?

Anyway, you played a good match.

1: Fuck you.

(*Beat.*)

2: Excuse me?

1: You think you won this?

2: Yeah. I do.

1: The call at break point in the fourth—

2: It was in!

1: It was NOT in! The linesman called it out—

2: And he was overruled half a second later, CORRECTLY,
'cause it was a shitbrained call from the far end of the court,
my grandmother was closer to the ball and she's in Phoenix
and she's been DEAD for six years.

1: Oh now you are being ridiculous.

2: AND the guy's a drunk—

1: I think—"You protest so much."

2: Don't get lippy with me. And it's "protest too much." If you
can't handle the loss get off the fucking circuit.

1: No, YOU get off the circuit! You are old man!

2: I AM getting off. I told you.

1: Good!

2: Yeah.

(*Beat.*)

I did you a favor. You forgot what losing feels like. I
reminded you.

1: Also your draw was ridiculous.

2: Fuck off.

1: Admit that at least. It was the joke of the tournament. For the last two weeks you could not have gotten a sillier bunch of babies to play. First round—a qualifier, ranked 205. Second round—American teenager with drug problem.

2: He doesn't have a drug problem.

1: He was arrested in Florida last summer!

2: He's been clean for months!

1: His agent says. I doubt VERY much. But nevermind. Round three—your opponent defaulted in the second set, twisted ankle.

2: Because I made him run down that SCREAMING backhand volley, shot of the TOURNAMENT—

1: You only play two sets! That is the fact! Fourth round—another old man like you, only not even in shape. Quarters—clay court specialist, shouldn't be here at all. Semis—he is playing injured all season, and HE had a TERRIBLE draw, five sets all the way so he meets you tired. Finals—ME, your first real opponent.

2: And I won.

1: No, I LOST. Bad calls. Bad crowd, assholes—they want to see "grandpapa" win one last time. Bad draw, bad weather. Bad everything. All of it. They robbed me.

2: Yeah, I'll tell them that when I cash the check.

1: (*Kicks his equipment bag.*) Fuck EVERYTHING. My coach flies up here to see THIS?

(*Beat. He calms down, retrieves his bag. They dress in silence for a moment.*)

2: How is your coach?

1: He is okay. Holding on. Somehow.

2: Girlfriend?

1: We broke up.

2: Ah.

(*Beat.*)

You ever buy any paintings?

1: No. Stupid idea. I don't want to be a pretentious art-snob shit, going to stupid galleries, drinking wine. Museums are FUCKING boring. I'm going to buy horses. I want a horse farm in Virginia. This will be MY "hobby." Fuck paintings and dealers. Fuck YOU. After today, all I can say: I have no respect for you.

(2 *looks at him. Beat.*)

2: Attaboy.

END OF PLAY

NEGOTIATION

Billy Aronson

Negotiation premiered at the U.S. Comedy Arts Festival in Aspen, Colorado, in 1997, featuring Marc Grapey and Kelly Connell under the direction of Michael Patrick King. It was subsequently performed in New York City at MCC, featuring Matthew Lewis and Christopher McCann under the direction of Evan Handler.

CHARACTERS
EMPLOYER
FREELANCER

EMPLOYER *sits behind a desk.* FREELANCER *sits in a chair.*

EMPLOYER: How much could you do the job for?

FREELANCER: What were you planning to spend?

EMPLOYER: What would you normally charge?

FREELANCER: I can work around your figure.

EMPLOYER: Give me a number.

FREELANCER: I could do the whole thing for, probably, twenty-five.

EMPLOYER: We can't pay anything like that.

FREELANCER: I could swing it for fifteen.

EMPLOYER: Sorry but

(*Simultaneously.*)

EMPLOYER: I'm not authorized to go over twelve thousand.	FREELANCER: I couldn't afford to go under twelve hundred.

EMPLOYER: You were talking hundreds?

FREELANCER: You were talking thousands?

EMPLOYER: Twelve hundred would be fine.

FREELANCER: When I said twelve hundred, I was just tossing out twelve hundred as a ballpark number, that I could take up front, as long as my total came to at least twelve thousand.

EMPLOYER: When I said twelve thousand, I meant the annual budget that I'm working within, since with all of the cutbacks, I'm stuck handling this whole project with a total of twelve hundred.

FREELANCER: I could approach it for seven thousand.

EMPLOYER: I couldn't possibly go above two.

FREELANCER: I'd be taking a loss below six.

EMPLOYER: I could dig up three if you'll start tomorrow.

FREELANCER: I'll start tomorrow for five.

EMPLOYER: I'll see if I can get you four.

FREELANCER: That's low for me, and it's the busy season, and another client is breathing down my neck . . .

EMPLOYER: I'll pay you under the table.

FREELANCER: Deal.

EMPLOYER: I like your stuff. You'll get half your total fee after each dozen transplants.

FREELANCER: Transplants?

EMPLOYER: You *do* do heart transplants?

FREELANCER: No, I'm a painter. I paint houses.

EMPLOYER: I see.

FREELANCER: I'd feel a little silly accepting four thousand under the expectation that I should perform two dozen heart transplants.

EMPLOYER: Five thousand.

FREELANCER: What am I supposed to do, stay up all night reading medical books and watching instructional videos and practicing on toads?

EMPLOYER: Six thousand.

FREELANCER: Under the table?

EMPLOYER: Deal. You've got what it takes. I'll get you the first thousand candy bars now.

FREELANCER: Candy bars?

EMPLOYER: We pay for all transplants in candy bars.

FREELANCER: I work for dollars, not candy bars.

EMPLOYER: Candy bars are more than a dollar in some states.

FREELANCER: I'm not going to stay up all night learning how to perform heart transplants for six thousand candy bars.

EMPLOYER: Seven thousand.

FREELANCER: Listen. It's one thing for us to sit here and talk about me becoming a competent heart surgeon overnight, but I think we both know that in reality I'm bound to botch a few incisions and get blood all over the place and kill a few people and get clobbered by angry relatives and wind up in jail.

EMPLOYER: Eight thousand.

FREELANCER: I have no place to put eight thousand candy bars.

EMPLOYER: Nine thousand.

EMPLOYER: I'd break out in pimples.

EMPLOYER: Nine fifty.

FREELANCER: I'd throw up all over.

EMPLOYER: Nine ninety.

FREELANCER: They'd melt, there'd be flies . . .

EMPLOYER: Ten thousand.

FREELANCER: Deal.

EMPLOYER: You're quite a person.

FREELANCER: I'm not a person, I'm a gorilla. See?

(FREELANCER *exposes furry belly.*)

EMPLOYER: I'm sorry, hiring a relatively inexperienced human is one thing, but this job is far too delicate for a gorilla.

FREELANCER: I'll do all twenty-four transplants for a single squashed candy bar.

EMPLOYER: Alright, but only if you'll be my one true love.

FREELANCER: Under the table?

EMPLOYER: Deal.

(*They go under the table.*)

END OF PLAY

CONTRIBUTORS

BILLY ARONSON's plays include *The First Day of School* (premiered at SF Playhouse and 1812 Productions, named Outstanding Original Script 2009 by Bay Area Theatre Critics Circle); *Light Years* (Playwrights Horizons); *The Art Room* (Woolly Mammoth Theatre and Wellfleet Harbor Actors Theater); one-acts produced in eight EST Marathons, published in five volumes of *Best American Short Plays*. TV scripts: *Beavis & Butt-Head*; *Wonder Pets* (Emmy Award; head writer); *Peg + Cat* (created with Jennifer Oxley). www.billyaronson.com.

DAVID AUBURN's plays include *The Columnist* (MTC/Broadway, 2012); *The New York Idea* (adaptation; Atlantic Theater Company, 2010); *Proof* (Pulitzer Prize, Tony Award, New York Drama Critics Circle Award); and *The Journals of Mihail Sebastian*. Films include *The Girl in the Park* (writer/director) and *The Lake House*.

PETE BARRY has authored and coauthored numerous plays, including *Drop*; *Nine Point Eight Meters Per Second Per Second*; *Hangman*; *The Banderscott*; *Sex with a Mathematician*; and *Signs from God*. He is a cofounder of the Porch Room, a film and theater production company. Pete lives in the Lehigh Valley, Pennsylvania, with his wife, Jean, and his daughters Lia and Violet.

NAVEEN BAHAR CHOUDHURY's plays have been produced and developed in such theaters as the Signature Theatre, the Ensemble Studio Theatre, the Second Stage Theatre, the Lark Play Development Center, and the New Federal Theatre, and aired on Northeast Public Radio. She was recently awarded a commission from the Ensemble Studio Theatre / Alfred P. Sloan Foundation Project. Member: Ma-Yi Writers Lab; Dramatists Guild.

ANTHONY CLARVOE has received the American Theatre Critics, Los Angeles Drama Critics Circle, Will Glickman, and Elliot Norton awards and the Edgerton Foundation New American Play Award; fellowships from the Guggenheim, Irvine, Jerome, and McKnight Foundations, the National Endowment for the Arts, TCG / Pew Charitable Trusts, and Kennedy Center Fund for New American Plays; and the Berrilla Kerr Award for his contributions to American theater.

STEVEN DIETZ is a two-time finalist for the Steinberg New Play Award (*Becky's New Car; Last of the Boys*). He received the Kennedy Center Fund for New American Plays Award for his Off-Broadway drama *Fiction*, the Edgar Award for Best Mystery Play for *Sherlock Holmes: The Final Adventure*, and the PEN USA West Award in Drama for *Lonely Planet*.

HALLEY FEIFFER is a playwright and actress whose plays include *How to Make Friends and Then Kill Them*; *Sidney & Laura*; and *I'm Gonna Pray For You So Hard*. Her work has been produced and developed by the Rattlestick Playwrights Theater, Labyrinth Theater Company, Second Stage Theatre, and elsewhere. She cowrote and stars in the film *He's Way More Famous Than You*, directed by Michael Urie.

SIMON FILL's full-length plays include *Little Fears* and *How to Marry a Punk*. His one-act *Night Visits* won the Heideman Award from Actors Theatre of Louisville and premiered there. He has been an A.S.K. American Exchange playwright with the Royal Court Theatre and a Yaddo fellow. His plays have been produced in New York City, regionally, and internationally.

FRANK HIGGINS is also the author of *The Sweet By 'n' By*, which was produced with Blythe Danner and Gwyneth Paltrow at the Williamstown Theatre Festival, and is published by Dramatists Play Service. His other published plays include *Miracles*; *Gunplay*; and, for young audiences, *The Country of the Blind* and *Anansi the Spider and the Middle Passage*.

DAVID IVES was nominated for a Tony for Best Play for *Venus in Fur*. Other plays of his include *All in the Timing*; *The School for Lies* (adapted and translated from *The Misanthrope*); *New Jerusalem: The Interrogation of Baruch de Spinoza*; and *Is He Dead?* (adapted from Mark Twain).

JACOB JUNTUNEN is head of playwriting at Southern Illinois University, Carbondale. His play *Under America* opened at Mortar Theatre after winning the Lee Blessing Scholarship and the Tennessee Williams Scholarship. His follow-up, *Joan's Laughter*, premiered at the Side Project Theatre. Juntunen's plays have been produced at the Vestige Group, the Source Festival, the Stages Repertory, Caffeine, and others. More information at www.JacobJuntunen.com.

EAN MILES KESSLER holds a Rutgers BFA in Acting. Acting credits include *Hamlet* (Hamlet, Player King, Priest), at London's Globe Theatre, and *King's River* (Marcus). Playwriting credits include *Brotherly Love* (Manhattan Repertory Theatre), *The B-Cam* (Inertia), *Beautiful Hands* (finalist, Samuel French Off-Off-Broadway Festival), and *King's River* (Foxhole Entertainment). Publication: *Brotherly Love* (in *Shorter, Faster, Funnier*, edited by Eric Lane and Nina Shengold). Ean would like to thank his mother.

NEIL LaBUTE is a writer and director for theater, film, and television. His plays include *Bash*; *The Shape of Things*; *The Mercy Seat*; *Fat Pig*; *Autobahn*; *This Is How It Goes*; *Wrecks*; and *Reasons to Be Pretty*. His films include *In the Company of Men*; *Your Friends & Neighbors*; *Nurse Betty*; *Possession*; *Lakeview Terrace*; and *Some Velvet Morning*.

ERIC LANE's plays have been published and performed in the United States, Canada, Europe, and China. Plays include *Ride*

(Dramatists Play Service), *Times of War* (Dramatic Publishing), *Heart of the City* and *Dancing on Checkers' Grave* (Playscripts). *Filming O'Keeffe*, a new play commission, premiered at the Adirondack Theatre Festival. Eric has won a Writers Guild Award, the Berrilla Kerr Award, and the La MaMa Playwright Award. www.ericlanewrites.com.

KITT LAVOIE is the award-winning author of more than thirty plays and musical books. His works have been performed in five languages and on all seven continents (including at the Rothera Research Station in Antarctica). MFA in Directing: Actors Studio Drama School. Member: Stage Directors and Choreographers Society; Dramatists Guild. Artistic director of the CRY HAVOC Company (www.cryhavoccompany.org). www.kittlavoie.com.

JACQUELINE E. LAWTON is the author of *Anna K*; *Bloodbound and Tongue-tied*; *Deep Belly Beautiful*; *The Hampton Years*; *Ira Aldridge: The African Roscius*; *Love Brothers Serenade*; and *Mad Breed*. Nominated for the Wendy Wasserstein Prize and the Lark's PoNY Fellowship, Lawton was named one of thirty of the nation's leading black playwrights by Arena Stage's American Voices New Play Institute.

MARK HARVEY LEVINE has had more than 850 productions of his plays from New York to Seoul to Prague to Cairo. Evenings of his work have been produced in Amsterdam, São Paulo, Sydney, Edinburgh (Fringe Festival), New York, Los Angeles, and elsewhere. *Surprise* and *The Rental* appear in other Vintage anthologies. He lives in Pasadena with his lovely wife, Sara, and son. www.MarkHarveyLevine.com.

ELIZABETH MERIWETHER wrote *The Mistakes Madeline Made*, which premiered at Naked Angels and was subsequently produced at Yale Rep and published by Dramatists Play Service. Other plays include *Heddatron*, an adaptation of *Hedda Gabler* featuring live robots, which was produced by Les Freres Corbusier and is published by Playscripts; *Nicky Goes Goth*, which premiered in the 2004 New York International Fringe Festival; and *Oliver*, workshopped by the Vineyard Theatre.

MICHAEL MITNICK's credits include *Sex Lives of Our Parents* (Second Stage Uptown); *Ed, Downloaded* (Denver Center); *Fly by Night* (Theatreworks USA and Dallas Theater Center); and *Lion. Pig. Wolf. Snake.* (developed at Berkeley Rep and Ars Nova). He is writing the book for the Broadway musical of *Animal House.* Commissions: MTC and Theater Masters with the Goodman. MFA, Yale School of Drama.

DARIA POLATIN's plays include *In Tandem*; *The Luxor Express*; *Guidance*; *That First Fall*; *D.C.*; and *A Fair Affair.* Her work has been produced at the Kennedy Center, Actors Theatre of Louisville, Naked Angels, Ensemble Studio Theatre, and Cape Cod Theatre Project. Residency with London's Royal Court Theatre; BFA, Boston University; MFA, Columbia University. Kennedy Center / ACTF Best One-Act Play. Daria also works in television. www.dariapolatin.com.

MARCO RAMIREZ has had plays produced at the Kennedy Center, the Juilliard School, Black Dahlia (L.A.) and Actors Theatre of Louisville's Humana Festival, where *I Am Not Batman* and *3:59am* each received the Heideman Award for Best Short Play. He trained at NYU and the Juilliard School. His TV writing credits include *Sons of Anarchy*; *Da Vinci's Demons*; and *Orange Is the New Black*.

KELLY RHODES is a recent graduate of Goucher College living in Baltimore, Maryland. *Heads and Tails* was her first work to be performed and is her first piece to be published.

JOSÉ RIVERA's screenplay for *The Motorcycle Diaries* was nominated for an Oscar in 2005 for Best Adapted Screenplay. He has won Obies for playwriting for *Marisol* and *References to Salvador Dali Make Me Hot.* Other plays include *Cloud Tectonics*; *Boleros for the Disenchanted*; *Sueño*; *Sonnets for an Old Century*; *School of the Americas*; *Massacre (Sing to Your Children)*; and *Brainpeople*.

PAUL RUDNICK's plays have been performed on and off Broadway and around the world. They include *I Hate Hamlet*; *The Most Fabulous Story Ever Told*; *The New Century*; *Regrets Only*; *Valhalla*; and *Jeffrey*, for which he won an Obie, an Outer Critics Circle Award, and the John Gassner Playwriting Award. His *Collected Plays* is published by HarperCollins, and he's a frequent contributor to *The New Yorker*. His screenplays include *Addams Family Values* and *In & Out*.

EDWIN SÁNCHEZ won the National Latino Playwriting Award for *La Bella Familia*. Other honors include Kennedy Center Fund for New American Plays, three New York Foundation for the Arts Playwriting/Screenwriting Fellowships, the Princess Grace Playwriting Fellowship, the Daryl Roth Award, and the AT&T On Stage New Play Award. He lives in upstate New York, where he writes, teaches, and mentors playwrights.

NINA SHENGOLD is an editor and writer in multiple genres. Her plays are published by Playscripts, Inc. (*Finger Foods*; *War at Home*), Samuel French (*Homesteaders*), and Broadway Play Publishing (*Romeo/Juliet*). She won a Writers Guild Award for her teleplay *Labor of Love*, an ABC Playwright Award for *Homesteaders*, and a Henry Miller Award for her novel *Clearcut*. www.ninashengold.com.

CORI THOMAS is an actress and playwright. A native New Yorker, she studied acting with the late Bobby Lewis and Lloyd Richards. Her work has been developed at the Goodman Theatre (Chicago); Playwrights Horizons, Ensemble Studio Theatre, Page 73 Productions, New Georges, New Federal Theatre, and Going to the River (New York); Pillsbury House Theatre (Minneapolis, Minnesota) and Penumbra Theatre (St. Paul, Minnesota); City Theatre Company (Pittsburgh); and Passage Theatre (Trenton, New Jersey).

DOUG WRIGHT's Broadway credits include the play *I Am My Own Wife* (Tony Award, Pulitzer Prize) and books for the musicals *Grey Gardens* (Tony nomination), *The Little Mermaid*, and *Hands on a Hardbody.* His play *Quills* won an Obie Award; he subsequently adapted it as a screenplay and the resulting film was nominated for three Academy Awards.

ABOUT THE EDITORS

ERIC LANE and NINA SHENGOLD have been editing contemporary theater anthologies for more than twenty years. Their other titles for Vintage Books include *Shorter, Faster, Funnier: Comic Plays and Monologues*; *Laugh Lines: Short Comic Plays*; *Under Thirty: Plays for a New Generation*; *Talk to Me: Monologue Plays*; *Plays for Actresses*; *Leading Women: Plays for Actresses II*; *Take Ten: New Ten-Minute Plays*; and *Take Ten II: More Ten-Minute Plays*. For Viking Penguin, they edited *The Actor's Book of Contemporary Stage Monologues*; *The Actor's Book of Scenes from New Plays*; *Moving Parts: Monologues from Contemporary Plays*; *The Actor's Book of Gay and Lesbian Plays* (nominated for a Lambda Literary Award); and *Telling Tales: New One-Act Plays*.

ERIC LANE's award-winning plays have been published and performed in the United States, Canada, Europe, and China. Plays include *Ride* (Dramatists Play Service), *Times of War* (Dramatic Publishing), and *Heart of the City* and *Dancing on Checkers' Grave* (Playscripts). *Filming O'Keeffe*, a new play commission, premiered at the Adirondack Theatre Festival. *Floating*, a Play-Penn finalist, was workshopped at the Raven Theatre. Eric's short plays are published in *Best American Short Plays*, *Poems & Plays*, and the Foreign Language Press (Beijing). He wrote and produced the short films *First Breath* and *Cater-Waiter*, which he also directed. Both films screened in more than forty cities worldwide. For TV's *Ryan's Hope*, he received a Writers Guild Award. Honors include the Berrilla Kerr Playwriting Award, the La MaMa Playwright Award, and fellowships at Yaddo, VCCA, and St. James Cavalier in Malta. Eric is an honors graduate of Brown University. He is artistic director of Orange Thoughts, a not-for-profit theater and film company in New York City. www.ericlanewrites.com.

NINA SHENGOLD's plays are published by Playscripts, Inc. (*Finger Foods*; *War at Home*), Samuel French (*Homesteaders*), and Broadway Play Publishing (*Romeo/Juliet*) and have been produced around the world. Her one-act *No Shoulder* was filmed by director Suzi Yoonessi, with Melissa Leo and Samantha Sloyan. Nina won a Writers Guild Award for her teleplay *Labor of Love*, starring Marcia Gay Harden; other teleplays include *Blind Spot*, with Joanne Woodward and Laura Linney, and *Unwed Father*. Her books include the novel *Clearcut* (Anchor Books), *River of Words: Portraits of Hudson Valley Writers* (SUNY Press, with photographer Jennifer May), and a growing posse of pseudonymous books for young readers from Scholastic, Delacorte, DK, and Grosset & Dunlap. A graduate of Wesleyan University, she's currently teaching creative writing at Manhattanville College. Nina lives in New York's Hudson Valley, where she has been the books editor of *Chronogram* magazine since 2004. www.ninashengold.com.

PERMISSIONS ACKNOWLEDGMENTS

David Auburn: *An Upset* by David Auburn, copyright © 2010 by David
  Auburn. Reprinted by permission of the author.
Inquiries contact: Paradigm Agency, Attn: Jonathan Mills,
360 Park Avenue South, 16th Floor, New York, NY 10010.

Billy Aronson: *Negotiation* by Billy Aronson, copyright © 1997 by Billy
  Aronson. Reprinted by permission of the author.
Inquiries contact: Billy Aronson, www.billyaronson.com.

Pete Barry: *Hearing Aid* by Pete Barry, copyright © 2012 by Pete Barry.
  Reprinted by permission of the author.
Inquiries contact: Pete Barry, petebarryplaywright@gmail.com.

Naveen Bahar Choudhury: *Skin* by Naveen Bahar Choudhury, copyright
  © 2012 by Naveen Bahar Choudhury. Reprinted by permission of
  the author.
Inquiries contact: Naveen Bahar Choudhury, naveen.choudhury@gmail
.com.

Anthony Clarvoe: *The Art of Sacrifice* by Anthony Clarvoe, copyright ©
  2005 by Anthony Clarvoe. Reprinted by permission of the author.
Inquiries contact: Broadway Play Publishing, Inc., 224 East 62nd Street,
New York, NY 10065-8201; telephone: 212.772.8334; fax: 212.772.8358;
ppi@broadwayplaypubl.com.

Steven Dietz: *Shooting Star* by Steven Dietz, copyright © 2010 by Steven
  John Dietz. Reprinted by permission of the author.
Inquiries contact: Dramatists Play Service, 440 Park Avenue South, New
York, NY 10016; telephone: 212.683.8960; www.dramatists.com.

Halley Feiffer: *Frank Amends* by Halley Feiffer, copyright © 2012 by Halley Feiffer. Reprinted by permission of the author.
Inquires contact: The Gersh Agency, Attn: Jessica Amato, 41 Madison